ENCYCLOPEDIA WALKING

POP CULTURE &
THE ALCHEMY OF ROCK 'N' ROLL

Jon Kanis

Eyes of Da Vinci Publishing
P.O. Box 84653
San Diego, CA 92138

Kanis, Jon, 1964–
Encyclopedia walking: pop culture & the alchemy of rock 'n' roll /
by Jon Kanis.
ISBN 978-0-9906578-0-4

1. Rock music. 2. Popular Culture. 3. Film.
4. Television. 5. Conspiracy Theory.
6. Singers—United States—Biography
I. Title.

Library of Congress Control Number: 2014948933

Author's website: www.jonkanis.com/blog

Book design by Frankie Frey

Printed in the United States of America

To Emily
and
the next seven generations

TABLE OF CONTENTS

FOREWORD
(FOREWARNED)

I met Jon a decade ago when he was doing a story on me. He seemed obsessed with my music at the time. The fact that there is no chapter in this book devoted to me and my music does not surprise me at all because I've come to know Jon. He's very easily obsessed. Especially about anything relating to music and its place in the heart of our culture. If all of Jon's musical obsessions from his entire life were written into this book, it would be a true encyclopedia. But it would not be walking. There would be no need for it to move about from place to place because it would already be in all places at once.

So I am very glad he was able to edit his immense life's journey of obsession with all its related flights of fancy down to a readable length. It will be nice to hold the well-abridged flight log like a chubby bird in my hands. And it will be nice to read the parts I haven't read. Yes, I admit I haven't yet read the entire digital version he emailed. The first time through, I was mostly skimming, skipping around, looking for my chapter (haha), but Jon did tell me there's no need to read it all linearly from beginning to end. I can take my time, grazing, mapping my own chron-illogical journey, which is what I intend to do. And so can you. In fact, feel free to skip the rest of this Foreword (which doesn't get much better from here) and proceed to Jon's informative (if lengthy) introduction.

Okay, since you chose to stay I will tell you what this book is NOT: it's not a compilation of music reviews and critiques. Nor is it a promotion or appreciation for one style or genre of music. It is the chronicling of one person's awakening through music. Extremely personal stuff. And also universal.

There's an old saying: "No statue was ever erected to a critic." It's a nice mantra, very useful in blowing off unwanted criticism. But I'm not so sure how true it is anymore. Sculptors are digging deeper and deeper for inspiration, so I wouldn't doubt there are statues to critics by now. For all I know, they flank the entryways to art museums like statues of lions once did. But aren't our most incisive critics more than mere guardians at the gate? Aren't they more like doormen guiding us deeper into to the subject matter through hitherto unopened points of entry? Cutting us new ones, so to speak (in a good way)? The greatest critic is a great fan, maybe not of the artist, but of the ART. And whether or not we agree with his evaluation of something we love or hate, his experience enhances ours.

The best parts of this book enhance my experience of music and its meaning in my life. They're exhilarating because Jon practices what I'd call The Journalism of Joy. Without jettisoning his critical faculties, he goes beyond criticism to a place where pettiness (what's hip, etc.) is stripped away, love dominates, and all is magnificent. Even failure. A good critique is useful in deciding which album or book to buy this week. But the joy in these writings is timeless, making them as useful tomorrow or next year as they are today in seeking answers to questions like, "What is the role of art and music in a world in conflict?"

I should make mention of Chapter 20 ("Check Your Ego at the Door: Transformation and Rejuvenation at Steel Bridge Songfest") about Jon's participation in an event that's dear to my heart. It's "my" chapter I guess (the one I jokingly said was missing), because it promotes something I'm deeply invested in: the Art of Collaboration. Art and music marketing thrives on the myth of the Lone Genius. But most (if not ALL) of what we attribute to individual genius is more collaborative than we think. Why not acknowledge this and celebrate it? It takes teamwork to create a community. And communities to change the world.

Music lover, be forewarned: this book builds a persuasive case for the holy trinity of Words, Music, and Beat as a world-changing force. Following Jon's journey through these joyful writings might inspire you to dust off those old Ludwigs or (worse) grab a ukulele. And if you're already a lifer musician like me who takes comfort in futility as an excuse for inaction, this book might motivate you to mark the page, set it aside (just for a while), go team up with somebody and write a song that will save the world. :)

pat mAcdonald
Sturgeon Bay, Wisconsin
July 27, 2014

THE INTRO AND THE OUTRO

Listen, the next revolution is gonna be a revolution of ideas.
— **Bill Hicks**

If there's *anything* I love, it's a good idea: full disclosure, the 45 rpm single, Paris in the springtime, a sunset in the Andes, Vindaloo curry, Acapulco Gold, free perpetual motion devices—*all* beautiful ideas to my mind. But primo at the top of the list is the exploration of consciousness; adapting new modes and behaviors, experiencing *vitalizing transmutations*. Very few things excite me more than the ability to incorporate a new idea into my psyche, all the while conjuring up as much fun as possible. Of course, your mileage will vary when it comes to defining the notion of what "fun" is, but being neither a sadist, nor a masochist, my idea of fun is experiencing as much bliss, love, and count-downs to ecstasy as I can possibly handle. Actually, make that *more* than I can handle. Does that make me a hedonist? If so, it's nice to make your acquaintance. You're welcome to relax and hang out for a while. Perhaps you'd like something to drink?

Writing is something you do alone in a room. Copy that sentence and put it on your wall because there's no way to exaggerate or overemphasize this fact. It's the most important thing to remember if you want to be a writer...[however] the only thing you really need is the talent of the room. Unless you have that, your other talents are worthless.

— **Michael Ventura,** *The Talent of the Room*
(*LA Weekly,* **May 21–27, 1993**)

☯

So, what is the big idea behind *Encyclopedia Walking* anyway?

Well, it's like this: when you're blessed with a bountiful existence, it's in everyone's best interest to share the bounty *equally* with the entire tribe. It's the compassionate, considerate, and polite thing to do. If I had the equivalent of a billion dollars sitting in my bank account, I would be embarrassed to sit down at the dinner table and only feed myself when so many others in the world are sick or dying from malnutrition. So it is with the world of ideas. Sure, life has its share of challenges that appear to be unbearable at times, but thank goodness everything is constantly morphing. That's the curse, and that's the blessing. As the man said: *All Things Must Pass.* George Harrison didn't invent that observation—he simply passed on that awareness through a mass communications medium. Because, when I bother to take pause, it's almost unbearable how many wonderful moments this life is teeming with. To quote Frank Zappa: "It's so fucking great to be alive!" So, in that sense,

Encyclopedia Walking is a reminder to count your blessings, because they're infinite.

The musical blessings for me have so far included witnessing over 2,000 live musical performances, and performing 600-plus gigs all over the world since 1976. Each one of those experiences has transformed me in some significant way, and I have a lot to be thankful for.

After traveling around in this incarnation for a half-century (you never know when your ticket's going to get punched, signaling you to move on to the next plateau) it seems like a decent time to reflect on what's gone down thus far.

Conversely, there's nothing conclusive about this book. It's WAY too early for that sort of thing. *Encyclopedia Walking* is an open-ended meditation, ticking off the possibilities of those things that strike one man's fancy. It's also an anthology of previously published feature articles, reviews, and social observations—a series of snapshots from one artist's perspective, measuring the distance from Arlington to Amsterdam, from Pono to the NWO, from SXSW to SBSF.

Encyclopedia Walking is modeled upon some other anthologies that I particularly adore: *Psychotic Reactions and Carburetor Dung* and *Mainlines, Blood Feasts, and Bad Taste* by Lester Bangs; *The People's Music* by Ian MacDonald; *Now Dig This–The Unspeakable Writings of Terry Southern*. Their selfless examples of bravely exposing themselves through their work remain an inspiration, prompting me to express myself as courageously and truthfully as possible.

My favorite types of prose have a conversational style— so it is with mine. Comfortable, face-to-face, keeping-it-real. While it's physically impossible to have a conversation these days with Lester Bangs or Ian MacDonald, when I sit down to read their words, I feel like they are speaking directly to me. The world of popular culture is such a vast sea of shared, universal reference points, I am constantly learning new ways of being in the world when I read someone else's take on our collective existence.

❧

One of the ideas central to J.D. Salinger's *Catcher In The Rye*, and an idea that is emphasized in the very first chapter of this book, is the notion of paying forward whatever you have of value to share with future generations. The greater our awareness is regarding ourselves, our collective history, the universe we live in, and how we create our reality through our thoughts and perceptions, the richer our existence. These are aspects to our journey that should never be taken for granted.

The first time I found myself busking in Amsterdam I haphazardly wandered around the city for weeks. The next time I came back I bought a map and studied it for an hour. Oh, it is so much easier to traverse the territory after grasping how all the elements relate to one another. I briefly berated myself for being so shortsighted and not seeing the bigger picture the first time around, as it would have certainly saved a lot of needless walking around in circles. *And so it is with the world of ideas.* It is a lot easier to make your way through the world once you've bothered to familiarize yourself with the lay of the land.

❧

So, why write a book? Honestly, I go back to the idea of compassion. And frankly, I didn't think I had it in me to sit down long enough to write 1,000 words, let alone tens of thousands. It will become obvious, in short order, that you have stumbled upon the den of an obsessed musicologist. It requires a substantial amount of discipline to sit in a chair and write, because whenever possible, I'd rather be raising a wild ruckus somewhere, anywhere—recording, rehearsing, or performing music. If I'm not *making* music, I'm likely listening to a piece of music that will inform my process somehow as a musician. If I'm sharing time with someone, we're probably either playing music together or discussing it. And the fourth option is an all-of-the-above, swirling assimilation of those aspects, dependent upon how well I am practicing *The Talent of the Room*: i.e. that ability to crystallize into word streams how certain sounds make you feel, and to express those meditations through syllables. In a not-so-small nutshell, that is what basically lies between the covers of *Encyclopedia Walking*: the meditative musings of an unrepentant music freak.

But **then** there's that side of me that aspires for all of humanity to evolve spiritually into a race of mystical avatars. Perhaps I'm setting the bar too high? But what are the other options? The church and state appear all-too-happy to have us maintain the status quo of behaving like post-modern barbarians, continuing to inflict violence upon one another, as well as on the planet that we depend upon for our very existence. Until something more revolutionary is placed on the table, I'm sticking with the evolving-into-avatars idea. And no, I'm not talking about anything having to do with James Cameron.

Of course, being born in the last year of the Baby Boom (1946–1964) and coming of age during the 1970s, my mind was deluded and polluted by watching as much television as inhumanly possible. By contrast, regular trips to the cinema also insured that I would enjoy a lifelong love affair with that unique art form which is film. Those three mediums: music, film, and television, are how I have taken in such a large degree of my sensory input. By my mid-20s, I was in a state of media over-saturation—I went on a prolonged sabbatical by exploring the world at large and experiencing different people and cultures firsthand, without those experiences being re-contextualized by an electronic box. Oh, the things you can learn by having a conversation with a complete stranger from another part of the world, in the bar car of a moving train, careening across the countryside of a foreign nation, thousands of miles away from your hometown. Sharing stories and swapping ideas: it's one of the ways we expand our horizons and potentially learn how not to think so small.

☯

One of the reasons I might be a hedonist, seeking out as much pleasure as possible in life, is to reasonably counterbalance the dualistic relativity inherent in the first of the Buddha's Four Noble Truths: the truth of *dukkha*, or suffering. Suffering is inherent to the duality of our existence here on good 'ol Mother Earth, at least as long as we remain anchored in the third dimension. A fellow hedonist, Pete Townshend, once said, "Rock 'n' roll might not solve your problems, but it does let you dance all over them."

Another way of saying the same thing is that once you understand the lay of the land (that life is suffering), and work within universal laws and principles (understanding how to transcend the suffering)—the rest is gravy. Ignorance of cosmic laws only exacerbates our plight as humans. So it's up to each individual to become aware and educated. If you wish to learn things the hard way, that's your prerogative. As for myself, I'd rather learn my lessons through the tried and true forms of sex, drugs, and rock 'n' roll, and when I arrive at my destination, I will then be justified in discarding my maps. But when will we arrive already? I suppose that's anyone's guess. In the meantime, we have a hell of a bar car to bounce around in while sharing our stories and interpretations of what this existence is all about. I do have a few ideas (and I have jotted them down for posterity) just in case I should need a reminder down the road.

As our self-knowledge and compassion grow, it becomes inherent within that awareness, for each of us to generously share the fruits of our labor with all beings, no matter what their station in life.

I love to exchange ideas and converse one-on-one with sensitive, intelligent creatures whenever possible. That idea of sharing conversationally influences my writing style. While there is plenty of third-person reportage to be found within the covers of this anthology, there are also a number of first-person, journal-type pieces to give the reader a "you-are-there" perspective.

At the beginning of this millennium, I had the great fortune to spend two weeks in Peru and Bolivia, as well as a month in Tibet—I must say those were truly life-altering experiences. Almost as life-altering as learning how to practice Vipassana meditation. *Arrive without traveling.* Practicing Vipassana is compassion in action: what you might call learning how to become the Bodhisattva.

I first learned about the nobility of the Bodhisattva by listening to Walter Becker and Donald Fagen, the mastermind duo behind Steely Dan. It's an unlikely place to begin a spiritual journey, but it has worked out pretty well for me. The Beatles, the Who, Bob Dylan, the Beach Boys, Love, Aerosmith, Neil Innes, Robyn Hitchcock— all of these artists, and SO many others, have transformed my consciousness by their words and music. Anyone can make "Art." But if someone's artistic statement is capable of causing a cosmic shift in the consciousness of their audience, then that's the greatest cause and effect I know of. Why do I experience such bliss when I listen to the Beatles perform "Rain?" Or why do I feel even better when I myself sing a song that is an expression of my heart and soul? Because: acknowledging and reaffirming life in all of its complexity is a beautifully simple task. All you have to do is allow yourself to feel, and then express those feelings unabashedly without one degree of shame, guilt, or regret. By living the example of love, you perpetuate love: and the really beautiful thing is that ANYONE can do it. After that, it all just boils down to elements of style.

I love this life and I am grateful that I get to share it with you. You are the actor, the director, the screenwriter, the producer, AND the audience in your particular production. Your thoughts set the stage for your entire trip. So come up with some righteous conceits and let's create something beautiful and pleasurable together.

As Joe Strummer, the frontman and spokesperson for the Clash, suggested throughout his body of work: *The Future Is Unwritten*. Unless, of course, time travel turns out to be possible, then all bets are off at that point. The only limitations we have are what we choose to dream about, and subsequently manifest into "reality."

Thank you for buying the ticket and taking the ride. See you on the flip side—and welcome to the show!

Jon Kanis
San Diego, California
August 26, 2014

ONE

The Beat Generation Is Now

Things are symbols of themselves. – **Allen Ginsberg**

Walking on water wasn't built in a day. – **Jack Kerouac**

Among other things, you'll find that you're not the first person who was ever confused and frightened and even sickened by human behavior. You're by no means alone on that score, you'll be excited and stimulated to know. Many, many men have been just as troubled morally and spiritually as you are right now. Happily, some of them kept records of their troubles. You'll learn from them, if you want to. Just as someday, if you have something to offer, someone will learn something from you. It's a beautiful reciprocal arrangement. And it isn't education. It's history. It's poetry. – **from** *Catcher in the Rye* **by J. D. Salinger**

Life is a mysterious adventure, a treasure hunt you might say, and making your way through it can be tricky business. That is why maps were invented. Maps give you a glimpse of the terrain and the potential treasures that await at your "destination." Awareness (intuitive, cognitive) can be its own type of map, and through the application of myth it becomes much easier to chart a course for yourself and still

1

allow for life's mysteries to unfold naturally. That might appear to be a contradiction, but merrily, life is full of them.

Life is also about the reconciliation of seeming opposites. 2,500 years ago, the Buddha taught that creating and maintaining balance is crucial to your personal sense of well-being if the Zen practitioner is to successfully integrate the material realm with the spiritual. Zen masters perpetually emphasize that the only moment that truly exists is the eternal Now. I'd even go so far as to suggest that the entire construct of "history" is a hype and that there really is no such thing if you are living in the here and Now. It's an idea that runs parallel to the relative truth within René Descartes' 17th century maxim "I think, therefore I am."

I've only recently become aware of the fact that in a reality based on symbol systems, the only meaning those symbols have is whatever I choose to project upon them. Words, pictures, objects—they're all symbols of a sort. And I may be a bit slow on the uptake, but I'm waking up to the fact that many of the beliefs I've formed are based upon what I've been told reality is, rather than what my direct personal experience has shown it to be. My perspective shifted profoundly as I learned how to navigate through life with my heart and go with the flow of my feelings. No one within my direct sphere of influence talked much about feelings or intuition as I was coming of age.

And that is one of the many reasons why role models and mentors are of such vital importance. If human beings are to live in a conscious manner, then it is crucial to have mentors along the way who are capable of setting a positive example. Everyone is looking for clues in the mystery of life, it's just that some people are better detectives than others.

Ultimately, how you perceive reality and what you choose to value will dictate the course of your own adventure.

Being in touch with your feelings and knowing how to maturely act upon those impulses is paramount if we are to live our lives beyond mere intellectualization. Bohemians throughout the ages have understood this and that is one of the qualities that sets the artist apart from the remainder of society. By being able to go into the uncharted wilderness (intellectually, emotionally, spiritually) and explore one's heart and psyche to the fullest, the artist embarks on a personal treasure hunt. And the "gold" that he or she returns with is the transcendent discoveries that they share with the rest of the universe. When an artist is capable of baring his soul, both the audience and the artist are enriched by the experience.

This is what writers and poets do and in the literature of the twentieth century few have done it with as much profound candor and vulnerability as the members of the Beat Generation. Call them naïve rebels in need of a bath and a haircut—in fact, hurl whatever insulting epithet you like—the Beats are a tremendously important link to the post-modern world as we know it. As a group of "crazy" and romantic idealists, the Beat Generation shared a vision. It is a vision that perpetuates the stance that nothing is more important than the liberty of every living thing—or more to the point, that everything is sacred. Being Beat is to transform conventions and refuse to accept the status quo. It is about teaching awareness and practicing the beatitude of love. It is a vision of unity, to create a social and spiritual revolution across the planet—a vision that is perpetually ripe in this eternal Now.

It's a worthwhile message that's never gone out of style, or persisted to the point of becoming a foregone conclusion. Are Christ and the Buddha fashionable? To a Zen practitioner it doesn't matter, because history doesn't exist, remember? Certainly the United States of America circa 1955 doesn't exist; the "America" of that space-time continuum is now within the realm of myth and legend. How can I really gain an objective perspective on "history" when most of it is just hearsay relative to my direct personal experience? I wasn't even conceived when Jack Kennedy was assassinated in Dallas, Texas, so how can I truly understand what post-World War II America is all about? History as a system of symbols can be difficult to fathom. One of the things I **do** know, however, is what lies on the printed page of Jack Kerouac's mind through the books that he authored. To bring that experience into the eternal Now, I don't require an historical context to feel those emotive tales of abandon and excess. The search for joy and freedom, the longing for spiritual connection—these are but a few of the timeless excursions into the human condition. For me, the Beats didn't happen sixty years ago, they're happening right Now. And all that is necessary to share in the experience of these eternal truths is a heart that feels and the vision to perceive. Of course, there will always be those who'll insist that the times have changed and you can't hitchhike the way you used to and blah, blah, blah—but it doesn't matter. That is the kind of mindset that believes history is something static and fixed. The Beat Generation is Now and it refuses to conform to any conceptual pigeonhole. Being Beat is a state-of-mind, and you can't blot out that truth by tearing out a page from a calendar. It's as eternal as your next breath or your first kiss. Dig what's on the page, baby. Listen with your eyes and feel.

Author Michael McClure says "I see two definitions of the Beats. I see Allen (Ginsberg), Gregory (Corso), (William) Burroughs and Jack (Kerouac). The Beats. That's it. You can add a lot of people to that list. Then there's the Beat movement, Beat consciousness. I literally see that Beat can be taken as romantic, classic, surreal. I think it can be taken as one of the larger frameworks of human statement."

Jack Kerouac famously referred to the Beats as a "swinging group of new American men intent on joy," and wrote as if he had integrated the spiritual epiphanies of the Buddha by understanding that we are all in this thing together—this thing called Life—and that's where the inherent contradictions of duality creep in. You can proclaim that "We're all One" and express that truth from the depths of your soul, but when you choose to live out those convictions and break away from the established conventions of society, there will always be opposing factions who are heavily invested in keeping things exactly the way they are. If you rock Caesar's boat too hard, you run the risk of being dumped overboard. The status quo has little (or no) use for authentic revolutionaries and that is precisely what the Beats helped stir into action with the freedom movements of the 1960s by mirroring what true liberation could possibly look like. Again, it's a message that never goes out of style regarding love, art, and the politics of conscious co-creation. To my way of thinking they are all interconnected.

Allen Ginsberg believed it imperative that all writers go with the flow of their feelings. His primary epigram remains: "First thought, best thought." This is a similar idea to André

Breton's theory of automatic writing. However, Ginsberg appended that idea by suggesting that in order to remove the illusory barriers between the Self and other beings, it would be useful to take off our clothing so that we might become psychologically naked. Through this act, the purity of our essence would, by default, ooze out. It would have to. Without the façade of clothing to hide behind, what else could be left? Why, merely your body and soul, bare for all to perceive and experience.

Like pure communism, that form of psychic openness has yet to be created on a global scale. But Ginsberg and other members of the Beat movement did their utmost as human beings to push that particular envelope—to look their illusions squarely in the eye and speak out and *act* against unjust social circumstances. That quality of courage and a system of mores based on compassionate values is to be applauded, for if the artist is not honest and open with himself and his audience, then he's just jiving. And we are on the receiving end of enough jive from politicians and other segments of society—we certainly don't need it from the psychic explorers who are creating the myths and symbols of our current age. The Beats understood this and their level of awareness boldly serves to mirror the hypocrisies within a so-called democratic society. It takes a prodigious amount of strength and love to create something of lasting benefit. The Beats tapped into that truth and they had the courage to share that vision with the planet. The Beats chose to draw a different type of map, a map of spiritual ideals that does not shrink in the face of hostility, fear or ignorance.

For me, the perpetual question remains: as we draft our map in this present moment, what sort of vision will we choose to perpetuate? I hereby nominate a world that celebrates diversity, supports solidarity, and performs every deed in the name of unconditional love. And, should you seek the quickest route to the land of self-realization, there are an infinite array of resources to draw from. Role models exist throughout the ages if you're looking for a stance to cop—unless you'd care to do something really radical and invent your own identity. Now that would really be Beat.

❦

THAT WAS ZEN, THIS IS TAO
SEVEN KEYS TO THE KINGDOM
(an auditory tour through the world of being Beat)

1. *The Jack Kerouac Collection* / **Jack Kerouac** (Rhino Word Beat). Possibly the finest single document of what Kerouac is all about, this trio of compact discs houses all three of the LPs that he recorded in 1959, along with several previously unreleased gems. Kerouac's reading of his "Origins of the Beat Generation" essay might well be the last word on the subject. Equally impressive are his readings from *On the Road* and *Visions of Cody* from *The Steve Allen Show*. For a visual accompaniment, screen the documentaries *What Happened to Kerouac?* and *Kerouac, the Movie*. And if these audio recordings merely serve to whet your appetite, *The Jack Kerouac Collection* contains a comprehensive bibliography of Jack's published work. Absolutely essential.

2. *Holy Soul Jelly Roll Poems and Songs (1949–1993)* / **Allen Ginsberg** (Rhino Word Beat). *Holy Soul Jelly Roll* is a staggering four-CD collection by master archivist/

producer Hal Willner that is the auditory equivalent to Walt Whitman's *Leaves of Grass*. The hardcore purists might argue about Ginsberg's relevancy past the 1960s, but the real truth of the matter is that up until his untimely death in 1997, Ginsberg continued to write mind-bending, soul-stirring verse. Ginsberg was a man of letters *and* a man of action, linking arms with all peoples of the world. He also serves as the literary link between the original Beats of the 1950s and the subsequent counterculture that emerged in the 1960s. But hey, don't take my word for it, listen to "After Lalon" and find out for yourself: "Allen Ginsberg warns you, don't follow my path to extinction."

3. *Howls, Raps & Roars (Recordings from the San Francisco Poetry Renaissance)* / **Various Artists** (Fantasy). In addition to housing Ginsberg's classic 1959 LP *Howl and Other Poems*, *Howls, Raps & Roars* includes a full CD of unreleased poetry from the legendary *Mad Mammoth Monster Poetry Readings*. And even though a full disc is unwisely parcelled out to present some of the weaker Lenny Bruce material that Fantasy owns, this collection has much to rave about. None of the material on *Holy Soul Jelly Roll* is duplicated here, so if four CDs of Ginsberg's work seems a bit daunting, this is an excellent place to start. And nowhere else will you find the recorded work of Gregory Corso, Michael McClure, Kenneth Rexroth, Lawrence Ferlinghetti, Peter Orlovsky, Philip Lamantia, Lew Welch, David Meltzer, and Philip Whalen, all housed under the same roof. This is literally the Who's Who of the Beat poetry movement. The booklet alone is worth the price of admission.

4. *The Beat Generation* / **Various Artists** (Rhino Word Beat). This collection deserves a big asterisk by it. If it

weren't for Rhino's Word Beat division, there might not be a spoken word section at your local record store. Rhino usually does a stellar job with all of its reissues, but this collection has so many misfires that it is impossible to give it an enthusiastic recommendation. Yes, there are a number of gems to be found in this three-CD box set, such as a previously unreleased interview with Jack Kerouac and several wonderful radio documentary segments. But a lot of space in this collection is dedicated to kitschy, rip-off merchants, lamely attempting to jump on the hip bandwagon. A question of aesthetics erupts when you hear Rod McKuen giving you his take on what the Beat scene is all about. Ditto when it comes to Edd Byrnes doing his Kookie schtick. Need I go on? *The Beat Generation* tries to cover so much ground that it barely manages to scratch the surface. If you're interested in learning about the timeless genius of Charlie Parker or Lenny Bruce, there are much better places to hang out and spend your bread.

5. *The Berkeley Concert* / **Lenny Bruce** (Bizarre/Straight). Produced by Frank Zappa and issued five years after Bruce's tragic expiration in 1966, *The Berkeley Concert* stands as **the** tribute to Lenny's brilliance as a free-form "word blower" and social commentator. This is the snapshot that speaks well over a thousand words. Bruce remains a central reference point to the Us vs Them mentality in America as the 1950s bled into the '60s, and his subsequent persecution by the powers-that-were perfectly illustrates the degree of corruption within the existing power structure. Lenny Bruce had the *cojones* to exercise his First Amendment rights, and it ended up costing him his life. Paranoia strikes deep indeed. Check out *The Midnight Concert* and *Let the Buyer Beware* as well.

6. *Bop.* **Any** discussion of the Beat aesthetic would be remiss without mentioning the jazz revolution that occurred in the middle '40s through the early '50s. In fact, they're nearly inseperable, with poetry evolving stride for stride with bebop in the realm of the Beats. Charlie Parker and Dizzy Gillespie are rightfully credited as the midwives of this genre-bending hybrid, but Thelonious Monk deserves equal credit for shaping bop into a full-blown movement. Be sure to check out Monk's *The Complete Blue Note Recordings* and ALL of the sides that Parker recorded for Dial and Savoy. Gillespie protégé Miles Davis' Prestige recordings and his earliest sessions for Columbia (i.e. *Round About Midnight*) are also essential if you care to slip into the mood of the times. It's as close to hanging out at Birdland circa '54 as you're likely going to get without a time machine.

7. *Bringing It All Back Home, Highway 61 Revisited, Blonde on Blonde* / **Bob Dylan** (Columbia). If Allen Ginsberg had never written "Howl" would "Like a Rolling Stone" exist? Who knows, but with "Subterranean Homesick Blues" Dylan sent out a clear message that he was no longer the folk troubadour whose answers were blowin' in the wind. Dylan simultaneously plugged in his guitar, AND into the surreal verse of the Beats, as his musical vision shifted into mystical overdrive. With an obvious nod to Kerouac (*The Subterraneans*), Woody Guthrie's greatest disciple is caught prying off the lid of existentialism in this holy triumvirate of Beat poetry set to rock 'n' roll. And the ads of the time said it all: "Nobody sings Dylan like Dylan."

Schlock, #14, 1994
reprinted in *Subliminal Tattoos*, #6, Fall, 1995

TWO

I'll See You in My Dreams: Looking Back at the *Concert for George*

It was a typical, sepia-toned, autumnal day on that particular Friday in London, November 29, 2002, with the sky a grey mist across South Kensington. However, **NO** amount of precipitation could have possibly dampened my spirits as I stood in queue to gain entrance into the Royal Albert Hall with several thousand other fortunate souls to witness one of the greatest evenings in music history. And I am speaking, of course, about the *Concert for George*—the granddaddy of all musical tributes, in honor of the late, great George Harrison.

This week marks the tenth anniversary of the concert (staged one year to the day of Harrison's passing on 11.29.01) and in seasonal homage of practicing gratitude, it seems appropriate to offer up some perspective on that historic night, and share why I feel the *Concert for George* to be one of the grandest evenings I will ever experience. Grand in the sense that it remains a mind-blowing example of how much joy can be created when thousands of human beings come together in a room to beam Love at one another.

Not to make too large a point of it, but I perceive music to be a combination of both sacrament and church, in its fullest expression nothing short of Divinity, and to walk into the Royal Albert Hall that evening—well, you want to talk about a room having energy? Jeez, I was completely sober and the walls were vibrating. My. Sweet. Lord. It was akin to an amnesiac stepping across a threshold and re-entering their spiritual home. It was certainly no less profound than my previous experience of reverberating with 60 Tibetan monks, all chanting in unison in a Himalayan monastery. In fact, change the locale to a Hindu temple, light a stick of Nag Champa, and it could have been the same vibe.

The evening began with the traditional Hindu prayer of *Sarve Shaam* before Eric Clapton offered these words: "We are here to celebrate the life and music of George Harrison. This is a blessed occasion for me because I can share my love of George with you. And I think most important of it all is that his wife, Olivia, and his son, Dhani, can experience and witness how much we loved him through his music tonight." Clapton then introduced Harrison's musical and spiritual mentor, "the maestro" Ravi Shankar, who told the audience, "I strongly feel that George is here tonight. I mean, how can he not be here when all of us who love him so much have assembled all together to sing for him?"

With two dozen Indian musicians conducted by Annoushka Shankar, the music commenced at 8 PM sharp, weaving an intoxicating spell of irregular rhythms and unfamiliar dialects, with sitar, tabla, strings, and vocalists in unison within the melody to create a deliriously serpentine sensation. This music is as exhilarating and exciting as any pile-driving rock 'n' roll on the planet, without a sneer or harsh word to be found. After seven minutes of amazing sitar work on Annoushka Shankar's "Your Eyes," Jeff Lynne takes the stage to sing "The Inner Light," the 1968 Beatles track that found Harrison setting the words of the *Tao*

Te Ching to a traditional raga. The Indian section of the program concludes with a brand new twenty-minute composition from Ravi Shankar titled "Arpan," described by its composer as a "offering, gifting, giving, and dedicating—all combined in one word." If I had to use one word to describe "Arpan" it would be "mesmerizing." All of the musicians are wonderful, but the solo that Eric Clapton takes toward the end is breathtaking.

And while I'm on the subject of Eric Clapton, allow me to add that his playing throughout this particular evening is nothing short of stunning. I must confess to having very little appreciation for 95 percent of what the man has chosen to release under his own name since 1971, and yet on the three unorthodox occasions I have managed to see him perform live (*Bob Dylan's 30th Anniversary Concert Celebration*, his 2000 induction into the Rock and Roll Hall of Fame, and the *Concert for George*), he absolutely burned the stage with an intensity and purpose that I don't usually experience from his recordings. It is clear from the onset that his performance at this gathering was extremely personal and its significance shows in every frame of footage from the event.

After a 35-minute intermission, the picture hanging over the center of the stage of "mature" George sporting a moustache (from the 1970s) is replaced with a picture of "Beatle" George (circa 1964) playing a Gretsch guitar. And as swiftly as you can possibly move from the sacred to the profane, an announcement comes over the PA proclaiming "Ladies and gentlemen, Monty Python's Flying Circus!" and on marches Terry Jones, Terry Gilliam, Eric Idle, and Neil Innes dressed as French waiters for the wonderfully bawdy "Sit on My Face." They conclude the number by taking a bow and revealing that none of them are wearing trousers under their aprons.

Which succinctly sums up the devilish dichotomy of George Harrison's wry Liverpudlian nature quite well; devotionally reverent one minute, cocking a snoot at conventional morality the next. Who else would simultaneously donate thousands of pounds to promote spiritual organizations throughout the world and then start his own independent film production company (Handmade Films) in order to finance one of the biggest piss-takes on religion that's ever been produced: Monty Python's glorious satire on Christianity, *Life of Brian*?

Just as Gandhi famously stated, "my life is my example," so it is with Harrison. The man walked his talk with countless examples of his generosity and exercised the belief that it is imperative to share your gifts with the world, a philosophy that is echoed in the evening's program notes. "From my point of view, the material world is not necessarily just down to money or gain or wealth or power, but material in the sense of the physical...the physical world as opposed to a spiritual world. So the material world is where we live. We live subject to the laws of relativity, which is good and bad and up and down. I wrote a song called 'Living in the Material World,' and it was from that I decided to call the foundation the Material World Foundation. Most people would think of the material world as representing purely money and greed and take offense. But in my view it means a physical world. It's the idea that if it is money and greed, then give the greedy money away in the material world." It was in this spirit of giving that Harrison lived his life and that the entire night was conceived, with the remainder of the evening strongly resembling the program that George created for 1971's *Concert for Bangladesh*, a milestone in social consciousness for rock's first major benefit concert.

As musical director, Clapton exercised great editorial judgment in the song selections, diplomatically allowing for all the major players in George's life to have a dignified segment in which to shine. Harrison's most consistent collaborator from 1987 and beyond was Electric Light Orchestra co-founder Jeff Lynne, who turned in great performances of "I Want to Tell You" and "Give Me Love (Give Me Peace on Earth)." Procol Harum's keyboardist Gary Brooker belted out a rollicking "Old Brown Shoe" and Clapton really nails it on "Beware of Darkness," with a soulful vocal and a guitar lead that is lyrical, sad, and beautiful, all in the same instant.

At 9:35 PM Joe Brown comes on and does "Here Comes the Sun" and "That's the Way It Goes," followed by his daughter Sam and keyboardist Jools Holland for "Horse to Water." If it feels at all like a slight lull, there is a complete sea change when Tom Petty and the Heartbreakers take the stage and perform a rocking three-song set of "Taxman" (from *Revolver*), "I Need You" (from *Help!*), and "Handle with Care," the song that served to catalyze Harrison, Lynne, Petty, Bob Dylan, and Roy Orbison into the Traveling Wilburys.

At 10 PM straight up the night takes an intensifying shift on "Isn't It a Pity," with Clapton sharing vocals with organist Billy Preston. At 10:08 PM Ringo Starr is introduced and the audience shrieks its approval. If there was ever a person destined to sit behind a drum kit it is Richard Starkey—the guy is definitely not front man material. But only a complete cad could not be warmed by Ringo's guileless manner, as he sways to and fro to sing "Photograph" (a 1973 number one hit, co-written with George), and the Carl Perkins standard "Honey Don't."

When Ringo steps up and says "it gives me great pleasure now to introduce another friend of George's: Paul McCartney," the place goes absolutely bonkers. It is a safe assumption that everyone in the building is a Beatles freak and now, for the first time since Harrison's death, the two remaining Beatles are on stage together among a dozen or so of the greatest musicians in the world—who incidentally also happen to be Harrison's best mates. McCartney turns on the charm and performs at the height of his powers, delivering a lovely performance of "For You Blue" and sharing a duet with Eric Clapton on "Something," arguably Harrison's most beloved song.

This performance of "Something" never fails to bring tears to my eyes—I find it so emotionally pure and beautiful. The contrast between the busky manner that McCartney employs for the first half of the song on ukulele and then—boom!—two snaps of the snare drum and Clapton is off into outer space accompanied by the London Metropolitan Orchestra, conducted by Michael Kamen in one of his last public appearances—less than a year later on 11.18.03, Kamen would suffer a fatal heart attack at the age of 55.

Bassist Klaus Voormann joins in as McCartney continues to soar on "All Things Must Pass" and shares vocals with Clapton on a passionate reading of "While My Guitar Gently Weeps." For "My Sweet Lord" and "Wah-Wah" to REALLY come to life, it requires the trademarked, over-the-top, Phil Spector "Wall of Sound," with not one, nor two, but three drummers (Ringo Starr, Jim Keltner, and Henry Spinetti) on stage with three more percussionists (including Ray Cooper and Jim Capaldi). Double horns, double electric bass, double keyboards, God knows how many guitars, two choirs, and an orchestra. It smacks a bit of overkill, but it is a HUGE adrenalin rush that can't help but bowl you over and leave you feeling emotionally drained.

Which is *exactly* how I feel after that rousing climax, as Joe Brown saunters back on stage for the encore. With George's favorite instrument, the ukulele, he croons the old jazz standard "I'll See You in My Dreams." It is as sweet a denouement as you could ask for, with all the musicians gathered together at the back of the stage swaying in unison, and thousands of red paper roses floating down from the heavens. I never tire of revisiting this performance on DVD, or the memory of this evening. It serves as a perennial reminder of how fleeting every moment is and just how dreamlike life can be. (The set list is in the **Appendix** on page 473.)

Namah Parvarti. And namaste.

So, how *did* I wind up in London on 11.29.02? When the Universe wants you to be somewhere, it conspires with all of its power to make it happen. It also helps to set intentions, follow through, be determined, and work your magic. I am forever grateful to Mike Campbell for making my attendance at the *Concert for George* possible. I met Mr. Campbell in the spring of 2002 when he was being inducted with Tom Petty and the Heartbreakers into the Rock and Roll Hall of Fame at the Waldorf-Astoria in New York. I was working the event as an consultant to the Hall during my time co-creating the archival music footage empire that is Reelin' in the Years Productions. Serendipitous bliss.

San Diego Troubadour, December, 2012

THREE

The Transformation of
John Lennon

October 9th marks the 73rd anniversary of John Winston Ono Lennon's birth. At this point in the narrative the cultural significance of Mister Lennon and the body of work that he left behind ought to be a given, whether in collaboration with the Beatles, as a solo artist, or with his wife and life partner, Yoko Ono. However, one of the least discussed (and most significant aspects) of Lennon's journey is how profoundly his consciousness was transformed in the 40 short years that he was alive on this planet. He was a twentieth-century Renaissance Man. If art and philosophy have any intrinsic value to our evolutionary voyage as human beings, then surely the ideas and symbols that Lennon left behind offer a timeless example of how much one person is capable of growing in order to express their divine essence.

Consciously or not, Lennon's entire life was about extreme transformation. Due in part to the disruptive nature of his upbringing, he spent much of his existence seeking out "the truth"—that elusively relative construct where perception is so subjective and yet allows (paradoxically) for so many points of view to be universal.

Lennon was a classic Libra, an astrological archetype that is all about seeking balance on a teeter-totter of hope and despair. Born during a blitzkrieg of the Third Reich that rained upon the council flats of Liverpool, England, in the fall of 1940, he came into the world literally rocking and rolling in a vibration of violence. Twenty years later he would return that energy from whence it came, back into the streets and nightclubs of Hamburg, Germany, as a Teddy Boy hooligan, eventually allowing himself to be made over by his gay manager in a bid to seduce the show biz world on its own terms. The campaign apparently succeeded.

Growing up without either of his biological parents (he was raised primarily by his mother's older sister, Mary), he sought emotional refuge from the pain caused by a father who abandoned him and a mostly absentee mother who was killed by a drunken, off-duty, police officer when Lennon was seventeen. His response to these tragedies in the stifling post-war conservatism of 1950s Britain was to become a knee-jerk rebel in the classic *Look Back in Anger* stance of the Angry Young Man. His deep insecurities prompted him to ridicule the infirm, with the chauvinistic attitudes of his teenage years being typical of males from the era.

"I always was a rebel," said Lennon. "But on the other hand, I wanted to be loved and accepted and not just be a loudmouth/lunatic/poet/musician. But I cannot change what I am not.

"But I'm not gonna change the way I look or the way I feel to conform to anything. I've always been a freak. So I've been a freak all my life and I have to live with that. I'm one of 'those' people."

What is *truly* freaky is the amount of artistic and psychological growth that Lennon's group, the Beatles, exhibited during their seven-plus years (1962–1970) of recording for

EMI. With the release of *A Hard Day's Night* in July of 1964, Lennon recorded what was arguably his first solo album, having penned ten of the album's thirteen originals himself. With two albums and three singles a year contractually due to EMI, plus the continuous strain of performing concerts throughout the world, the demands of being in the most successful pop group in history were intense. Numerous substances were used to cushion the pressure and fulfill the need for endless creativity. The booze and pills that had fueled the Beatles music from their earliest days in Liverpool and Hamburg eventually gave way to marijuana by the end of 1964 (famously introduced to them in New York by Bob Dylan). By 1966 the influence of LSD could be discerned throughout the *Revolver* and *Sgt. Pepper's Lonely Hearts Club Band* albums, with cocaine, speed, and heroin floating through the ether during the sessions for *The Beatles, Let It Be*, and *Abbey Road*.

Towards the end of his thirties Lennon wrote that "being a Beatle nearly cost me my life and certainly cost me a great deal of my health—the drinking and drugs having started before we were professional musicians—all in the effort to reach 'out there.'

"I think the basic thing nobody asks is why do people take drugs of any sort? Why do we have to have these accessories to normal living to live? Is there something wrong with society that's making us so pressurized that we cannot live without guarding ourselves against it?

"We've been through the drug scene and there's nothing like being straight. You need hope and hope is something that you build up within yourself and with your friends. The worst drugs are as bad as anybody's told you. It's just a dumb trip. I can't condemn people if they get into it, because one gets into it for one's own personal, social, and emotional reasons. But it's something to be avoided if one can help it."

You name it and Lennon tried it in an almighty attempt to erase his conditioning, float downstream, and explore the mysteries of inner space. Drugs eventually gave way to transcendental meditation. By 1968, with the sixties reaching a peculiar crescendo of unparalleled violence and unrest across the globe, Lennon found a person that would help to steer him out of the cul-de-sac of his own mind: conceptual avant-garde Japanese-American artist Yoko Ono.

"She's me in drag" is how Lennon described the former Fluxus artist, a woman who challenged him at every turn regarding the antiquated ideas he held about himself, women, race, and spirituality. She turned out to be a mirror that saw right through him. "I'd never met a woman I considered as intelligent as me. And I always had this dream of meeting an artist, an artist girl who would be like me. And I thought it was a myth, but then I met Yoko and that was it."

Their union created a scandal (both of them being married when they met) and their disruption of the status quo caused resentment within the Beatles and to many of the group's fans, who unjustly blamed Ono as the cause of the quartet's disintegration in the spring of 1970. Lennon: "I started the band. I disbanded it. It's as simple as that."

They wed on March 20, 1969, and for the next eleven years the Lennons became performance artists *par excellence*, producing an extraordinary body of work (both together and apart) that confounded as much as astounded, flipping numerous social conventions on their heads. With Ono and Lennon, East met West and the prejudice that confronted them in the media and within various social circles, was a shock to their utopian idealism. As their addiction to drugs dissipated in the face of Dr. Arthur Janov's primal scream therapy, so did junk food and red meat give way to a macrobiotic diet. After leaving Great Britain in 1972, they came to the United States, embracing New Left politics and guerrilla theatre. Gradually, Lennon morphed into a feminist, putting forth the unpopular viewpoint that women are the niggers of the world. Songs, slogans, and media campaigns were all conscious attempts to shift the awareness of the masses by chanting jingles such as "Give Peace a Chance," "Instant Karma," and introducing the "subversive" notion of imagining a world without heaven, money, or war, and living a life of peaceful co-existence. Playing those "Mind Games" as it were.

"I'm a peacenik," said Lennon. "War is big business and they like war because it keeps them fat and happy. The thing is to protest, but protest non-violently. Violence begets violence. If you run around wild you get smashed, that's the law of the universe. It's up to the people. You can't blame it on the government and say, 'Oh, they're going to put us into war.' We put them there and we allow it and if we really want to change it, we can."

Lennon and Ono understood the power of the media and using one's psyche to project and visualize an alternative to the agenda of the ruling class that keeps people divisive and at war with each other. Religion, racism, sexism, class— all of these aspects of society were brought out onto the public stage in the work of these two "holy fools."

"I think our society is run by insane people for insane objectives," said Lennon. "And I think I'm liable to be put away for expressing that. That's what's insane about it."

☯

It's the same with the Christians (so called). They're so busy condemning themselves and others, or preaching at people, or worse, still killing for Christ. None of them understanding, or trying in the least, to behave like a Christ. It seems to me that the only true Christians were (are?) the Gnostics, who believe in self-knowledge, i.e., becoming Christ themselves, reaching the Christ within. Christ, after all, is Greek for light. The Light is the Truth. All any of us are trying to do is precisely that: turn on the light. All the better to see you with, my dear. Christ, Buddha, Mohammed, Moses, Milarepa, and other great ones spent their time in fasting, praying, meditation, and left "maps" of the territory of "God" for all to see and follow in our own way. – **from** *Skywriting by Word of Mouth* **by John Lennon**

☯

Convinced that the Lennons were going to disrupt the Republican National Convention, the U.S. government tried to deport them in 1972. The FBI and the CIA had their phones tapped, reporting daily on their activities, and assembled a massive dossier, based on the perception that John and Yoko's peace efforts would undermine the military-industrial complex's stranglehold on the world at large. The neo-conservative far right (Nixon, *et al*) believed that the Lennons were capable of swinging public opinion away from their fear-based, war-mongering agenda, and fought to suppress their activities. Only after President Nixon's resignation did they manage to successfully petition for the legal right to stay in the country, on July 27, 1976.

Nine months earlier, on Lennon's 35th birthday, the couple became parents with the birth of Sean Ono Lennon on October 9, 1975. For the next five years Lennon transformed himself into a "househusband," and surrendered all business matters to Ono.

A conspiracy of silence speaks louder than words.

— Dr. Winston O'Boogie

In the summer of 1980, the Lennons returned to the recording studio and on November 17, 1980, released *Double Fantasy*, a meditation on family values and domesticity. Two weeks earlier Ronald Reagan was elected as the 40th president of the United States. On Monday, December 8, 1980, Lennon's ultimate transformation occurred when he was murdered in the archway of the Dakota apartment building in New York City where he and Ono lived. The murder suspect, Mark Chapman, made no attempt to flee from the crime scene and pled guilty to the charge of first-degree murder—insuring that no official investigation would ever occur. In the book *Who Killed John Lennon?*, author Fenton Bresler makes the argument that Lennon's killer was a product of the CIA's MK ULTRA program of mind control, becoming a Manchurian Candidate-type patsy. Eliminating Lennon preemptively removed a potential impediment to the Republican right's shift back into power. It's a point of view that Lennon's youngest son shared.

"He was a countercultural revolutionary, and the government takes that shit really seriously historically," said Sean Lennon to Rebecca Mead of *The New Yorker* in 1998. "He was dangerous to the government...these pacifist revolutionaries are historically killed by the government, and anybody who thinks that Mark Chapman was just some crazy guy who killed my dad for his personal interests is insane, I think, or very naïve, or hasn't thought about it clearly. It was in the best interests of the United States [government] to have my dad killed, definitely. And, you know, that worked against them, to be honest, because once he died his powers grew. So, I mean, fuck them. They didn't get what they wanted."

Is it truly possible that Lennon was perceived as enough of a threat that he could have harmed anyone within the political arena? What sort of motive could there have been to assassinate John Lennon? Had his stance as a pro-active pacifist earned him those kinds of enemies? Is that the reason why José Sanjenis Perdomo, a Cuban secret police agent (who doubled as an operative for the CIA), was working as a doorman at the Dakota the night Lennon was killed?

John Lennon: "Nothing will stop me, and whether I'm here or wherever I may be, I'll always have the same feelings and I'll say what I feel. My role in society, or any artist or poet's role, is to try and express what we all feel. Not to tell people how to feel. Not as a preacher, not as a leader, but as a reflection of us all.

"I still believe in love. I still believe in peace. And where there's life, there's hope."

San Diego Troubadour, October, 2013

The Beach Boys
Made in California 1962–2012

It's never been easy being a Beach Boys fan. Those hodads from Hawthorne, California were never the hippest dudes in the world and their relevance to contemporary music pretty much ceased over thirty years ago. That said, the surviving alumni of Brian Wilson, Mike Love, Al Jardine, David Marks and Bruce Johnston celebrated the milestone of their 50th anniversary last year with a world tour and an irrelevant album of new material (*That's Why God Made the Radio*), underscoring why Capitol records fiscally churns out a "best of" Beach Boys collection with the regularity of the summer solstice. With easy corporate justification too, because as long as there is a need to be transported to a mythical, bygone era, unsullied by the demands of a modern-day world gone wacko, there will always be an audience for the simplistic, choirboy ear candy of the Beach Boys.

At first glance it would appear that *Made in California* is yet another exercise in fleecing a devoted fan base and continuing to cash in on the legacy of the Wilson brothers, their cousin Mike and their legions of devoted colleagues who have pitched in along the way (there are over 700 other musicians and collaborators listed in the accompanying credits to this 174-song collection). However, you might want to do a double take because looks can be deceiving. If you already own 1993's *Good Vibrations* four-disc box set, then why would you want to shell out another 125 dollars to largely repeat the experience? Additionally, novices would be better served looking elsewhere in order to navigate the labyrinth of the Beach Boys mystifying musical output.

The undeniably great news about this six-disc package is that the sonics have never sounded more full, and if you play back your music on equipment more upscale than a cellular phone, then *Made in California* is an epiphany of immense proportions. As digital technology keeps improving, so does the luster and punch of these timeless classics. Many kudos to engineer/producer Mark Linett for his groundbreaking work remixing many of these songs from their original multi-track reels. Selections most benefiting from the facelift are: "Do You Wanna Dance," "Do It Again," "Country Air," "Wild Honey," "Darlin'," "Let the Wind Blow," and "Meant for You" (with an additional section unique to the original version on *Friends*). Other rarities such as "Sail Plane Song" and "Soulful Old Man Sunshine" also sound great in the context of this collection.

The bad news is that if you are a Beach Boys completist, by definition you HAVE to own this set because many of the unreleased songs, alternate takes, remixes and rarities, are an absolute godsend. Hardcore fans will also appreciate how *Made in California* offers up ample proof that the dark horse of the Beach Boys, middle brother Dennis Wilson, was as accomplished and expressive a singer and songwriter as his lionized older brother Brian. Both sides of Dennis' 1970 solo single ("Sound of Free" b/w "Fallin' in Love") make their digital debut, as well as the previously unreleased gem "Wouldn't It be Nice (to Live Again)," that was incomprehensibly left off of 1971's *Surf's Up*.

The first two discs of *Made in California* cover the years between 1962 and 1967, where five yokels from the suburbs took the regional fad of surfing, added the teenage obsessions of cars, girls and uncomplicated fun, and managed to become an international sensation. Brian Wilson's melodic gifts, together with his determination to beat both Phil Spector and the Beatles at their own games, pushed the Beach Boys music to the absolute zenith of emotional expressionism in mid-'60s American pop. Disc two is pretty much immaculate, providing incontrovertible evidence as to why we should care about this group in perpetuity. After the artistic success of *Pet Sounds* and the delayed gratification of the *SMiLE* project, Brian became the proverbial Icarus, compromising his angelic characteristics by flying too damn close to the Sun. Forever afterwards the Beach Boys became a democracy and disc three (1967–1971) suggests that for a short time the new program of diversification was an unqualified success. Disc Four (1971–1979) starts off strong, but by 1973's *Holland* the enterprise was becoming creatively bankrupt and save for 1977's *The Beach Boys Love You*, the remainder of their back catalog (1978–2012) remains for the appreciation of fanatics who are incapable of recognizing a dead horse as it continues to be flogged.

The main justification for the existence of *Made in California* lies in the rarities to be found on discs five and six: fifteen previously unreleased live tracks spanning 1965–1993, demonstrating that at their peak the Beach Boys were a great live ensemble, especially during the period of 1968–1973 with Carl Wilson at the helm. Disc six *From the Vaults…* contains studio outtakes, demos and remixes that are essential to the overall big picture (some of which will be familiar from bootlegs): an alternate vocal for "Don't Worry Baby," the backing track for "Guess I'm Dumb," "Sherry She Needs Me," "Mona Kana" and a demo for "Be With Me" (both *20/20* outtakes), "Where Is She?" (a great *Sunflower* outtake), "I Believe in Miracles" (a brief vocal snippet from *Smiley Smile*), *a cappella* mixes for "Slip on Through" and "This Whole World," and two beautiful Dennis Wilson tracks from 1974, "Barnyard Blues" and "My Love Lives On."

There is a cornucopia of cool, previously unpublished photographs in a well-designed book that cops the vibe of a high school annual, evoking the days when Brian, Mike, Dennis, Carl, Al, and David all passed through the halls of Hawthorne High ("onward Cougars, onward Cougars"). Under the caption of "Never to Be Forgotten" are pictures of the late Dennis and Carl Wilson, bringing to mind the grand irony that, after all the punishing self-abuse Brian Wilson laid upon himself during the 1970s, he should be the last man standing of the Wilson brothers.

Ultimately, *Made in California* is a mixed blessing for the true diehards who will really appreciate this material from the archives, and yet are being asked to fork out once again for the greatest hits that they have likely purchased at least ten times over the last 50 years. In spite of the undeniable genius of so much of their best work, THAT is ultimately why it isn't easy being a Beach Boys fan.

Ugly Things, #36, Fall/Winter, 2013

FIVE

Scribe of the Tribe:
The Ballad of Paul Williams

Each man creates himself. Do not be afraid to love. The only sin is self-hatred. It is the act of self-negation. Words contain no awareness. They can only trigger awareness. It does no good to try to impress a man with some thought he can't relate to. But if you can make him realize the obvious, that might change his life. – from *Das Energi* by **Paul Williams**

Don't ask me nothin' about nothin'
I just might tell you the truth.

"Outlaw Blues" – **Bob Dylan**

In the mythic psyche of the vast American landscape known as the Wild West, there are few things as celebrated as the archetype of the pioneer: the staunch individual who takes risks where others fear to tread. *The Hero with a Thousand Faces* who opens up new vistas of perception for the benefit and preparation of others. As revolutionary trailblazers basking in the adventure of the unknown, pioneers possess a vision of how to transform the world into something grander than what has come before. When we celebrate the innovations of the pioneer, we simultaneously promote the evolution of the race by allowing our most progressive ideas to prevail. And call it being "educated" if you like, or simply being aware, but for any sort of evolution to occur a sense of our back story is crucial—because how can we know where we are going if we don't understand where we've been? History is our moral compass (Joseph Campbell tagged it *The Power of Myth*) and it is through these stories that we know ourselves as a people.

Thankfully, every tribe throughout the ages has a learned wanderer who goes out into the world and reports his findings back to the village—for the past twenty years San Diego played host to one of the twentieth century's most pioneering scribes: Mister Paul Steven Williams, who passed away on March 27, 2013 due to complications sustained from a traumatic head injury in 1995. As the author and editor of over 30 books covering a range of topics, from science fiction fandom to the underground rock 'n' roll counterculture, Williams was also passionate about progressive politics and expressed his spiritual observations through the "practical philosophy" of his cosmic blank verse. He is considered by many to be the father of rock journalism with the creation of *Crawdaddy!* magazine, the first American publication to write about rock 'n' roll as a serious art form, predating the similar enterprise of Jann Wenner's *Rolling Stone* by eighteen months. As a seventeen-year-old freshman at Swarthmore College (near Philadelphia, Pennsylvania), Williams was an atypical wünderkind. Inspired by the grassroots broadsides being published for the science fiction and folk music communities, he took it upon himself to fire the first shot in declaring the good news that innovations within the world of rock 'n' roll had reached a new plateau. And he wanted to tell the world about it.

Williams: "The first issue of *Crawdaddy! [The Magazine of Rock]* was printed on Sunday, January 30, 1966, in a basement in Brooklyn, New York, on the mimeograph belonging to and operated by Ted White. I wrote everything in that first issue myself. The cover featured a quote from a new British group, the Fortunes, talking to a London music paper after returning from their first U.S. tour: 'There is no musical paper scene out there like there is in England. The trades are strictly for the business side of music and the only things left are the fan magazines that mostly do the 'what color sock my idol wears' bit.'

"My vision of the magazine [was to provide a forum] where young people could share with each other the powerful, life-changing experiences that we were having listening to new music in the mid-1960s. Since I didn't have a way to get my new magazine into the hands of thousands of young music lovers immediately, my short-term focus was to get the attention of the radio station and record company people to whom I planned to mail complimentary copies of the first issue. In truth, I really was interested in whether a record would be a "hit" or not and if that was something I could predict or influence. I had been fascinated by Top 40 artists since I was ten years old, impatiently bicycling to the record store every week on the day the local radio station's new Top 40 handout sheet would be available. (Where's 'Charlie Brown' by the Coasters this week?)

"We printed 500 copies of that first issue. The first copies were mailed from New York (five cents apiece for first-class mail then) on Monday before I hitchhiked back to Swarthmore, carrying the rest of the magazines, many of which I soon mailed to music business names from *Billboard* magazine's annual directory. The total budget for the first issue, including postage, mimeograph stencils, paper, ink, fifteen-cent subway fares, peanut butter sandwiches, and the one album I bought and reviewed (Simon and Garfunkel's *Sounds of Silence*) was less than 40 dollars.

"The most noteworthy response to the new magazine came later in the week when Paul Simon called me at the freshman dormitory to say that my review was the first 'intelligent' thing that had been written about their music. Perhaps he also gently corrected my false idea that Garfunkel was the guitar player of the duo (I'd figured he had to be, since Simon wrote the songs and sang the leads). I was invited to meet them on my next trip to New York. They introduced me to their manager and brought me along to a concert and a radio interview."

Beware means be aware.

Born in Boston, Massachusetts, May 19, 1948, it seemed inevitable that Williams would come to the West Coast as he later claimed to have "California in his blood. My dad [Robert] is from Palo Alto. He met my Brooklyn mom [Janet] at Los Alamos, working on the atomic bomb [i.e. the Manhattan Project]." Small wonder that with a nuclear physicist for a father it would be natural for Williams to become passionate about the ideas contained in the literary realm of science fiction. Not to mention the explosive fissions occurring in the world of rock 'n' roll.

Williams: "The reason why I started *Crawdaddy!* is because it had never been done before. I was seventeen and heavily influenced and inspired by the two scenes that I'd hung out in during my teen years: science fiction fandom and the Cambridge, Massachusetts folk music thing. Science fiction fans are readers who get involved in a conversation with each other and soon become more interested in the conversation than in the SF stories that brought them together in the first place. They [we] invented the word fanzine. I used to publish a science fiction fanzine when I was fourteen and fifteen, so I knew that the freedom of the press belongs to anyone who owns a typewriter and can cut a stencil and has access to a mimeograph.

"I read an article by Jim Warren about how to become a magazine publisher. He got across to me the idea that what you needed was to find an audience that had a keen interest in something that was not yet being covered in a professional magazine and go forth and fill the niche.

"So I discovered girls and Dave Van Ronk and Howlin' Wolf and didn't publish any fanzines for awhile. I heard Skip James perform at Club 47. Then the Rolling Stones converted me to rock 'n' roll and I was off to my freshman year in college and I started thinking that if there were folk music magazines, why not a rock 'n' roll magazine? I thought I'd call it *Crawdaddy!* after the club in London where the Rolling Stones and the Yardbirds got their start."

After publishing a few issues of *Crawdaddy!* Williams dropped out of college, moved to the Philadelphia suburbs, went back to Boston for awhile and eventually landed in Greenwich Village. Williams: "Within a month of arriving in New York, *Crawdaddy!* was written up in Howard Smith's "Scene" column in the *Village Voice* and the next thing I knew I was at a meeting of Interesting People and Richard Alpert (*aka* Ram Dass) was telling us about the Human Be-In that had just been held in San Francisco and we were there to talk about bringing it out east. Four of us of like mind detached ourselves from the rest of the conversation and went ahead and organized the first New York Be-In for Easter Sunday, 1967 in Central Park. It was really great. We believed in no agenda, no explanation, no entertainment— just let people show up. And they did. It was the first time that I saw really serious energy surfacing.

"There was a sense that something was happening and it just seemed to feed on itself. I saw the Doors at Ondine in New York and Buffalo Springfield at the Whisky before their first album came out and the Airplane and the Dead and Janis at the psychedelic ballrooms in San Francisco. I first smoked dope with a guy from a group called the Lost in Cambridge in September of '66 but I didn't get off and didn't try it again until I was interviewing Brian Wilson in his meditation tent in his living room in Bel Air a couple of days before Christmas that same year." During that visit to Los Angeles, Williams wrote about the tracks that Wilson was currently working on, being one of the first people to hear the album-in-progress that he and Van Dyke Parks were creating under the working title of *Dumb Angel*, later to be called *SMiLE*. When Wilson shelved the project in the spring of 1967, the myth around *SMiLE* grew to immense proportions, in part by Williams' excitations about the material in the pages of *Crawdaddy!* No one knew at the time that it would be another four decades before those legendary tracks would be officially released.

By the end of 1968, after three years of publishing *Crawdaddy!* (where the readership jumped from its initial 500 copies per issue to a staggering 25,000), Williams decided to walk away from the enterprise—and say goodbye to New

York City. "I just wanted to go on to the next thing," he said, "which turned out to be a cabin in the woods in Mendocino."

After handing the reins of the magazine off to some friends, Williams was still interested in doing freelance assignments. In early 1969 Jann Wenner asked him to interview Timothy Leary for *Rolling Stone*. One thing led to another and the next thing he knew he was a charter member for a day in the Plastic Ono Band, clapping and singing along on their debut single "Give Peace a Chance."

Williams: "Tim and I got to know each other a little and after a few months he said he was going to run for governor of California and would I like to be his campaign manager? I held the post for about ten days. We found out that John Lennon and Yoko Ono were planning to do a bed-in for peace in Montreal, so of course we had to go to Montreal.

"We had a fabulous visit. Tim explained his gubernatorial platform (something about a marijuana tax) and said that he and his wife Rosemary were really running together as a couple and that he/they tremendously admired John and Yoko's revolutionary expression of coupleness and their campaign slogan was "Come Together, Join the Party!" And would John please consider writing a campaign song?

"The next day [June 1, 1969] John and Yoko got us and the Hare Krishnas and Tommy Smothers together in a small hotel room converted into a recording studio [Room 1742 at the Queen Elizabeth Hotel] and we all sang "Give Peace a Chance." You can see me swaying and clapping in the video, which was shot more or less over my shoulder. Then it was time to go."

Participating in the energy flow is the only satisfaction there is in life.

Eventually, a greatest hits anthology of Paul Williams' early *Crawdaddy!* work was compiled under the cover of *Outlaw Blues: a Book of Rock Music* in 1969. It was the first in a long line of tomes. If it seemed like Williams had dropped out of conventional social circles by 1970, it was because he had, as reflected in the publication of 1972's *Time Between*. "The theme of the book is transition," writes Williams. "The sense of being caught between the old world and the new. I wrote it in a burst of energy between December 27, 1969 and February 19, 1970. It starts by describing the goings-on around me (mostly sex and LSD, enthusiasm and conflict) in the commune I was then living at in Mendocino, northern California. It continues through a disjointed cross-country rap on [Robert A. Heinlin's] *Stranger in a Strange Land*, Charlie Manson, Mick Jagger, breaking free of the old world, love between men, moving to Canada—and settles into a visit and series of adventures in another commune, the Total Loss Farm in Vermont. The book ends with the author's awareness of and suggested cure for his own schizophrenia [combined with final comments on the messiah myth, another recurring theme]." It's somehow telling that Williams refers to himself in the third person as comment on his "schizophrenia." If *Time Between* chronicles the period of Williams having a breakdown, his next book, *Das Energi*, would prove to be the breakthrough of his publishing career.

When your space is clear the whole universe functions at its best.

Williams: "When I was living on an island commune in Canada in 1970, I found myself writing this strange book called *Das Energi*, a few lines a day, feeling very guilty because I should have been working in the garden or otherwise making myself useful. *Das Energi* was turned down by lots of publishers and finally Elektra Records decided to put it out, their first and only book, in 1973. It turned into a word-of-mouth bestseller and it's been through 23 printings in the United States and has sold at least as many copies as all my other books together."

Despite the feel-good/new-age vibes present in *Das Energi*, *Remember Your Essence*, and his other works of philosophy, Williams could also be quite confrontational with his prose (he did, after all, participate in the march on the Pentagon in 1967). Hardly a doe-eyed flower child, he retained a righteous indignation throughout his life about the social imbalances inherent in the political status quo. He was frequently insistent that "the People" get off of their complacent, apathetic asses and correct the injustices of the world. In 1995 he railed in print against the "American bankers and stockbrokers [and their political and media puppets] and the sucker game they're running. I want to talk about it, except I honestly feel that no one wants to hear it, which is depressing. Why are we nostalgic for a time when people tried to find out the truth and do something about what was going on, but we resist following the same course now, this decade, this present moment? We're moral idiots and it's going to cost us."

The 1970s found Williams' book projects moving further away from the world of rock 'n' roll and more in alignment with his spiritual and political interests. Before the seventies were over he wrote five more chronicles of his emerging consciousness: *Pushing Upward* (1973), *Apple Bay or Life on the Planet* (1976), *Right to Pass and Other True Stories* (1977), *Coming* (1977), and *Heart of Gold* (written 1978, published 1991). In 1979 he merged his philosophical explorations with his love for music in *Dylan—What Happened?*, where he pondered the implications of Bob Dylan's then-recent conversion to born-again Christianity.

A prolific run of titles continued into the '80s with *The Book of Houses* (co-authored with Robert Cole in 1980), *The International Bill of Human Rights* and *Common Sense* (1982), *Waking Up Together* (1984), *Remember Your Essence* (1987), and *The Map or Rediscovering Rock and Roll (A Journey)* (1988). *The Map* is perhaps the most significant of these titles because it documented Williams' return into the world of music after a fifteen-year lack of interest.

The Map reads like the journal of someone who fell out of love with their first girlfriend, and takes a fifteen-year Homeric odyssey away from her. But brazened by life's experiences (that take him from the age of 25 to 40), he discovers that not only is he still in love with her, he actually loves her more than ever. Such was the muse of music for Williams, and it was this rekindled affection that inspired him to undertake the deepest project of his career, a three-volume series of Bob Dylan's recorded output chronicled in *Performing Artist*.

Performing Artist is in many ways the crowning achievement of Williams career. It is certainly the most sustained meditation that he undertook in all of his writing projects. In *Performing Artist* Williams becomes the virtual fly on the wall, and all he has to base his perceptions on are the same records and tapes that any other fanatical Dylan collector might possess. But somehow he conveys to the reader startling insights into Dylan's process, insisting that not only is Bob Dylan rightly considered the William Shakespeare of our time as a writer, but also that his abilities as a performer are of an equal caliber.

If a picture is worth a thousand words, then these sound paintings that Williams draws from are a museum's worth of impressions that will build a cathedral in your consciousness—raising your awareness to unforeseen heights. This is what the best writers and artists do through their word and picture symbols. Bob Dylan is a master at it. And Paul Williams is a master at chronicling the process of a master at work.

Volume One of *Bob Dylan: Performing Artist* covers the years of 1960 through 1973 and was published in 1990. *Volume Two*, covering the middle years of 1974 through 1986, quickly followed in 1992. In 1993 Williams undertook the impossible task of personally choosing his favorite rock 'n' roll singles of all time and writing a brief essay about each record. The result was the wonderfully eclectic offering *Rock and Roll: the 100 Best Singles*, including a Foreword by his future wife-to-be, Cindy Lee Berryhill.

Energy flows through all things; it rests in none of them.

In addition to the spiritual philosophy of *Das Energi* and all of his work regarding how rock 'n' roll music made his heart sing and his spirit soar, there is, of course, the long shadow cast across Williams' entire career as an author by his first true love: science fiction. As a teenager he was entranced by the work of writer Theodore Sturgeon, and would later serve as the authoritative last word on Sturgeon's work by editing, compiling, and commenting in *The Complete Stories of Theodore Sturgeon*. As Sturgeon's literary overseer, it was a function that Williams would also undertake for another of science fiction's most acclaimed writers: Philip K. Dick.

Williams became aware of Dick's writing in 1967 after being turned on by fellow enthusiast Art Spiegelman. "Phil and I met at a science fiction convention in 1968 and were close friends until his death in 1982, the same year that *Blade Runner* came out based on his novel *Do Androids Dream of Electric Sheep?*" In 1975 Williams wrote a profile on Dick for *Rolling Stone* magazine, eventually expanding the manuscript in 1986 to book length for *Only Apparently Real: the World of Philip K. Dick*. It's a fantastic document that demonstrates how the two writers related to each other as friends. It offers an overview of Dick's career, focusing on the multiple theories as to why Dick's San Rafael, California house was burglarized on November 17, 1971 (take your pick: it was either the extreme right or the extreme left. Or it was the local police. Or it was rival neighbor gangs. Or the Black Panthers. Or...). The two writers enjoyed an easy dialog with each other and the affection between them is palpable. When Dick died on March 2, 1982, Williams became Dick's literary executor, getting several previously unpublished manuscripts placed with printers and editing and publishing a newsletter for the Philip K. Dick Society.

The ringing of the mindfulness bell.

It's true that writers require large amounts of solitude to perform and perfect their craft. Conversely, there are also the social dictates of business meetings, interviews, and travel that require being out in the world. Williams found a stable foundation for this dichotomy of demands in the three-act scenario of his marriages, where he performed the classic roles of husband, father, and friend. In 1972 he married Sachiko Kanenobu, a Japanese singer-songwriter with whom he raised two sons, Taiyo and Kenta (causing him to relocate for a second time to New York City). In the 1980s he moved to Glen Ellen, California and married artist Donna Nassar (a chiropractor/healer by profession), where Williams served as stepfather to her two children Eric and Isabelle (and also served for ten years as a volunteer fire fighter). Sometime in 1992 he fell in love with singer/songwriter/musician Cindy Lee Berryhill, which led to his relocation to Encinitas, California in 1993. After the two wed in July of 1997, their union produced a son Alexander Berryhill-Williams in 2001.

His relocation to Southern California coincided with the decision to revive the *Crawdaddy!* imprint as Williams once again began self-publishing a quarterly newsletter in the winter of 1993, in many ways picking up where he left off in 1968. The newsletter was a success and introduced Williams' writing to a new generation of music fans who weren't around for the first incarnation. Everything was flowing in his personal and professional career until Saturday, April 15, 1995—when everything came to an abrupt halt.

Cindy Lee Berryhill: "It was tax day. Because he was riding his bicycle to the post office to drop off the taxes and he was on his way back and there's this treacherous hill that you go down and if you want to get up the other one you go down the first one fast. So he was going too fast and he didn't have a helmet on.

"At the time *Garage Orchestra* was out [Berryhill's fourth album from 1994]. I'd been touring for that album and was just starting to put together some songs for the next one, and when Paul's accident happened it kind of exploded whatever I was going to do. I became a caregiver for like three months. But he did remarkably well and had a miraculous recovery. And because he was such a genius already, losing a few brain cells didn't seem to alter things too much. In fact, a mere three months or so after his accident, he had a book tour to do in Europe and I accompanied him and actually played a few songs on his tour: I was his opening act sometimes. It was that kind of thing. He was mostly talking about Bob Dylan.

"My focus was really on him that year, and then I recorded the next album, *Straight Outta Marysville*. A song like "Unknown Master Painter"—I wrote that in the couple of weeks of Paul's return from the hospital, and I had this overwhelming feeling at the time of wanting to get in the car and drive east as far and fast as I could and just escape. But I'm not that kind of person, so I'm not going to do that. But I wrote the song, and it was a way for me to escape."

Williams did indeed manage to make a miraculous recovery, as evidenced by the remarkable output of projects that he completed during the last half of the '90s. In addition to continuing with the responsibilities of writing and publishing *Crawdaddy!*, he also published seven more titles between 1995 and 2004: *Fear of Truth (Energi*

Inscriptions) (1995), *Bob Dylan: Watching The River Flow* (1996), *Neil Young: Love to Burn* (1997), *Brian Wilson and the Beach Boys—How Deep Is the Ocean* (1997), *How to Become Fabulously Wealthy at Home in 30 Minutes* (1999), *The Twentieth Century's Greatest Hits* (2000), and *Bob Dylan: Performing Artist Volume Three: Mind Out of Time, 1987–2000* (2004).

However, by 2009 Williams was suffering from Alzheimer's disease and dementia, the early onset caused by his accident. Berryhill documents the tragic, grueling process of watching her husband drift away in stages on *Beloved Stranger*, the name of her blog site and the title of her extremely riveting sixth album from 2007. Berryhill eventually created a website (paulwilliams.com) to promote awareness of her husband's work and to solicit financial assistance for the enormous medical bills.

A retrospective curated by Johan Kugelberg titled *Paul Williams: a Science Fiction and Rock and Roll Trufan* at the Boo-Horray gallery in New York City was held on March 24th just three days before Williams left his body, giving up the ghost of a compromised vehicle that had housed his tremendous spirit for over six decades.

Berryhill: "Johan proposed the idea three weeks before it happened. He wanted it to happen quickly and for it to be a celebration of Paul and his work. At that point Paul had started hospice, so it was a thoughtful thing to do.

"I was able to share with Paul over the phone how beautiful his show was. There were so many writers that were there and everyone was saying that they couldn't believe how much he'd written...and that was only a fraction of his stuff. The other news I had for Paul was that two very impressive libraries were interested in taking his books and papers, thanks to Johan.

"When you read an essay that he wrote about a song, he said these things that you were thinking and that you felt about the music but you could never articulate it the way he could. As a musician you just thought, 'I gotta write something that good! I gotta write a song as good as that.' Because he could actually come up with the words to talk about 'Don't Worry Baby,' I'd think that if I could say it, that's exactly what I'd say. He was like the perfect listener for us musicians. He really listened. And as somebody who got to live with him, if I tried out a new song on him he was very much the same as he was as a writer. He either really liked it: "That's powerful!" or he wouldn't say anything [laughs]. Or he would say, 'I haven't listened to it enough to know. I don't know if I have an opinion about it.'"

Sort of from the If-You-Don't-Have-Anything-Nice-To-Say school?

"Yeah, definitely. He said to me, 'Why would I waste my time?' It needed to be music or a piece of writing that really talks to him.

"But, ultimately, what he writes about is transcendence."

A Celebration of Life for Paul Williams memorial was conducted at Pilgrim United Church of Christ in Carlsbad, California on April 7, 2013 with a second memorial in San Francisco on April 13, 2013.

Engaging in a Form of Prayer: Remembering Paul Williams

It has been an incredible whirlwind these past few weeks, meditating on Paul Williams's life and legacy. I am humbled by the task of writing his story, and left with such a range of emotions: giddy one minute, sad the next. But when I pause and take a deep breath, what I mostly feel about the guy is triumphant about what he managed to create in his short time here on Earth. Another emotion that I could add to the palette is frustration, because shy of a 10,000 page multi-volume compendium, there is just no way to portray the full range of his literary gifts.

I believe Paul thought this trip was largely about communication—in order to create communion. One of the thoughts he committed to paper, and made an example of in his life, was that: "The only way to enjoy the show, to enjoy life, is to be a participant. Perhaps it's the people who think they're spectators who spread the idea that all pleasure must be paid for. Don't pay for anything—life is free." Not exactly what you would call the thinking of a free-market capitalist.

Part of the beauty of Paul's words are that they offer a window into a period of personal and collective history as well as a glimpse into the timeless possibilities. His words are an evocation and an invitation of how to see, think, and BE, suggesting that if you're willing to take action and responsibility for your personal vision, then you can change yourself and, by doing so, subsequently change the world. The best art is inspirational and suggests that by being bold and courageous you can do anything. So, (I can hear Paul saying) get cracking, kid!

I also believe in the law of magnetism, which perhaps accounts for how I found myself on June 9, 1986, on Jerry Weddle's couch in University Heights talking about the great, lost Beach Boys album *SMiLE* with Paul. I came prepared by bringing a bootleg copy of *SMiLE* on cassette, unbeknownst to me that he hadn't heard the material since 1966. In appreciation for the tape, he whipped out a copy of *Dylan—What Happened?*—signed it, and handed it to me. I was only 21, but already an appreciator of Paul's work, and I felt that his writing, regarding the mysterious power and spiritual sway of rock 'n' roll, is as substantive and significant as the very sounds that inspired him to write in the first place. You could look Paul in the eye and know that you had a confidante who held a paradigm-shifting secret that he was dying to share with the world. He was endowed with a compassionate fervor that wanted to hip everyone to the awareness that music could expand your consciousness and had the power to heal your soul and affirm the beauty of existence. In his essay on the Rolling Stones single "The Last Time," he makes it clear that music wasn't just a pastime or background noise, that it was no less than Existence Itself: "We're talking holy noise here, sacred writ," adding that a great 45 rpm record could contain "sex and death and humor and an attitude and a great beat and guitar piano vocal orchestral rock and roll music to die for." Jeez, no wonder I loved the guy.

The day I met Paul I happened to have an extra ticket for the inaugural San Diego date of a 41-city North American tour by Bob Dylan, who was touring at the time with Tom Petty and the Heartbreakers. Paul had an extra ticket for a show in Berkeley a few days later so we swapped. I had never seen Bob Dylan before and when the week was over I experienced four spectacular shows with Paul in San Diego, Berkeley, and Costa Mesa. Over the next decade I would see Dylan another 30 times and the frequent post-concert ritual would find many of us sharing notes about which songs were played and how well the evening came off. Most times I witnessed Paul in what seemed to be a state of ecstasy after seeing Dylan play, and over time I came to share his conviction that, beyond his obvious genius as a writer, Bob Dylan is also one of the greatest singers in the history of popular music.

Paul was a spiritual brother in every sense of the word. While it was music, music, music that brought us together I also learned a great deal about Zen philosophy, astrology, and the *I Ching* from him. He was the first person I ever witnessed to throw a hexagram when grappling with the uncertainty about how to handle a particular situation. He was an old-school hippie, a wise magician, a science-fiction geek with nerd glasses—and he knew how to use words as a divination tool. You heard music differently after Paul's sensibilities had zig-zagged through your skull; astonishing pictures could emerge from the previously unconnected dots that his prose drew together, turning your mirror maze of a mind into a cultural playground as profound as the discovery of fire or the invention of the wheel.

Once in awhile I would get a postcard from Paul when he was out in the world traveling. One card dated March 13, 1995, sent from Prague reads: *Totally in love with this city—five days not enough! Wallet stolen but I don't care. Dylan reinventing self by putting down his guitar—he always surprises! Love, Paul*

Thinking about his passion always makes me smile and it was a joy to witness his process. I have a slew of happy memories from when he was immersed in the writing and research of *The Map* or *Rock and Roll: the 100 Best Singles*. I couldn't help being pleased by his acknowledgement for helping him out with the *Bob Dylan: Performing Artist* series. There were other cool times as well having "postage parties" where we mailed out issues of *Crawdaddy!* to the subscribers in '93, '94, and '95—listening to records or cassettes, swapping stories, arguing over the relative merits of this LP or that artist, and always while passing around the peace pipe.

We were hanging out together in July of '88 when we heard the news that the singer Nico had died from a freak bike accident in Ibiza. Paul got extremely upset by the news and slammed his fists into his knees crying out "No! No!" and fired off a few choice expletives to express his anger and sadness. Well, that visceral response was exactly how I felt when I received the news around Paul's own bicycle accident in April 1995, and after visiting him in the hospital a couple of weeks later with Cindy Lee, I was stunned by how quickly (and profoundly) things can change on a dime. I am grateful for the generosity of Paul's spirit and that I was privileged to bear witness to all the beautiful energy that he poured into the world. He is definitely missed and yet his ideas will be with us in perpetuity. I look forward to meeting up again in the next lifetime. Thanks for making a difference, man.

San Diego Troubadour, May, 2013

SIX

Neil Young
Taking Group Art on a Solo Trip
Archives Vol. I 1963–1972

Cinéma vérité? I got into audio vérité. The concept of capturing the moment on the camera? I just translated that right into the recording studio. And when I started doin' it, I found all these other reasons why I was doin' the right thing. But the original thought was audio vérité. Why not make records like that? Capture the moment.

Q: Is rock 'n' roll the devil's music?

A: Rock 'n' roll is everybody's fuckin' music...I would certainly hope that it's the devil's music, but not just *the devil's music. I think that's where God and the devil shake hands—right there, heh heh heh.*

– Neil Young to biographer Jimmy McDonough in *Shakey*

We live in a dynamically strange time regarding our relationship to information. Marshall McLuhan coined the maxim "The medium is the message" and at the moment there is seemingly no limit to the amount of information that can be accessed at the touch of a button—so what does **that** say about the so-called medium? For music enthusiasts who came of age prior to the digital revolution, tracking down a recording or connecting with other musicians and fans could prove a huge logistical challenge that was both time-consuming and expensive in the effort to exchange information and create grass roots connections with the world-at-large. And those dynamics continue to morph in this future-shock acceleration of technology that we are currently in the midst of here in good 'ole two thousand and ten A.D. (after-digital).

There is a beautiful example of how recording technology (and indeed, Life itself) has changed and evolved over the last half-century—it is an eleven-disc behemoth of a box set that came out in the summer of 2009 entitled the *Neil Young Archives Vol. I 1963–1972*. In the foundry of rock archeology I believe that this package is unprecedented in its breadth, design and imaginative use of technology. Perhaps most important is that no recording artist's back catalog has ever sounded this sonically superior before, and to that end I have to say that this first installment of the *Neil Young Archives* series is about as cool a multi-media music project as I have yet to lay my eyes and ears upon.

In fact, this is Art with a capital A as well as the minutiae of one man's life taken to a whole new level of artistic commerce. Why should we care this much about Neil Young and his process? Is the guy really that great a musician or songwriter? Producer David Briggs certainly thought so, proclaiming "that when it's all written down, he will unquestionably stand in the top five that ever made rock 'n' roll...the only guy other than John Lennon who can actually go from folk to country to full orchestra. The only guy."

Young has certainly led a colorful existence these past 65 years, and for anyone seeking evidence as to just how colorful, your first educational foray should be to investigate *Shakey*, the superb above-mentioned biography of Neil Young by writer Jimmy McDonough. McDonough's telling of Neil's life flies by with one chillingly hilarious anecdote after another (with comedy and tragedy frequently dancing together in the same sentence), and it provides a fairly exhaustive context in which to enjoy the *Archives* box set. Believe me, when you are presented with this much information in one wallop, context is crucial in being able to fully appreciate and dig what is being put down here.

And it's not just about the information to be found in this box set, it's also in the novelty of how the information can be accessed and what kind of experience can be drawn from the *Archives* once you get your hands on the right kind of hardware. Much as Young may document and love the bygone era of putting a scratchy piece of vinyl on a portable record player back in the 1960s, we now live in an age where Young has his post-modern audience (ironically?) watching a video screen with a replication of a record player spinning a piece of plastic, while state-of-the-art audio pours out of the speakers. We have taken virtual reality and the illusion of sound reproduction to a whole other level. Then there are the "Easter eggs," hidden tracks that you have to hunt for that are sprinkled throughout the entire box set, with at least 85 audio and video elements not to be found in the main programs. Should you be itching to learn more about the technical aspect of things, you are encouraged to check out the official public relations hype online at www.neilyoung archives.com. And no matter how impressive the *Neil Young*

Archives is from a technological point of view, none of this would matter if the music being featured on these discs wasn't so fucking brilliant most of the time. And while we're on the subject, I would suggest that you don't even consider buying the compact disc version of the *Archives*, because you are cheating yourself out of what really makes so much of this collection unique: primarily the various multi-media surprises that come from navigating through the menus (the 1967 video clip from *Where the Action Is* with Dick Clark interviewing Buffalo Springfield managers Charlie Greene and Brian Stone is one such gem to be found on Disc 1).

When Young started talking about the *Archives* project he apparently had a clear vision of how he wanted to organize and present his musical and personal history—and he refused to release the *Archives* until technology conformed to that vision. The concept was fairly simple: create a virtual filing cabinet with folders housing every song from his career in chronological order, potentially containing music, typed and handwritten song lyrics, relevant period photographs, film and video footage, and newspaper and magazine clippings. Another important function was allowing the listener to page through the visuals simultaneously as the music played. Finally, Young wanted a format that allowed the filing cabinet to incorporate new data into the system, and to insert that information into the proper place of chronology. And now, via the internet, while interfacing with the Blu-ray system, it is possible to do all of the above.

Lord knows how many more volumes of the *Archives* series will come out in Neil's or our lifetime, because after hearing him talk about it for thirty plus years, I thought it would never be released. However, this premiere set, covering the first decade of Mister Young's recorded output, is pretty staggering in its quality. Although much of this material is previously unreleased, three of the eleven discs in the set were actually available months before the box set came out. Young's website suggests buying the titles separately if you already bought the first three *Neil Young Archives Performance Series* discs, but if you did that you wouldn't get the poster of the virtual filing cabinet, the leather-bound scrapbook (which is an awesome document in its own right), or the seven-inch Squires 45 rpm single. The scrapbook covers Neil's life from the time of his birth (November 12, 1945) through 1972, providing visual clues to Young's existence to accompany the sonics. Here's how it all lays out:

Disc 0, Early Years (1963–1965) sets the stage for what was to come, with Young learning licks from local Winnipeg legend Randy Bachman and finding inspiration from Hank Marvin of the Shadows and Jimmy Reed (to name but two), as he cut his teeth playing guitar in instrumental groups such as the Stardusters, the Classics, and ultimately, the Squires, who recorded a single in the summer of 1963 titled "The Sultan" b/w "Aurora." The single flopped and it would be another three years before a record label released any new Neil Young compositions. And Young would have to leave his native Canada for that to happen.

Disc 1, Early Years (1966–1968) has Young setting off for California in a black hearse named Mort Two, fortified with musical gear, raw talent, a modest supply of marijuana, a head full of dreams, and a handful of friends, including bassist Bruce Palmer. Within a couple days of hitting Los Angeles, the hearse crossed paths with Stephen Stills and Richie Furay.

With the quick addition of drummer Dewey Martin—the Buffalo Springfield were born. During 1966 and '67 they produced two classic LPs (*Buffalo Springfield* and *Buffalo Springfield Again*), with Young coming into his own as a writer, with some of the finest tunes of this magical era including: "Nowadays Clancy Can't Even Sing," "Flying on the Ground Is Wrong," "Mr. Soul," "Expecting to Fly," and "On the Way Home." If you dig the sounds on this particular disc, then it's mandatory to seek out the four-disc *Buffalo Springfield Box Set* from 2001. That collection lays out in its entirety the beautifully tragic saga of the Springfield. As breathtaking as **Disc 1** may be, this is merely a snapshot.

But still, what a tantalizing snapshot it is, with several unique, period surprises to be found: a previously unreleased Buffalo Springfield song "Sell Out," a newly discovered superior acetate of the original "Mr. Soul," an historically important (i.e. distorted sounding) live montage of songs from the very last Springfield concert in Long Beach, California on May 5, 1968, and "Slowly Burning," a plaintive, twangy instrumental that Young began but never finished with Jack Nitzsche on the same day that the dynamic duo recorded "Expecting to Fly" in 1967. And there is much illumination regarding Young's tenure with Buffalo Springfield from the interview that DJ Tony Pig conducted with him at KSAN-FM in San Francisco, California on his 24th birthday (November 12, 1969). It is great to hear Young this unguarded, but it requires a bit of effort to find this hidden Easter egg track. In that sense the *Archives* is a bit of a hunt, and in typical Neil Young fashion, he is more than happy to give you all kinds of cool information, but he'll frequently make you work for it.

Sugar Mountain Live at Canterbury House Ann Arbor, Michigan (November 9, 1968) is considered "disc 0" in the *Neil Young Archives Performance Series* and is included in the box set as a "bonus disc." *Sugar Mountain* documents the brief pause between the break-up of Buffalo Springfield and the start, in earnest, of Young's solo career.

Disc 2, Topanga 1 (1968–1969) is where Young landed after signing a solo deal with Mo Ostin and Reprise Records. His self-titled debut from January of 1969 was the first (and last) time Young would adopt the approach of crafting a slick studio creation, forever after adopting producer David Briggs' ethos that when it comes to capturing rock 'n' roll on tape "the more you think, the more you stink." After getting *Neil Young* out of his system, he was prepped for a lifetime of audio vérité recording. Yet in spite of Young's later misgivings about excessive overdubbing in the studio, I think "The Loner" turned out pretty great, and I must say kudos as well to arranger and producer Jack Nitzsche. One of the more amusing hidden tracks on the box set is of Neil and Jack goofing around in the studio while recording strings for "The Emperor of Wyoming."

Disc 3, Live at the Riverboat Toronto (February 7–9, 1969) captures Young in acoustic troubadour mode a month after the release of his solo debut. Archivist Joel Bernstein observes that "the Riverboat series is very important, unquestionably. He's retelling the Buffalo Springfield songs in a way that's very poignant."

Disc 4, Topanga 2 (1969–1970). For the next two years Young lived in the Topanga Canyon section of Los Angeles, where he encountered a rough and tumble six-piece rock 'n' roll band called the Rockets, who made a name for themselves around town playing at a local watering hole called the Coral. After recording their one and only self-titled LP in 1968 on the White Whale label (*The Rockets*), Young "borrowed" three of it's members: guitarist/vocalist Danny Whitten, bassist/vocalist Billy Talbot, and drummer/vocalist Ralph Molina. Almost immediately, the quartet went into the studio and within a week cut one of the classic LPs of the era—*Everybody Knows This Is Nowhere*. Rockets' guitarist George Whitsell: "My understanding was Neil was gonna use the guys for a record and a quick tour, bring 'em back and help us produce the next Rockets album. It took me a year and a half to realize my band had been taken." Young, however, must have understood that on some level the birth of Crazy Horse meant the death of the Rockets. Hell, he wrote a song on *Everybody Knows This Is Nowhere* titled "Running Dry (Requiem for the Rockets)" so the writing must have been somewhere on the studio wall. Oh, and by-the-way, 1969 also marks Woodstock, Altamont, the recording of *Déjà Vu*, and the musical (and off-stage) antics of Crosby, Stills, Nash, & Young. This period is indeed a "Sea of Madness," with CSNY a relative footnote in the grand scheme of things.

Disc 5, Neil Young & Crazy Horse Live at the Fillmore East (March 6–7, 1970) is proof positive that the original Crazy Horse with Danny Whitten is one of THE all-time great live bands in rock 'n' roll history. "Winterlong" and "Wonderin'" are real treats, and it is superb to hear "Come On Baby Let's Go Downtown" in the context of its original performance, as opposed to being relocated to *Tonight's the Night*. Jack Nitzsche joins the Horse on electric piano. It's a damn shame that the magic wasn't destined to last.

Disc 6, Topanga 3 (1970) is the beginning of the end as far as Neil's tenure in Topanga goes, and the archetypal Topanga Canyon document has to be *After the Gold Rush*, the 1970 LP that Young recorded in the basement of his house on Skyline Trail. Right about this time, Washington, D.C. musician Nils Lofgren traveled west and joined the fold as Young performed a balancing act between the demands of performing with CSNY and dancing to the beat of his own drummer, which in Young's case happened to be Ralph Molina. CSNY and Young's solo career were both building steady momentum and it wasn't long before something was going to give from the combined stress. Too bad it was destined to be Young's first marriage. On May 4, 1970 the Kent State shootings happened and Young responded immediately by writing the song "Ohio," easily the most visceral track that CSNY ever cut. This period contains some of Young's most enduring tunes: "Only Love Can Break Your Heart," 'Don't Let It Bring You Down," "After the Gold Rush," and "I Believe in You."

Disc 7, Live at Massey Hall Toronto (January 19, 1971) was intended to be the follow up to *After the Gold Rush*. Producer David Briggs was given that brief and he recorded and edited this show with that intention. But when Young went to Nashville to perform on the *Johnny Cash Show* and spontaneously wound up recording some new songs with producer Elliot Mazer, this fantastic performance was unfortunately shelved. This is one of the gems of the series, and this performance displays quite clearly why Young was poised for the multi-platinum success that followed with *Harvest*, and why Briggs was so understandably pissed off for being slighted in the process.

Disc 8, North Country (1971–1972). In September of 1970, Young moved near San Francisco, California and bought a 140-acre property that he christened Broken Arrow Ranch. This is where he has lived ever since. And with the various artisans he has attracted to his inner circle over these past four decades, Young has had the luxury of creating *his* art whenever he wants to. A lot of that is due to the financial success of the 1972 LP *Harvest*, which spawned the hit single "Heart of Gold," the only record in Young's career to reach number one on the *Billboard* Hot 100. As he famously wrote in the liner notes to his *Decade* anthology: "This song put me in the middle of the road. Traveling there soon became a bore so I headed for the ditch. A rougher ride but I saw more interesting people there." Ever the perverse one, the moment that Young reached the top of the heap he made a wild left turn, leaving his audience in a lurch that is well documented by the LP *Time Fades Away*, one of the few albums in Young's back catalog that enjoys the distinction of never being released on compact disc. It will allegedly be included on *Vol. II* of the *Archives*.

And then, of course, there were the self-destructive habits of Danny Whitten. After working on *After the Gold Rush* and the 1971 *Crazy Horse* LP, Whitten's depression and dalliance with heroin got the best of him, and on November 18, 1972 he died of an overdose, taking the spark of the original Crazy Horse with him. Young would remark to Sandy Mazzeo that "Every musician has one guy on the planet that he can play with better than anyone else. You only get one guy. My guy was Danny Whitten."

The tragedy of Danny Whitten's early demise is multiplied when you consider that there is zero film footage of the original Crazy Horse. There are, however, some incredible film segments to be found in the *Archives* from this period with footage of Young and Nitzsche recording "There's a World" and "A Man Needs a Maid" with the London Symphony Orchestra. Other highlights include footage at Broken Arrow of the Stray Gators recording "Are You Ready for the Country?" and "Alabama" in Neil's barn and an interview conducted by Wim Vander Linden for a Dutch documentary. There's also Neil's performance from the aforementioned *Johnny Cash Show*.

Commercially unavailable since its theatrical release in April 1973, **Disc 9, Journey Through the Past** is an elaborate, self-indulgent mess of a motion picture on a lot of levels, but that doesn't mean it isn't without it's charms. You might even say that it's charming because it is a bit of a mess. Young hijacked a pre-existing CSNY documentary and that provides much of the concert footage and behind the scenes action. It is certainly a great time-capsule piece and it captures some of the flavor of what it was like to be in Young's orbit circa 1970–72. A couple of great outtakes include one sequence where Young banters with a record store clerk before walking out of the store without paying for a bootleg recording of one of his own performances.

By the end of 1972, Neil Young's path had reached such a plateau that it left him with basically two career choices. He could pander to the audience who had fallen in love with the soft-spoken folkie and continue to crank out the same kind of material that brought him success as both a solo artist and as one-fourth of Crosby, Stills, Nash, & Young— OR continue to follow his artistic whims and his musical muse wherever it took him, even in the face of commercial suicide, which is arguably what Young chose to pursue in 1973 when he insisted on playing a bunch of bleak and aggressive unreleased songs for an audience who had come to hear the *Harvest* LP reproduced live. Young famously loves to confound audience expectations. In fact, hidden on one of the video clips of the box set, Young goes so far as to proclaim to Joel Bernstein and Gary Burden "Fuck the audience," in regards to their desires and expectations. "If I'm going to survive, they're going to have to fuckin' eat it. That's been the balance that I've had to play." Sounds like a true Scorpio to me (a double Scorpio in fact).

What the audience didn't realize was that they were at the start of a full-on Irish wake, because a month-and-a-half before the *Time Fades Away* tour started, Danny Whitten died, casting a funereal pall that influenced the overall vibe within Young's circle for the next two years.

It will be fascinating to see how Young chooses to tackle *that* period of his life when he gets around to the next installment of the *Archives* series. As a passionately interested witness to Mister Young's process, I pray that it doesn't take him another thirty years to get around to *Vol. II.*

Ugly Things, #30, Summer/Fall, 2010

SEVEN

Living on Tulsa Time via
The Road to Escondido
J.J. Cale Remembered

On July 26, 2013 the world lost one of its most respected songwriters and guitarists with the unexpected death of J.J. Cale at Scripps Green Hospital in La Jolla, California. Cale passed away after suffering a heart attack. He was 74.

During his lifetime Cale released over 25 albums in a career that spanned more than five decades (his first release was in 1958 with the single "Shock Hop" under the name Johnny Cale). Many listeners, however, will be familiar with his work through the numerous cover versions that were recorded by scores of famous appreciators, including Johnny Cash, Waylon Jennings, Captain Beefheart, the Allman Brothers, Tom Petty, Dire Straits, and Phish. Most notable of them all is Eric Clapton who covered several of Cale's tunes including: "After Midnight" (a #18 hit from 1970's *Eric Clapton*), "Cocaine" (a #30 hit from 1977's *Slowhand*), "I'll Make Love to You Anytime" (from 1978's *Backless*), "Travelin' Light" (from 2001's *Reptile*), "River Runs Deep" and "Everything Will Be Alright" (from 2010's *Clapton*), and "Angel" (from 2013's *Old Sock*). "Eric's been paying my rent for a long time," said an appreciative Cale. "I'd probably be selling shoes today if it wasn't for him." The two guitarists eventually teamed up in 2006 to record *The*

Road to Escondido, which won a Grammy award for Best Contemporary Blues Album in 2008.

Lynyrd Skynyrd recorded a version of Cale's "Call Me the Breeze" on their 1974 LP *Second Helping* and "I Got the Same Old Blues Again" on 1976's *Gimme Back My Bullets*. When asked what he thought of Skynyrd's version of "Call Me the Breeze" Cale responded with, "Oh, I just love that. That also helped my bank account too. Yeah, Lynyrd Skynyrd, I knew them guys. They cut it before the plane crash that killed two or three of them."

"Basically, I'm just a guitar player that figured out I wasn't ever gonna be able to buy dinner with my guitar playing so I got into songwriting, which is a little more profitable business," he said.

John Weldon Cale was born on December 5, 1938 in Oklahoma City and was raised 100 miles away in Tulsa where the shuffling, melodic sounds of Chet Atkins, Les Paul, and Clarence "Gatemouth" Brown first pricked up his ears. Cale is so identified with his hometown that his music is often described as the "Tulsa Sound," a hybrid of rockabilly, blues, jazz, and country. If there were ever a musician who was the very definition of laconic, it was J.J. Cale. "Mellow and laid-back are the two terms most applied to my style and I guess I go along with that," he said. "Most of it is medium, slow-tempo, not really an aggressive, in-your-face thing. When I was young I played a lot more rock 'n' roll but when I got into songwriting and had to sing, since I only have a two-note range, it was easier to do mellow."

As an acclaimed engineer, many of the tracks that he recorded sound like glorified demos after he discovered drum machines in the early 1970s. On his first solo album,

Naturally (1972), Cale said that the sound was born from a practical necessity: "In addition to vocals and guitar I'm also playing piano and bass. On "Crazy Mama" and "Call Me the Breeze" those were electric drum machines. I first started out doing that because of the economics—I didn't have enough money to hire a band. Now that I have enough money to hire a band I still like that. It's kind of an art form in itself."

The only time Cale ever had a chart hit of his own in the U.S. was with the song "Crazy Mama" in 1972, peaking at #22 on *Billboard's* Hot 100.

Throughout his career Cale shunned the spotlight and did not like to tour, proclaiming, "send me the money and let the younger guys have the fame. Fame elevates your ego to the point where you start believing your own bullshit." With an attitude like that it wasn't too surprising that when Cale left Tulsa in the early sixties and moved to Nashville, he ended up struggling to make ends meet for over a decade. In 1965 fellow Tulsa musician Leon Russell suggested to Cale that he come out to Los Angeles where he could find regular work. During this period he cut three singles for Liberty records, including a B-side titled "After Midnight." In 1967 he also recorded with a group called the Leather-coated Minds and made an album of psychedelic covers called *A Trip Down the Sunset Strip*, which he subsequently described as "terrible." It was during this period that he took on the moniker of "J.J. Cale" so that he wouldn't be confused with Welsh musician John Cale, co-founder of the Velvet Underground.

By the end of the '60s, after failing to make a go of it in Los Angeles, he considered giving up music completely.

When Delaney Bramlett played some of Cale's demos for Eric Clapton in 1969, Clapton responded by recording Cale's "After Midnight" for his solo debut. Cale wasn't even aware of Clapton's recording of the song until he heard it on the car radio. "I almost drove off the road and I thought, 'oh, boy I'm gonna buy me a new car.' I was dirt poor, not making enough to eat, and I wasn't a young man. I was in my thirties, so I was very happy. It was nice to make some money."

When the single hit the Top 20, it served as a catalyst for Cale to land his own recording contract with Leon Russell and Denny Cordell's Shelter records, beginning a long association with the Tulsa-based label. A string of albums followed: *Naturally* (1972), *Really* (1973), *Okie* (1974), *Troubadour* (1976), *Five* (1979), and *Shades* (1981).

In his autobiography, Eric Clapton writes that he was "tired of the guitar hero thing, and I was starting to follow the example of J.J. Cale. When I listened to his records I was impressed by the subtlety, by what wasn't being played. He's one of the most important artists in the history of rock, quietly representing the greatest asset his country has ever had. It's all about finesse."

She don't like, she don't like, she don't like…cocaine.

Clapton was also quick to point out that Cale's "Cocaine" is actually an anti-drug song, saying that "it's no good to write a deliberate anti-drug song and hope that it will catch. Because people, in general, will be upset by that. It would disturb them to have someone else shoving something down their throat. So the best thing to do is offer something that seems ambiguous. But if you study it or look at it with a little bit of thought it is quite cleverly anti-cocaine." Although Clapton had the bigger hit with the song throughout most of the world, Cale's version actually went to number one in New Zealand of all places.

In the Neil Young biography *Shakey*, Young told biographer Jimmy McDonough, "What is it about J.J. Cale's playing? I mean, you could say Eric Clapton's the guitar god, but he can't play like J.J. Cale. J.J.'s the one who played all that shit first. And he doesn't play very loud, either—I really like that about him. He's so sensitive. Of all the players I ever heard, it's gotta be Hendrix and J.J. Cale who are the best electric guitar players. J.J. is my peer, but he doesn't have the business acumen—he doesn't have the idea of how to deal with the rest of the world that I do. But musically, he's actually more than my peer, because he's got that thing. I don't know what it is."

In his autobiography, *Waging Heavy Peace*, Young wrote that "J.J.'s guitar playing is a huge influence on me. His touch is unspeakable. I am stunned by it."

After Cale's association with Shelter records ended, he moved to California and recorded two albums for Polygram: *Grasshopper* (1982) and *Number 8* (1983). When neither of those albums sold, he asked to be released from his contract and became a recluse, living in a trailer without a telephone. Asked how he spent his time during the 1980s he said: "Mowing the lawn and listening to Van Halen and rap music." It would be seven years before he released another album with 1990's *Travel-Log*.

Two more albums for the Silvertone label followed with 1992's *Number 10* and 1994's *Closer to You*. He released a pair of albums for Virgin records: 1996's *Guitar Man* and 2001's *Live*. *To Tulsa and Back* came out on Sanctuary records in 2004, and his final record, the spectacular *Roll On*, was released in 2009 for the Rounder label.

While promoting *To Tulsa and Back*, Cale spoke to National Public Radio. When asked if any contemporary music was influencing him he responded by saying that he "tried to steal a little bit from everybody [laughs]. I'll hear a rap record I really like and I'll go, 'Wow, that bass drum really has a nice tone to it,' and I'll try to pull that tone off of it, like a Juvenile's record or a 2Pac record. I'll take it in little sections because I am an engineer. And maybe I'll hear a country song and I'll go 'I like the way the voice sounds on that so I'll try to emulate that.'"

Responding to critics who suggest that all of Cale's records sound the same he said, "When I made the first album *Naturally*, that was probably my most popular album and then all the rest of the albums I made they said, 'Well, that's great, but he's not doing anything new,' which in the commercial record business you're supposed to keep changing, you know, and mystifying and surprising your audience. I never tried to do that—well, let me put it this way, I did try to do that but I'm not any good at it so I just try to do what I know. The nice thing about that is there's 400 million other records out there they can also get, but I agree with my critics that most of my albums have a sameness to them, but that's me," he says with a laugh.

In a 2009 *Los Angeles Times* interview Cale says that the Escondido city fathers tried to contact him after *The Road to Escondido* won a Grammy. "They wanted me to talk to the chamber of commerce," he recalled. "And I said, you know, I'm not a chamber-of-commerce kind of guy."

"I kind of write songs hoping that musicians will take them and make them better and more accessible," he said. "When my songs started raking in some funds I thought, 'What's the use of working all the time?' I believe in no work at all if you can get away with it. I'd recommend writing songs. You get all of the money and none of the bother."

On Cale's website it says he "was a great lover of animals, so if you like, you can remember him with a donation to your favorite local animal shelter." It seems a fitting gesture for a man who lived an unpretentious existence and sang about the simple pleasures in life.

J.J. Cale is survived by his wife and musical collaborator Christine Lakeland Cale.

San Diego Troubadour, September, 2013

EIGHT

Coming Down Again:
Keith Richards' *Life*

There's always a bit of voyeurism involved whenever you crack open anyone's life story, and that has never been more apparent than in the recently published autobiography of Keith Richards. Much as a steak lover might not wish to know how that piece of meat ended up on the end of his fork, appreciators of the Rolling Stones' music might not want to learn of the circumstances that led to the creation of some of the greatest rock 'n' roll music from the last fifty years. *Life*, if anything, can certainly be viewed as a cautionary tale and I personally find it fairly easy to laugh along with all of the depravity. But it frequently begs the question—would **you** enjoy these tales of excess if you were personally implicated in these scenarios? *Life* presents a classic case of the reader having to make the distinction between an artist's lifestyle and the art itself, a debate that has been around for ages. Does the fact that Pablo Picasso was a brutal chauvinist diminish his genius as an innovative artist? Of course not, the work has to be judged on its own merit. And just because Keith Richards has lived the life of a proud outlaw, with more than one foot in the gutter for many of his 67 years, that does not diminish his impact on the cultural landscape of the twentieth century. As a contemporary of Davies, Dylan,

Lennon, McCartney, Townshend, and Wilson, he deserves to be mentioned in the same breath, but in addition to all of the classic art he made, the reader will also know the subject from the trail of the dead.

All of the mythic greatest hits are here, confirmed and/or debunked: the rise and fall of Brian Jones and the "theft" of Anita Pallenberg, a naked Marianne Faithfull accessorizing her vagina with a Mars chocolate bar (even Keef declares that one "a classic"), his fractious "marriage" to songwriting partner Mick Jagger, his monumental run-ins with the local constabulary—including, of course, his infamous 1977 arrest for the possession of heroin in Toronto where they almost put him away for ten years. No matter how murky the proceedings get, Keith claims to remember it all. And much as it may be difficult not to judge the man, Keith rarely seems able to judge himself. By the way, if one were ever curious about what causes a junkie to OD, Keith officially sets the record straight. It isn't so much the ingestion of heroin that kills, apparently it's the "greed" of trying to get higher than your constitution can handle. I trust that Richards knows what he is talking about when he insists that it's really all about proper "maintenance."

Yes, Dartford's most famous son relates what it is like to live your life in the eye of a drug-infused hurricane while playing guitar in the "world's greatest rock 'n' roll band." He finally got off hard drugs after the Toronto bust but complains that his public image still hasn't left him, even though he's been "clean" for the past three decades. He does admit to exercising lousy judgment at times and was sensitive enough to feel slighted when Jagger stopped consulting him on the Stones' business affairs after a decade or more of Keith's supreme negligence to the business side of the enterprise. You can't really blame Mick for refusing to entrust a multi-million dollar organization to the whims of a junkie. Still, at the end of the day, I'd rather hear Keith sing his version of the blues than any other member of the Rolling Stones. *Life* is a fantastic read by a great artist, but after feasting away carnivorously for the last 550 pages, I'll admit to sticking to vegetarianism for a while.

Essential Keith: Selected Tracks
Connection (from *Between the Buttons*) (1967)
Salt of the Earth (from *Beggars Banquet*) (1968)
You Got the Silver (from *Let It Bleed*) (1969)
Happy (from *Exile on Main Street*) (1972)
Coming Down Again (from *Goats Head Soup*) (1973)
Memory Motel (from *Black and Blue*) (1976)
Before They Make Me Run (from *Some Girls*) (1978)
All About You (from *Emotional Rescue*) (1980)
Little T&A (from *Tattoo You*) (1981)
Take It So Hard (from *Talk Is Cheap*) (1988)
Slipping Away (from *Steel Wheels*) (1989)
Wicked As It Seems (from *Main Offender*) (1992)
Thru and Thru (from *Voodoo Lounge*) (1994)
Losing My Touch (from *Forty Licks*) (2002)

Ugly Things, #31, Spring/Summer, 2011

NINE

The American Folk Blues Festival

It is February once again ladies and gents, a time when we traditionally celebrate African-American culture in this country with Black History Month. Being born and raised in the Washington, D.C. metropolitan area, I can attest that everyday is a day to celebrate Black culture in America and yet I can easily understand how some folks might take offense at such ethnic designations and might simply prefer being called "American." We are ALL part of a greater melting pot and I often think of myself as an all-American mongrel boy—one part this, three parts that, and a whole lot of mystery as to what it all adds up to. Humanism, perhaps. I also have a strong aversion to anyone who wraps themselves in the stars and stripes and parades about in a jingoistic fashion. However, if there is anything to be proud about regarding this diverse country of ours, it is definitely the music that has spilled out from every sector of this continent over the past century (or five) and when I think of "American music" there isn't a finer representation of it than the artists who were involved with the *American Folk Blues Festival*, documented on a series of DVDs and compact discs that celebrates its tenth anniversary this summer.

The *American Folk Blues Festival* was a succession of annual tours throughout Europe in the 1960s, which featured the absolute cream of the blues scene in America at a time when most domestic audiences were unfamiliar with these musical giants. Over the course of several years two enterprising German promoters, Horst Lippmann and Fritz Rau, engaged the services of master songwriter and musician Willie Dixon to organize a traveling road show of the best blues artists in the world. Not that Dixon thought of it that way at the time—he was mostly lining up friends that he knew from the blues clubs around the south side of Chicago. But what a circle of friends the man had! Included on the 1962 inaugural tour were the likes of T-Bone Walker, Sonny Terry and Brownie McGhee, Memphis Slim, John Lee Hooker, and Dixon himself. Lippmann and Rau channeled their deep love of jazz and blues into (ironically) providing a forum for all of these masterful artists who were otherwise suffering a tremendous amount of hardship back at home—due to apathy and overt racism. As Charlie Parker once stated, "If you don't live it, it won't come out your horn," and the authenticity of these artists is a testament that each and every one of them were very much indeed living the blues.

And I say ironic because it was only eighteen years previously that Lippmann had been arrested by the Gestapo for publishing a broadsheet promoting American jazz during a time in history when the Nazi party had declared jazz and blues music to be strictly prohibited. So, what a delightful turning of the tables that these two German men should be so respectful of these American artists, where back home they could barely score a gig, let alone be treated like royalty and featured on national television. As with many a BBC documentary on American culture, leave it to a European to teach you how to appreciate your own history.

What I particularly love about this conceptual enterprise that we call America, is the spirit and ideals that are projected through much of our musical heritage. And while we may like to cheer on the original declarations of our founding fathers, in reality this hasn't exactly been the land of milk and honey for many of its inhabitants. Obviously, when the slaves from other countries, and all women, regardless of color, were deigned to have three-fifths the status of a free white male, it's hardly what you'd call the foundation of a fair and balanced democratic society.

However, one of the unexpected side effects of all that imbalance and oppression throughout the ages is this cumulative musical form that we've come to call the blues, a form that we've been celebrating for almost a century. Its influence can be found in nearly every strain of popular music since 1920, around the time it evolved into its own genre as a derivative of jazz. A popular exercise over the years has been to define which diverse forms of music came together to create rock 'n' roll, and there is an equally divergent melding of musical styles that came to be known as the blues. Whether it be songs from minstrel shows, vaudeville, opera, Tin Pan Alley, field hollers, gospel, ragtime, folk ballads, or call-and-response chants—all of this and more went into the cast iron cauldron that influenced the formation of jazz (arguably America's first true indigenous art form) and its subsequent evolution into what we now call the blues.

Significantly, it was the *American Folk Blues Festival* that directly inspired the British blues boom of the mid-1960s, due to the fact that when the tour traveled through Britain in 1962 and '63, in attendance were such young devotees as Brian Jones, Keith Richards, Mick Jagger, Eric Burdon, Paul Jones, Long John Baldry, Alexis Korner, Cyril Davies, and Jimmy Page. All of those musicians (and many more), spearheaded by the international success of the Beatles, took all of that American blues music, digested it through their British art college sensibilities, and brought it all back to a primarily white audience in America. Americans were unaware that much of the British pop pouring out of their radios in 1964 and '65 was largely interpretations of the type of music that was heard on these fabled tours.

Part of the arrangement that Lippmann and Rau made with Dixon for the *AFBF* was, in addition to the gigs scheduled throughout Britain and the European continent, the troupe would also be captured on tape by Südwestfunk (SWR) in Baden-Baden, Germany, for a one-hour television special. The initial response in 1962 was so positive that the tour became a yearly tradition for the remainder of the decade, boasting among its lineups some of the greatest musicians of all time: Muddy Waters, Big Mama Thornton, Lonnie Johnson, Sonny Boy Williamson, Howlin' Wolf (with Hubert Sumlin), Lightnin' Hopkins, Skip James, Big Joe Turner, Koko Taylor, Little Walter, Hound Dog Taylor, Bukka White, Son House, Otis Spann, Buddy Guy, Otis Rush…the list goes on and on.

In a way it is a miracle that this footage even exists for us to be talking about 50 years after the fact. By all rights it should be lost, like so many other great ephemeral moments of television history. But unlike so many other broadcasts from America and abroad, where the ravages of time have either destroyed these documents through sheer neglect or willful abandonment (i.e. thrown into a dumpster due to space limitations), the good people at SWR recognized the historical and cultural value of this footage and kept it properly stored for more than four decades. During my six-year stint at Reelin' in the Years Productions (RITY), where I co-created the single greatest library of music performance footage under one roof, along with my comrade, David Peck, we auditioned an astonishing amount of footage. SWR was one of the 30-plus archives that we gained the privilege of representing for worldwide commercial distribution, and they were sitting on a goldmine of footage. We knew it the moment the tapes came in from overseas. Once the initial shock and awe of seeing this footage wore off, it became a matter of how to best capitalize on it. The real work of getting this footage released began with an arduous year-long process of initiating a dialog with each artist (or their estate's representatives) and coming to terms with a favored-nations contract that fairly compensated each of them for their contribution to the project. No one gets rich on a project like this and that was never our goal. The true objective was to get this historic material into the hands of the general public, but to do so in a manner that was fair to the artists and licensed properly.

A key aspect in getting the *AFBF* out onto the market was establishing a relationship with John McDermott, a writer who had become central to the success of Experience Hendrix, the company that was created to curate the vast (and lucrative) musical catalog that was eventually awarded to Jimi Hendrix's father, Al, after a court battle that took years to resolve. In 2001 Experience Hendrix and RITY partnered up to produce the *Experience* DVD (quickly earning a gold disc in the process) and other projects soon followed. Thanks to the already established relationship that Experience Hendrix enjoyed with Universal Music, it was an easy sales pitch to convince the powers that be that the *AFBF* should find a home there. McDermott made some invaluable contributions from a technical standpoint by enlisting famed engineer and producer Eddie Kramer to supervise the digital transfer of the material and to clean up the audio tracks. Once the contracts were signed it became a matter of how to present the material and to make sure that all the proper clearances were in order. That took months to accomplish but when it was all over we had a product that everyone involved was thrilled with.

Coordinating the graphics for this three-volume series was another labor of love that put San Diego front and center in this history-defining project. The brick wall that was used as the backdrop for the memorable cover art was photographed by Randy Hoffman at Dick's Last Resort in the Gaslamp Quarter with vintage guitars and amps provided by Jim Soldi of Valley Music fame. We had the good fortune to have master art director Vartan coordinate the visuals for the entire project and by happenstance managed to get Bill Wyman (the Rolling Stones), Robert Plant (Led Zeppelin), and Ray Manzarek (the Doors), to contribute to the package's liner notes. The exhaustive historical essay contained in the DVDs, and their companion audio discs, was authored by Canadian writer Rob Bowman.

As I wrote in the booklet's original production notes, after 20 years of archiving music performance footage and seeing thousands of hours of material spanning the last century, nothing has impressed me quite like the *American Folk Blues Festival* has. This material is a national treasure worthy of the Smithsonian and all that it asked for was to be presented in a respectful manner. When the project was finally released in the summer of 2003 it became an immediate worldwide sensation.

And a critical success it turned out to be as well—at the exact moment that Martin Scorcese produced *The Blues*, his seven-part series honoring the idiom, the *American Folk Blues Festival Volumes One & Two* went on to be honored with the Keeping the Blues Alive Achievement in Film award from the Blues Foundation, a Grammy nomination for Best Long Form Music Video, and an Honorable Mention from the *MOJO* Magazine Music Awards. Volume Three of the series was also honored with Best Music Anthology from the *DVD Entertainment* Awards and won the Best Compilation Award from the *Home Media Retailing* Awards.

There are some seasons when everything you touch turns to gold and, as a co-producer of the *AFBF* series, I found out what it is like to don a tuxedo and walk down the red carpet at the Grammy Awards—as well as step up to the podium in Memphis and accept an award from my music industry peers at the Blues Foundation. It was a lot of work for everyone involved and I am forever grateful for the experience. But, what pleases me most is that these legendary artists have been preserved at the peak of their artistry, for the edification and enjoyment of future generations.

San Diego Troubadour, February, 2013

TEN

East Greets West or the Sun Also Sets
Ravi Shankar's Memorial
December 20, 2012

*In the beginning was the Word and the Word was with God
and the Word was God.* – **John 1:1**

*Say the Word and you'll be free. Say the Word and be like me.
Say the Word I'm thinking of. Have you heard the Word is love?*
   – **"The Word" John Lennon and Paul McCartney**

Tuesday, December 11, 2012—One of the most profound
musical and spiritual teachers of the 20th century is gone
this week with the passing of Pandit Ravi Shankar at the age
of 92. In spite of his failing health over the past several years,
he still managed to perform regularly in public, including a
concert four weeks earlier on November 4, 2012, in Long
Beach, California, with his daughter Anoushka, which
turned out to be his final public performance.

Because he was a long-time resident of Encinitas,
California, a memorial was held on December 20 at Paramahansa Yogananda's Self-Realization Fellowship—a pillar
of spiritual influence in the San Diego community that
Shankar embraced during the last three decades of his life.
Memorial services for such a renowned figure typically turn
into a sensationalist media circus but Shankar's memorial

was as tasteful and profound as the example set forth by his life and music. In a concise, one-hour program there were a dozen distinguished guests and family members who spoke lovingly of his deeply spiritual heart and compassionate nature, mirroring the energy that Shankar himself put out into the world. One of his disciples spoke of Shankar's wit and his playful use of puns, inspiring the wisecrack "that's why they call me a pundit!"

Born a Bengali Brahmin on April 7, 1920 in Varanasi, India (his birth name was Robindro Shaunkor Chowdhury but was later changed to the Sanskrit version of Ravindra), Ravi was the youngest of four brothers who was raised by his mother in impoverished conditions and did not meet his absentee father until he was almost eight years old. His eldest brother Uday transplanted the family to Paris in 1930, where, for the next decade, Ravi was a member of Uday's troupe, developing into a consummate professional as he mastered the classical and folk traditions of Indian dance. Through his travels he rubbed shoulders with some of the most influential people of the time, including the likes of Gertrude Stein and Cole Porter.

In 1938 Shankar became the student of his musical guru Ustad Allauddin Khan and studied with him under the same roof for seven years, eventually marrying Khan's daughter, Annapurna Devi (resulting in one son, Shubho, before divorcing). During the 1940s and '50s, Shankar became a national sensation in his native country and was responsible for synthesizing many elements of music from India's northern region with aspects drawn from the Carnatic discipline, prominent in the south of India. When filmmaker Satyajit Ray asked Shankar to compose music for his *Apu*

Trilogy (1955–1959), his fame reached global proportions in recognition of India's unique contributions to the arts.

Those gifts truly are unique and quite emblematic of the cultural and philosophical divide that separates the great spiritual disciplines of the West and East. The twelve-tone scale, used in most of Western music, has an underlying foundation of Christianist thought embedded within— filtered through the notion that human beings are borne of "original sin" requiring redemption through a spiritual and/ or psychological "Christlike" transmutation. Hinduism, by complete contrast, contains no such construct. However, one of the many precepts that unite these two great religions is the notion of the divine Word. In the case of Hinduism the Word is the cosmic sound of "Aum" (or *Om*) as the combined vibration of the three phases of nature: creation, preservation, and dissolution. When human consciousness is properly aligned with spirit in the Hindu paradigm, the sound of "Aum" literally contains the power to make manifest everything in our physical world—and the ragas that Ravi Shankar composed and performed were a living manifestation of this spiritual principle.

On his seminal 1968 LP *The Sounds of India,* Shankar provides insight as to how to musically define a raga: "Ragas are precise melody forms. A raga is not a mere scale, nor is it a mode. Each raga has its own ascending and descending movement [containing] those subtle touches and usage of microtones and stresses of particular notes.

"The Western listener will appreciate and enjoy our music more if he listens with an open and relaxed mind, without expecting to hear harmony, counterpoint, or other elements prominent in Western music. Neither should our music be thought of as akin to jazz, despite the improvisation and exciting rhythms present in both kinds of music."

With the tambura, the drone instrument in the background, there is a sense of suspended animation: of not quite being grounded, with space and time in a permanent state of rubato. That can be unsettling to the western mind firmly rooted in a four-on-the-floor aesthetic.

When the Beatles were making their second feature-length film *Help!* in 1965, George Harrison happened upon a sitar on the set and it was through this chance encounter with the exotic instrument that he became curious about Indian culture. Within the next few years Harrison's personal and spiritual awakening led to a worldwide renaissance of exploring Eastern thought and, more specifically, Indian culture as a whole. Enter Ravi Shankar as his friend, mentor, collaborator, and guru.

As an example of how unusual Indian music was to Western ears a mere 40 years ago, after spending a minute and a half tuning up and receiving a round of applause for his efforts, Shankar famously told the audience in 1971 at the *Concert for Bangladesh*: "Thank you. If you like our tuning so much, I hope you will enjoy the playing more."

Harrison once referred to Ravi Shankar as "the Godfather of world music." Did Harrison have any idea when he wrote one of his most famous songs that the English translation of Ravi is "Sun"?

Of the numerous words spoken at Shankar's memorial, some of the most heartfelt were by conductor and musical director of the Israel Philharmonic Orchestra, Zubin Mehta: "As a musician I've always felt like a little crumb in his presence because every night, whichever stage he was performing on, he was composing simultaneously. That is something that doesn't exist in my world. We just try to recreate what masters have left us for hundreds of years. Working with Ravi in New York, knowing that he could not read or write the Western notations, it was my honor to sit next to him when he was composing his concerto for the New York Philharmonic and take dictation from this great master. These are hours I will never forget. And the humility with which he approached the great musicians of the New York Philharmonic who were dying to hear him improvise in the sections, that we would sit quiet and he would say now just go on let me hear the orchestra and I would say 'no, we want to hear you.' And so it went through all the rehearsals. And we performed this great piece of his in quite a few cities in the world, always to such standing ovations for this master, that I, as a musician, have always looked up to from the first recordings I heard of his—and he was always positive, always smiling. You know, each raga starts with such a plaintive, meditative, introspective mood, and ends in victory. Until he achieves this victory he takes you through a gamut of emotions—it's the cosmos opening up.

"I was once at a recital in Carnegie Hall that didn't finish 'till way after one o'clock in the morning. It was only around midnight that he really got into his inspirational high points, and not one person in the public left. These were thousands of Americans glued to what guruji took all over the world. Ravi was opening up our country to everyone when India was an unknown quantity in the world."

In 2002, a year after George Harrison had passed away, Shankar had the opportunity to honor his friend with a major composition ("Arpan"), a highlight of the *Concert for*

George. He told the audience how George "was like a son to him," a sentiment echoed by Harrison's widow Olivia at Shankar's memorial: "I met Ravi in 1974, in fact a few weeks before I met George. Of course, his relationship with George is a story that encompasses so many things that went on to inform and change the world we grew up and grew older in. Its music, beliefs—lofty realms of thought, multiculturalism, and the power of friendship. He guided a young George and helped satiate his desire for a more meaningful life. He did this through Indian classical music, literature, and travel.

"Ravaji laid the stepping stones from west to east that led George to new concepts, alternative philosophies, and completely transformed his musical sensibilities. Both of them stepped outside their cultures and, in the spirit of true adventurers, immersed themselves in each other's customs. They exchanged ideas and maladies, until their minds and hearts, east and west, were entwined like a double helix. And I believe that we will carry a molecule of a hybrid gene that today has opened our minds and tuned our ears to different sounds, making familiar what once seemed so foreign.

"They were like father and son as well as brothers. They made each other laugh as if they shared a secret. And I'm sure they did. Their common bond was music and they collaborated many times. Sukanya and Dhani and Anoushka and Norah and I were rather in awe of their bond. Of course, Anoushka studied with her father and George said he felt so sorry for her because she could never escape practice like he did. Then one day, many years ago, he brought his young daughter Norah over, not telling us she was a musician, and just before they were leaving, she sat down at the piano and began to sing. She never saw Ravi's face standing behind her beaming as our mouths fell open. Once, Ravi had written a short [song], a devotional A-side if you will. George said "Ravi! You should write more of these." Raviji said, "George, I've been trying NOT to write them for years." From the terrestrial to the celestial, his music will flow on— within you and without you. He will be with us in morning, afternoon, and evening ragas."

Ravi Shankar is survived by his wife, two daughters, three grandchildren, and four great-grandchildren.

San Diego Troubadour, March, 2013

ELEVEN

Infested Whitewash:
The History of Channel 13's
SOUL!

Dear Sir:
My family has a five-hundred dollar color television set that we turn on once a week. Thursday—9 PM—Channel 13—Soul! *Because it's the only for-real thing on TV. Dig it?*
— **Ann Minor, Long Island, New York**

People's stories fall through the cracks in time. One chapter missing from the history books is on a television program called *Soul!*

Initially conceived in 1968 as an hour-long musical-variety show by and for African-Americans, *Soul!* was an olive branch of appeasement from the white establishment. But more than just a reflection of the civil unrest of the era, *Soul!*'s no-nonsense eclecticism offered a bold, new canvas of expression for the Black nationalist feeling rising up and out of the urban communities.

Part clarion call town-hall meeting, part café poetry reading, *Soul!* offered up a street theater club-performance cabaret and gave African-Americans their first significant television forum. And ever since it was yanked from the airwaves in 1973, it has never been seen again. What happened to *Soul!* and how did it come into being in the first place?

The program was masterminded by Ellis Benjimin Haizlip, a Howard University graduate whose deep interest in the performing arts led him to New York City. Haizlip made a name for himself after working behind the scenes with the Harlem YMCA, and producing a world tour of Langston Hughes' gospel song-play *Black Nativity.* He subsequently formed his own production company, organizing several world tours with an all African-American theater group that produced Eugene O'Neill's *The Emperor Jones* and James Baldwin's *The Amen Corner.* When Haizlip's 1967 production of the Donald McKayle Dance Company's *Black New World* caught the eye of independent television station WNET (Channel 13), it was subsequently telecast, and Haizlip began a fourteen-year relationship with the station, eventually serving as executive producer.

Not long after Haizlip joined the staff at WNET, riots were erupting across America's inner cities. The Kerner Commission appointed by President Johnson determined that "America was moving toward two societies—one Black and one white—separate and unequal, with segregation and poverty creating in the racial ghetto a destructive environment totally unknown to most white Americans."

The commission's findings struck a chord in Channel 13's Director of Cultural Programming Christopher Lukas. Lukas says that "Among the recommendations [that the commission made] were that the media had a responsibility. The report stated that there were no Black people on most newspapers, that there were no Black people in television and no Black people **on** television and I looked around me at Channel 13 and I noticed that they were absolutely right." This realization inspired Lukas to produce a show called *Talking Black*, showing life in the inner cities of Boston, Pittsburgh, and New York. Lukas wanted to show that African-Americans "weren't just out in the streets rioting—that they have their own lives, with their own responsibilities." The show was well received and its success paved the way for another idea that Lukas had.

"I went to the head of the station and said that I wanted to do a Black *Tonight Show*. I asked Ellis' advice and he said that he'd like to produce it. So, Ellis and I discussed it and it quickly became apparent to me that he thought a Black *Tonight Show* was ridiculous. It is not how Black people would do a show. And I said 'Design the show, I'll make my comments, but essentially it will be your show.'" And *that* became *Soul!*

Soul! debuted over the New York airwaves on September 8, 1968. Initial shows were broadcast live, giving the show a gritty, hit-and-run appeal which caused one journalist to remark that "if some of the language was a bit strange and some of it not generally considered suitable for polite conversation, it succeeded splendidly in conveying the writer's meanings. And that, baby, is what language is all about."

By the end of *Soul!*'s first season the show received enough support and praise to be broadcast nationally—when WNET became part of the Public Broadcasting System. Over the next four years, *Soul!* forged its unique voice and helped others to find theirs. "The creativity of realism can only lie in that creativeness of the aware" wrote one viewer, and that is what *Soul!* accomplished—it made people aware of the African-American experience. Ida Lewis, publisher of

Encore magazine, wrote that "the problems of Blacks reflect the whole panorama of our human needs in microcosm. The Black struggle is related to the natural aspirations of society as a whole." *Soul!* zeroed in on those aspirations and managed to bring as much history, art, and truth about the black experience into American living rooms as could be thoughtfully orchestrated into the space of 60 minutes.

The diversity and range of talent that *Soul!* presents is breathtaking. And with no other avenues available on television, *Soul!* became, by default, **the** showcase for Black artists of the day.

One artist to receive his first national exposure through the program was author and poet Quincy Troupe. Currently (1995) a professor of creative studies at University of California, San Diego, Troupe confirms that "at the time there was nothing out there for African-Americans. There was no show for African-Americans and there still isn't. Because everything is segregated in this country. People are so tribalistic. Irish are for Irish, Jews are for Jews, and you don't get this innerflow, what I call a cross-fertilization that makes the country really unique. So you get Black-owned networks, and you get Black-owned radio stations, and that is what becomes the norm. And that has become the model, because it is easier to do it that way for the advertisers, because you can target markets, but you end up segmenting everyone. What we should be working towards is fusion, but people don't think about it in that way.

"What Ellis wanted to do with *Soul!* was put something out there reflecting African-American culture. It was a revolutionary idea then and it is *still* a revolutionary idea. He was combining poetry, fiction, music, politics, and everything else into one forum. Now, you tell me that's not revolutionary. That's not happening now. No show on television does that."

Describing a typical episode of the show is nearly impossible. One program might feature an hour of music by Al Green or Stevie Wonder in a nightclub atmosphere dubbed "Club Soul." Another might seamlessly weave the verse of Amiri Baraka or the Last Poets between musical numbers by the Delfonics or Gladys Knight and the Pips. Then a dance company might bust out some free-style movements.

Haizlip felt a responsibility to offer viewers a sense of the richness and beauty of African-American heritage. "It's not all finger-poppin' time" he remarked in a 1971 interview. "And I feel good when I realize that I have presented over 300 artists to the public."

One viewer wrote in, "After viewing your show I saw just how ignorant I was about anything that concerned Blacks"—and he praised Haizlip for "helping to keep this infested whitewash from taking over our intelligent minds, and replacing it with more productive insights of ourselves."

Haizlip suggests that the main reason African-Americans weren't represented on television was for "a lack of regard for all things Black. Our future in the mass-media lies in removing the profit motive from our motion picture, television, and other productions. I don't say that they should be non-profit. We hope that a project will pay for itself and its artists, writers, producers, and contributors. But it is the profit *motive* which cheapens and downgrades the American product."

Haizlip's *Soul!* wasn't fixated with presenting marquee artists or musicians that guaranteed ratings. If he thought that someone had an important and/or relevant statement to make to African-Americans, he gave them a forum. Perhaps the high water mark of *Soul!'s* civic-minded audacity came when it broadcast two complete hours of author James Baldwin conversing with poet Nikki Giovanni, a simultaneous triumph for African-Americans, homosexuals, and women.

Listen, in my day, older women would get their wagons in a circle and when a girl-child came of age they'd school her in the ways of men folks; same with the men and boy-childs. My father was a master in the community. His motto was: "Knowing how to treat a woman is the root of all knowledge." Heavy stuff. Of course, for my money there ought to be courses in this kind of thing. 'Cause this stumbling trial-and-error business is a terrific strain on the heart. And why-the-hell should every generation have to scuffle through thirty or forty years of improvisation just to learn what the last generation already found out? We all get turned around and put to sleep and someone has to wake himself or herself up and put their very life on the line to remind us of something basic. We need schools in a bad way.

– from *The Johnson Girls* by **Toni Cade Bambara**

The show made you think and, ultimately, that's what led to its removal from the airwaves in the spring of '73. Troupe suggests that *Soul!* may have become too powerful an influence in strengthening the militant outlook of African-Americans. It was suggested by one staff member on *Soul!*

that PBS felt that an all-Black show "was no longer necessary since racism was no longer a problem in America by 1973."

If *Soul!* was initially funded as a gesture of placating the African-American community after the riots of the late '60s, did the PBS higher ups believe the necessity of representing Blacks on television had outlived its purpose? The newspaper stories that ran in May of 1973 spoke of PBS withdrawing funds because of low ratings and to make room for other types of programming.

Haizlip accused the Corporation for Public Broadcasting of attempting "to destroy all Black programming" on PBS. PBS claimed that the money that would have funded *Soul!* was being allocated to another Black show called *Interface. Interface*, it was argued, was a show geared to an "interracial" audience.

"We will mount as aggressive a campaign as the situation calls for," Haizlip announced in the press. "We'll do everything in our power to bring this to the attention of the people."

Soul!'s last episodes address the cancellation by encouraging a heavy letter-writing campaign to provide a show of support. A similar plea to the viewership at the end of the second season (May 1969) had succeeded in keeping the show on the air for three more years. Viewers sent in poignant appreciations of what *Soul!* meant to them, and on *Soul!*'s final program, entitled "To the People, Thank You," Haizlip offered, "Five years ago there were some uprisings in the United States and these uprisings created an atmosphere that allowed most, if not all, Black programs that are on television to exist. But sometimes it is necessary in the evolution of things to disappear, reorganize and to reunite.

"However, the communication has been established— we cannot cut that off. Because it has been expressed to us over and over again that people are reaching out and accepting and responding to the communication that has been laid down before."

Soul! has never been syndicated or rebroadcast once it was taken off the air in 1973.

After *Soul!'s* demise, Haizlip worked on many projects, notably a twelve-day arts festival at the Lincoln Center in the early '70s, "Soul at the Center." He stayed on at WNET until 1981, and created another television show called *Watch Your Mouth*, a language skills development series for adolescents. He maintained a high social profile, participating in the political campaigns of both Jesse Jackson and David Dinkins. He died of lung cancer in 1991.

Looking back, Troupe says that *Soul!* "gives us a good reference point of what was happening in that period and it sets up a model of the possibilities of what a television show can be.

"You don't have that now. You don't have poets on television shows. You don't have that kind of combination and *Soul!* showed that it can be successful.

"It's important history. It's real history rather than revisionist history." And if your mind gets too blown out from thinking about all that heavy stuff, it's also a hell of a lot of fun to jump out of your chair and dance to. Bring it.

San Diego Reader, September 28, 1995

TWELVE
1992

Terry Southern once said that a hipster was someone who had deliberately decided to kill a part of himself in order to make life bearable. He knows that by doing this he is cutting himself off from many positive emotions as well as the negative, destructive ones he seeks to avoid; but on balance he feels that the sacrifice is worthwhile. By this definition Bruce was (and is) authentically, indelibly hip. – **Kenneth Tynan, in his introduction to** *How to Talk Dirty and Influence People* **by Lenny Bruce (taped to the inside of my road journal for the** *Six Pack of Love* **tour)**

Seek ye first the kingdom of God, and His righteousness; and all these things shall be added onto you. – **Matthew 6:33**

Genius is simply knowing who you really are. – **Peter Case to Phast Freddie, en route to Asbury Park, New Jersey**

I was feeling desperate. And I didn't know where to turn. I was desperate for the winds of change to blow me **anywhere** toward some "positive" direction, but I lacked the conscious will, or understanding of what was truly positive, in order to steer the winds "just so." Unaware of the game-changing significance represented by my astrological Saturn Return coming up around the bend, I grew obsessed with how to go about changing my circumstances in life. Or, at the very least, I was obsessed about changing my attitude toward my circumstances. And then…isn't it funny, how things can seemingly turn on a dime—attaining critical mass with your visions, by investing enough energy into your hopes and dreams, wishes and prayers, to make them manifest and become reality.

From the time I was sixteen, I knew I wanted to be an artist—but not just any type of artist. Like spokes on a wheel, I wanted to practice multiple artistic disciplines, with each path sustaining and supporting the others. This multitudinous approach appeals to me primarily because: a) I've always loved exploring as many options simultaneously as possible, and b) because the Lord knows how much I enjoy the universal applications of diversification. Or, perhaps another way of saying it, being an archetypal Virgo, is that God is in the details. Furthermore, why would anyone wish to pigeonhole him or herself and compromise their fullest potential? There are enough people and institutions in the world that are delighted to play out that role for you. I certainly don't see the need to waste energy with any further self-imposed limitations. After all, there ARE ideals and standards to be maintained.

Of course, the cosmic sounds of the spheres— MUSIC—will forever serve as the source prime number in my particular equation—as a musician, natch, plus pulling a trifecta additionally as a DJ and musicologist. I find numerous other disciplines *almost* as attractive: writing, acting, photography, and the visual art of multi-media assemblage/collage. With the encouragement of several teachers and a couple of girlfriends, by the time I hit high school, poems, song fragments, and stories began emerging. And when I stopped long enough to ponder and fantasize about the future, I imagined myself a writer. That was, of course, with all of the perceived glory and none of the economic constraints. I imagined how every day would be an adventure—a life spent in motion and reflection, investigating new cultures through travel, and interacting with people from all walks of life. Always open, forever curious, and constantly learning—it was upon those lofty principles that I was chomping at the bit to write. Or more to the point, I was chomping at the bit for some life experiences that were worthy of documenting. Steady, dear boy, steady.

And then one day you find, ten years have got behind you. Well, a decade swept by in an instant, and it felt like the bow had been strung back long enough. It was time to LET GO AND LET 'ER RIP—for once and for all. At 26, it felt like I was in a terrible rut, and that life was passing me by. My *hipster* side found me dropping out and sidelining my artistic aspirations—I'd become a part-time hobbyist for the most part. I had allowed myself to become complacent and overly preoccupied with the concerns of paying the rent, eating, maintaining a car, and spending the majority of my waking hours at a dead-end job in order to pay for those "necessities." I also had dependency issues. I was a vinyl/music junkie and had an unquenchable desire to discover/hear as much compelling new music as possible, either on record or preferably, through live performance. These were the golden years before the cultural freefall/free-for-all of the Internet.

The vibration of sound is something that has nurtured me since before my first breath, and music sustains my spirit in ways that are inexplicable. Yet, I've spent decades spewing immense amounts of verbiage in the attempt to commune and communicate the sensations, feelings, and ideas that wail away within, seeking to make sense out of the chaos. To appreciate the abstract wonder and beauty of life is complex, and simple, and absurd. If I've managed to settle on a worldview, then life to me is, if anything, Dada-esque to the nth degree.

But *something* vital was missing from my life circa '91, and until I summoned the ability to listen to my heart and have the courage to act upon its dictates, nothing was going to sate the restlessness: then, a series of revelations allowed me to hit the reset button on how I was living my life.

☯

Those revelations began in the spring of 1991, when I took my very first overseas adventure from San Diego, California, with a motley group of five musicians calling themselves Manual Scan. The idea was go to over to Great Britain for seven days and perform four gigs, with three in the city of London proper, and a fourth gig 101 miles to the west (nearly in Wales), in the market town of Chippenham.

It really is true about who you know and the types of doors those relationships can sometimes open for you. Thanks to Kevin Ring and Bart Mendoza, I was brought on board as Manual Scan's road manager and opening act for this one-week mini-tour. The four gigs were a blast, and after spending seven days in London, I managed to stay on for another week of solo adventuring, taking in Birmingham, Liverpool, Manchester, Amsterdam, and Paris, before returning to London and flying back to San Diego. I discovered that I really liked being abroad. In fact, the experience shattered my preconceptions about how I was choosing to live. It felt like I had become a complete slave to my materialistic existence. Actually, it was worse than that. I had become the protagonist in T.S. Eliot's *The Love Song of J. Alfred Prufrock:* one of those miserable wretches who measure their lives out in coffee spoons, in quiet desperation, waiting for the five o'clock whistle to blow so you can have a respite from the tedium before having to report to your post—and repeat the dreadful process again and again. Traveling abroad for the first time was a tremendous shot in the arm. It reinforced my sense that I was wasting my life in the rat race, because as everyone knows, even if you win, you're still a rat. I related ever more to Thomas Jefferson's council to his nephew Peter Carr in 1787: "Travelling. This makes men wiser, but less happy."

Being on the road for two weeks abroad as a traveling musician had left me with the feeling that all I really needed in life was a clean set of clothes, a modest amount of money, a place to sleep for the night, a good meal, and my guitar. This isn't, of course, strictly true, but at that time I trusted that the rest would somehow sort itself out.

There's nothing like having goals that you are rabidly foaming over, giving you more than just cause to be in a perpetual state of excitation. I had zero savings in the bank, but a boatload of determination that the time had come to hatch a plan and procure some monetary resources in as timely a fashion as possible.

After spending a week back at my secure, but boring, job as a technical writer and editor at *Mitchell Manuals* (an after-market publisher of automotive repair manuals for independent garages and mechanics), I decided that some drastic action was in order. It was time to commercially release a record, and go out on the road to promote it. I had entertained the fantasy of being a professional musician for longer than I had dreamed about being a writer. I dabbled with public performance, composing songs, and occasionally going into the studio to see what I sounded like on tape, but my initial results had been raggedly discouraging. However, with the help of my studio-savvy friends Darian Sahanaja, Nick Walusko, and Steve Kobashigawa, I released my first EP on cassette at the beginning of 1992—a six-song excursion into the void called *Walk Without Me*. I networked and started sending out as many promotional packages as I could to any connections that I had at clubs across the U.S. who were willing to book an unknown artist. There were not, and still aren't, many clubs who are willing to take a chance on somebody who's not likely to draw very many people. It's plain capitalism. Learning how to build your audience is the most challenging and important thing to know in order to make it as a professional musician. That's, of course, AFTER assembling an arsenal of great songs, and developing the ability to put them over in a compelling manner in front of a room full of people.

As I embarked on this solo adventure I received some invaluable advice and made a few choice connections via songwriter and musician Peter Case. I first met Peter in 1983 at a Plimsouls gig at SDSU. I was instantly bowled over by his passionate attack, intense energy, and raw talent.

He's a classic Aries in so many ways. Over the next six years I saw Peter perform as much as possible, frequently making trips to L.A. to catch him in action. After a show at the Belly Up Tavern, we concocted the idea backstage to create a newsletter called *travellin' light*, in order to maintain contact with his fan base. Such were the days before the Internet, and in the twilight of desktop publishing. Happy to do anything to help Peter out with his career, I volunteered to publish, edit, and distribute said broadsheet. Doing publicity for Peter was an education, and it eventually taught me how to fish for myself after getting into the nuts and bolts of tour management and contract negotiations. But I get ahead of myself.

By the summer of '91 I had formulated a plan and wrote out the following intentions:

1) Pack a bag of clothes, a guitar, a box of tapes, and three thousand dollars.

2) Get an open-ended ticket to London with a maximum six-month period of stay.

3) Sell my car, quit my job, and say *au revoir* to all my belongings.

4) In mid-January '92 start making my way via the Greyhound bus across the country, visiting Austin, Dallas, Baton Rouge, New Orleans, Nashville, Charlotte, Northern Virginia/ Washington, D.C., New York City, and Boston, before leaving for Great Britain.

5) After arriving in Great Britain, stay with friends in Birmingham and Manchester, then make my way back to the continent. If I can find work I will take it, for I am looking to stay as long as my money can hold out, and I want to see as much of Europe as possible.

6) By September of '92, I need to be back in the States because my brother in Dallas is getting married and I am in the wedding party. So that is as long as I can stay, for this time at least.

☯

Cartoonist Bill Griffith, of *Zippy the Pinhead* fame, frequently delivered some kind of abstract profundity in his work. He is definitely someone whom I would call a Dadaist. One strip in particular called *Get a Mid-Life* absolutely NAILED my state of mind circa 1991, so much so that I clipped it out and used it as artwork on a gig flyer that summer. It more than expressed how desperate I was to blow this Popsicle stand.

Griffy pensively emotes *"I want to be someone else Zippy..."* "Oh, yeh? Which celeb?" *"I want to be on 'th road...I want to live in hotels. I want to go to some unspecified place & do vague things for an indeterminate period of time."* Zippy responds, "You're making a huge mistake!" *"I want to be alienated and alone...waiting for a train to nowheres-ville..."* "Can I be Susan Sarandon?"

You know I don't even know what I'm hoping to find. I related COMPLETELY and utterly to the existential crisis of needing something so badly but not being able to put your finger on exactly what that is. All I knew was that I couldn't face the prospect of doing the same, exact thing with my life a year from now. It was unbearably unthinkable. I needed to shake things up in the worst way, harvesting the patience of a saint while putting my ducks in a row. It wasn't easy biding my time, but I needed to build as much of a financial nut as possible, without so much as a penny to fall back upon once I returned. Or, if I returned—who could say?

❦

I spent the first two months of 1992 working my ass off and managed to sell my red Honda CRX to divest myself of my monthly car payment and insurance. I rode my bicycle everywhere after that point, including biking 35 miles roundtrip to work most days. I didn't care. I was relentlessly pursuing my game plan and nothing was going to stop me.

On Saturday, February 22, I played my last gig of the year in San Diego, to a packed house at Caffé Fiore, in Hillcrest. Two weeks later I was at the Metcalfe House, a youth hostel in Phoenix, Arizona, and making a new best friend every 24 hours. It was non-stop fun, but I took pause long enough to capture the occasional thought in my journal:

03.06.92, Friday afternoon, 3:50 PM still finds me in Phoenix, where I'm having a much greater time than I expected. The American Youth Hostel has been so warm, like a huge pair of arms welcoming me on my journey. The morning was spent with Sue, the den mother of the AYH, Mare Ashely, and all the really cool artists who are staying here: Eric (from France), Andrew (from Australia), Brad (the South African who weaved my hair), and, of course, Russell, the Irishman. Mare is talking of going back to Downey but would rather spend a few days traveling with me towards Austin. Everyone in the house is hanging out, with the artists painting and/or drawing, with the others sprawled out conversing. Sue brought out her guitar and Penelope brought out her Bob Dylan songbook, so I proceeded to play "I Threw It All Away," "Tonight I'll Be Staying Here With

You," "Living the Blues," "Idiot Wind," "Clothes Line Saga," "You're a Big Girl Now," "Hurricane," "Million Dollar Bash," "Shelter from the Storm." Later, Mare and I walk over to a local mall and by the time we get back to the hostel everybody wants us to elope. She drops me off at the bus station and I give her the last two cookies that my mom baked for the road. Wait for the bus to take me to Austin feeling happy and melancholy.

Happy and melancholy—that is pretty much the theme of '92 in a nutshell. Before leaving San Diego I managed to line up a few gigs along the way and I had several friends and relatives to stay with as I crossed the country on the Greyhound bus, which greatly reduced my traveling expenses. March 8 and 9 were spent in Dallas visiting my brother Craig and his fiancé Missy, where I was able to check out Dealey Plaza and the infamous School Book Depository firsthand. The vibe there is positively spooky because anyone who has seen the Abraham Zapruder film and has actually observed the angle from where Oswald allegedly shot JFK knows that it is physically impossible to have shot the president from that window. I don't wish to diss the entire city of Dallas, but the place feels "sinister" to me.

KEEP AUSTIN WEIRD

Half the musicians in this town wouldn't be where they are today if it weren't for waitresses. Arrive in Austin on March 11 and it strangely feels like I'm no longer in Texas for some reason. As home to the University of Texas, as well as the state's capital, Austin has a bohemian vibe that is unique unto itself. I manage to hit town right in the middle of the sixth annual South by Southwest (SXSW) music conference and have pre-arranged to get together with PC's friend, Bill Morrissey, when he plays Marcia Ball's club La Zona Rosa. Bill is a fabulous songwriter and he turns out to be a gracious and humble man. After his set, I catch one of my all-time favorite bands at the Terrace: Timbuk3, in their native Austin, promoting their album *Big Shot In The Dark*. Also on the bill is Michelle Shocked and John Trudell/AKA Graffiti Man. I did some busking during SXSW, sold a couple of tapes, and by Friday the 13th, get back on the bus for Baton Rouge.

St. Patrick's Day is celebrated early with my Aunt Nancy on Saturday the 14th with the Chickasaw Mudd Puppies playing a block party on the back of a flatbed truck at LSU. I end up playing an impromptu house concert on Monday the 16th before getting back on the bus for another house concert scheduled in Nashville on the 19th.

Over the next four weeks, between staying with friends, I play a series of shows in Charlotte, NC (the Foundry), Arlington, VA (private party), New York City (Blondie's and the Life Café), and Boston (at Park Center). On April 17, I end up meeting songwriter Mary Lou Lord busking at Harvard Square, and for the next two days, she shows me the ropes of playing the subway stops on the red line of the "T." Since I'm leaving the country for England in couple of days, and pose no future threat as her competition, she's willing to share some of her secrets of how to succeed on the street as a performer. Otherwise, I'm sure she wouldn't have given me the time of day. She's a scruffy ball-of-fire, and I'd later cross paths with her again in 1995, after she released her debut CD *Mary Lou Lord* on the Kill Rock Stars imprint.

❦

Much as I loved crossing the U.S., and seeing so many friends and family, I was really happy to be back "across the pond" to see Great Britain again. I bounced up and down the country a few times and ended up playing one of the most unusual gigs of my life at the National Association for Teachers of English in Birmingham on April 23. As a solo, acoustic American rock 'n' roller I was sandwiched on the bill between an Irish Gaelic Folk band and a group of Pakistanis playing Beatles and Chuck Berry covers. The experience was thoroughly surreal. I met a young English teacher from Croydon named Jane Barnes and we danced three or four Irish jigs, even though I had no idea what I was doing. I ended up seeing much more of Jane while I was in the country, after she determined that I wasn't a "psychopath." She even graciously introduced me to a couple of friends who were happy to host me in London and Copenhagen.

After spending a week in Sale with fellow Bob Dylan fanatic and author Clinton Heylin, I connected with my roommate Phil from San Diego in London, catching a superb They Might Be Giants show on May 6 at the Family Cat Town & Country. The next day I entertained a group of twenty uniformed French schoolgirls with my guitar in front of Westminster Abbey. They spent the entire time giggling and taking pictures, and were completely adorable. After a week of sightseeing in London, the two of us took the ferry from Dover to Ostend. After a three-hour train ride through Belgium and the Netherlands, we arrived at Centraal Station. We are at last in Amsterdam!

We spend a week tirelessly exploring the canals, visiting museums, and finding out how much hash can be consumed before Phil has to return to San Diego. One memorable afternoon found us sitting in an out-of-the-way bar with four or five locals, when a jovial man in his 40s comes bounding through the door, enthusiastically proclaiming "Ring the chicken!" The barman obliged his request and grabs a rubber chicken hanging from the wall that covers up a ball to strike a bell. "Ringing the chicken" means that he was buying everyone in the pub another round of whatever they were drinking at that exact moment. The Dutch are a crazy lot, and I love 'em!

06.01.92—I sit taking notes in the Frisco Inn, a hotel in the red-light district of Amsterdam. It is just past noon in room 20. Svenja is lying asleep next to me. The last 24/36 hours have been even more insane than the previous two weeks in Amsterdam. That is saying something. The week that I spent with my roommate as a tourist doesn't begin to compare to what has happened since he left town to go back to San Diego.

Last Saturday when I came down to breakfast at the Shelter, I met a gal from Bremen, Germany: Svenja Slinka. She was on the terrace writing in her journal when I sat down to eat. After a few minutes we started talking and decided to set out together for the day, with the idea that I would show her where the Van Gogh Museum is located. But we never made it there because...

We ended up buying some beer and sitting in the grass at Rembrandt's Plein sipping our suds while I played my guitar. Two hours after we were scheduled to meet, Victor finally shows up with his guitarist friend Frank and we move down to the Pavilion, next to Mister Coco's restaurant. Frank and I jam on "Melissa," "While My Guitar Gently Weeps," "Hey

Joe," and "*After Midnight.*" Victor hustles the passing patrons for loose change by passing the hat—he calls it "bottling," as in raising enough money as a busker to buy another bottle for the musicians.

We make enough money for Svenja and I to buy a bottle of Chardonnay at the market. In an alley on the way back from the store we sit down and talk, embrace, and kiss. Then we make our way back to the group.

Victor pulls out his violin and the two of us play a café terrace together. Linda, Cynthia, and Bill—all from San Francisco—are hanging out. We disperse and meet up an hour later at De Saloon for a few more drinks where Frank, Victor and I play the terrace. Our set sounds great: "Summertime," "While My Guitar Gently Weeps," "Hey Joe," and "Hey, Good Lookin'," with another hat full of silver resulting. We split the take three ways and set out for the Gollom.

Once at the Gollom we alternate between sweating profusely inside the pub and cooling off outside. At the end of the alley (Daam-Steeg) lies a canal. Svenja, her friend Menage, and I sit down in a couple of chairs and then this incredibly drunk and tall Dutch guy comes sprawling down the street, wailing on a harmonica. I run back inside the Gollom, grab my guitar, and play the "Mannish Boy" riff for ten minutes while this guy wailed and screamed "I'm a Hoochie Coochie Man!" at the top of his lungs. Then two cyclists coming from opposite directions crashed head-on right in front of us—cacophonous surreal ecstasy.

We finally go inside the Gollom and set up to play a 45-minute set. We pass the hat and drink Guinness outside. Victor plays Bach's greatest hits for ten minutes and keeps saying re: Svenja *"Look, I like the lady…"* Pause. *"Okay?"* Victor's seal of approval is laced with the tinge of a come-on.

As it gets closer to 1 AM (curfew time back at the Shelter), Svenja and I start heading back to the hostel. After we get there I ask her if she really wants to sleep? *"No."* *"Well, I've having too much fun to want to sleep either."* So we grab a few things and decide to rough it outside for the night.

We walk back to Rembrandt's Plein, set up a blanket and make out on the grass for a while. During this moment of losing ourselves, someone comes by and steals Svenja's purse. Twenty minutes later we find it over by the bushes (thanks? to a French guy, was he in on the theft?). She lost all her money (100 dollars), but recovered her train ticket and passport and everything else. I gave her some money to make up for it but that sort of put a damper on things. We broke camp and ended up spending 4:00 to 8:00 AM sleeping in the bushes near the Rikjsmuseum. Svenja woke up very groggy and practically fainting until we managed to get some water and oranges, which wasn't easy on a Sunday morning. Went back to the Shelter. Showered and had breakfast.

Have three hours before Svenja has to go back to Bremen. We hang out on the docks until someone shoos us away. We sit on a public bench with hypodermic needles lying underneath it. Nice. I play my guitar, make out on a bench, and get stroked to a climax. Walk to the station, play my guitar on the platform, and wave goodbye until the train disappears into the distance. Roll credits, end of Wild Weekend—Part One. Stay tuned until next Saturday for Part Two.

☯

There are numerous entries in my journal duplicating those types of antics during the merry month of May in Amsterdam, as I learn the ways of the world and figure out how to survive on the terraces as a street musician. I would soon become pals with Bill Costa, a fiercely independent musician who transplanted himself from the bay area, east of Berkeley, after deciding that he had had enough of America and her culture. Twenty-two years later, to the best of my knowledge, he is still there. Bill is quite a character and helped me to get my sea legs in A'dam; he's a consummate musician with more integrity than anyone I had ever met. Speaking of characters, the other person who set the tone for my tour of duty in A'dam was Victor. I never did catch his last name, but Victor was in his 40s, born and raised in the Middle East (Saudi Arabia, I believe), and claimed to belong to a "royal family." It was impossible to discern where the reality ceased and the bullshit began with Victor. What I DO know is that he is a genius musician who speaks upwards of seven languages. I spent several weeks observing him as he simultaneously insulted and charmed the tourists, depending upon his schizophrenic moods. This was likely to have been caused by his enthusiastic fervor for alcohol. But I learned that if I didn't expect too much from Victor in terms of punctuality or conventional behavior, we got along great. He made such a magical sound with his violin that it was easy to overlook many of the things that ordinarily would have pissed me off. Like the one afternoon that he called a German tourist a "cunt-face," and then proceeded to charm the wallet off him with his recital of Bach for fifteen minutes, to the point where the man is throwing ten guilder notes on the ground around his feet, in appreciation for his talents.

As May gave way to June, it was time to be thinking of leaving town—an excruciating thing to contemplate. I was simultaneously lonely and yearning for some profound change to sweep into my life, and at the same time I had never had so much fun. My days and nights were filled with an incredible assortment of musicians, expatriates, and bohemians from all the world: a roving cast of lead and bit players left over from a Fellini production. All I had to do in order to make a living was open my guitar case and sing for the passing tourists. I spent the month of May at the Shelter, a Christian youth hostel that cost less than ten dollars a night for a bed, shower, and breakfast in the AM. The staff was full of young, Dutch, fundamentalist Christians who didn't ram their beliefs down anyone's throats. But you were always welcome to join them for their nightly prayer meetings and discussions of the *Bible*.

One morning in the first week of June, a young man came walking down the stairs. We hadn't really spoken the entire month I was there, but he stopped me for a moment with the words "I had a dream about you last night." "Oh, yeah? What was it about?" "Well, I can't really get into the details, but what I can say is that if you want your life to remain exactly as it is right now, then don't leave Amsterdam." Really? Thanks for the cryptic message, universe.

After five weeks in Amsterdam it felt like I needed to expand my parameters a bit. Before I left the States in April, I bought a Eurail pass that was good for three weeks of consecutive travel anywhere on the continent. Much as I adore Amsterdam, I knew that if I ended up back in California from my second trip abroad, and hadn't visited any other countries beyond Britain or the Netherlands, I was really going to be mad at myself. After two straight weeks of playing the terraces and pubs with Victor, and a proper gig with bassist Jeroen Schouten at the Café Zoetter on June 5, I started making plans to leave town. But not before catching Def Leppard, at the Paradiso, with Jeroen on June 6.

On June 8 I took the night train to Copenhagen and met two fabulous women from Long Beach, Paulene and Lynn. I played my guitar for them all night long in our car. It is on this particular leg of the journey that I make a pact with myself that no matter how painful it is to forge emotional connections with people and then let them go within a day (or sometimes hours), I'm not going to let the pain of separation stop me from bonding as deeply as possible with my fellow travelers while on the road. I always seem to walk away richer for having had the experience.

I say goodbye to the two of them in Copenhagen and then continue on to Oslo, where I busk in the town square with a female violinist I just met. We make enough coinage to buy ourselves an ice cream cone apiece. I then travel another seven hours north to Verdal and visit Stein and Solveig, a couple I met at the Greyhound station in New Haven, CT. After spending a couple of days in the land of the Midnight Sun (they are 190 miles south of the Arctic Circle), I end up wishing that I had come in September when you can see the Aurora Borealis.

After spending three days in Norway I make my way to Copenhagen and stay at the house of Diane McKelvey, a friend of Jane Barnes, who is on assignment from the British Embassy. We see Tivoli Gardens and the place is lit up like Christmas in June.

06.13.92 Diane is quite a straight arrow, a devoted Christian and someone who leads a pretty straightforward and straight-laced life. You know, goes to church on Sunday, believes that Jesus died for our sins, doesn't swear, doesn't drink, doesn't use drugs—in other words, is pretty much the opposite of me. We had some interesting conversations centering on religion and other items of controversy. We spent Saturday walking through Copenhagen and finding Christiana. Christiana is a commune that has been in operation since the early '70s after it was abandoned by the city in 1963. There is the open selling of hash and marijuana within its gates, and because it keeps the activity centered to one locale, the city tolerates and allows the selling and consumption to occur without incident. I met a guy from San Diego there (of all things). He had on a UCSD T-shirt, plays violin in a bluegrass band called the Floyds, and hangs out at Megalopolis all the time. Small world.

I spend Sunday further sightseeing in Copenhagen and leave the next day for Berlin. I check out the Brandenburg Gate and take a boat ride around the city. I met a musician from a band called the Scaries, who is kind of interesting, before taking the subway to Berlin-Lichtenburg so I can make my way to Prague. Berlin doesn't do much for me, but it would probably be much different if I had been able to connect with some of the locals. But I decide to move on and utilize my Eurail pass while I can.

06.15.92, Monday. Once on the platform to go to Prague, I meet a very attractive nineteen-year-old woman from La Coruña, Spain named Cecilia. We started talking on the platform, said goodbye, got on the train from opposite sides of the car and somehow ended up in the same compartment. Her English skills were less than fluent, but not bad, and she spoke

German in addition to her native Spanish. *Between her English and the crash refresher course my mind was conjuring from my two years of high school Spanish, we were able to communicate with each other. And, of course, the music and the guitar, which have broken through so many other communication barriers, helped out as well.*

The journey from slightly-bland Germany to beautiful Czechoslovakia was amazingly scenic. Arrived in Prague around 8 PM, with Cecilia and I planning on staying at a hostel, but we were shanghaied on the train platform by a 35-year-old guy named Freebort. He explained to us that he made a few extra dollars by finding travelers who were in need of lodging and placing them into the homes of local families who have extra rooms in their house or apartment. After listening to his spiel, he seemed legit, so we decided to go along with him. We rode the Metro out to the furthest stop on the red line to Haje (pronounced High-Yea), walked to the apartment house and met the family that we would be staying with: a mother and father who spoke almost no English and a fourteen-year-old daughter who spoke very little. English has only been taught in Czechoslovakia for the last seven years, so subsequently most of the citizens who speak English are teenagers. Between the slight limitations of communicating with Cecilia, and the complete inability to communicate with our host family, it became a VERY interesting exercise to convey an idea—utilizing sign language, pantomime, drawing pictures on the wall—whatever it took sometimes.

After being introduced to the family, we all sit down in the living room and a round robin of conversation begins, with Freebort the only person who is able to translate for all the parties. After a few moments, Freebort turns to me and says "I've been learning how to play the guitar and I'm trying to learn this particular song. Could you show me how to play it?" I say "sure" and ask which song? He pulls a Xerox copy of sheet music out of his bag to "I'm a Loser" by the Beatles. After laughing for half a minute at the absurdity of the situation, I play "I'm a Loser" for three Czechs and a Spanish woman after being in Prague for an hour. After playing the song, I then go line-by-line explaining what the text means, because of all the colloquialisms within the lyrics. It was quite an interesting exercise, because I was able to utilize several different skills at the same time, and it was so much fun. Can I get a job doing THIS for a living: teaching ESL courses and Beatles songs at the same time?

I spent three days hanging out in Prague with a beautiful free spirit and had an awesome time taking in the sights: the Prague Castle, the Karlov Most (Charles Bridge), the Franz Kafka Museum, and drinking a fair amount of cheap Czech beer. By Friday, I had to leave for the weekend and go back to Amsterdam to play some pre-arranged gigs with Jeroen and Victor. When I arrive on Friday June 19 at the Café Zoetter, Victor is sitting at the bar and he hands me a letter.

Amsterdam, 9th of June '92

Hello Jon!
How are you? I hope you're fine. I was looking for you, but unfortunately you are in Norway now (nice for you, anyway!).
I wanted to say thank you! You'll probably wonder why. I'll explain. After the lovely afternoon with you, and Victor, and the other musicians, I started thinking about my life. I found out I've always lived the life of other people. I mean, the influence of the way my parents, teachers, etc. etc. wanted me to live was

so strong that I didn't recognize my own wishes anymore. After last Tuesday I discovered myself again. And that feels good! So, thank you, for showing me that having fun and living the way your heart tells you to live are the most important things in life! Here is my phone number, in case you'd like to spend another afternoon in Amsterdam with me! Marie-Anne

I'm not sure what chord this letter struck in me, but it made me smile and cry at the same time. This gal Marie-Anne was someone whom I met on the Rembrandt's Plein one of the afternoons hanging out with all of my musician pals. I told her my story about quitting my job to follow my bliss and going on the road and apparently that served as a catalyst for her to do the same. It is one of the sweetest letters I've ever received. I never saw Marie-Anne again, but I will always remember that one afternoon, where under the right set of circumstances, someone's perspective was altered completely. I found it to be a blessing.

After another round of gigs and assorted mayhem (*de rigueur* when you hang out with Victor), I took the train back to Prague for the remainder of the next week, spending another three days with Cecilia. After picking up the English language newspaper *The Prognosis*, I find out about the John Lennon Wall, and on Tuesday, June 23, Cecilia and I make our way over to check it out.

The **John Lennon Wall** has an assemblage of murals, graffiti, and scrawled tributes dedicated to the late musician, with a symbolic altar/grave underneath it where people leave flowers and candles and hand-written messages. Apparently, it's a landmark/hangout for Beatles fans to congregate. At that time they couldn't get records there. It's like the Soviet Union used to be, but they have bootleg tapes that are copied and passed among friends. I met a sixteen-year-old Prague girl who had tapes of the entire Beatles catalog. After discovering I was a musician, she asked me to sing a song *a cappella*, which I did. All of a sudden, it started raining, and the four of us took shelter underneath some nearby scaffolding.

Within ten minutes, another TWENTY kids joined us, one of whom, a Canadian named James, had a Spanish guitar. Only one of the girls spoke English very well, but all of them knew the lyrics to every single Beatles song, and we ended up singing Beatles tunes for about three hours until the rain slowed down to a drizzle. We must have sung 40 songs! It was at that moment that I realized how lucky I am to be able to sing and play the guitar, as it was the only means I had of communicating with these people who have such a great, generous spirit about them. It was a really magical, transcendent experience—the kind of thing that made it extremely difficult to leave.

☯

But leave I had to do, if I was to make it back to the U.S. in time for my brother's impending nuptials back in Texas. After spending a week back in London, I spoke to my roommate on the phone long-distance the day before heading back to the States and he tells me that Peter Case is trying to get a hold of me. I give PC a call in L.A. and find out that he will be taping the *Late Night with David Letterman Show* the following evening in New York, performing "Dream About You," his latest single from his brand new album *Six Pack of Love* with Paul Shaffer's band. After the *Letterman Show*, he has a gig in Boston, where serendipity has me arriving the day before, so we make a plan to meet up at the club.

The first thing I do after arriving at Boston's Logan International Airport with my bags and guitar in tow is go to a pay phone and call my brother Craig in Dallas. I ask him how things are going and he tells me in a slightly heavy breath that his wedding has been cancelled. "What?! That was the only reason I came back to the States! You mean that I could have stayed in Europe longer? Fuck!" Almost on cue, the words of the Christian dude at the Shelter come creeping back into my ear. "If you want things to remain exactly as they are right now, then stay in Amsterdam…"

Well, it was too late for that, and there was no use in wasting my time getting angry. I felt bad for my brother, but at the same time wanted to know: *why* was I back in the U.S.?

After spending the night near Harvard Square, I take the bus the next afternoon and meet up with PC at Johnny D's. The notorious Phast Freddie is also hanging out. He's hipper than hip and I take an instant liking to him. I tell Peter all about my adventures from the past five months and he seems surprised, interested, and pumps me for further information. After a while, he tells me that he's about to go on the road—a 45-city North American tour with a band and that he needs a road manager. Would I be interested in the gig? I said "I don't know, man. I just spent five months away from my own bed and I kind of want to just be stationary for a while." He then tells me that with the band he's forming he'll be playing piano on a couple of numbers. Perhaps on those songs I could come out and play some guitar? Maybe even open a couple of shows during the tour, who knows? I tell him to let me think about it. I'm pretty weary, but flat broke, with no job prospects on the horizon. But it sounds like a once-in-a-lifetime offer and, ultimately, too tempting to pass up. I accepted the gig the following morning.

☯

Everybody should have a wife somewhere.
— **Bob Dylan to Kinky Friedman (1975)**

When I get back to San Diego I need something to organize the impending details of the *Six Pack of Love* tour. I grab a red spiral notebook off the shelf that was briefly employed the year before for a film class at San Diego City College. On the first page is written:

Kubrick/Rubric
There are five ways to establish character:
1) What people say about you.
2) What you say about yourself.
3) What you do (i.e. your actions).
4) What you look like (i.e. your physical appearance).
5) Symbols (i.e. the things that you surround yourself with).

For some reason they seem like apt reminders for what is about to go down. Holy reminders.

Peter Case
The *Six Pack of Love* Tour Phase I

Wednesday, July 15: Johnny D's, Boston, MA
Thursday, July 16: Fastlanes, Asbury Park, NJ

07.16.92. Spend the evening chewing Peter's offer over. It looks like I could spend the next four months on the road. The gig is pretty wonderful, with Peter in great form, dedicating a song to me ("Travellin Light"), and announcing on the mic: "We're trying to talk Jon into going on the road with us."

The next morning, Peter and Phast Freddie pick me up in Harvard Square at 10 AM. We eat breakfast at a diner. Drive, drive, drive. Stop in Bridgeport, CT to buy pants for Peter (he left his in NYC after the David Letterman Show*). Pick up airline ticket in Glastonbury, CT. Freddie gets out on the side of the freeway as we pass by NYC. Continue on to the gig in Asbury Park, NJ. Upon arrival in the land of Springsteen, PC says "This place is so strange, it's like a ghost town."*

After driving 270 miles from Boston we arrive at the venue at 6 PM, to be greeted by a surly old man, drunk with no shirt on. When we inquire about loading in and doing a sound check, he responds with "Nobody tells me anything! I'm so pissed off! I'm getting more pissed off every minute!" Peter and I exchange knowing glances: this guy is a nut. Go around the corner and eat Mexican food for dinner. We are summoned for a sound check. Afterwards, we go to our hotel and check-in to room 711. Peter jumps on the phone with his wife Diane, and I go for a jog through the neighborhood, before it's off to the gig.

Wait for the second opening act to finish their set by going for a drink next door at the Mexican place. 25 minutes later I set up the stage and introduce PC by saying "Ladies and gentlemen, direct from the Late Night with David Letterman Show, *won't you please put your hands together and welcome Geffen recording artist Peter Case."*

The show goes relatively well with the exception of a photographer using a flash that bugs the hell out of Peter, and a drunken, over-zealous female fan who blurts out: "I have to talk to you—it's not like I can get to Bob Dylan." Outside the club she continues by spraying her spittle at Peter and emotes "that song 'Put Down the Gun' saved my life. I was gonna blow my brains out." To which Peter replied, "You're blowing your brains out with booze. Get out of my face!" Apparently (even as a small 'c' celebrity), fame is not what it's cracked up to be.

Thursday night ends with footage from the Democratic National Convention. It looks like Bill and Al in '92.

Friday morning we awake without an alarm in a stuffy room. Drink pineapple juice, shower, and leave. Check out of hotel, pack the car and eat breakfast at the Blue Swan diner. French toast and coffee. Listen to Bob Dylan on Folksinger's Choice en route to JFK—a 70-mile drive. When we pass Coney Island, Peter learns that his Long Island gig is "blown out" (cancelled) and he is really pissed off about it. For 10 minutes we think we are lost and this merely adds fuel to the fire. We make it to JFK and part on the premise that we will speak on Monday, when the two of us are back in California. On Saturday, Peter plays Atlanta, and then flies back to L.A. on Sunday.

After being away for four months, I had a few things to attend to upon my arrival back in San Diego. But I only had 72 hours before I needed to be up in L.A., and during that three-day window I had to prepare, publish and distribute the third edition of the *travellin' light* newsletter, in order for Peter's fans to know about the upcoming tour dates and the release of several new CDs. 1992 was the season of *Six Pack of Love*, Peter's third album as a solo artist. After building a reputation playing bass and singing in the power pop trio the Nerves, Peter formed the Plimsouls in 1980 and between the two groups recorded two EPs and two LPs. In

1986, he continued his association with Geffen records as a solo artist, releasing the critically acclaimed debut *Peter Case* that same year. His sophomore effort came in 1989 with *The Man With the Blue Post-Modern Fragmented Neo-Traditionalist Guitar*. While the arrangements on Peter's first two solo albums were heavily reliant upon his acoustic guitar, *Six Pack of Love* attempted to breach the gap between the rockingly rapturous Plimsouls and his more folk-tinged contemplative side. With an assortment of studio cats including bassist Bruce Thomas from Elvis Costello's Attractions, *Six Pack of Love* is a mixed-bag, with some cool songs having some questionable production techniques. Producer Mitchell Froom, and his highly suspect "house of keyboards" production style, brings the entire affair into the radio-ready digital domain—and that isn't necessarily appropriate for someone as gut-bucket and earthy as Peter David Case. Ultimately, with the lateral move to Vanguard Records in 1994, *Six Pack of Love* turned out to be quite an anomaly in PC's discography. Or perhaps this quote from Denise Sullivan on the Allmusic website says it best, calling *Six Pack of Love* "a failed attempt at expanding his folk roots and augmenting it with the tricky production of Mitchell Froom—Case's simple songs were lost in the morass." That just about sums it up.

I went up to L.A. on Tuesday, July 22. The next day I drove over to a rehearsal space and meet up with PC and his rhythm section for the *Six Pack of Love* tour, which includes drummer Jerry Angel and bassist Tony Marsico. After showing me the chords to "Why Don't We Give It a Go" and "Deja Blues," and running through the songs a couple of times with PC on piano and myself playing

Peter's electric guitar, PC gets a phone call from his label rep at Geffen Records. It turns out that because "Dream About You" isn't performing on the charts the way the label had hoped, Geffen is yanking its financial support for the impending tour that starts next Wednesday. The rest of rehearsal is cancelled and Jerry and Tony pack up to leave. The next few days drag out with no news forthcoming. I meet up with Mike Keneally on Friday, as he is currently living in North Hollywood with his wife Viv, and he plays me a cassette of his latest demos for his debut solo LP, *hat*. Even on a measly little four-track recorder, the songs sound incredible. On Saturday, July 25, I spend a long weekend with Darian Sahanaja and have one of the greatest birthday party/impromptu musical jams EVER. In retrospect it seems like a grand bon voyage to an era of remarkable friendships, as we all begin embarking upon our singular destinations after traveling together as a tribe for the better part of the last decade—those otherwise dreaded '80s.

Reach Out in the Darkness. The idea on this evening was to have a Spinal Tap-themed birthday party for Lisa Mychols, who performed an awesomely-rocking set with her all-female band, the Mozells. After they formally conclude their presentation, the remaining musicians, including Steve Kobashigawa, Nick Walusko, Darian Sahanaja, Probyn Gregory, several others, and myself started jamming on anything we could think of: Cheap Trick, Raspberries, Van Morrison, Sex Pistols, the Carrie Nations, you name it. After one particularly great number Darian said to me: "Damn, dude you really obtained some vocal chops over there in Amsterdam." This went on for hours at the Montrose Bowl in North Hollywood until they finally kicked us out. After that magical evening, things were never really the same after that weekend. Everyone in our clique seemed to morph into a different person, or perhaps it seemed that way. Either way, it made me think of what Jack Kerouac's Sal Paradise says at the end of *On the Road*, regarding his pal Dean Moriarty: "We're still great friends, but we have to go on to later phases of our lives." Sigh.

☯

Do you ever get the feeling that you are merely an extension of other people's narcissism? – **Peter Case**

After a long weekend of worrying and wondering about what was going to happen with Peter's tour, he was finally able to give me an update on Monday morning. He made me a fresh offer. Without Geffen underwriting some of the road expenses, Peter couldn't afford to take an entire band out on the road, so he decided to fulfill his tour commitments as a solo act. I stayed on as his road manager, with the enticement that I would get a $20 per diem and ten percent of whatever Peter earned at each one of his gigs. And there was still the possibility that I would open for some shows. This wasn't as exciting as the initial offer back in Boston, which included performing in Peter's band, but I decided that it was still a pretty attractive option, especially in lieu of having no others. At least I knew what I would be doing with the next four months of my life.

From the end of July through the middle of November I drove over 10,000 miles, in addition to thousands of air miles while meeting dozens of club owners in the U.S. and

Canada along the way. I "advanced" every one of the gigs, which included booking our hotels (PC: "Whine for the lower rate."), hiring rental cars, booking the plane tickets, dealing with our booking agent and the contracts, settling the finances with the club owner at the end of the night, setting up the equipment, monitoring the stage during performances, and breaking down and packing up the gear afterwards. So you wanna be a rock 'n' roll star? Well, get in the van and find out what it's all about.

Wednesday, July 29: Greek Theatre, Los Angeles, CA
Thursday, July 30: Great American Music Hall, San Francisco, CA
Friday, July 31: Malarkey's, Sacramento, CA
Sunday, August 2: Sweetsprings Saloon, Los Osos, CA

The first leg of the tour found PC opening for Paul Weller at the Greek Theatre. Weller is a short dude and turns out to be much nicer then I've been led to believe by the press. His dad is backstage and is quite jovial, offering me a lager. The next day on July 30 we drive 380 miles north to San Francisco for a gig at the Great American Music Hall where Peter is triple-billed with John Wesley Harding and Chuck Prophet. July 31 we drive 90 miles to Sacramento, with the Porcupines as support act. Saturday, August 1, drive 215 miles to Squaw Valley to have a "day off" at a writer's convention that Peter's (then) wife Diane is attending. On August 2, drive 170 miles to Los Osos for a gig at the Sweetsprings Saloon. On August 3, drive 210 miles back to L.A. August 4–6 are days off in San Diego. Welcome to the road.

The *Six Pack of Love* Tour Phase II

Friday, August 7: Bogart's, Long Beach, CA
Monday, August 10: Denver Zoo, Denver, CO
Wednesday, August 12: First Avenue, Minneapolis, MN
Thursday, August 13: First Avenue, Minneapolis, MN
Friday, August 14: Shank Hall, Milwaukee, WI
Saturday, August 15: Majestic Theatre, Detroit, MI
Sunday, August 16: Peabody's Down Under, Cleveland, OH
Monday, August 17: Horseshoe Tavern, Toronto, Ontario
Wednesday, August 19: The Bottom Line, New York, NY
Thursday, August 20: T.T. Bears, Cambridge, MA
Friday, August 21: Maxwell's, Hoboken, NJ
Saturday, August 22: 23 East Cabaret, Ardmore, PA

After three days off, drive 110 miles to Long Beach for a great gig at Bogart's, with the Swamp Doctors and the Bed-Shredders as support. Hang out over the weekend and fly on Monday AM from LAX to Denver to spend a week on the road opening shows for Los Lobos, who are out promoting their brand new, and career highlight LP, *Kiko*. PC goes way back with these guys, with David Hidalgo playing on his second solo album, and everybody in the Los Lobos camp is particularly welcoming. Wally Hanley, their road manager, and Victor Bisetti, the drum tech who doubles as additional percussionist on stage, are particularly cool to work with. Our first gig of the week is at the Denver Zoo. We stay at the nearby Motel 6, behind the Waffle House. On Tuesday we fly to Minneapolis for two nights at First Avenue, the club where *Purple Rain* was photographed. We stay at the Best Western Northwest Inn. Wednesday night is a great show. After Peter and Los Lobos perform their respective sets, they bring Peter back on stage for the encores and Victor grabs me to play percussion with him behind the congas. I am one smiling fool as I shake a tambourine on the Rascals' "Come on Up" and Larry Williams' "Dizzy Miss Lizzie." Both songs feature Peter singing with Los Lobos and the feeling is pure adrenalin—it's exhilarating to be on stage with all of that energy, when a couple thousand people are screaming in your direction. Who needs drugs? Thursday's show goes even better, after Los Lobos spend the day at Paisley Park studios enthusiastically recording a version of CCR's "Run Through the Jungle" for the 1993 box office flop *Gunmen*. We all go up for the encores once again, this time performing "Come on Up" and the Troggs' "Wild Thing." *You make everything groovy...*F-U-N! (Both nights are captured off the soundboard on cassette, see the **Appendix** on page 471 for the set lists.)

On Friday, August 14, we drive 340 miles to Milwaukee to play at Shank Hall. Above the front entrance is a miniature Stonehenge monument, a tribute to Spinal Tap, who named their fictional Milwaukee venue in *This Is Spinal Tap* "Shank Hall." It's an inside rock 'n' roll joke. Stay at the Astor Hotel. On Saturday, August 15, we drive 380 miles to Detroit for the final show on this leg with Los Lobos. Stay at the Radisson, thanks to Wally. These five shows are incredible, and henceforth, I have nothing but respect for Los Lobos. (The Milwaukee and Detroit shows are captured off the soundboard on cassette, see the **Appendix** on pages 471-472 for the set lists.)

On Sunday, August 16, drive 170 miles to Cleveland's Peabody's Down Under, where the support act is the Clarks.

Stay at the Holiday Inn, and noticing some of the rather unevolved specimens around the dining room, PC observes during dinner "Someone's been pissing in the gene pool." The gig is sparsely attended. Goodbye Cleveland. The next day, August 17, we drive 290 miles to Toronto, having to endure a border-crossing inspection of our vehicle that eats up at least an hour. Stay at the Ibis Hotel and have a great gig at the Horseshoe Tavern. Musician and author Paul Myers of the Gravelberrys (who also happens to be Mike Myers' brother) is the support act, and he is a very nice chap, truly enjoyable to talk to. But, man, talk about a fellow "pop geek." He is wearing a Partridge Family T-shirt and plays "Come On Get Happy" during his opening set. Tuesday, August 18 drive 475 miles to New York City and promptly install the car into an exorbitantly-priced garage (no one parks their car on the street) after checking into the Manhattan Journey's End. On Wednesday, August 19, PC plays two shows at the Bottom Line, with Pal Cezaar as support. PC's friend Aldo Perez gets me stoned outside the club and then Peter invites me up on stage in the middle of his second show to play a song while Peter Buck and Mike Mills from R.E.M. are in the audience. I play "Think It Over" from my EP and Aldo gets up and plays a song as well. It was super nerve-wracking to play the Bottom Line stage in front of such notorious company, but it all seemed to go down well. Afterwards I say, "Isn't it cool that Peter and Mike came out to see you perform?" PC: "Why do you think they're out in the clubs right now? Where do you think they're getting ideas for their next album?" (Both sets are captured off the soundboard on cassette, see the **Appendix** on page 472 for the set list.)

Thursday, August 20 drive 215 miles to T.T. Bears in Cambridge, MA. Support acts are Super Atomic Power and Skeggy. Stay at the Cambridge Best Western. Friday, August 21, drive 215 miles to Maxwell's in Hoboken, NJ. Support act is the Shams. This is the first of several times I cross paths with singer/songwriter Amy Rigby, and I think she's great. But I much prefer her solo work. On Saturday, August 22, drive 105 miles to 23 East Cabaret, in Ardmore, PA. Support act is Peter's Cathedral. On Sunday, August 23, we fly back to LAX from Philadelphia. Make my way back to San Diego for two and a half weeks off before gearing up for Phase III.

☯

The *Six Pack of Love* Tour Phase III

Thursday, September 10: Cactus Café, Austin, TX
Friday, September 11: Cactus Café, Austin, TX
Sunday, September 13: Poor David's Pub, Dallas, TX
Monday, September 14: Juanita's Cantina Ballroom, Little Rock, AR
Wednesday, September 16: Bluebird Cafe, Nashville, TN
Thursday, September 17: Variety Theatre, Atlanta, GA
Saturday, September 19: 40 Watt Club, Athens, GA
Thursday, September 24: Pacific Amphitheatre, Costa Mesa, CA
Saturday, September 26: McCabe's Guitar Shop, Santa Monica, CA

During the lull, I turned 28-years-old on August 26. I also produced the fourth edition of the *travellin' light* newsletter to let Peter's fans know about his upcoming gigs.

My cryptic notes are titled **ROBBING BANKS: MAIL FROM JAIL**. There is much to read between the lines:

A few words while I'm (not) thinking about it. The Midwest was a lot of fun until we reached Ohio, then it became something completely different. We lost something nearly every day and recovered it all except the blood, the money, and the broken tooth. We spent seven days on the road with Los Lobos and had such a great time that we still owe Wally for the hotel room in Detroit. The encores were a blast: after "Marie, Marie" everybody joined together for rousing renditions of "Come on Up," "Wild Thing," and "Dizzy Miss Lizzie."

On Wednesday night, September 9, I made my way up to West L.A. via Amtrak and Super Shuttle. Thursday, September 10, is a comedy of continual errors, except that none of it is particularly funny. Fly from LAX to Austin with Peter, Diane, and their newborn daughter, Leah. Discover en route to LAX that PC has forgotten his and my plane tickets. That costs $100 in duplication fees. Then our plane is diverted to San Antonio because of flooding at the Dallas airport. Peter decides to get off the plane in San Antonio, rent a car and drive the 80 miles to Austin, where we check-in to the Driskill Hotel on Brazos. The only problem is that our luggage, and Peter's guitars and gear, are still on the airplane. But we never would have made it to the gig if we hadn't gotten off the plane in San Antonio. For the show at the Cactus Café this evening, Peter is in the unenviable position of having to borrow some gear for his performance. PC is to play two shows tonight and two shows on Friday with Paul Rodriguez as support for all four shows. (Friday night's set is captured off the soundboard on cassette, see the **Appendix** on page 472 for the set list.)

After much checking with the airline, our gear finally comes in around midnight, which is good because there is a lot of promotion to do on Friday: an 1:00 PM appearance at KSTB-FM at the University of Texas, a 3:30 PM appearance at KGSR-FM, and an afternoon appearance at Austin Cable Access where Peter is taping a performance for the *Knee-Jerk Show* and I meet fellow archivist Kent Benjamin for the first time. When their three-camera crew in the studio is a cameraman short, they have me fill in on one of the cameras. Fourteen years later in April of 2006, I would perform the same duty in that exact studio for the *Twine Time* program when they film pat mAcdonald.

In spite of all the hassles, the shows in Austin go really well but it is definitely a different vibe and a bit more of a strain having two extra people traveling with us, particularly with a baby. Saturday is a day off in Austin, and the next day Diane and Leah go back to L.A. On Sunday, September 13, we drive 195 miles north to Poor David's Pub in Dallas and stay at the Hilltop Inn. PC gets food poisoning from the Two Pesos taco stand across the street from the club. By the time we get to Little Rock he is paying for it. Ugh. I feel bad for him.

Monday, September 14, we drive 320 miles to Little Rock, AR for a gig at Juanita's Cantina Ballroom. At 7:00 PM PC plays two songs and does an interview at KABF-FM with Robert Bowen. After the gig we crash at the Best Western. On Tuesday, September 15 drive 350 miles to Nashville, Tennessee, and check in to Shoney's Inn. PC stays with songwriter Fred Kohler. Get a massage to alleviate some of the tension from doing so much driving. On Wednesday, September 16, PC performs at the Bluebird

Café. John Prine shows up and hangs out after the show. One of his more memorable comments is: "No one ever stopped having a good time to go and write a song about it." On Thursday, September 17, drive 250 miles to Atlanta for a gig at the Variety Theatre. 3:00 PM appearance on WRAS-FM/Georgia State University, where PC performs "Wonderful 99," "Never Coming Home," "Broke Down Engine," and "Punch and Socko." Instead of staying over in Atlanta, we make the 75 mile drive after the gig to Athens and check into the Campus Inn. (The shows in Nashville and Atlanta are captured off the soundboard on cassette, see the **Appendix** on page 472 for the set lists.)

Friday is a day off in Athens; eat at the world-famous Walter's Barbeque, notorious for the patronage of local legends R.E.M. and their B-side instrumental homage "Walter's Theme." Saturday, September 19, PC does some promotion at WUOG-FM/University of Georgia. The gig at the 40 Watt Club goes very well, and during sound check I see Michael Stipe over at the bar fiddling with a camera. Settle up finances with Berry Buck (Peter Buck's first wife) at the end of the night. She comps me a 40 Watt Club T-shirt and the entire experience is pretty cool. (The show is captured off the soundboard on cassette, see the **Appendix** on page 472 for the set list.) The next morning (Sunday) is the world premiere of the R.E.M. video for "Drive," the lead single from their soon-to-be-released, mega-platinum smash *Automatic for the People*. Athens certainly is the hip place to be at the moment, but we've got to be moving on.

Particularly as Peter has a plane to catch from Athens to Charlotte, and Charlotte to Charleston, WV so he can perform on the National Public Radio *Mountain Stage* program. He's only in Charleston seven hours before flying to Pittsburgh and back to LAX. Meanwhile, I am tasked with driving the rental car from Athens, Georgia back to Austin, Texas, where this whole crazy leg began. The upside is that I get to visit my Aunt Nancy in Baton Rouge on the way back for a night, but it is a long solo journey, 980 miles. On the drive west from Baton Rouge, one hour outside of Austin, the worst downpour I have ever witnessed was unleashed from the heavens. Talk about your Texas floods! Jeezus. I had to slow down to twenty miles per hour on the freeway, but I didn't dare stop. I eventually out ran the storm but, damn, it was hairy there for a while.

The next day I returned the rental car and boarded the plane back to LAX. As other people start filtering on, I recognized Johnny Van Zant walking down the aisle, swinging on the seats like a jungle gym. Then guitarist Ed King strolls on. And then keyboardist Billy Powell. Holy shit! Lynyrd Skynyrd is getting on this flight! It makes me excited, and at the same time fills me with a slight sense of unease, as they are the most famous band in the history of rock 'n' roll to be in an airplane crash and have most of their members live to tell the tale. It's criminal that lead vocalist and mastermind of the group, Ronnie Van Zant, wasn't one of the survivors. I go over to Billy Powell and introduce myself and ask him if he minds me sitting down and talking to him for a few minutes. He graciously waves me into the seat next to him. Mr. Powell is a sweetheart and answers my queries with candor. I ask him "What sort of influences did you have while learning how to play the piano?" Sounding like a cross between Slim Pickens and Foghorn Leghorn, he responds with "I listened to the classics, son." I'm expecting

Professor Longhair or Dr. John, or some other boogie-woogie, stride piano master, but he continues by ticking off the groups one-by-one on his left hand: "Yes, Genesis, King Crimson..." Really? I was expecting other influences. I ask him if flying in a plane bothers him much after the events of October 20, 1977, near McComb, Mississippi, and he says "Heck, no. Why statistically speaking, flying is still the safest way to travel. I just kick back and enjoy the flight." As we are rolling down the runway, he does a countdown from ten to one and is able to guess precisely when our wheels will leave the ground. Before I say goodbye and leave him in peace, he graciously offers to put me plus one on the guest list for their show the next night at the Pacific Amphitheatre, in Costa Mesa, California. Guests of Billy Powell, hmm…It turned out to be a fun show, even if it is hard to call any band without Ronnie Van Zant at the helm "Lynyrd Skynyrd." They DO turn out to be one hell of a tribute band, particularly as they have Blackfoot's (and one-time Skynyrd drummer) Rickey Medlocke on guitar and vocals, Gary Rossington and Ed King on guitar, Billy Powell on keyboards, and Ronnie's youngest brother on vocals. Two nights later on the 26th, PC does two fantastic performances at McCabe's Guitar Shop in Santa Monica, CA. (Both sets are captured off the soundboard on cassette, see the **Appendix** on page 473 for the set lists.) Have five days rest in San Diego and then it's off to the Midwest.

☯

The *Six Pack of Love Tour* Phase IV

Friday, October 2: Lounge Ax, Chicago, IL
Monday, October 5: State Theatre, Kalamazoo, MI
Tuesday, October 6: The Milestone, Rochester, NY
Wednesday, October 7: Marquis at the Tralf, Buffalo, NY
Thursday, October 8: Graffiti, Pittsburgh, PA
Friday, October 9: Stache's, Columbus, OH
Saturday, October 10: Canal Street Tavern, Dayton, OH
Friday, October 16: Madison Square Garden, New York, NY

Make my way up to L.A. on Thursday, October 1. On Friday, October 2, leave at 9:00 AM from LAX to Chicago's O'Hare airport. Upon arrival, pick up rental car and check in at the Comfort Inn on Diversey Parkway. Make it to Lounge Ax for soundcheck at 6:00 PM. The show at 11:15 PM is fantastic.

There are two off days in a row when a potential gig in Detroit does not happen, so PC flies to Nashville to hang out and write with John Prine. When he returns 48 hours later for a gig in Kalamazoo he has a new song called "Space Monkey" that resulted from the collaboration, written on October 4. PC says he and Prine just kept playing Hank Williams' track "The Log Train" over and over again until they came up with "Space Monkey." Peter immediately began playing it in his set, and he quipped that when he ran into a familiar face in line at a hotel the following week his acquaintance said that he had been trying to get Prine to return his phone calls so they could collaborate. But after hearing "Space Monkey," the acquaintance said with a tinge of sarcasm, "Well, maybe I shouldn't be so concerned that John's not calling me back."

My mother's entire side of the family is from the great state of Michigan, and while PC was away in Nashville, I had two days where I was able to visit my grandparents, L.D. and Julie, in Grand Rapids. It was a lovely visit and was fated to be the last time I would see either of them in this lifetime. I was also able to visit my mom's older sister Myrna (the last time I would see my aunt alive as well), and my step-cousin Rhonda, whom I had a wild crush on at age fourteen. In 1978, we wrote letters to each other every day for an entire year. It's useful to check in with your memories, and find out how much your fantasies are in stark contrast to how other people's lives have actually turned out.

After driving 150 miles to Kalamazoo from Chicago, pick up PC at the K-Zoo airport on Monday, October 5 for a gig that evening at the State Theatre with Brian Vanderack as support act. We stay over at the Radisson on West Michigan Avenue, two blocks away from the venue. Do an in-store appearance at Boogie Records at 5:30 PM. Sound check is immediately after the in-store, with the show at 8:00 PM.

On Tuesday, October 6 drive 520 miles to Rochester, New York for a gig at the Milestone. The venue recently changed their name from the risible moniker of Jazzberry's. After checking in to the Holiday Inn at Genesee Plaza, we head straight over to WITR-FM for an on-air interview with Hal Horowitz. The show goes well. On Wednesday, October 7 drive 75 miles to Buffalo and stay at the house that PC grew up in. Meet his mother Ethel and think she is a sweetheart. Don't really talk much to his father, Wilbur.

End up sleeping in the room that PC had when he was younger—there is a framed picture of the Plimsouls that is hanging on the wall above the bed. Pretty endearing. PC has an interview on WBNY-FM with Rich Wall at 7 PM before going over to the Marquis at the Tralf. This is quite the homecoming, as PC grew up in nearby Hamburg, thirteen miles from Buffalo. Many people from Peter's past come out for the gig and there are a lot of stories from the early days. One friend talks about a particular adventure that involved walking through the snow on LSD as teenagers, arriving late at night at another friend's house and listening to the *Are You Experienced?* LP by the Jimi Hendrix Experience. PC says they were so high that they weren't able to tell if the record had finished playing or not.

On the afternoon we arrived in Hamburg I decided to go out for a jog around town, and when I ran through the town square I could actually see most of the local landmarks that Peter sings about in his song "Small Town Spree" (from *Peter Case*). Over there was Gate's Liquor Store and Miller's Drug and across the square was the big church, St. Peter's and Paul's. As I kept jogging, the lyrics played out in my head, and there was a movie forming before me. Ultimately, our time in Hamburg offered up a little bit of insight into PC, and it is really cool to see where his roots are. But after spending 24 hours there I could also sense why he had to get away and go 3,000 miles west to the bohemian grove of San Francisco. *As Far As You Can Get Without a Passport* indeed.

On Thursday, October 8, we drive 205 miles to Graffiti in Pittsburgh, Pennsylvania, and stay over at the Howard Johnson's on the Boulevard of the Allies. The next day is John (and Sean) Lennon's birthday and we drive 185 miles to Columbus, Ohio. This day sticks out in my mind as being particularly beautiful. The leaves are turning "all chimney red and Halloween orange," and as we dip and slide through the hills of Ohio, I experience Miles Davis' 1959 classic *Kind of Blue* for the very first time. The rhythmic cadence of "All Blues" and the irrepressible shuffle of the beat is mesmerizing, and the impression this work of art makes on this day is monumentally life-changing. But, it wasn't nearly as monumental as what I would learn the following day.

The gig in Columbus is at a place called Stache's and we stay at the Park University Hotel. The next day, Saturday, October 10, we drive 72 miles to the Canal Street Tavern in Dayton, Ohio. The owner, Mick Montgomery, is a nice guy who takes the two of us out for dinner before the show and puts us up at the Spring Brook condominiums. The shows go very well but before the gig happens I get a phone call at the club, which is highly irregular. It turns out to be Carolyn, the woman back in San Diego that I have been seeing off and on for a couple of years. Even though we decided that we weren't going to have a "serious, monogamous relationship," that didn't stop us from still seeing one another and engaging in sex. Just as the roller coaster ride that was 1992 was beginning to crest, she just had to call me during sound check at the Canal Street Tavern to tell me she was pregnant. And that she was certain she was going to have the baby. It was at that precise moment that my head went into a prolonged state of vertigo for several months. My foot loose and fancy days appeared to be coming to an end. Or were they? In either case, now what? For years afterwards, PC would reference this day with "hey, you remember that night in Dayton when you received that phone call?" "Yeah, how could I ever forget?"

Peter and I spend the evening back at the condo staying up late talking, and the conversation is comforting. Peter is like a big brother offering some sage advice and being willing to listen as I get a few things off my chest. As confused as I was, I really appreciated Peter's feedback. (Tonight's show is captured off the soundboard on cassette, see the **Appendix** on page 473 for the set list.)

Funny how things turn on a dime. On Sunday morning, the 11th, we get up early and drive 300 miles to Chicago to return our rental car from its place of origin and I accompany Peter to his terminal at O'Hare so he can fly back to LAX. The next day he has an in-store appearance at Rhino Records and then two days later he, Diane, and Leah take off for ten days in Mexico.

In the meantime…when we were in NYC back in August for the Bottom Line gig, I ran into my buddy Steven Keene, a very talented songwriter and musician in his own right. After sharing a drink and getting caught up with each other he excitedly remembers something and spits out "Oh! Where are you on October 16?" "I don't know, I think I have a break from the tour with Peter then, why?" "You HAVE to come back to New York. There is going to be a show at Madison Square Garden for Dylan's 30th anniversary of recording for Columbia Records. EVERYBODY who is anybody is going to be performing. You have to come!" "Do you think you can get me a ticket?" "Yes." "Would it be okay if I crashed on your couch?" "Yes." "Well, I'll be there then. Thanks, man!"

I stay over in Chicago at a cheap hotel and have an interesting visit with Robin Brack's Aunt Irene. On Monday, October 12, I make my way to the Greyhound bus terminal and take the bus 792 miles from Chicago to the Port Authority Bus Terminal, arriving seventeen hours later on Tuesday, October 13. Spend a couple of days in NYC with Steven, and on Friday night we go down to Madison Square Garden for the big concert. Tickets are a then-unheard of sum of $80, but the experience turns out to be priceless. The biggest thrill of the evening for me was seeing George Harrison perform "If Not For You" and "Absolutely Sweet Marie." A close second was seeing Stevie Wonder sing "Blowin' in the Wind." Tied for third was seeing Johnny & June Carter Cash and Lou Reed perform. It was a tremendous night. Several of us go back to Steven's apartment after the show and stay up past 4 AM, partying and listening to Dylan records, reliving the concert. It was truly one of those magical nights that only happen once. And boy, were we there, baby! (See the **Appendix** on page 474 for the set list.)

On Saturday, October 17, I take the train out to Ronkonkoma on Long Island and visit my friend, singer/songwriter Andrew James Fortier. I met Andy the year before when he was out in California making a record with Peter's then manager, and co-producer, Steven Soles. Andy lives on a huge boat, a "1938, 42-foot Humphrey Bogart looking cabin cruiser" that is parked in the front yard of his parents' property. He calls it 1517 Dream Street. I meet his girlfriend, we eat dinner together, and Andy plays me some of his new songs since recording his album *Early Midlife Crisis*. He has an obvious love for fellow Long Islander Billy Joel, so much so, that he hired Joel's bassist Doug Stegmeyer to play on his album. Stegmeyer passed away three years later, but while he was alive he was a thoroughly awe-inspiring musician.

On Monday, October 19, I travel 225 miles south to spend four days in Washington, D.C., visiting my friend Jeff Lee, and I fly back to San Diego on October 22. I have three days to get my act together and rehearse the Shambles (actually four/fifths of "Manual Scan" that went to Britain the year before), on a song that I wrote in Clinton Heylin's attic back in June called "It Is & It Isn't." We go in to record between 7:00 and 11:00 PM on October 26 and this is the very first time I would produce my own recording session with a full band. I book Blitz Studios for the occasion, and Richard Livoni, the owner and engineer, does a great job at capturing the band, even if he's a bit aggressive in telling everyone what to do and how to perform. But the important thing is that the track turns out great and winds up on the *Staring at the Sun 2* compilation CD before the end of the year.

☯

The *Six Pack of Love* Tour Phase V

Yeah, it's been a really weird season, and you've been a big part of the weirdness. – **Peter Case**

Wednesday, October 28: the Town Pump, Vancouver, Canada
Thursday, October 29: Harpo's, Victoria, Canada
Friday, October 30: Backstage, Seattle, WA
Saturday, October 31: Satyricon, Portland, OR
Monday, November 2: Rock Candy, Seattle, WA
Wednesday, November 4: Paradise Lounge, San Francisco, CA
Thursday, November 5: the Palms Playhouse, Davis, CA
Friday, November 6: the Starry Plough, Berkeley, CA

Wednesday, November 11: Belly-Up Tavern, Solana Beach, CA
Thursday, November 12: the Palomino, North Hollywood, CA
Saturday, November 14: House at the Top of the Hill, Solvang, CA
Sunday, November 15: Big Music, San Luis Obispo, CA

The day after recording "It Is & It Isn't," I take the train up to L.A. and meet up with PC for the final leg of the *Six Pack of Love* tour. On Wednesday, October 28 we fly from LAX to Seattle, Washington and rent a car at the airport. Then we drive 140 miles across the border to Vancouver where PC has a gig that night at the Town Pump. We stay downtown at the Chateau. The next day on Thursday, October 29, we travel 69 miles and take the ferry over to Victoria for a gig at Harpo's. On Friday, October 30 take the ferry back and drive 110 miles south to Seattle for a gig at Backstage. Stay at a lovely bed and breakfast on First Avenue called the Pensione Nichols. Eat lunch at one of the funkiest places I have ever been that serves authentic "soul food" with a killer jukebox of 45s that includes the likes of Little Walter, Muddy Waters, and Sly and the Family Stone. Pure heaven. On Saturday, October 31, we spend Halloween in Portland, Oregon, driving 175 miles south to the Satyricon club, which has spray paint all over the walls—looking, and smelling, a bit like a toilet.

On Sunday, November 1, we drive the 175 miles back north to Seattle so that Peter can fly back to LAX. Drop off the rental car and I stay over for a few days with my friend Rebecca Fitzpatrick at her house on 73rd Street NE. It rains the entire time I'm there. On Monday, November 2, we catch the Breeders at the venue Rock Candy. During the evening, I run into Ken Stringfellow of the Posies, as he is following a line of females into the women's bathroom. When he comes out several minutes later, he sidles up and asks "What are you doing here?" Ken and I spend fifteen minutes getting caught up, before Kim Deal and company come out and rip our heads off sonically.

On Tuesday, November 3, I fly back to LAX from Seattle and spend the night at Darian's. On Wednesday, November 4, PC and I drive 380 miles up to San Francisco for a gig at the Paradise Lounge. In the middle of the set, PC has me come up and play a couple of songs. This feels a lot more natural than sweating it out in front of the guys from R.E.M. Stay over at the Phoenix Hotel on Eddy Street. Thursday, November 5, we drive 75 miles to Davis for a gig at the Palms Playhouse, where I get to see my dear friend Karen Eng. At the time the Palms was in a barn-like setting, with a very cool, rustic vibe to it (there's an old farm tractor as part of its décor). Very funky. We stay over at a Motel 6. On Friday, November 6, we drive south 65 miles to the Starry Plough in Berkeley, CA, and stay at the Campus Motel. On Saturday, November 7, we drive the 380 miles back south to Los Angeles.

Have a couple of days off before gearing up to perform as PC's official opening act at the Belly-Up Tavern, in Solana Beach, CA on Wednesday, November 11. I actually make $100 on the gig as a performer. The same occurs the next night when I drive 125 miles north on Thursday, November 12, to the Palomino in North Hollywood, where I get another opening slot, this time with David Rodriguez also supporting the bill. Hang out with Nick and Darian on Friday and drive 125 miles north from L.A. to Solvang on Saturday, November 14, for a house concert at the House at the Top of the Hill. David Rodriguez is the support act. Actress Cheryl Ladd is in attendance with her husband and, boy, does she look stunning at 42. On Sunday, November 15, we drive 67 miles north to Big Music, a record store in San Luis Obispo, for the final performance of the *Six Pack of Love* tour. On Monday, November 16 we drive south 200 miles back to Los Angeles and I make my way south via Amtrak to San Diego.

As I told journalist John D'Agostino for the *San Diego Reader* in December: "This has been the best year of my life, but I'm glad to be off the road for the first time in nine months." After 4,000 miles on the Greyhound, three months traveling through Europe, road managing 45 gigs and logging 10,675 miles driving on the road with PC, not counting all the additional air miles back and forth across North America, I was definitely in need of a break. I didn't know what the future held, or if I even had a future. It felt like the weight of the world was now hanging over me, like the Sword of Damocles, with fatherhood, poverty, and probable homelessness looming for the New Year. A million feelings and issues came flooding through. But 1993 turned out to be nothing like 1992, and as that Saturn Return came around to knock me square between the eyes, there was an entirely different set of lessons to be learned. And, oh boy—did I learn them?!

Hold on tight, babe 'cause this ride doesn't last for long
Guess this town ain't big enough for the both of us
Sending you good wishes and luck and love from wherever I am
Can you meet me next week, next year for coffee in S.F.?

www.jonkanis.com, July 4, 2014

THIRTEEN

Jimi Hendrix
Blowing His Public Saxophone
in *Jimi Plays Berkeley*

No one knew that Jimi Hendrix only had 25 more performances left in him when he took the stage with drummer Mitch Mitchell and bassist Billy Cox for two performances at the Berkeley Community Theatre on May 30, 1970. Since his death on September 18, 1970, the continuing demand for fresh Hendrix product has ensured that as long as there is a buck to be made from the archival material left behind in the vault, *someone* will be happy to exploit it (Hendrix's back catalog still shifts a dependable 500,000 units annually). Forty-two years on, it continues to be business as usual. Having moved distribution from Universal to Sony in 2009, the Experience Hendrix team is updating the back catalog, which means new reissues of the *Jimi Plays Berkeley* film on DVD, with the complete audio of the second set available for the first time in a 5.1 remix by Eddie Kramer. The second set is also available as a stand-alone compact disc.

As a sonic experience *Live At Berkeley* bristles with energy, as listeners are treated to works-in-progress versions of "Straight Ahead" and "New Rising Sun" before ripping into the one-two punch of "Lover Man" and "Stone Free." "Hey Joe" and "I Don't Live Today" are both focused and taut before the trio launches into an amazing version of "Machine Gun" that's even more electrifying than the version to be found on the *Band of Gypsies* LP. "Foxey Lady" lightens the mood and sets up the "Star-Spangled Banner" (Hendrix: "The American anthem the way it really is in the air that you breathe every day...oh, our flag was still there—big deal!") before "Purple Haze" and a ten-minute version of "Voodoo Child (Slight Return)" that is as great as any other live Hendrix performance out there. He pulls out all the stops, demonstrating his inventive use of feedback and signal distortion, falling to his knees, playing between his legs and soloing with his teeth, masterfully twisting and braiding the tonal clusters and scales to be found in every form of the blues. A shaman with an electric guitar, this performance is simply riveting. With no overdubs or edits, mind you, just three guys in a room doing it all right before your eyes and ears. It's a pity that technical problems prevent us from hearing the complete first set as well.

You can, however, see some of the performances from that first set in the film of *Jimi Plays Berkeley*, which is an essential document if we are to appreciate the full scope of Hendrix's career. As a disheveled cinematic object there is much to criticize, but the historical significance cannot be over-emphasized. Three weeks before the Berkeley concerts, the shootings at Kent State University occurred, mirroring the tensions that had been escalating in Berkeley since the police killed a People's Park protester the year before. With countercultural political vibes revving to an all-time high, Hendrix manager Michael Jeffrey thought it was a good idea that his client be captured on film among the Berkeley radicals, to capitalize on the high profile that Hendrix was enjoying, coming off of his performances in *Monterey Pop* and *Woodstock.* At the time of the Berkeley concerts Hendrix was also in the middle of creating his fourth studio offering, ostensibly titled *First Rays of the New Rising Sun,* a record that he would not live to complete. The footage shot by cameraman Peter Pilafin's team sat dormant until Hendrix's death virtually guaranteed a return on the investment and Jeffrey instructed Pilafin to create a composite out of the Berkeley shows.

What Pilafin and editor Baird Bryant came up with is a snapshot of the cultural tidal wave sweeping across America in the spring/summer of 1970, interspersed with some of the last footage ever shot of Hendrix. There are times when Hendrix looks a bit washed out—i.e. tired and/or stoned—but his playing is on fire this evening, particularly during "Hear My Train a Comin'" (from the first set) and the afore-mentioned "Machine Gun" and "Voodoo Child," which is particularly nice because those are three of the songs that have benefited the most from this newly expanded version. If you already own the CD of *Live At Berkeley* you needn't bother replacing it. The DVD, however, is another story. An artistic afterthought, the evolution of the film's haphazard manifestation is explained quite thoroughly in John McDermott's excellent liner notes. Profiteering might have been the motivating factor from the get-go for the *Jimi Plays Berkeley* project, but the silver lining is that some of Hendrix's most inspired playing exists for future generations to marvel at and enjoy.

Ugly Things, #34, Fall/Winter, 2012

FOURTEEN

Listen, Whitey!
The Sounds of Black Power
1967–1974

According to comedian Eddie Murphy, "Black people lost their minds in the '70s," presumably (in part) for sporting natural "Afro" hairstyles and embracing the polyester bell-bottom fashions of the day. Another inference, perhaps, is the residual insanity left over from 400 years of slavery and racial inequality. To understand the birth of the Black Power movement (circa 1967–1974), I highly suggest checking out *Listen, Whitey!*, the brand new compact disc by producer/writer Pat Thomas which serves as an audio companion to the coffee table book of the same name.

There are already several excellent compilations that musically illuminate the struggle for Black Emancipation (*Say It Loud! A Celebration of Black Music in America*, *Rhapsodies in Black* and *Black Power*) but *Listen, Whitey!* could be the slice of the revolutionary pie that cuts the deepest when addressing this unique period of American history. Thomas' liner notes are detailed and well-written, and the cover photo says much about the content: a buff and shirtless Huey Newton holding a copy of Bob Dylan's *Highway 61 Revisited* LP. There are scores of progressive ideas throughout the proceedings as this disc rails, screams, prays, admonishes, and soothes the savage soul with observations that could only be made by the disenfranchised. Check out the passionate oratory of Stokely Carmichael and Dick Gregory as they speak out on what Black Power really means. There's also the in-your-face street poetry of Gil Scott-Heron (poignantly on "Winter in America"), the Watts Prophets (amusingly on "Dem Niggers Ain't Playing"), or the Last Poets (devastatingly on "Die Nigga!!"). Refreshingly, as a curator, Thomas crosses the color line by including tracks from Roy Harper ("I Hate the White Man"), John Lennon and Yoko Ono ("Angela") and the aforementioned Dylan (with the acoustic version of "George Jackson"). Each one of these activist/artists understood what it truly means to be an American by exercising the freedom and the right to speak out against the injustices perpetrated by the State.

To that end, *Listen, Whitey!* is a Molotov cocktail, exploding with sixteen superb examples of why it is crucial to exercise your civil rights AT ALL TIMES. Sure, some of these folks were jailed (and many more were murdered) for speaking out against institutionalized oppression. There is certainly a lot of (justifiable) finger-pointing going on in this set, but there is also a sense of empowerment, and a fierce determination not to play victim to anyone, regardless of the power that they might wield. It's no tall surprise that the Nixon administration sought to suppress many of these voices, and it is certainly sobering to consider how much of this collection is still relevant in 2012, suggesting that until the struggle is truly over, being a revolutionary never goes out of style. "Power to the people, right on!"

Ugly Things, #33, Spring/Summer, 2012

FIFTEEN

Stew *Is* the Negro Problem

They'll never play in my club. Can you imagine the kind of trouble a band with that kind of name would attract?
— Anonymous San Diego Club Manager

There is no Negro problem. — Lyndon B. Johnson (circa 1965)

If you keep doing the same weird thing over and over again, people will eventually get it.
— Mark Stewart, the Negro Problem

From the Echo Park/Silver Lake area of East Hollywood comes the Negro Problem, a group as musically enigmatic as their name, returning to San Diego this Saturday for a performance at Java Joe's in Ocean Beach. Fronted by African-American singer/guitarist Mark Stewart, TNP refer to their music as sounding like "the Fifth Dimension in grad school." The rhythm section includes drummer/vocalist Charles Pagano and bassist/vocalist Heidi Rodewald, who "funnel the swirling vibe" around Stewart's genre-defiant songs. His subterranean sarcasm rarely abates, with Stewart suggesting that his songs are "miniature psychedelic political documentaries shot with a camera that only records daydreams." If that seems a tad too self-consciously clever, their recent (1997) debut CD *Post Minstrel Syndrome* nevertheless offers up ample evidence that this is a band worth paying attention to.

The Negro Problem begins and ends with its "deconstrunctionist" frontman and namesake Mark Stewart (he prefers to be addressed by the self-selected nomenclature of "Stew," lest he be confused with the British Mark Stewart of Tricky and Portishead fame). Stewart has taken a rather strange and loopy musical journey over the last decade, with a long history of being unconventional.

"I wrote what you would call 'normal' pop tunes when I was younger," says Stew. "But when I moved to New York in 1982 I stopped doing that and moved into weirder, noisier stuff." After two uneventful years in New York, Stew gypsied across Europe for several months and eventually settled in Berlin.

"When I arrived in Berlin I thought that I was going to play in the normal rock clubs like everybody else did. But the group that I was in got adopted by this squatted museum and when they heard our tape they said 'Oh, you guys are arty—you belong with us.' So we just fell into this complete art clique and suddenly these artists started hanging around us and we began to do art installations with our music and we got further away from the music and more into the art, with the band becoming an actual installation piece. We did nutty things. We did a show once where we were being videotaped in an adjacent room so you could only see us on television—sometimes we got pretty extreme. We did a show once on Hitler's birthday (April 20) and sent invitations to this neo-Nazi group daring them to come to our show, which was in a predominantly Turkish neighborhood. But we knew that they wouldn't come because they would've gotten their asses kicked."

As much fun as Stew was having stoking his bohemian soul in Germany, the political climate went through a radical shift when the Berlin Wall came down (November 9, 1989) and he decided that it was time to head back to his native Los Angeles. "Before the Wall fell, it was nothing [to be a Black in Berlin]. But after the Wall fell it was *way* too significant. [laughs] I mean, after the Wall fell you could get the shit beat out of you by skinheads on the subway. That would have never happened before the Wall fell. Berlin was a very cosmopolitan place; people were almost too jaded to be openly racist like that. But after the Wall fell it was completely different—it got ugly, and that is why I left, because I wasn't there to deal this archaic shit."

Upon returning to L.A., Stew quickly fell in with another group of improvisational musicians and formed the group Primal Synthesis. After performing at the LACE gallery in downtown L.A., he met drummer Charles Pagano, and it wasn't long before the two were working together. United by a mutual love of progressive rock, orchestral music and absurdity, Stew and Pagano created the foundation for what would later become the Negro Problem.

"When I got back to Los Angeles and got into Charles' clique it was with all of these people who were fairly un-pop," says Stew. "We were playing the type of music where you really didn't know what was going to happen next, kind of like John Cage with some hidden pop influence. It was a real gradual process. Seven minute tunes would be whittled down to four and we just kept kicking people out who weren't into it, so that by the time we called ourselves the Negro Problem we had decided 'Yes, we're doing songs.'"

The move into a pop context became solidified when Stew and Pagano wanted to put an accordion track on one of their songs and they enlisted the help of accordionist Jill Meschke. They dug the results so much that Meschke ended up becoming a full-time collaborator. It was a relationship that would last a full five years (Menschke left TNP in August of '97). Stew admits that "Jill was the one to point us out of our progressive rock orientation." Once the threesome decided to take a more listener-friendly, song-oriented approach, they invited bassist Gwynne Kahn to join the band on the strength of her garage/punk rock roots. Kahn's musical pedigree includes a stint in the seminal L.A. garage band, the Pandoras—not to mention her familial lineage. Her grandfather is lyricist Gus Kahn, who wrote a plethora of classic Tin Pan Alley songs: "Makin' Whoopee," "Yes, Sir That's My Baby," "It Had to Be You," and "I'll See You in My Dreams" to name but a few. It also didn't hurt that Kahn's irreverent attitude perfectly suited the temperment of the band. When asked about their "controversial moniker" she quipped that the band wouldn't change their name "until the United Negro College Fund changed theirs."

Armed with a provocative muse and a fistful of great songs, TNP took their perfect balancing act of race and gender out into the L.A. underground club scene. Their initial outings met with a fair amount of resistance to their name, with some club owners refusing to list the band in its print ads or on the marquee. "Can you imagine someone getting upset about a band name?" asks Stew. "It should be as innocuous as the Fifth Dimension." The name did, however, help them to get some press in Los Angeles. "It was a good way to get attention," Stew admits. "Because with our name, people are curious. They want to see if it's a bunch of skinheads or a Black guy. If they see me I think they get it."

A series of recording projects followed over the next three years, and the Negro Problem began to receive attention on the national level, with invitations to play at the South by Southwest music festival in Austin, Texas (which they accepted) and the CMJ show in New York City (which they turned down). The personnel of the band went through a period of musical chairs for a while when Menschke took a sabbatical to play with Elastica on their Lollapalooza tour (keyboardist Carolyn Edwards filled in for her) and bassist Marc Doten sat in for the frequently absent Kahn. By the time the full-length disc *Post Minstrel Syndrome* was released in the summer of 1997, both Menschke and Kahn had permanently split the band and TNP was reduced to a trio with Rodewald entering the fold. Stew says that the new TNP feels "pleasantly naked" and that the goal is to "shift the baroque nature of things away from the instruments and towards the vocals." When TNP played Java Joe's with the new lineup in September, the songs actually benefited from the addition of Rodewald and the stripped-down arrangements (they continue to utilize long-time sideman Probyn Gregory on trumpet, percussion, and the occasional keyboard). Stew: "Someone told me that back in the days of Tim Buckley and Bob Dylan, when a singer/songwriter would make a record with a full-on band, that it was considered something special when you would see this person live and their band would be pared down so that you could actually hear the songs. For me, the different stuff that you hear on the records, whether it's a keyboard or whatever—it doesn't make that much of a difference if I hear that stuff live or not."

Whether on stage or in the studio, the music never takes itself too seriously, as Stew often deflates the very subjects that inspire him to write in the first place (their sonic irreverence is underscored by Pagano's cinematic/John Cage-like arrangement ideas). Far from using pop-culture references as a crutch, Stew nonetheless draws a great deal of lyrical inspiration from that most obvious pitfall of life in L.A.: the mass-media. "The Los Angeles news has got to be the most satanic local news ever," he says. The hilarious "Birdcage" (as in birdcage-liner) rips on the irrelevance of the *Los Angeles Times*, while several of his songs use television personalities to get a particular point across. "It's not that I'm fascinated by these newspeople," says Stew. "This is where the information comes from, from this ridiculous, buffoonish forum. And that's what I'm fascinated by—that these people are supposedly telling you the truth." He's careful to add that "it would be missing the boat if it seemed like I had a fixation with media personalities." Still, in Stew's universe you can easily run into the likes of Mia Farrow, Sting, Sebastian Cabot, Oprah Winfrey, Montel Williams, or Peter Jennings. And if namedropping doesn't do the trick, then perhaps the snatch of a TV theme song will convey a particular idea (such as the loss of innocence) when they quote "The Fishing Hole" from the *Andy Griffith Show* in the TNP tune "Camelot." But does all that cleverness fly over the heads of an audience that primarily goes to a club to enjoy an ordinary night out? Stew believes that those types of subtleties are probably lost on most of his audience.

"I'm convinced that most of the people that come to the clubs who dig us don't particularly know or care that our music is kind of like Frank Zappa or Jimmy Webb or Burt Bacharach. And I know where I am right now—I'm in a rock club competing with, for the most part, frustrated single people. And the subtext of their being there really is to get laid. And to get drunk. And I'm competing with every woman and man in there and how they're dressed and the price of the beer so I know what I'm up against. The club for me really is about figuring out ways to make a connection with people."

But once a connection is established, what do you do with it? Stew blanches at the suggestion that he has a specific agenda or message to impart through his songs. "I think that maybe we have to define the term 'message.' Because there are definitely ideas in there, but that's different. 'Message' implies that I'm sending you a message and that you have to receive it in order to validate the idea. An idea can just sit there. But in order for it to work it has to communicate to you in some way even if you don't know anything about it."

So, no messages, just ideas. It's a paradox as simple as the "idea" behind Stew's brilliant song "Heidigger in Harlem."

"I was talking to and reading about these really hard core black nationalists who were really into "Black essence," meaning that there is a distinct essence about being black. And I was reading Heidigger and he was basically saying the very same thing about Germans. The only problem with that was when the Nazis came into power Heidigger took a job at the head of a university under the Nazis and held hands with them and said that Hitler was some kind of incarnation of the German will. He philosophized and

justified Hitler's existence through this very highly intellec-
tualized mode of thinking. He was a jerk, basically.

"But I saw similarities in the way that he justified
that [Nazi] ideology. Because some of his ideas are really
beautiful and he was really a deep thinker—so in my mind
I had this contrast between Heidigger and these so-called
oppressed Blacks who turned to nationalism as a way of
somehow combating the racism that they had been dealt.
It was a fun idea to me that these Black guys had a similar
ideology and point of view as this German philosopher who
tried to be a Nazi."

Message or not, there is the vibe that runs through most
of TNP's songs that **something** is being said. "And that's just
it," says Stew. "The idea is to throw out all these images.

"After songwriting and the lead vocals, comes background
vocals in order of importance," says Stew. "It's what I hope
will separate us from all these non-singing slacker bands
with their soccer crowd background vocals. I want to assault
people with the raucous beauty of lowbrow collective
singing and make them question themselves for feeling
slightly uncomfortable about how much they are enjoying
the goofy sing-song melodies. I want to come to them as
this strange little urban(e) tribe with these odd ritual songs.
And challenge them to see where they might fit into this
music. See, that's the message. The message is not politics
this—Black that—heavy lyrics, blah, blah, etc. The message
is that we simply exist here and now in all our complexity
and simplicity and are doing this in front of you and are
celebrating everything and inviting/challenging you to find
your way into it.

"But the bottom line is that this is all entertainment. Even with the films that I really like. I mean, [Jean-Luc] Godard is my favorite filmmaker, but the reason that his films are still watchable to me is because I find that stuff entertaining. I don't think I would go back to it if it bored me in some way. And I know *that* is the reason why some people like us. Because it is entertaining."

The Negro Problem/Stew: Selected Discography
Silver Lake What a Drag! (1995)
Their General Suave Guys Request (1996)
Post Minstrel Syndrome (1997)
Joys and Concerns (1999)
Guest Host (2000)
Sweetboot (2000)
Muddy Sweetboot (2002)
The Naked Dutch Painter and Other Songs (2002)
Welcome Black (2002)
Something Deeper Than These Changes (2003)
Passing Strange (2008)
A Midsummer Night's Dream (2009)
Work in Progress (2010)
Making It (2012)

San Diego Reader, November 13, 1997

SIXTEEN

Careening in the Back of a Big Black Car—Deconstructing Big Star in *Nothing Can Hurt Me*

Unless you were cognizant in the summer of '83, it is nearly impossible to explain just how bland and soulless the programming of Top 40 and AOR radio had become throughout the majority of America. In the era that begat MTV and the business merger, the odds of finding anything passionate, intelligent or inspirational from the national musical mainstream were becoming practically nil—and tuning into corporate radio had become comparable to taking all of your meals at McDonalds.

Well, being a precocious teenager, it wasn't long before I became enmeshed within a vast underground grapevine of other disenfranchised musical fanatics—as I continued the lifelong pursuit of sifting through the pop cultural detritus of whatever I missed out on firsthand from the '50s, '60s, and '70s. However, in 1984 I happened upon a quartet from Memphis, Tennessee, who recorded a trio of obscure LPs between 1971 and 1975. After passionately absorbing their supernova burst of creativity it seemed incredible to me that the music of Big Star remained largely unknown, outside of a small circle of burgeoning powerpop freaks. Their music was, and remains, a revelation, and *damn*—I haven't been the same since.

To me Big Star was like some letter that was posted in 1971 that arrived in 1985. It's just like something that got lost in the mail really. – **Robyn Hitchcock**

A lot can change in 30 years, and now a rather large cult of devotees are well aware of just how ground-breaking Big Star was, as evidenced by the current documentary *Big Star: Nothing Can Hurt Me.* Director Drew DeNicola and his production team do an excellent job of deconstructing the myths and exploring the mystery as to why Big Star didn't become one of the biggest acts of its day.

Egotism, neurosis, spiritual crisis and a lack of managerial guidance—it all reads like a textbook example of how NOT to run a successful enterprise. Like any group, Big Star did not emerge out of a vacuum and *Nothing Can Hurt Me* goes a long way toward explaining the backstory of all the principals involved, and how Big Star was the invention of musician and songwriter Chris Bell. Conversely, part of what makes Big Star's music so compelling is the push me/ pull you dynamism between Bell and his musical sparring partner, Alex Chilton. Emulating the song craft partnership of Paul McCartney and John Lennon, it was Bell who asked Chilton to join his group, in a ploy that ultimately backfired on him.

Sometimes lack of success forces you deeper within yourself.
– **Lenny Kaye**

Four years before the formation of Big Star, Alex Chilton was already a pop star. Fronting a quintet of Memphis teenagers called the Box Tops, Chilton was only sixteen when he sang lead on "The Letter," which held the number one spot for four weeks on the *Billboard* Hot 100 in the fall of '67. Even though they went on to score seven more Top 40 hits, by the end of 1969 Chilton had grown weary of his role as a corporate puppet and as soon as he was of legal age to quit the group, he did.

At the same time there was a brand new recording facility in Memphis called Ardent Studios, created by electrical engineering wizard John Fry. When Fry designed a state of the art, sixteen-track studio, superior to the recently refurbished Stax studio across town, Ardent began recording the overflow from their roster of soul giants (Booker T. & the MGs, the Staple Singers, Isaac Hayes, *et al*). And when Fry couldn't handle the additional work load by himself, he started recruiting and training additional engineers for his staff, including a guitar-playing Beatles fanatic by the name of Chris Bell.

"You couldn't grow up around here without being in the middle of soul music culture," said John Fry. "But we were also real English music fans, to the extent that when the British Invasion started, I had a subscription to the *New Musical Express*."

Before the success of the Box Tops, Chilton and Bell had known each other from childhood. While Chilton was touring the country and racking up the hits, Bell pursued the British-infused sounds in his head, playing guitar in a group called the Jynx. One of the invaluable perks that came from working at Ardent was having unlimited access to the studio when it wasn't in use. Bell took full advantage of his training, and after hooking up with bassist Andy Hummel and drummer Jody Stephens, they started amassing a stack of demos under the names Icewater and Rock City. After splitting the Box Tops, Chilton made some recordings at Ardent (later released as *1970*) and it wasn't long before he agreed to join Bell's trio. Throughout the winter of 1971, over a dozen Bell/Chilton compositions were laid down. John Fry loved what he was hearing and thought that the group would be perfect for Ardent Records, the new rock-based subsidiary label that Stax was organizing. After swiping their name from a neighboring supermarket chain, Big Star's debut LP, *#1 Record* was released in April of '72. It quickly became apparent, however, that the premier soul label in America had no idea how to promote a rock 'n' roll band. In spite of a fair amount of airplay and rave reviews in the press, you couldn't find Big Star's record at your local store.

We could have been jinxing ourselves by calling our band Big Star and our first album #1 Record. – **Jody Stephens**

Dominated by the "heavy rock" of its day (Grand Funk Railroad, Led Zeppelin), when *#1 Record* came out it was a complete anomaly. With a sonic blueprint that drew upon the harmonies of the Beatles, the chiming Rickenbackers of the Byrds, the intensity of the Who, and the sensitivity of the Beach Boys, Big Star possessed an enigmatic quality—what Robert Gordon later referred to as "an underlying menace." Producer Jim Dickinson noted "if Big Star was anything, it was dangerous. In an almost imperceptible way—yet you knew it was there, like a switchblade ready to pop."

Also crucial to the mix was a certain type of spiritual and emotional angst—due in no small part to the closeted homosexuality of Chris Bell—a subject that is completely skirted in *Nothing Can Hurt Me*. The closest the film gets to this sticky subject is when Bell's older brother David relates how Chris told him that he "should do drugs, because they take away your sexual urges." Bell's lifestyle was complicated by the fact that he had embraced born-again Christianity. Unfortunately, being gay and occasionally indulging in Dilaudid didn't seem to jibe with the tenets of his church. And then there was the not-so-small matter of all the media attention Chilton was receiving.

"Things started going sour for Chris when he started reading reviews of *#1 Record*," says Jody Stephens. "[Big Star] was such a large part of his creative vision that when the press started coming back and focusing on Alex, he thought he might have to live under that shadow from that point." Andy Hummel agreed: "I'm sure that was a factor in the emotional problems he started having at that time. I mean the guy poured his heart and soul into this thing, so I guess he felt kind of betrayed."

Bell's lack of recognition caused him to snap, and according to his brother and John Fry, he attempted suicide with an overdose of pills—but not before going into Ardent Studios and wiping the multi-track masters for *#1 Record*. Bell survived the episode and went on to pursue a solo career, but the seeds of his dissolution were sown and he never did recover from his sense of being slighted. In a peculiar synchronicity, on December 27, 1978, Bell died in a car accident at the age of 27—the eve of Alex Chilton's 28th birthday.

As substantive as *Nothing Can Hurt Me* is, it does veer off onto a few fruitless tangents, such as a detour through the late Jim Dickinson's property with his widow Mary. There is also an overabundance of screen time dedicated to the Rock Writer's Convention, a publicity stunt dreamt up by promotion man John King in order to present a reconstituted Big Star (sans Bell) to the rock press.

From the documentary, Bruce Eaton: "Okay. Chris left, took the tapes, the band broke up. Then you were asked to play the [1973] Rock Writer's Convention and you went out and kicked ass and then decided to get back together…"

Alex Chilton: "Well, I would really say that the general idea was that—okay, Chris was the main first guy in this band, and if he's gone then I guess we won't do anything. But the moment when I decided that we **would** do something more together, I was speaking to John King, who said 'You know, we did well in a lot of ways with that first album and I think if we do another one we can really make some success out of it.'" John Fry counters that assertion with "There was no question that we weren't gonna do another Big Star album."

With Bell's departure, Chilton became Big Star's de facto leader and his songs, no doubt, are exemplary throughout the sophomore offering in February of '74 of *Radio City*. But a sense of equilibrium was somehow lost in the process. A black and white video by photographer William Eggleston entitled *Stranded in Canton* captures the careening drunkenness of the times, suggesting that the entire scene was inevitably heading for a cliff. A favorite place for much of the Memphis music scene to hang out was Thank God It's Friday (TGIF), the location where Eggleston's lens captured the iconic sleeve images of *Radio City*.

Writer and musician Rick Clark: "I look at *Radio City* as a transitional record. It's the pristine brilliance of the first record, but it's the beginning of the unfraying and the sound of falling apart."

Journalist Billy Altman: "That second album to me was almost a perfect record. All the songs had a sensibility and a feel and a certain kind of mystery. This was not a record that revealed itself fast. When you listen to these songs, they're complicated."

Alex Chilton: "It's like they're not really even rock 'n' roll songs. I don't know what they are. They're some kind of psycho-dramatic tunes about something that doesn't have any particular place in music."

Whatever the relative merits of *Radio City*, the band continued its exceptional run of bad luck when copies of the album sat idle after a distribution deal between Columbia Records and Stax fell through. Shortly thereafter, Stax filed for bankruptcy and the ever-practical Andy Hummel jumped ship to go back to school. For a brief spell Chilton's friend John Lightman filled in on bass.

"We often played to rooms that were almost empty," Lightman relates in the film. "And I felt really awful for how disappointed they were in the lack of response that they got. It was sort of chaotic at Ardent. The future was all unknown, sort of in limbo. We had a rehearsal set up there. Jody and I arrived at 2 PM and we waited and waited and about 5:30 Alex comes sauntering in. 'Well, here I am, but I don't have my guitar, what do you wanna do?' That would be a typical day. After a while of this sort of thing going on Alex said to me: 'My attitude about music is I can take it or leave it.'" At this point, it's arguable that Big Star continued to exist. A string of Chilton/Stephens sessions from 1974–75, produced by Jim Dickinson, were eventually released in 1978 as *Big Star 3rd*, wherein Chilton appears to be cheerlessly and willfully losing the plot—and slamming the psychic accelerator in an attempt to create some distance between himself and the failures of the immediate past.

The sum of Chris Bell's post-Big Star work was posthumously released in 1992 as *I Am the Cosmos*. And in a typically perverse maneuver, in April of '93 Chilton confounded everyone by spontaneously agreeing to reform Big Star with Jody Stephens, Jon Auer, and Ken String-fellow of the Posies—a lineup that lasted for seventeen years of intermittent gigs, and produced one new studio LP, 2005's *In Space*. The Big Star story came to a full stop when Chilton suffered a fatal heart attack on March 17, 2010, and Hummel succumbed to cancer on July 19, 2010.

Nothing Can Hurt Me is a mixed bag of emotional cues—ecstatic praise by numerous alt rock luminaries and writers, contrasted with the melancholic expressions of those who were directly involved. Nevertheless, the shimmering alchemical brilliance and achingly gorgeous yearnings of Big Star inspired scores of other artists, including R.E.M., Let's Active, Game Theory/the Loud Family, the Replacements, the Bangles, Teenage Fanclub, Elliott Smith, and Matthew Sweet. Their music is timeless and *Nothing Can Hurt Me* serves to contextualize why Big Star is a national treasure. Check it out when you get the chance.

Ugly Things, #36, Fall/Winter, 2013

SEVENTEEN
Scott Miller
MUSIC: What Happened?

In 1989 I subscribed to a quarterly newsletter entitled *True Gamesters*, the official mouthpiece for '80s alternative rock group Game Theory. The motivation was simple; I had become obsessed with this conglomerate from the Bay Area after having my mind blown by their sprawlingly ambitious, 1987 masterpiece *Lolita Nation*, and I wanted to find out more about its songwriter and chief ringleader Scott Miller (also responsible for the '90s ensemble the Loud Family).

By the time *True Gamesters* started hitting my mail slot I discovered that not only had Miller written several LPs worth of catchy, intelligent, classic rock/power pop, he was also capable of some of the most conversational, humorous, and deftly knowledgeable musings in the realm of rock 'n' roll that you'd ever want to read. I consider him a sort of fourth-generation rock 'n' roll Renaissance Man, capable of making the printed page jump and sing as triumphantly as the complex conversations that his Les Paul conducts with a Marshall stack.

Which brings us to the recently published *MUSIC: What Happened?*, meditations on Miller's favorite recordings from the past 53 years (1957–2009). Very much in the spirit of the list-making freaks that populate the world of Nick Hornby's

High Fidelity, the self-selected guidelines for this exercise allow that no artist may be represented by more than one song per year, even if he occasionally bends that rule. And each year's countdown compilation must fit onto a single compact disc.

Miller's unique POV of the experience of music is expressed with succinct observations and jokey one-liners. I'm thinking rim shots here, that make me howl with recognition from our shared cultural zeitgeist. The chapter on 1981 begins with "the first salvos of eighties annoyance. The most deadly was the 'New Romantic' movement, where the romance was with drum machines, thin, washy synthesizers, grandiose, brayed vocals, bad hair, and bad clothes." Miller concludes his commentary on Black Flag's "TV Party" by suggesting that "the lesson of Henry Rollins is probably that with a sufficiently engaging personality, the issue of technical merit will eventually take care of itself."

Miller's writing demonstrates a level of skill, intelligence, sensitivity, and wit that I'm nearly jealous of: he pulls it off so well. Also, this isn't the type of book you need to read straight from cover to cover, skip around, be non-linear. Check out 1977 as punk was heating up, or 1993 when *Exile In Guyville* was the order of the day. It's obvious that Miller loves the Beatles, Big Star, Led Zeppelin, and Chris Stamey, but he also has the superb aplomb to applaud the work of XTC, the Posies, the Negro Problem, Mike Keneally, and scores of other artists who are an eargasm awaiting your senses.

MUSIC: What Happened? is an inspiration to dig that much deeper into your own collection with relish and to seek out some new favorites with a fresh perspective.

Ugly Things, #32, Fall/Winter, 2011

EIGHTEEN

Paul Myers
A WIZARD, A TRUE STAR:
Todd Rundgren in the Studio

Sometimes I just don't know what to feel about Todd Rundgren—one minute I think he's an unparalleled genius, and the next that he's some spoiled dilettante with complete contempt for his audience. At least that's the impression I've walked away with on more than one occasion when I have been "lucky" enough to catch the Prince of Upper Darby live in concert. Be that as it may, I have no ambivalence regarding Paul Myers' wonderful new book that focuses exclusively on Rundgren's production work in the recording studio, the locale where the self-proclaimed "Wizard and True Star" truly shines. Navigating his way through a career of twenty-plus LPs under his own solo imprint while simultaneously negotiating a parallel career with the groups Nazz and Utopia, Rundgren has also managed to apply his awe-inspiring prowess upon the work of a stunning list of collaborators. In fact, in strictly commercial terms you could easily claim that Todd Rundgren has been FAR more successful as an outside producer than as a performing artist—if only for the fact that he produced two #1 singles for Grand Funk Railroad: "We're an American Band" and "The Loco-Motion." Rundgren should have been able to retire for several lifetimes from his points on *Bat Out of Hell* alone: Meatloaf's 1977 surprise mega-hit that has sold over 34 million copies worldwide. Instead, he ended up pouring most of his millions into his audio and visual production company.

A large measure of *A Wizard, a True Star*'s success is, of course, due to the access that Myers was afforded by Rundgren. Focusing exclusively on the oeuvre without any sensationalistic detours, there isn't one whiff of anything salubrious, with Myers interviewing all the right principles to give us the skinny on how such seminal LPs as Badfinger's *Straight Up*, the *New York Dolls* self-titled debut, and XTC's *Skylarking* got made. Equally thrilling is learning how such underrated gems such as Sparks' *Halfnelson*, Daryl Hall and John Oates' *War Babies*, and The Tubes' *Remote Control* were produced. I did, however, find myself wondering: how did Myers keep a straight face when he interviewed Jim Steinman about *Bat Out of Hell*? I hear Steinman's compositions and insist that the guy must be putting me (and everybody else) on, but Rundgren apparently got the joke and managed to turn this overblown opus of a teenage wet dream into commercial gold.

Oh, and I'd be remiss if I failed to mention how tickled I was to discover how "Dancing Barefoot" by the Patti Smith Group, "Love My Way" by the Psychedelic Furs, and "I Can't Take It" by Cheap Trick were all committed to tape as well. And while I'm not that much of a gearhead I did love learning about the tricks of a master. Getting down to the nuts and bolts of all those outside productions is fantastic, but the real meat of Myers' book is learning how Rundgren came to produce himself, creating such timeless gems as

Runt: the Ballad of Todd Rundgren, Something/Anything?, A Wizard, a True Star, Todd, Initiation, and *Hermit of Mink Hollow.* After the recent twin follies of the New Cars and recording the shallow-sounding *Arena* CD on a laptop, here's hoping that Todd gets the gist of Myers' tribute to him: that when it comes to making music in a brick-and-mortar studio, with real live human beings all playing together in the same room, Mr. Rundgren has few peers.

Ugly Things, #32, Fall/Winter, 2011

NINETEEN

Louise Goffin
Songs from the Mine

When was the last time you heard an album that changed your life in some significant way? Perhaps it was that summer romance when the Beach Boys' *Pet Sounds* was constantly on the box, coloring your moods and articulating your feelings. Or maybe it was that beach party where the DJ played "Hey Ya!" from Outkast's *The Love Below* five times in a row because it sounded so great—and now it brings back such wondrous memories when you hear it again. The evocation of music is a glorious phenom. In the bygone era where music held pride of place in our cultural pantheon as a sanctified art form, it was appreciated on a mass scale, not relegated to the realm of cultural wallpaper and background noise—or something to disturb the unbearable stillness of your personal space. We've become so used to noise pollution in our contemporary culture that most folks expect and/or require *any* sort of electronic pablum to reassure themselves and feel comforted within this chaotic slice of eternity. These modern day contrivances are the antithesis of what music is intended to be. At its glorious core, music is a decoration to the expanse of space and time, and in the hands of a master, it transmutes your consciousness to a dimension that it has never before perceived. That is what timeless art does. It speaks to the soul, reaches into the heart and explores the endless paradoxes of what it means to be alive, to be human within the full spectrum of contradictory emotions. As peculiar animals, uniquely aware of how transient our existence is, most of us would rather bury our heads in the sand and blithely ignore that fact. But for the brave and the willing and the true adventurers among us, we revel and are revealed by looking into that mirror which has the power to sustain us in its fount of inspirational truth and beauty. By developing the ability to look deep within oneself, a piece of another person's soul reflects our universal existence together.

Great art often demands that you meet it more than halfway if you are to truly appreciate the gifts on offer. Sometimes it is merely arriving at the proper state of mind to appreciate Cézanne or the writings of Emmett Grogan. At other times, their genius seems so obvious that you wonder why the entire world isn't celebrating their exemplary output. And years from now, when I conjure up memories from the summer of 2014, I will smile sweetly and remember the profundities evoked by *Songs from the Mine:* the latest sonic adventure from composer/musician/producer Louise Goffin. As the title intimates, it took a lot of living and exacting toil to extract these nuggets from the darkest recesses of the psyche and bring them into the light, where all are invited to share in their beauty, strength and encouraging wisdom. But be forewarned, it may take more than a superficial glance, or a cursory listen, to appreciate what's happening here.

❧

If your first response to hearing Louise Goffin's name is bewilderment, or slipping into a Pavlovian daydream and wondering if she sounds anything like her parents—I suppose that's a reasonable response. As the eldest daughter of Gerry Goffin and Carole King, such is the cursed blessing of living in the incomparable shadow of arguably the greatest songwriting duo of the twentieth century. And should you require validation of that claim just ask Messieurs Lennon and McCartney, or numerous other masters within the field.

But really, what sort of masochist would wish upon themselves the comparisons to their notoriously famous parents? Just ask Sean or Julian Lennon, Robert Downey, Jr., Jakob Dylan, Chynna Phillips or Carnie and Wendy Wilson, what that particular exercise is like. If nepotism can only take you so far, then that's certainly been one of the perceptual obstacles that Goffin has been up against since the release of her debut LP, *Kid Blue*, for Elektra Records in 1979.

Okay, masochist is the wrong adjective, perhaps "fated determinist" is a better description: because it would seem inevitable that, if you had that caliber of DNA coursing through your veins, karmically influencing your thoughts and dreams, it would be criminal to deny the world of all that unexplored potential. But is it possible for the prodigy of compositional legends to be received and appreciated with a Zen-like beginner's mind, by the general public? Most likely not, because in this celebrity-drenched culture that spills over our awareness like a shroud of mystification, how do you experience any art form without preconception? Everyone brings their own personally monogrammed baggage to the table of the eternal now. And man, it must be wearisome to be jaded and feel like you've seen and heard it all.

If you've been following Louise Goffin's career since its inception, you would have noticed that, with each successive record she's made, there are discernible arcs and dips to the moods, techniques, and performances that she has put forth before the lions of public opinion. After two LPs (*Kid Blue*, and her eponymous follow-up, *Louise Goffin*) of rather conventional fare, other titles followed including 1989's *This Is the Place*, and 2002's extremely compelling *Sometimes a Circle*. At first glance, *Sometimes a Circle* has the appearance of an artist who has truly arrived and can't believe that she's living the dream (i.e. husband, kids, home, career). But by 2008's *Bad Little Animals*, it became apparent that there was a downside to the fantasy come true—with the illusion of having it all collapsing in the face of reality. As a clue to how much things had changed, listen to the track "Hurt People" and that pretty much says it all.

But now, six years on, all of the hard-earned wisdom of learning how to be self-reliant (both on stage and off), and figuring out how to pierce the veil in the land of dashed hopes and dreams, comes a masterpiece of reinvention. This latest record is a conversation with your best friend— it serves as a reminder that just because your dreams came tumbling down, it's still okay to keep on dreaming. And even though your heart's been broken, it doesn't mean that after taking a sabbatical to lick your wounds and regain your equilibrium, you can't emerge from the experience stronger and wiser.

Some records feel like they're chasing trends, while others are completely oblivious to the whims of fashion. If you're seeking something snide, aloof and stylistically detached in the name of appearing "cool," then look elsewhere kids, 'cause this isn't it. *Songs from the Mine* feels like a long, lost letter of reassurance from someone that you haven't spoken to in years. And no matter how long it's been, the conversation picks up naturally from the last time you crossed paths—feeling as comfortable as your favorite pair of jeans.

Songs from the Mine has a sweetness that is rare these days. With one song building upon the next, a narrative forms throughout, without the pretense of being a concept album. No two songs sound alike, either in structure, production, or the emotions that they exude, and yet there is a continuity that carries you from the first song to the last. The album starts off with an epic pep talk ("Everybody but You") that never fails to make my heart sing, especially with the triumphant chord change that occurs when the verse goes to the chorus. Sometimes I can't help but wonder if the singer is speaking to herself.

There are cautionary tales of what life can be like out in the weird, wild world, with some particularly sage advice in "Some of Them Will Fool You," a song about perception and how the stories we tell ourselves are oftentimes self-defeating. So be careful about what you think: "When they sing you don't have to sing along, it's only true if you believe them. So **don't** believe them."

"Follow My Heart" is a sly demonstration of what happens when you don't live in an intellectual cocoon of self-protection. There is earnest vulnerability and a yearning in the perpetual search for someone or something to believe in and trust: that somehow these ideals and myths will magically manifest, and the ills of the world will be transformed, trumping all the odds. Woven within this mosaic of faith and hope is an acceptance of love as **the** guiding factor—and that's the mortar that holds *Songs from the Mine* together. Whatever life has wrought, there is always a new day ahead and another shot at redemption from the self-imposed shackles of the past.

Although she's written plenty of songs by herself in the past, one of the attributes that Goffin shares with her parents is a proclivity toward writing with other songwriters. All eleven tunes on *Songs from the Mine* greatly benefit from the input of other writers. A trio of collaborations went down at the Steel Bridge Songfest in Sturgeon Bay, Wisconsin. "Main Street Parade," written with Lynda Kay Parker and Dustin Welch, is a breezy summation of losing your lover amid the hustle and bustle. "We Belong Together," written with James Hall and Chris Aaron, offers up some atypical, Stones-like swagger, proving that, even if the protagonist has been burned in the past, the need for connection, affection, love and the arms of protection are worth pleading, fighting and working towards.

One of the crown jewels of the record is "Deep Dark Night of the Soul." Composed at Steel Bridge Songfest with Corinne Lee, who contributes some marvelously absurd French to the proceedings, and Craig Greenberg, "Deep Dark Night of the Soul" is a whimsical treaty with the past, demonstrating how much Goffin has changed: "I'm a bad-ass bitch with my shit together, make my bridges out of steel." These are but three of the reasons why songwriters throughout the land are seduced by the cosmic situations that create such catalyzing art in the hallowed confines of the Holiday Music Motel.

2013 found Goffin exploring a duo with songwriter/ musician and sometime actor, Billy Harvey, with the two of them dubbing the enterprise A Fine Surprise. There are two soulful collaborations with Harvey on *Songs from the Mine*. Inspired by a book on Gandhi and non-violence, the meditation within "Sword in Your Heart" is deep, knowing that peace shall never come as long as any feelings of malice persist. "If only you would listen to all it has to say. When you start to feel that everything you do is in vain. The sword in your heart is pointing the way."

"Here Where You Are Loved" is simply beautiful (with lovely harmonies by Harvey) that serves as the core of reassurance to the entire album. "Get With the World" has a killer lyrical hook ("get on back to who you are and get with the world, get with the world, before the world gets to you"). "Watching the Sky Turn Blue" is the catchiest song I've heard all year: it ought to be burning up the request lines at your local Top 40 station. The album ends on the philosophically upbeat "Good Life," making me want to return to the top and experience this reaffirmation all over again.

After producing and writing songs for Carole King's *A Holiday Carole* in 2011 (with the record receiving a Grammy nomination), comes the high point of Goffin's professional career so far. And it should be noted that the segues on *Songs from the Mine* are positively sublime and play a significant part of why this set adds up to such a singular experience. Like the most classic of expressions on that extended canvas of the long-playing album, *Songs from the Mine* is a glorious slide through a kaleidoscopic range of emotions. Caressing, provoking and expanding your awareness, it ultimately soothes the savage impulses of self-destruction, caring enough to talk you off the ledge and suggesting how to love yourself in a brand new way. If summer means new love after a long and lonely winter, here's to the happily ever after evoked by the muse of Louise Goffin.

San Diego Troubadour, September, 2014

TWENTY

Check Your Ego at the Door: Transformation and Rejuvenation at Steel Bridge Songfest

Every June for the last nine years a musical miracle occurs in the ship building port of Sturgeon Bay, Wisconsin. Nestled just to the west of Lake Michigan and 42 miles to the northeast of Green Bay, this relatively modest community, in the heart of Door County (population 9,144), celebrates the onset of summer by throwing a week-long party that takes over the entire town. Championing its unique cultural heritage, while simultaneously crafting a bacchanalian vibe of intense proportions, musicians and songwriters from all corners of the globe converge annually to create the unique zeitgeist that is known as Steel Bridge Songfest (SBSF)—the world's only collaborative, interactive songwriting festival.

Not to be selfish or small-minded, but I'm sort of tempted NOT to tell you about how incredible Steel Bridge Songfest is, out of fear that it will become so popular (like perhaps what happened to the Burning Man Festival) that it will somehow end up forfeiting its immense charm. But you know how it is when you're transformed by an experience and you just have to share the news with whomever you come in contact with. You run the risk of becoming a proselytizer. And just ask anyone who has been lucky enough to be involved with SBSF and they'll no doubt sing you a similar tune because: **there's nothing like it anywhere else in the world.** And I must say that after 30-plus years of interacting with the (oft-times gargantuan) egos of numerous musicians, the degree of humility and sense of community that SBSF and this sleepy little hamlet inspires, is nothing short of miraculous. It's awe-inspiring really, and it all came into being when a group of concerned citizens from Door County exercised their sense of civic duty and insisted on taking action when part of their local heritage was under threat of being destroyed: namely the Michigan Street Steel Bridge that connects downtown Sturgeon Bay with the rest of the region. In the interest of "progress," some powerful players in the area decided that it was time for a change, and they sought to shut down and replace the last operational steel bridge on the planet.

Unfortunately, by 2005 that point of view wasn't entirely without justification. As the debate became heated among the locals there was no arguing that the bridge was in dire need of substantial repairs. Some people argued that constructing a new, more modern bridge would alleviate traffic snarls and keep the flow of cars and boats moving much more efficiently. At the same time, there was a large number of people in Door County who took great offense at the notion that the Michigan Street Bridge was an antiquated symbol from a time past. Eventually, a win-win solution was created in 2008 with the construction of the brand new Maple-Oregon Street Bridge, in addition to the restoration of the Michigan Street Steel Bridge.

Progress vs. Tradition

Dedicated to honor those of Door County who answered their country's call and gave their services in time of emergency.

One of the main issues, when it came to the discussion of demolishing the Michigan Street Bridge, was the fact that the bridge was dedicated on July 4, 1931, as a memorial to all the military veterans of Door County who had served the United States in times of war. To even whisper of demolition and of revoking this patriotic symbol of appreciation was akin to sacrilege for a lot of folks, and it sparked a political crusade that lasted for years—the unlikely silver lining being the creation of SBSF. One of the primary voices of dissent, in the initial push to keep the bridge from being torn down, was Sturgeon Bay resident Christie Weber (*Citizens for Our Bridge*). It wasn't long before she was joined in her fight against city hall by the energies and passion of her brother, renowned singer/songwriter and musician pat mAcdonald.

It was in the spring of 2006 that the politics of Sturgeon Bay became personal for me when I was fortunate enough to cross paths with mister mAcdonald, an artist whose work I'd been enchanted with since the release of *Greetings From Timbuk3* in 1986 (featuring the ubiquitous Top 20 hit single "The Future's So Bright, I Gotta Wear Shades"). At the time we met, mAcdonald was on the cusp of unleashing *Troubadour of Stomp*, the 17th release of his illustrious career, while at the same time organizing the second Steel Bridge Songfest. Even though the premiere festival in 2005 was a big success in terms of raising money and promoting awareness, it was a modest one-day affair. By 2006, mAcdonald decided to expand the parameters of the festival by upping the ante and having three days of music throughout the town, and creating what he dubbed the "Construction Zone."

During his time at I.R.S. Records, the label that Timbuk3 was signed to during the 1980s and early '90s, mAcdonald became involved in a songwriting roundtable that was instigated by I.R.S. president Miles Copeland. Copeland's pitch was simple: at a locale in the south of France dubbed "the Castle," Copeland invited a broad cross section of professional tunesmiths to congregate and cross-pollinate their talents for a fortnight, with the provision that whatever material was created during their time together would be 50 percent owned by Copeland. You could think of it as a working vacation, and the arrangement produced some unlikely bedfellows, with mAcdonald collaborating with scores of other writers including Keith Urban, Imogen Heap, and Cher.

Talent Borrows, Genius Steals

No doubt there was plenty of fun to be had at the Castle, but it still was a business arrangement at the end of the day. When it came time to put together the second Steel Bridge Songfest, mAcdonald drew upon the model of the Castle and adopted all of the appropriate aspects for the Construction Zone. Simultaneously a social and artistic experiment, the first Construction Zone was birthed within the confines of the Holiday Motel, an eighteen-room lodge that was built in 1952, which sits at the foot of the Michigan Street Bridge. In 2006, a special arrangement was made with then owners Pete and Marilyn DeVaney to commandeer the motel for an entire week, with a makeshift studio installed in Room 124 by ace Milwaukee-based recording engineer Steve Hamilton. The first group of songwriters were 25 in number and the general idea was to have everyone get together in a circle and play spin the bottle. The fate of the spin would break the songwriters off into groups of two or three or four, and each group was to follow a very simple brief laid out by mAcdonald: write a song that somehow relates to the bridge. The options were as endless as your imagination. You could write about the bridge literally, figuratively, or metaphorically, not to mention take in aspects of the local culture in Door County, and write about that as well. By 2006, mAcdonald had already provided a number of stellar examples of what he was possibly going for, including "The Bridge Hater Song" and "Steel Bridge Song" (both from *Troubadour of Stomp*) and "Steel Yourself" (a collaboration with Jackson Browne).

If you think that it's easy to write a song on demand about a particular subject, you ought to try it sometime. It takes discipline and focus. But amazingly, that is what every group of writers for the last nine years has done in the Construction Zone. As evidenced by the nine volumes of compact discs that document each year's output, the bridge motif has been twisted around so many times that the variations on the theme appear infinite.

Of course, it's highly encouraged to stick to the suggested subject matter of the bridge but it's not mandatory. Scores of "other" types of songs get written at SBSF that have nothing to do with the bridge or Sturgeon Bay. Sometimes you have to write from pure inspiration and set the bridge motif aside for a song or two—but eventually, all songs bring you back to the bridge.

Transformation Day

The first Construction Zone was such a success that mAcdonald and a consortium of others decided to purchase the Holiday Motel from the DeVaneys and turn it into the Holiday Music Motel, with the intention of transforming it into a destination location for musicians and tourists alike—to soak up the natural beauty of Sturgeon Bay and/or make recordings while staying on the premises. The motel has had its share of growing pains since the acquisition, including a major fire and subsequent renovation in 2008, but in 2013–14 the property is in fine fettle, boasting a fully operational recording studio that's available 365 days a year.

So how does one become involved with Steel Bridge Songfest and the Construction Zone? Well, this extremely unique group of individuals all get together primarily based upon the alchemical instincts and aesthetics of one guy: creative director pat mAcdonald. I think of him as an "artistic firewall," who possesses an intuitive, discriminating wisdom of who will be able to function as a productive team member.

At SBSF 2013 there were three fully functional studios that ran pretty much 24/7, with the stellar engineering talents of the aforementioned Steve Hamilton, Billy Triplett, and Dan-O Stoffels. The protocol for recording material is fairly simple: once a songwriting team feels that it has a song worthy of recording, they audition the song for mAcdonald. mAcdonald might suggest a change or two or feel that the song is fine the way it is. At that point the song goes onto a signup sheet (first come, first served), and then that group goes into the next available studio to record. Each group of composers is responsible for assembling their "band," choosing who will play on their track, and they also need to give their transient outfit a moniker. The idea is to capture the material as quickly as possible so that the next band can get in and do their thing. Rarely does a group spend more than an hour or so on a particular track. Considering these field conditions, the quality of the material that is created is astonishing.

After spending Sunday through Wednesday writing and recording, it then becomes necessary to shift gears into rehearsal mode so that these brand new compositions can be taken into the streets and out to the clubs and performed in bars, cafés, theaters, and on the main stage at the all-day concerts, which take place on Saturday and Sunday in the parking lot of the Holiday Music Motel. All told, there are over 150 acts that perform in twelve different venues over the course of four days.

The bottom line of SBSF, and what brings all of us together in the first place, is a sense of community that is created within the town and among all of the people who are inspired to congregate here. As for the compositions and the recordings that are generated at the Holiday Music Motel during the week of SBSF, they are also a kind of community property. The music made at the Holiday Motel is free to be used by the artists who create it, provided that proper credit is given to the respective writers and musicians, as well as within the SBSF organization to help promote awareness of the festival and to underwrite some of the substantial expenses that are incurred each year. The festival and motel play host to many of the artists who are involved, which includes the housing and feeding of the artists while they are creating during the week.

In addition to the scores of volunteers who make the festival possible each year I must make a special mention of melaniejane, pat mAcdonald's "partner in crime," who serves as the manager and "air traffic controller" of the Holiday Music Motel. She keeps this train of wildly creative and delightfully eccentric personalities from derailing from its chosen course. In addition to collaborating on the motel, mAcdonald and mj also make dangerously beautiful music together as the duo Purgatory Hill, listed in the Steel Bridge program as being from "Heaven/Hell, WI."

To neatly summarize the entire range of feelings regarding my Steel Bridge experience this year is impossible, as evidenced by the stream of 8,000 words that I managed to journal during these ten transformative days from June 8–17. I was one of 73 kindred spirits who came together for reasons shared and for reasons known only to ourselves. I was blessed to co-write six songs while in attendance, perform bass duties on another three songs that I didn't compose, and came back with the beginnings of another song that was completed when I was back home in San Diego. I renewed ties with old friends, made countless new ones, and had experiences that you could never put a price tag on. By putting myself out there in service with others, I managed to be a part of something that is way bigger than any individual—co-creating and participating in a community happening that transcends mere personal gratification.

Here's a blow-by-blow/day-by-day acount of what went down at SBSF9. Personnel credits for each of the tracks recorded can be found in the **Appendix** on pages 450–451. Readers are also encouraged to go on the Internet and watch the smattering of videos offering a glimpse of what a unique event Steel Bridge Songfest is, and how beautiful the people of Sturgeon Bay, Wisconsin, are. I can't wait until the next one. And the next...

SKETCHES IN A JOURNAL
from Steel Bridge Songfest 2013

Fueled by elation, sleep deprivation, and the proximity of respected peers, droves of driven souls churned out yet another year's worth of tributes, tall tales, and ragged anthems. Fortuitous leaps of illogic brought chance continuity, driving this song cycle up into orbit, then gently back down again for its dazed and lovely last hoorah. However inspired the last batch of songs was, I see there's always more where those came from and find myself increasingly looking forward to Volume Seven, Eight, Nine and TEN! – pat mAcdonald, liner notes from *Steel Bridge Songs Vol. 6* (2011)

Saturday, June 8th, 2013

6:30 AM PDT. Take off from San Diego and arrive safely in Green Bay, via Chicago. Picked up at the airport by SBSF volunteer Nicole Henquinet (who is as sweet as could be) and have a pleasant drive before being deposited on the front steps of the Holiday Music Motel. Meet melaniejane and immediately upon arrival I find out that I will be staying in Room 230 and that my roommate for the week is Craig Greenberg (from New York, NY). It took me about five minutes before I accepted these cosmic arrangements and then—poof!—I surrendered my seven-year-long, petty-minded grudge with him from SBSFII. It feels liberating and from that moment forward I instantly know that I have that much more creative juice available to bring to the table. I unpack and then decide to take a walk around town. Not much has changed since I was here last in 2006. Check out the Nautical Inn and end up at Poh's where I run into Charlie Cheney (Fremont, MI). After sharing a drink together Charlie leaves Poh's for Egg Harbor and, unbeknownst to me 'till the next AM, immediately totals his van by hitting a deer. I bounce over to the Stone Harbor hotel for a bit where the bar is hopping with a trio grinding out "Save the Last Dance For Me," "Brown Eyed Girl," and "Twist and Shout." The clientele seem to be having fun but I decide to go back to my room for one last blast of solitude before the deluge.

Sunday, June 9th, 2013

Wake at 9:30 AM. Feel like I'm still on California time. Spend the morning acclimating, changing guitar strings, and mentally preparing for the week that lies ahead.

pat: "90 percent of this process is about listening." I come down to the lobby around 2:30 PM and see pat behind the front desk and his greeting to me is "welcome home." The two of us go over to Kick Café on Third Avenue for lunch until 4:30 PM. We discuss his new book *Space Kitty Blues* and get caught up after not laying eyes on each other for seven years.

At 6:30 PM there is a PA on the front lawn of the Holiday with tunes pouring out of the speakers from previous songfests. Everyone grabs a plate of food, pat makes some introductory comments and then melaniejane goes over the house rules for the week. pat asks everyone who is present (73 different songwriters) to pass the microphone around and introduce themselves. After those formalities are addressed we all form a circle in the parking lot—the welcome mat from the motel is placed in the center and James Hall (Atlanta, GA) initiates the proceedings by spinning an empty Jameson Irish whiskey bottle (the moment is captured beautifully by photographer Ty Helbach). Songwriters in groups of three split off and eventually I form a team with Stephen "Coop" Cooper (Fond du Lac, WI) and Jimm McIver (Seattle, WA), both of whom I've never met before.

I grab my acoustic guitar and Jimm grabs his and we all retire to the diner to start writing. After searching all over the property for a quiet spot this location feels like it has the appropriate "mojo," particularly for me, as this was where the "Holiday Motel" song was written with Allan MacPhee back at SBSFII. The three of us talk for a bit, throwing out suggestions as to what we should write about. I recall pat's first words to me from earlier in the day (not to mention being Chris Aaron's as well) and I suggest the title of "Welcome Home" and the next thing you know the three of us are tossing around ideas like a well-oiled basketball team. Within 90 minutes we are finished with our first song of the festival. We track pat down and perform it for him while he videos us with his camera. pat asks me to read the lyrics aloud and after a couple of questions tells us to put the song on the sign up sheet for the next available studio. Unbelievably, there are already five or six songs on the list.

Monday, June 10th, 2013

After pat approves our first song I go into the diner feeling adrenalized about what we just created together and I immediately get to revving with Vee Sonnets (Chicago, IL) on the Who's "A Quick One (While He's Away)," ("cello,

cello, cello, cello...."). Vee is an absolute freak of nature (I mean that in the most complementary way possible), and a force to be reckoned with—a left-handed guitarist and multi-instrumentalist who plays the guitar strung for a right-hander and plays his chord shapes upside down (and sideways for that matter). We continue bonding over a 30-minute Who medley in the diner and I continue singing cover songs with him on the front porch of the Holiday until 3:30 AM. I have clearly met a soulmate. Jim, Coop and I get the call from Steve Hamilton to record "Welcome Home" at 4 AM and we grab Dan-O Stoffels (Madison, WI) to play drums. We run the song down twice and after a couple of overdubs (acoustic guitars, harmony vocals, and handclaps) are finished within an hour. When the session is over I hang out at the fire pit on the front lawn until 5:45 AM with my soon-to-be new buddies Charles and Renée Boheme (Madison, WI), where I witness the sunrise for the first time in ages. It feels amazing to be up at that hour. Exhausted but exhilarated, it takes all of my will to drag myself off to bed.

Wake at 10:30 AM. I find out from Steve Hamilton that he has a fifteen-minute window of opportunity (from 1:15-1:30 PM) and we overdub Vee's Farfisa part onto "Welcome Home" where it is deemed "finished."

Spend most of the afternoon with Danielle French (Calgary/Alberta, Canada) on the front lawn talking, writing and drawing runes from her bag of sorcery. We witness a baby bat fly right by our heads (landing in the bushes behind us) and we talk about the Abraham-Hicks book *The Law of Attraction*. It leads into a conversation about monetary resources and not living a life based out of fear, all serving as fodder for our song "Transformation

Day." We get most of it written (two verses and the chorus) with Danielle thinking it should "modulate" and that Vee somehow holds the missing link. We find him, go back to room 230 and Vee throws in that classic Pete Townshend D major chord that runs up the neck and I spontaneously start singing "ooh-la-la-la" and the song pretty much completes itself. After dinner pat hears the song in the diner, makes a couple of suggestions that slightly tweak and improve the lyric, and it is approved for recording.

At 7 PM all of the writers gather on the front lawn of the Holiday for our first listening party. There are something in the neighborhood of seventeen songs already recorded— tunes that did not exist at this time the day before.

Miss Meagan Owens (Maui, HI) is one of the songwriters in the Construction Zone and her very talented brother Connor (Brooklyn, NY) has been given carte blanche to video any and all activities at the SBSF. When he's not shooting a performance or a recording session he can usually be found in the lobby on his laptop editing together some of the footage that he has captured. He then posts his completed videos online, which of course serve to promote the SBSF to the world at large. One of the songs that was written and recorded on day one is "Little Black Ninja," and Connor's video for it conveys the vibe of SBSF beautifully.

After listening to the new material and hearing a brief anecdote about how each song was created by its respective writers, we gather into another circle and spin the bottle again, this time in groups of four. For this second round I team up with Mike Bleck (aka "Digger") (Sturgeon Bay, WI), Kory Murphy (Rockford, IL), and Troy Therrien (Sturgeon Bay, WI). It is great to see Digger and Troy again after working with them both in 2006. Kory and Troy take off on an errand involving a guitar amp pedal for 45 minutes and Digger shows me some lyrics that he was working on from the day before. It's called "Jack" and it deals with Monstanto and their odious GMOs by metaphorically weaving in the Jack and the Beanstalk fable. By a fantastic synchronicity, pat and I were talking at lunch on Sunday about Jack and the Beanstalk, and there's something about the song that feels weirdly pre-ordained. I immediately love Digger's entire concept and when Kory and Troy come back all four of us work up a musical arrangement, concluding that each one of us should sing a verse and then together as a group on the choruses. By 11 PM it is finished. pat hears us wailing on the front lawn, videos us in the dark and approves it for recording after suggesting a title change from simply "Jack" to "Jack & the Fox." It goes on the sign-up sheet, which is starting to get quite backed up by now.

Tuesday, June 11th, 2013

After writing "Jack & the Fox" I walk over at Poh's with Johnny Hvezda (Rockford, IL), Sarvin Manguiat (Ontario, CA), Ronnie Sanchez (Ontario, CA), and Alex Mitchard (Madison, WI), drinking beer and eating some pizza until George (Poh's owner) kicks us out at 2:00 AM. The previous night's sing-along around the fire pit is becoming a nightly routine and we all hang out 'till 5:45 AM. Witness sunrise #2.

Wake at 10:30 AM. Rehearse "Transformation Day" with Danielle and audition it a second time for pat in Danielle's room. It's ready to record so we assemble our group, which thanks to Danielle, now includes the GrooveSession rhythm section of Ronnie Sanchez on bass and his brother Manny on drums and we go in with Steve Hamilton at noon and lay it down in three takes. After assembling and recording a vocal choir it is deemed finished by 1 PM. I thank Ellie Maybe (Chicago, IL) for singing on the track and she nonchalantly drawls "Of course, darling. I'd ooh-la-la for you anytime."

Over the last couple of days I have seen very little of my roommate Craig Greenberg (he was feeling a bit under the weather upon arrival), but by Tuesday we've talked about our past differences and have arrived at a really cool place. During the past 24 hours I hear him fooling around with a brand new song on the toy piano in the motel and it's starting to sound fantastic and I offer to play bass on it whenever he gets around to recording it.

At 6:30 PM everybody assembles on the front lawn for dinner and listening party #2. Another fifteen or more songs are auditioned from the previous 24 hours of activity. The third (and last) spin of the bottle sends us off into groups of four again. This time I am in a group with Robin Bienemann (Chicago, IL), Carley Baer (Portland, OR), and Shiri Gross (Chicago, IL), but the timing is unfortunate as I am immediately called into the studio to record "Jack & the Fox." On-air radio personality James Larsen is in attendance. We have a slight bit of behind-the-scenes drama when there are differences of opinion as to who should be singing lead vocals on the track. Eventually, to everyone's satisfaction, Digger sings the first two verses, I sing the third, and Kory sings the last verse. After a couple of false starts the song is nailed on the third take and I am positively elated to be playing bass with Wally Ingram (Joshua Tree, CA), whom I feel is one of the greatest drummers in the world. Troy overdubs a little guitar, we finish off the vocals, and then we are out. Steve Hamilton's rough mix sounds fantastic.

As soon as the session for "Jack & the Fox" is complete I walk down the hall to Dan-O's studio and play bass on Craig Greenberg's "I Won't Leave It Alone." By the time we are done recording I feel that it has all the hallmarks of a classic and it is great to lay down another track with Vee, Danielle, and Dan-O.

Wednesday, June 12th, 2013

After finishing off Craig's tune a large number of folks congregate into Dan-O's bathroom to record vocals on Danielle French's song "This Is Why I Drink." It is just my luck to walk back into the studio at the precise moment to see Dan-O in his birthday suit. What a hunk, a hunk of burnin' love the man is. They clearly have everything under control in the vocals department and I retreat to the fire pit where someone hands me a guitar and I am more than happy to sing songs once again until 5:45 AM. Witness sunrise #3.

Wake at 10:30 AM. I go downstairs to find an assortment of groups spread out all over the property: in the diner, in the lobby and outside on the front lawn—with everyone rehearsing their latest material, getting prepared to go into the studio to record. I hear Walter Salas-Humara (Flagstaff, AZ) playing a power-pop tune called "Like a Satellite" on an acoustic guitar in the lobby and I instantly fall in love with it. I offer to play bass on it and Walter says "sure." I make a copy of the lead sheet, run it down with him once and it instantly sounds great. Then I go outside and hear Clayson Benally (Flagstaff, AZ), Vincent Gates (Seattle, WA), and Robin Bienemann working on a bad-ass, hip-hop/rap tune titled "Battle of the Bridges." It is a Beastie Boys-styled pastiche that has a "battle" going down between the old Michigan Street Steel Bridge and the newer Maple-Oregon Concrete Bridge. This tune also sounds fantastic and I ask if they need a bass player for the recording. "As a matter of fact, we do." I go grab my guitar and run the tune down a few times and then go *immediately* into Dan-O's studio to record. Clayson lays down a drumbeat that gets looped into ProTools and I start laying down my bass part. Clayson insists that I play with my thumb (sans pick) and within the hour I have a blister, but the track sounds great. The *very* second that I'm finished recording my bass I walk out into the hall and I'm told they are ready in Billy Triplett's studio to record "Like a Satellite." I walk in and there is Caleb Navarro (Sturgeon Bay, WI) and Charles Boheme sitting in chairs with acoustic guitars in their laps, with Walter behind the drum kit. Lena MacDonald (Sister Bay, WI) is singing lead in the control room live. We run it down once and it sounds great. The song requires three takes and is basically done, save for Tarl Knight (Green Bay, WI) overdubbing his harmony vocal and keyboard part.

When I walk out of the session for "Like a Satellite" I am disappointed (but not surprised) to find that Robin, Carley, and Shiri have written and recorded an on-the-fly performance of the song "Under the Bridge," a beat-poetry/ be-bop type of song that I had nothing to do with, other than to completely stand out of its way. I'm sorry that I didn't get to participate in the session because it's a really cool recording. They are generous and gracious enough to insist on giving me a writer's credit. I consider protesting and then figure who am I to argue? Still, I'm sorry I missed out on the collaborative process. But I could only be in so many places simultaneously. Damn.

After recording "Like a Satellite" and hearing "Under the Bridge" I'm walking towards the entrance of the Holiday and "Johnny Rockford" (Mr. Hvezda) and Troy Therrien are playing their guitars and working on a new song and they ask if I'll help them out with it. I go grab a notepad and after an hour or so we have an *El Mariachi*-type of scenario with Ennio Morricone-like overtones on a new tune entitled "The Bridge of Cruelty." We appropriately call our group the Banditos and it is whipped into shape by 5:00 PM. The three of us perform it for pat and it gets approved for the studio sign-up sheet. And just in time, because we need to get ourselves over to the Cherry Lanes bowling alley for dinner and our third (and last) listening party for the week.

I catch a ride to dinner with Chris Aaron (Sturgeon Bay, WI), Wally Ingram, and Landon Capelle (Sturgeon Bay, WI). The Cherry Lanes bowling alley is a place where time has truly stood still: the ball returns, for the half-dozen lanes that are still functioning, are relics from the mid-'70s, and they belong in a museum, they look incredible. When we smoke on in (after smoking out in the van), most of our fellow collaborators are already there. There is a feast of pizza and fried chicken on the pool tables for dinner. The listening party this evening includes nearly 30 songs that were written and recorded in the previous 48 hours. Once again, pat asks everyone who is involved with each particular track to go up to the stage and have a band spokesperson talk about how their particular recording came together. It feels a bit like an awards ceremony and the vibe in the room is incredibly warm.

After the listening party breaks up everyone goes their separate ways. I am told that there is an open mic going on at Poh's so I go back to the Holiday and grab my acoustic and walk over to the bar to find Bruce Reaves (South Bend, IN), his son Jeremy, Chris Aaron and Wally Ingram on stage TEARING IT UP, loud with three guitars and no bass but kicking complete ass. I haven't heard Bruce sing since 2006 and he sounds really great. I park myself at the bar digging the music, order a pint of Point lager and the bar starts to fill up. I realize before long that it isn't so much an "open mic" as a free form jam that Chris Aaron seems to be running, and soon guitarist Jim Schwall (Madison, WI) is up on stage, peeling the paint off the walls with his shredding, and I realize that if I felt like performing, it's not going to happen here. It's a supremely cool scene, but just shortly before midnight my gut tells me to take my guitar back to the Holiday Music Motel. So I did.

Thursday, June 13th, 2013
Door County Appreciation Night

When I enter room 230 Craig is sitting on my bed in front of a borrowed Wurlitzer, with Corrine Lee (Atlanta, GA) stretched out behind him writing down lyrics, with Louise Goffin (Los Angeles, CA) sitting in a chair over in the corner. I come in, open the fridge, take out a Pabst Blue Ribbon, and sit down opposite Craig and Corrine. Louise: "Well, now that we have an audience I guess we better get this thing together." I sit quietly and listen to the song that they're working on, but after a while it appears to me that the three of them are stuck, even though the tune is 75 percent (or more) complete. I am impressed by the take charge way that Louise seems to be running the session, but I eventually start asking questions about what is going on with the action of the characters in this song: where are they going, what is being said, what is the story and how does it end? The lyrics continue to be tweezed, and I make a few suggestions, with a couple of them actually ending up in the finished version. When the song is finally deemed "complete" I type up Corrine's handwritten lyrics and send them to Louise via email. Before we break for the night I tell Louise that I'd like to play bass on this track and she says "sure" and the next morning tells me "Hey, why don't you put yourself down as a co-writer on that song we wrote last night." "Cool, thanks." It's nice to be acknowledged. And I'm really glad that I listened to my intuition and left Poh's the night before. What a supremely cool time back in room 230 and all because I was rooming with Mister Greenberg.

After finishing up our writing session for "Call Me at 3 AM" nearly everyone from the Construction Zone has come back to the Holiday, after all of the bars had closed, to congregate in Dan-O's studio. For the next two hours, with Dan-O and Wally taking turns drumming, everyone is dancing up a storm and singing at the top of their lungs a ditty that Wally came up with, the entire lyric consisting of: "Come on baby, let's go out tonight. There's a party going on and it feels all right. Uh huh huh uh huh huh." They manage to sing these two lines for TWO STRAIGHT HOURS without a break. It's, uh, incredible. Words fail, and one of those moments where you truly had to be there.

I pop my head in and out throughout the proceedings but it is a distorted funhouse of madness and reverie, and I decide to go downstairs to the front lawn and commiserate with Charles,

Renée, Vee and the scant few that either aren't asleep or dancing and singing at Dan-O's. Hang out round the fire pit until 5:30 AM for the now mandatory witnessing of sunrise #4. Wake at 10:35 AM. Go outside and rehearse "Through These Eyes" with Liv Mueller (Milwaukee, WI) on a song that we wrote together in 2006 at SBSFII, to be performed on Saturday evening at the Third Avenue Playhouse "All-Star Revue." Also hanging out with us is Delaney Davidson, the only member of the Construction Zone from outside North America, hailing all the way from New Zealand.

Thinking that there might be an opportunity to perform the "Holiday Motel" song with Chris Aaron, we go up to Room 229 and run that down a couple of times as well. Unfortunately, that never happens, but it is always fun to play with Chris in ANY situation.

Although we didn't do much work together this year, I could write another 10,000 words about my time playing and hanging out together with Chris from the summer of 2006. After bonding together at SBSFII, I came back to Wisconsin for the entire month of August where he, his wife Lisa Bethke and myself performed as a trio at a dozen gigs throughout the state. We talked about forming a band together, but I wasn't prepared to leave San Diego for Wisconsin—but I sure have missed Mister Aaron and it is really great to see him.

After rehearsals I go back to Room 230 and start writing the lyric to a song entitled "Ready. Fire! Aim..." My time with Charles Boheme is beginning to leave a mark on my psyche. After writing the first verse I am called away and I don't have time to finish it while I'm in Sturgeon Bay but I make sure to complete it within the week I get back to San Diego.

At 5 PM I find myself down in the diner and the next thing I know I'm rehearsing with Chris Aaron and Louise Goffin for her gig at Glas Coffeehouse. I have 90 minutes to absorb the structure and chord changes to two of her tunes. I grab my acoustic guitar and Ronnie Sanchez's bass and catch a ride across the bridge and hang out at Glas until it is time for Louise to play. The venue is hosted by Anna Sacks (Santa Barbara, CA) and is packed beyond capacity. Louise finds out that she can only play three songs instead of four, so we end up cutting "New Year's Day" from the set. When she gets up on stage she performs "It Started a Long Time Ago" on ukulele, "The Heart Is the Last Frontier" on piano, and "Clicking to the Next Slide" on acoustic guitar, with Chris Aaron on slide guitar, Wally Ingram on percussion, and myself on electric bass. It sounds great and you wouldn't believe that this quartet has never performed together before this moment.

Many other performers come and go throughout the night, all of them superb. I sit still long enough to catch James Hall perform his three-song set, including his classic "Here Comes the Trick," and he sounds incredible. I stick around to perform with Jimm McIver on his set and we do a duet version of "Welcome Home" with me on lead vocal and the two of us on acoustic guitars and it is well received by the audience.

I pack up my guitar, grab Ronnie's bass, and go out to the parking lot, where I approach a woman who is getting in her car. "Excuse me, m'am. But you wouldn't happen to be going over the bridge into downtown would you?" "Yes, I am." "Would you mind please giving me a ride, as I have a gig I need to get to?" "Sure, hop in." This sort of familiarity with a "stranger" is rare in the big city, but not so in Sturgeon

Bay. This is my first time traversing the Maple-Oregon Street bridge, and the lady in question tells me after a minute or two of conversation that she remembers me from seven years ago when I was playing in town with Chris Aaron. Incredible. Her name is Kathleen Finnerty, but her friends call her "Finn." I'm delighted to meet her once again. So much for us being "strangers." And to think that I wasted any energy worrying for the past 45 minutes about being late for my performance at Untitled Used & Rare Books—this lovely lady drops me off right at the door and I end up being fifteen minutes early. Berta Benally (Flagstaff, AZ) is on stage when I get there, singing a song with political overtones that I really like. Charles Boheme is acting as MC and Untitled's owner Steven P. Link is being an incredibly gracious host to all of the musicians. The walls are teeming with classic literature and art of every stripe, and I instantly fall in love with the place. Cariad Harmon (New York, NY), Victoria Vox (Baltimore, MD), and Carley Baer perform their brand new song "Echo," and it makes my night. In my sight they are three goddesses, who look and sound like angels.

At 10:30 PM I am scheduled to perform and do a four-song set: "Holiday Motel," "Where Is Joe Strummer When You Need Him?," "Jack & the Fox," and "Welcome Home" (again as a duet with Jimm McIver).

Friday, June 14th, 2013
After my set Robin and Jenny Bienemann (Chicago, IL) perform. Everyone sounds wonderful. I can't believe how much talent keeps passing through the bookstore and I'm enjoying the moment so much that I can't bring myself to leave. When the show officially ends at Untitled, a group of

twenty-plus patrons and artists congregate in the "backstage area" where Vee and I play Beatles songs until we are all dismissed by the generous Mr. Link at 3:45 AM (even Steven has to sleep at some point). The sing along continues back on the front lawn of the Holiday Music Motel until 5:45 AM. Witness sunrise #5.

Wake up at 11 AM. Coffee. Spend the afternoon recording the basic track for "Call Me at 3 AM" with Louise, Craig, Corrine, and Dan-O. After tracking is complete, rehearse for the Third Avenue Playhouse gig this evening.

Construction Zone Songwriters in the Round hosted by James Hall at the Third Avenue Playhouse from 7-10 PM.

1) Bridge Will Bring Us Home (Carley, Robin, Meaghan, Anna, Mojo)

2) Echo (Cariad, Victoria, Carley)

3) Battle of the Bridges (Vincent, Clayson, Robin, Landon, Jon)

4) Ocean in Twelve Notes (Vincent, Jimm, Andrea)

5) Little Black Ninja (Kim, Liam, Dan-O, Haydee)

6) Summer Love (Haydee, Ruby, Brittany, GrooveSession)

7) The Way Things Go (Geri X, Johnny Rockford)

8) Brighter Day (Chris A, Johnny Rockford, Kyle Collins, Wally, Jenny, Tony)

9) Fall in Lovers (Ruby, Coop)

10) Like a Satellite (Charles, Walter, Caleb, Lena, Tarl, Jon)

11) Build This Bridge (Liam, Tarl, Shiri, Lena, Haydee)

12) Passenger Side (Louise, Alex, Freddy, Coop, Alex, Wally)

13) Be My Bridge (Tomcat, Delaney, Wally, Coop, Steve Smith)

14) 1,000 Songs to Save the Bridge (Kim, Meaghan, Berta, Jeneda)

15) Welcome Home (Coop, Jon, Jimm, Vee, Dan-O)

16) Child of the Swallows (Jeannie, Tomcat)

17) Walk Away (Jimm, Vee, Jeannie, Greg, Jim Schwall)

18) Sweet Short Life (Jenny, Craig, James)

19) This Is Why I Drink (Danielle, Shiri, Dan-O, Alex, Statler)

20) Giving Up the Ghost (Liv, Delaney, Newski, Tomcat, Corinne)

21) Cross Me (Victoria, Carley, Ellie, Manny, Wally)

22) Home (Cariad, Kim, Berta, Ellie)

23) Mad, Mad World (Geri X, Corinne)

24) Sixteen Hours (Bruce, Sarven, Manny)

25) Old Steel Bridge (Kory, Delaney)

26) Conversation Between Pirates (Liam, Tarl, Ronnie, Michael)

27) Back in My Day (Cariad, David, Danielle)

28) Transformation Day (Danielle, Jon, Vee, Ronnie, Manny)

29) Curve of the Earth (Newski, Vee, Alex)

30) Hollow Bones (Lena, Caleb)

31) Keep in Mind (Lena, Statler)

32) Water Into Wine (Kory, Carley)

33) I Won't Leave It Alone (Craig, Jon, Vee, Danielle, Dan-O)

This performance is one of my favorite moments of the entire week. It is a truly wonderful evening, with **everyone** on the show sounding tremendous. The entire affair is pulled off with the utmost professionalism, with the changeovers from act to act running particularly smoothly, and I'm delighted at the opportunity to participate so much, performing on three songs in the first half and two in the second.

After the show is over at TAP, I run into my old friend Roberta Chevalier in the lobby and we walk over to Rock's Music Store where I am scheduled to perform a set at 10:45 PM. Danielle French is acting as MC, and All Good Things, a duo from Green Bay, WI, are on stage when I get there. They sound really good. Next up, the incomparable Charlie Cheney, who asks Danielle to stay and sing with him on a song, before asking me to come up and harmonize with him on his classic from SBSFII "Steel Bridge Tender." Charlie does a couple more songs and then I perform my set: "Holiday Motel," "Welcome Home," "Transformation Day" (with Danielle) and "Where Is Joe Strummer When You Need Him?" I also catch sets by Cariad Harmon and Carley Baer, who both sound fabulous.

While I am performing at Rock's there is a wild jam session going down at Poh's where Louise gets up and plays drums. Mojo Perry (Milwaukee, WI) is so impressed that he wants her to join his band.

Saturday, June 15th, 2013

It is drizzling lightly just after midnight when I take my guitar back to the Holiday Music Motel. I have a drink at Cherry Lanes with Roberta and her friend Jac, and a fight breaks out between a very drunk woman and some skinhead motorpsycho Neanderthal. Outside, the Sturgeon Bay cops are prowling around en masse keeping the streets safe. Several of them do eventually parade through the bowling alley after word of the fight reaches them. Things calm down and I end up at the Nistebox burrito stand with twenty other musicians and share a burrito with Louise and Carley circa 3:00 AM. Then it's back to the Holiday Music Motel fire pit where the regulars are hanging out (Charles, Renée, Vee, and many others). Play guitar and we trade off singing songs until 6:30 AM. Kim Manning (Los Angeles, CA) jumps up and does a few cheerleader moves (she was, in fact, a cheerleader back in high school) which includes the highly entertaining chant of: "Be aggressive, not passive aggressive!" For the first time in the entire week pat comes out and implores all of us to "please go to bed." Twice. Witness sunrise #5.

Wake up at 11 AM. Get over to Billy's studio by noon to do overdubs on "Call Me at 3 AM." I suggest to guitarist Freddie Lee (Milwaukee, WI) to "think like Steve Cropper" and the next thing you know magic is coming out of his axe. His first take: call. His second take: response. Then Louise overdubs her organ and all of a sudden we're in church. After that Clayson and I overdub a tambourine track before a choir of ten come in to triple-track vocals and handclaps. The song is deemed finished and Billy produces a great rough mix of the track.

No sooner do we finish up with the amazing Mr. Triplett then Steve Hamilton is ready to record "The Bridge of Cruelty" in his studio from 2:30-4:00 PM. By the time the Banditos are finished the track sounds really rich—but unfortunately there isn't sufficient time for us to walk away with a rough mix. Dang. It eventually happens at SBSF10.

From 4:00–5:30 PM I walk over to the Stone Harbor hotel with Louise and hang out in Room 124 to get caught up with email for the first time in several days, as the Internet has been down at the Holiday due to excessive traffic. While I'm online Louise cuts together her "Saturday Morning Gospel" video for YouTube. It's a great snapshot.

At 5:45 PM as I'm walking out of the Holiday Music Motel to MC at Kimz Café & Gallery (from 6:00-8:30 PM) I run into Jackson Browne (Los Angeles, CA) who is munching on a burrito. We exchange a few pleasantries and then I'm off to Kimz. Lena MacDonald performs and she asks me to play acoustic guitar behind her while she sings her new song "Like a Satellite." Fun. Also on the bill are Becca Richter (Waukesha, WI), Cariad Harmon (with Chris Aaron joining her for a song), Holly Olm with Nicole Henquinet (Sturgeon Bay, WI), Sara Zacek (Green Bay, WI), and Bill Gonnsen (Sister Bay, WI). I leave for the Third Avenue Playhouse at 8:15 PM after passing off the hosting duties to Corey Power (Houston, TX).

Get over to TAP for the "2013 Steel Bridge All-Star Revue" to find that the "Young Songwriters Showcase" is running an hour behind schedule. This causes some slight mayhem backstage, which can't be helped by the fact that it is now pouring rain outside. I practice my guitar backstage and there is an eleventh-hour decision to cut some of the songs from the All-Star Revue, no doubt causing a few hurt feelings. I'm grateful that Liv and I get to perform "Through These Eyes." When we get out on stage I introduce our ballad with "here is a song that Liv and I wrote together in 2006, at the very first Construction Zone. It is still unreleased but perhaps one of these days pat will eventually put it out on the thousand song box set," which receives a few chuckles. [*Ed. note*: the song is now available on the *All-American Mongrel Boy (1989–2014)* anthology CD.] We perform the song beautifully and I relish the moment, spending most of the song looking at Liv, because, let's face it, she's gorgeous. Two minutes and ten seconds later (blink!) and it's over.

After our performance I wonder aloud to pat backstage about disappointing anyone by missing my set at Kimz and he is insistent that the main priority is for all of the performers in the revue to be on stage as a group for the big finale of the traditional set closer "Party on the Bridge," as led by James Hall. It turns out to be a truly electric moment and is captured in all of its glory by the lens of Ty Helbach.

After the TAP performance it is STILL RAINING HARD and I end up at Rock's Music store again, hosted by Craig Greenberg. I perform a solo acoustic version of "I Love You More Than Words Could Ever Say" and "I Won't Leave It Alone" with Craig on piano. Craig performs a couple of songs solo and then Louise performs two songs, including "The Heart Is the Last Frontier." Louise and I walk over to the Red Room and en route pat and melaniejane are helping a white van on Third Avenue get a jump-start. The Red Room is crazy packed with revelers, hot and sweaty as they groove to the Freddie Lee Band, who are blistering on stage. Freddie is shredding like Hendrix, and Tony Menzer (Madison, WI) is laying down some righteously bad-ass bass, but I decide to bow out with Louise and James when they depart for Poh's. When we get there Delaney Davidson is on stage and he sounds positively ethereal in the washes of his digital guitar loops. I go out onto the street and run into Andy Lubahn (Oshkosh, WI) of Andy's Automatics, who is beaming with his new girlfriend on his arm. I also talk to Sara Zacek for a bit, whom I met earlier at Kimz. She has the most soulful brown eyes, and she keeps thanking me profusely for coming to Sturgeon Bay. Charlie Cheney pops by and I decide to go back into Poh's where Liv has taken the stage, blowing my mind with her three-song set, which includes a Dark Song composition with James Hall about a babysitter who seduces her charge entitled "It's OK." They are positively riveting. Jimm McIver asks me if I wants to perform "Welcome Home" and I ask James Hall to borrow his guitar: "It would be an honor." After Jimm does his three-song set, Craig grabs a keyboard and does three tunes of his own. Afterwards, Craig and I do three shots of whiskey at the bar to celebrate and cement our newfound camaraderie. Then James performs another amazing trio of tunes that conclude with an extremely inebriated white boy rapper stumbling through the door and interrupting him in the middle of a slow, emotional, soul ballad. The sea change is instant—with Mr. Hall making the most of the moment by breaking into a hip-hop song and inviting the "rapper" on stage with him to demonstrate his skills. Unfortunately, the kid isn't very, uh, together shall we say, and with tongue planted firmly in cheek, James manages to simultaneously support the kid and subtly take the piss out of him at the same time. The kid is elegantly whisked off the bandstand, and without missing a beat, James picks up at the exact same spot in the ballad where he was interrupted ten minutes earlier. I am stunned by how amazing this moment is musically and spiritually, causing Craig Greenberg to spit: "That was epic! Top three Steel Bridge moments EVER." Mr. Hall is a Baptist preacher disguised as a musician who could convince an atheist to go to church eight days a week—after tonight I am a true believer. We all close Poh's and linger on the sidewalk and Craig and I say that we will reunite in a while, but that plan never comes off and he ends up partying with the Groove-Session guys until sunrise.

Sunday, June 16th, 2013

At 2:30 AM I walk down Third Avenue with Vee and we run into a guy and a rather buxom woman who keeps bending over and asking Vee to smack her ass REAL hard, which he obligingly does. Her companion Tony refers to his nationality as "Blaxican." He lifts up his shirt and has a tattoo running vertically down the right side of his chest from his nipple to his waist that reads B-L-A-X-I-C-A-N. Go figure. For a moment I ponder the need of writing a song entitled "Antonio the Blaxican." What can I tell you, once this songwriting thing gets in your blood...

Vee and I arrive at Untitled Rare & Unused Books and Haydee Irizarry (Chicago, IL) is on stage playing piano and singing a beautiful version of the Smiths' song "Asleep," weaving it into a medley with "You Are My Sunshine." I love it. People in the audience are talking about how Haydee is a star in the making and they may very well be right. The gal is gorgeous, talented, extremely mature, and well-mannered for being only seventeen years old.

Tonight at Untitled, Kory Murphy is the MC. Danielle French performs "This Is Why We Drink." Charles Boheme is prowling around (with his better half Renée, of course) and he has Steven Link show me "The Globe," an antique contraption that elegantly holds a treasure trove of high quality liquor. Some premium scotch and tequila appear and Charles gets up on stage with Troy and Kory to perform his spoken word composition "El Whiskey." Charles' love for Jim Morrison is never more apparent to me than at this moment. The poetry, and no doubt the tequila nightcapping the evening, have me feeling introspective and I wind up reflecting on how differently some people in the world think, act, and relate. I grab a piece of paper and write:

How to be more selfless in order to create a community of people who care for each other, look out for each other, and have a common goal in mind with shared values that allows everyone to feel like they are contributing to the common good and are either recognized for their contribution or no longer have an ego that needs to be recognized.

As it gets closer to 3:00 AM, limericks start flowing. Steven gets up and reads two of his poems. They are really cool and thought-provoking, causing Mr. Boheme to remark "Keats be damned." At 3:45 AM Steven closes the bookstore and I walk back to the Holiday for one last pass around the campfire.

I hang out on the wall of the parking lot at 5:30 AM before walking across the Michigan Street Steel Bridge, for the first and only time on this trip, with Lena, Haydee, and Alex at 6:30 AM—witnessing my sixth and final sunrise in a row. Sleep from 7:00 to 11:00 AM. Up by lunchtime. Sit in the diner area having coffee and a bagel and Carley Baer hands me her iPhone and asks me if I'll video her performing her new song "All Roads Lead You Home." I'm more than happy to oblige and another great performance is captured for posterity.

Meanwhile, the Holiday Music Motel is BUZZING with people and activity, as THE BIG SHOW in the parking lot is about to begin at 1 PM. The question on everyone's mind is "will it rain?" Either way, insanity reigns.

There is a main stage with lots of great performances going on. I'm whirling around all over the place and not really capable of keeping track of them all. In between the set changes on the main stage there are short, two and three song sets being performed on the balcony of the Holiday. Various Construction Zone performers are signing up to perform on the breaks and somewhere around 2:30 PM Coop, Jimm, and myself (aka the Come Ons) get up to do "Welcome Home."

Afterwards I get into a long conversation with James Hall about having kids and the joys and occasional traumas of being a parent. After a while Louise shows up and I end up playing bass on the balcony on "We Belong Together," with James on vocals and guitar, Louise on vocals and tambourine, Chris Aaron on guitar, and Wally Ingram on drums. It is one of the highlights of the week and a total blast.

Unfortunately, right before our performance on the balcony, I discovered that I somehow lost my prescription eyeglasses in all of the activity rushing around the grounds, and I never ended up finding them. Oh well, the show must go on.

Jackson Browne takes the main stage at 5:00 until 6:30 PM and he is in great form this year. As a good friend of pat's, Jackson has been a tremendous supporter of the SBSF and the Holiday Music Motel, headlining the first four festivals between 2005 and 2008. This time around Jackson brought his own guitarist and drummer with him from L.A. and has pat taking care of the bass duties. I'm disappointed that the threat of rain caused Purgatory Hill's set to be cancelled at the very last minute, but that's the way it goes.

Jackson has Craig Greenberg and Stephen Cooper come up and join him on the encore, before the three final numbers on the main stage, including killer versions of "Battle of the Bridges" and "Party on the Bridge." It is another highlight of the festival to perform bass duties on "Battle of the Bridges" and I somehow maintain my composure as Vee dances around dressed up as a panda bear with starburst sunglasses in a blue pajama jump suit borrowed from Kim Manning.

I am invited to dinner at John Morton's by Joe Owens and his wonderful family, and later catch a ride to the Hitching Post in Valmy where the afterparty for SBSF is going down. It feels triumphantly bittersweet. It's tough getting around without my eyeglasses after dusk but I manage to make the best of it. After passing the peace pipe with Billy Triplett, James Larson, of Steel Bridge Radio, interviews me in the parking lot for nearly fourteen minutes and it captures my state of mind perfectly: excited and ecstatically buzzed. After talking with dozens of old and new friends I get called to the stage with the Come Ons for one last rendition of "Welcome Home" before we all call it a night. The bar shuts down at 2:00 AM and I catch a ride back to the Holiday Music Motel in the GrooveSession van. For the first time in seven days I hit the sack before sunrise at 3:45 AM.

Monday, June 17th, 2013

Wake at 9:30 AM. Start saying goodbye to everyone and it can't help but feel a bit on the melancholy side. I catch a stimulating ride to Green Bay with Tony Menzer at 3:00 PM and arrive at the airport around 4:30 PM. Hop from Green Bay to Chicago, and from Chicago to San Diego. I can't remember ever feeling so fried or elated and yet when

I get home all I can do is take out my guitar and play all of these new songs (that didn't exist eight days before) for my girlfriend and wonder how I will ever get back to sleeping regular hours again?

A day or two later I read a post by Craig Greenberg on Facebook where he managed to summarize what I'm sure many of us feel about the SBSF experience:

I had talks with a couple of the other songwriters at Steel Bridge this year about how will we be able to integrate the week we just had into our "normal" lives? How you go from spending a bunch of days in the Holiday Motel "Construction Zone," a truly alternative reality, where your only priority is writing (and recording) songs, back to doing things like buying groceries?? How do I refrain from replying to a normal everyday question like "Cash or credit?" with a line like "You just might regret it..." A response like this in normal society would draw looks of confusion and possibly contempt...

In the CZ we're 50-plus songwriters sleeping in close quarters, eating, breathing, crapping music. Conjuring up and putting down structured sound where there was none before. Any passing phrase or sound can spur a song at any minute, and with so many creative individuals about, sparks are just flying around the place at all times, and it's just a matter of lassoing it in. It's a creative cocoon, and different rules and laws apply... as long as the music is being well-served, everything else sorta takes care of itself.

So again I ask, engulfed in dismay, how do we do it? But nothing comes, and I throw up my hands...ehhh screw it!"

☯

So, after eight days of activity I left Sturgeon Bay with a thumb drive containing 67 MP3s of rough mixes from the collective efforts of everyone at Steel Bridge Songfest 2013. Steve Hamilton told me that there were five more songs that were recorded, but not mixed, and another five songs that were written, but not recorded.

Mere words are insufficient to express my undying gratitude. SBSF would not be possible if not for the Herculean efforts of pat mAcdonald, melaniejane, and the staff and volunteers at the Holiday Music Motel. A huge hug of appreciation goes out to engineers Steve Hamilton, the late, great Billy Triplett (who died tragically on 08.11.13), and Dan-O Stoffels. Blessings and boons to Ronnie Sanchez of GrooveSession for allowing me the use of his bass, and to Craig Greenberg for helping to make the week so transformative. A big thanks also to James Larson and Bruce Reaves for all that they do to promote SBSF. And most of all, thanks to Frankie Frey for encouraging me to take this leap and for supporting me in the endeavor.

I love each and every one of my amazing collaborators, not to mention all of the other wonderful songwriters and musicians that I didn't get the chance to perform or write with—next year I hope!

I raise a glass to the amazing spirit and generosity of the people of Sturgeon Bay and to the magic that resounds in the walls and foundation of the Holiday Music Motel. Thanks for an unforgettable experience and for welcoming me back so warmly. I carry you all with me wherever I go. Peace. & Love. xo

San Diego Troubadour, August, 2013

TWENTY-ONE

Living in the *Head*

Hey, hey, we are the Monkees, you know we love to please,
A manufactured image, with no philosophies.
We hope you like our story, although there isn't one,
That is to say there's many, that way there is more fun.
You told us you like action and games of many kinds
You like to dance, we like to sing, so let's all lose our minds.
We know it doesn't matter, 'cause what you came to see
Is what we'd love to give you, and give it one-two-three.
But it may come three-two-one-two or jump from nine-to-five
And when you see the end in sight the beginning may arrive.
For those who look for meanings in form as they do fact,
We might tell you one thing, but we'd only take it back.
Not back like in a box back, not back like in a race,
Not back so we can keep it, but back in time and space.
You say we're manufactured, to that we all agree,
So make your choice and we'll rejoice in never being free.
Hey, hey, we are the Monkees, we've said it all before,
The money's in, we're made of tin, we're here to give you more.
The money's in, we're made of tin, we're here to give you...?

So. There it is. Should you require a Rosetta Stone road
map to explore the surreal notions within the loop-de-loop,

skyscraper citadel that is the motion picture *Head,* I suggest looking no further than the "Diddy Diego–War Chant" that appears near the top of the film. The grand conundrum that is *Head* is also a cinematic masterpiece, uniquely representative of the esoterica contained within our collective consciousness—with the added bonus of demonstrating how relativity makes it impossible for us to pinpoint or precisely agree on what exactly constitutes consensus "Reality."

Head was at the vanguard of a radical movement of brilliant, maverick filmmakers coming into prominence during the late '60s and early '70s. It was the first feature film directed, produced, and written by Bob Rafelson, who later found acclaim directing *Five Easy Pieces* (1970), *The King of Marvin Gardens* (1972), and *The Postman Always Rings Twice* (1981). In addition to starring in the three above-mentioned titles, Jack Nicholson co-scripted and produced *Head,* in tandem with all four Monkees (Micky Dolenz, Davy Jones, Mike Nesmith, and Peter Tork), who each contribute equally to the dadesque, funhouse interior of *Head.*

When *Head* was released on November 6, 1968 (the day after Richard Nixon was elected to the presidency), its symbolism apparently sailed right over the scant few who cared to comment about it in the mainstream media. Taking the inference from the street slang "head," as in someone who has "turned on" their cerebellum through chemical means—some critics believed it was a drug movie, with the *New Republic*'s Stanley Kaufman remarking "I've been hearing that in order to enjoy *Head,* you have to be high on pot. I enjoyed it while smoking a cigar." The *New York Times* Renata Adler missed the boat completely and wheezed that *Head* "might be a film to see if you have been smoking grass or if you like to scream at the Monkees, or if you are interested in what interests drifting heads and hysteric high-school girls."

Whatever your particular drug of choice (coffee, tea or... television?), *Head's* freewheeling sense of style comes from a nonlinear, psychedelic, stream-of-consciousness dreamscape, resembling the astral plane far more than the physical. The thoughts inside *Head* reverberate and resonate with cosmic consciousness, projecting a message synonymous with the vibrations of its time: love your brother, love the planet, respect all living things, and wow, isn't this a silly Box that we've locked ourselves inside of, as our love affair with science and technology grows out of control. More about the Box later.

Five years after *Head* first appeared, Charles Champlin of the *Los Angeles Times* reassessed the film and asserted that "you have to wonder how the critics and the early audiences could have missed the film's fierce visual energy and perhaps even more the film's tart, iconoclastic point of view." That "fierce, visual energy" makes many deliberate points about civilization circa 1968, and does so with candor, humor, and complete irreverence. Teeter-tottering between taking itself too seriously and taking nothing seriously at all (there are no sacred cows herein), *Head* lampoons everything that comes across its depth of field—drawing its greatest breath by deflating and satirizing the pre-fab construct of the Monkees themselves.

The film opens with a blast of feedback, while journalists mill around at the christening of a newly constructed bridge. A nondescript, middle-aged mayor from central casting begins the dedication, and—BAM!—out of nowhere, our four principals (Micky, Davy, Mike, and Peter) tear through the red tape/ribbon, simultaneously concluding and beginning a marathon. As they rush to the highest spot on the bridge, Micky initiates a collective suicide leap into the waters below. Cue Goffin and King. Call Jack Nitzsche. And by the time the majestic "Porpoise Song" climaxes on the soundtrack three minutes later, it should be obvious to anyone watching the screen that the Monkees were through pandering to the prepubescent audience who had paid them such royal tribute during the golden years of 1966 and '67. With the cancellation of their TV show, the game had changed completely, and *Head* became a sly/deliberate/perverse attempt at killing the Concept entirely, and to distance the group from their public image as pre-fabricated puppets.

Unfortunately, *Head* never stood a chance of connecting with a contemporary audience. The film sits outside of time and is very much a High Concept Artistic Statement aimed at the *avant-garde* New Left underground, offering up the Monkees as symbolic silly putty upon a pyre—to be used and abused as much as Rafelson, Nicholson and the group themselves saw fit. The film had an appallingly short run of three days in New York City when it premiered and it never received a general release. Part of this could be blamed on the way the film was marketed. In the initial print, radio, and television adverts, the Monkees weren't even referenced. Instead, Rafelson employed mixed-media promoter John Brockman to appear in a "head shot" for the film's advertisement, with simply the word HEAD superimposed across his forehead. The campaign was minimalist to a fault, you might say. And contrary to what Pauline Kael wrongly asserts in her piece for the *New Yorker*, Brockman does appear briefly in the film, although he is hardly what you could call the "star" of *Head*. In the democratic omniverse of *Head*, everyone and no one is the star, with Brockman earning the right to serve as the film's poster boy as much as anyone.

From the Monkees' dive into the water below (a leap into the sub-conscious), the film's tone is established. With one brilliant match cut after another, a rhythmic pace is established that never allows the viewer to remain lodged within a particular scenario for longer than three minutes. The cuts **can** be jarring, but that is an integral point of the big picture. Anyone who has meditated, or merely sat and observed their thoughts for a spell, knows how easily the mind can jump from one landscape to another with disarming frequency. From that perspective, *Head* serves as an incredible visual metaphor for the inner workings of the mind, subsequently suggesting much more to its audience than most films do with a linear plot and storyline. *Head* certainly works as passive entertainment, but to reap its greatest rewards the film asks that you become a participant with the action on the screen.

As for the images within the film, the free-floating montage that Rafelson has constructed is so rich that one hardly knows where to begin. The audience's perception of reality is constantly being challenged. Are we watching a film or are we in a film? Are we watching a film about making a film about being in a film? Is the film a metaphor for life itself? Reality has become so convoluted that the lines of distinction no longer exist.

Someone holds a remote control and keeps changing the channels. In one sequence Micky finds himself stranded in a desert, shirtless and parched, until he happens upon a

Coca-Cola machine. With salvation merely a sip away, it turns out that the joke's on him, as this symbol of American imperialism is "out-of-order" (exactly like the television enterprise of the Monkees themselves). Out of frustration, he blows up the very Box that helped to create his present circumstances. Oh, how the ironies abound in *Head*.

The public image of the Monkees as a plastic construct is the film's central theme, and it crops up everywhere. In the cantina of the movie studio set within the film, the Monkees are branded as pariahs and the stench of their arrival instantly clears the room. The only person left who is willing to interact with them is a fellow freak of a transvestite waitress, greeting them cheerily with: "Well, if it isn't God's gift to the eight-year-old?" "Just trying to please" retorts Nesmith. After doing a Las Vegas-style song-and-dance routine to Harry Nilsson's "Daddy's Song," Davy walks out to a sea of applause (it's the only time in *Head* that one of the Monkees garners anyone's approval). Davy is greeted by the Critic, played by an appropriately typecast Frank Zappa, who sneeringly tells him "That song was pretty white." Davy shoots back, "Well, so am I, what can I tell ya." "You've been working on your dancing though," observes the Critic. "It doesn't leave much time for your music. You should spend more time on it because the youth of America depend on you to show the way." May we please have a bucket to catch the dripping sarcasm?

From public image to personal identity, the concept of the Box is central to *Head*. In the parlance of the '60s it was extremely fashionable to refer to people by what sort of "bag" they were in. This cliquish approach is taken several steps to the extreme by pursuing the subliminal questions of what sort of Box have I placed myself into with my perceptions? And exactly how AM I using my free will as a human being?

As the channels keep flipping towards the end of the film, Micky states that "this Box right now composes our universe." How big is this Box and is there room for growth? Judging from the collective suicide that begins and ends the film, it would appear that the Box of television and the cage of public perception were a bit too confining to breed any hope that the Monkees could escape from the straightjacket of their own built-in limitations. Of course, in this particular universe, a coffin comes with the territory.

But I suspect that is nothing to be afraid of. In death, just as in a dreamscape, situations meld into one another, with characters from one scene changing costumes and linking arms within adjacent scenarios. Continuity is only an illusion and in this particular reality everything happens simultaneously. Life is also an improvisatory theatre piece, a theme that Carole King and Toni Stern's liltingly beautiful "As We Go Along" serves to underscore.

The sequence for "As We Go Along" weaves a stunning visual tapestry of the four principals wandering through the terrestrial beauty of unspoiled wilderness, only to have the song's climax come crashing down in a modern day travesty of what man has wrought out of the natural, phenomenal world. Cast out of Eden indeed. We find that mankind has littered the horizon with tacky billboards to sell meaningless trinkets, plundered from the bosom of beautiful Mother Earth. It's subtly subversive, with Rafelson employing a litany of images that deserve a standing ovation.

From that series of images we move into the lion's den of a giant factory, with a tour guide explaining to our four principals the enormous benefits that await them in the industrial revolution. "Leisure," their overseer tells them, is "the inevitable by-product of our civilization. We are creating a new world, whose only pre-occupation will be how to amuse itself. The tragedy of your times, my young friends, is that you may get exactly what you want." He later goes on to explain "to the degree that we are capable of understanding these mechanical, electrical devices as separate extensions of our brains, to that same degree we are capable of using these machines productively." Having planted the seeds of understanding to our current dilemma within the atomic age, he then ushers them into a dark room (yet another Box) and slams the door behind them. They do manage to make their way out, only to walk right back in. Or does **this** particular Box only appear to be the same?

Your mind can be a trap, and that's why reality, as a concept, keeps getting shuffled around in *Head*. Continuing with the Box motif, Peter peers through the bars of an existential jail cell, where a mystical swami offers council through the fog of circumstance: "We were speaking of belief. Beliefs and conditioning. All belief possibly could be said to be the result of some conditioning. Thus, the study of history is simply the study of one system of beliefs deposing another. And so on and so on and so forth. A psychologically tested belief of our time is that the central nervous system, which feeds its impulses directly to the brain (the conscious and sub-conscious) is unable to discern between the real and the vividly imagined experience—if there is a difference, and most of us believe there is." The swami turns to Peter and asks "Am I being clear?" He goes on to add that "to examine these concepts requires tremendous energy and discipline. To allow the unknown to occur and to occur requires clarity. And where there is clarity there is no choice. And where there is choice there is misery." The next time the Monkees get caught in the Box (it happens several times), Peter remembers what he has learned from the swami and interprets him in the following manner: "Psychologically speaking, the mind or the brain, or whatever, is almost incapable of distinguishing between the real and the vividly imagined experience. The sound and film, of music and radio—even these manipulated experiences are received more or less directly and uninterpreted by the mind. They are catalogued and recorded and either acted upon directly or stored in the memory or both. Now, this process, unless we pay it tremendous attention, begins to separate us from the reality of the now." Echoing the swami, Peter asks "Am I being clear? For we must allow the reality of the now to just happen as it happens. Observe and act with clarity. For where there is clarity, there is no choice. And where there is choice there is misery."

Without ever repeating itself the film comes full circle several times over, and in the final analysis begs the question: who *really* controls the world of *Head?* Victor Mature's omnipotent character sits in the director's chair at the end of the film with the Monkees trapped in their final Box—an aquarium, encased within a body of water once again. In *Head,* even the end credits are lampooned, with the film stock catching fire, and when it is all over the film ends with a glorious giggle—suggesting that in the end, it was all done for a laugh.

❧

Cast

Peter Tork .... Peter
David Jones .... Davy
Micky Dolenz .... Micky
Michael Nesmith .... Mike
Annette Funicello .... Minnie
Timothy Carey .... Lord High 'n Low
Logan Ramsey .... Officer Faye Lapid
Abraham Sofaer .... Swami
Vito Scotti .... I. Vitteloni
Charles Macaulay .... Inspector Shrink
T.C. Jones .... Mr. and Mrs. Ace
Charles Irving .... Mayor Feedback
William Bagdad .... Black Sheik
Percy Helton .... Heraldic Messenger
Sonny Liston .... Extra
Ray Nitschke .... Private One
Carol Doda .... Sally Silicone
Frank Zappa .... The Critic
June Fairchild .... The Jumper
Terry Garr .... Testy True
I.J. Jefferson .... Lady Pleasure

and

Victor Mature .... as The Big Victor

❧

Schlock, #12, 1994
reprinted in *Subliminal Tattoos*, #5, Summer, 1995

TWENTY-TWO

Harvey and Kenneth Kubernik
A Perfect Haze: the Illustrated History of the Monterey International Pop Festival

I think that maybe I'm dreaming... unless you were born before 1960, chances are pretty slim that you were in attendance at the Monterey International Pop Festival on the third weekend of June in 1967. There is a LOT of mythology and a fair amount of hype surrounding this hallowed occasion, with all present and accounted for placing this event as the epicenter of that fabled "Summer of Love" that went down a mere 45 years ago. When Monterey happened, *Sgt. Pepper's Lonely Hearts Club Band* had been in the racks for only a fortnight. It was in this particular milieu that a couple of L.A. music biz entrepreneurs performed a financial coup d'état and co-opted a one-day commercial concert, morphing it into a three-day, charity, music festival. Monterey unflinchingly mirrored the zeitgeist and established the template, which persists to this day, of how to present big business rock 'n' roll spectacle. For better or worse, without Monterey you wouldn't have had Woodstock. Or Altamont. Or a thousand other rock festivals.

So how *did* producer Lou Adler and Mamas and the Papas ringleader John Phillips end up pulling off this logistical improbability? The answers are all here with the publication of Harvey and Kenneth Kubernik's *A Perfect Haze*:

a glossy, coffee table scrapbook with a plethora of dazzling photographs, making it easy to cop the vibe. Were we really ever this freckle-faced, wide-eyed, and innocent? Perhaps it was the batch of Monterey Purple acid that Owsley brewed up for the occasion; there certainly is an unmistakable gleam in everyone's eyes. There are cool period reproductions of concert programs, telegrams of artist confirmations, periodicals from '67, as well as a ton of fresh interviews that sit comfortably with eyewitness observations of the day. And while a number of important players have written in their memoirs about what being at Monterey meant to them, no one has documented how the event came together, and how the *behind* the scenes activties influenced what audiences saw from the main stage. For that reason alone, *A Perfect Haze* is a vital and long overdue piece of rock archeology.

Make no mistake, Monterey was a game changer and it tickles the funny bone to learn about the delicate dance of egos that managed to pull off this historic weekend. Rolling Stones' manager Andrew Loog Oldham speaks dismissively about visiting *San Francisco Chronicle* writer Ralph J. Gleason in a public relations maneuver with Adler, Phillips, and Derek Taylor in order to bridge the gap between the L.A. "constituency" and their highly suspect neighbors north in the Bay Area. "I did not take to him; he was like a schoolteacher I was lucky enough not to have. He almost gloated like he was marking our term papers, which, of course, he was."

Prior to the arrival of *A Perfect Haze* the Monterey experience has been chiefly represented by the 1968 D.A. Pennebaker film *Monterey Pop* (greatly expanded in 2002 on the Criterion Collection three-DVD edition), and the four-CD audio-only box set that Rhino put out in 1992. Both of these documents offer up a generous amount of music but precious little context about how the event came together. Regarding the structure of *Monterey Pop* Pennebaker claims that he "didn't want to do a lot of interviews. I wanted it to play like a record. Interviews didn't interest me. I didn't want to take the time." I dig the concept, but the finished product leaves me a bit wanting. With 31 different acts performing over three days, the majority of the musicians are not represented in the original film. And the Kubernik brothers' research shows that not everything was recorded on tape or captured on film. It would be great to find out what the Paupers or Beverly sounded like or if the Group with No Name was really as bad some folks have written. There are at least some cool photos of them in action.

On Saturday night of the festival, Otis Redding asked the audience "This is the love crowd right? We all love each other don't we?" echoing the words at his feet **Music, Love and Flowers**. It's laughable that anyone would use a phrase like that today and yet in June of '67 it seems that there was never a more appropriate sentiment for its time. Flower Power and loving your fellow human was all the rage. Even the local cops put flowers in their helmets and no one brandished a pool cue all weekend.

Of course, Monterey made the reputations of Jimi Hendrix, Janis Joplin, the Who, and Otis Redding, and it demonstrated to the world at large that you could put on a large rock 'n' roll spectacle and make a lot of money if it was exploited properly. The canniest move that Adler and Phillips pulled to attract such high-caliber talent was turning the event into a charity to benefit music scholarship programs—a foundation that continues to this day. All of the artists involved at Monterey donated their services (they did get first class expenses covered), knowing full well that the resultant exposure would be priceless to their careers. Adler: "It wasn't about the weather or traffic jams. It was, and will always be, about the music." *A Perfect Haze* doesn't let you hear the music, but the historical significance of the Monterey International Pop Festival sings throughout these pages and it sets the record straight on what an important and vital time this was as rock 'n' roll came of age and had the greatest coming out party ever.

Ugly Things, #33, Spring/Summer, 2012

TWENTY-THREE

Nothing New Under the Sun:
The Eternal Life of Jeff Buckley

For never was a story of more woe
Than this of Juliet and her Romeo.

There is nothing quite so romantic, nor as great a career move, as that of the premature, untimely death of an artist. With countless examples of this phenomenon in our youth-obsessed culture (James Dean, Buddy Holly, *et al*) the Old Globe Theatre in Balboa Park, San Diego, California, is launching its 2013–14 season with the marriage of two of show businesses' most enduring tragic motifs: William Shakespeare's *Romeo and Juliet*, and the songs of the late Jeff Buckley, in a musical amalgamation titled *The Last Goodbye*.

The success or failure of *The Last Goodbye* rests largely upon the execution of ideas brought to the stage by the creative team of director Alex Timbers, choreographer Sonya Tayeh, musical director Kris Kukul and Michael Kimmel, who conceived and adapted the entire enterprise. *The Last Goodbye*'s main creative challenge is finding an original and effective approach to the material, as Shakespeare's classic 1597 scenario has weathered numerous interpretations over the centuries for both stage and screen (most notably Franco Zefferelli's 1968 masterpiece, the reconfiguration of the text into Robert Wise and Jerome Robbins' *West Side Story* (1962), and Baz Luhrmann's 1996 radical reappraisal).

While the Old Globe has high hopes for *The Last Goodbye*, calling it a "remarkable fusion of the classic and the modern," it looks to be (on paper at least) another nostalgic bait-and-switch exercise, for our current generation of theater goers and music lovers, to hear the songs of an artist who is no longer capable of speaking for himself. Going back to the mid-seventies with the staging of *Beatlemania*, there are many examples of taking a popular music act's back catalog, hanging the flimsiest of narratives upon a collection of their greatest hits, and treating contemporary audiences to what is primarily a musical revue. The idea of a plot seems to be an afterthought when it comes to such productions as *Mamma Mia* (ABBA), *Jersey Boys* (The Four Seasons), *Movin' Out* (Billy Joel), and *Smokey Joe's Café* (Jerry Leiber and Mike Stoller). Perhaps most telling is that the success of these productions proves that the audience cares little about the paucity of ideas contained within the book, and is more than satisfied by the razzle-dazzle staging of the music, with songs they have already embraced long before entering the theatre.

And that is where perhaps *The Last Goodbye* has the edge over all the above-mentioned competition. By employing the classic tale of *Romeo and Juliet*, there is a depth and simplicity in the irrational feud of the Montagues and the Capulets, and the adolescent, star-crossed lovers who fall victim to forces that appear to be beyond their immediate control. Shakespeare's tragedy is at heart a morality tale, serving to illustrate the supreme futility of blind hatred and jealousy. It offers a glimmer of hope at the play's conclusion that the death of the principals has not been in vain and indeed has served a noble purpose—creating peace within the streets of Verona and building a bridge of compassion where once there were only walls.

In a way Jeff Buckley's songs are the perfect complement to such a dramatic conceit. For who is more dramatic or short-sighted to the effects of such impulsive decisions than an adolescent? Which is certainly what the principles of *Romeo and Juliet* are. Caught in the first flush of teenage lust and the surging hormones that come with the territory, the text of *The Last Goodbye* will no doubt resonate deeply with the musical material because Buckley was an archetypal adolescent: emotional, paradoxical, and lacking enough maturity to understand the full impact of his impulses. His life and music beautifully reflect upon the action that is central to *Romeo and Juliet*. It is a match made in theatrical heaven. The only lingering concern is: can the production team pull it off in a manner that is both tasteful as well as effective?

☯

Born on November 17, 1966, Jeffrey Scott Buckley was the product of a teenage romance in Anaheim, California between Mary Guibert, an aspiring actress, and singer/songwriter Tim Buckley. When Guibert became pregnant and the imperatives of adulthood came calling, the relationship quickly unraveled, with the songwriter bristling at having his freedom stripped away. Buckley bolted from his wife and unborn child for a life on the road as a touring musician, making an epic statement of renunciation on his debut LP with the song "I Never Asked to Be Your Mountain." Except on a few rare occasions, he spent precious little time with his biological son, and when Tim Buckley died on June 29, 1975, due to the combined ingestion of heroin and alcohol, it ensured that the primary way Jeff Buckley would ever know his father was through the nine studio albums that Tim recorded for Elektra Records between 1966 and 1974.

Music was my mother. It was my father. – **Jeff Buckley**

Apparently Tim's proclivities carried over through his DNA because ultimately the younger Buckley proved to be as formidable a talent as that of his absentee father. Growing up in a rather nomadic existence in Orange County, California, Jeff was inspired at a young age to become a musician. After one failed attempt at living in New York City, Buckley eventually relocated there for good, after receiving an invitation in the spring of 1991 by producer Hal Willner, to participate in a night of music celebrating his late father—it was called "Greetings from Tim Buckley." That evening at St. Ann's church in Brooklyn would have profound reverberations: Jeff ended up stealing the show, and, by reluctantly accepting the mantle of his father's legacy, he ironically found himself in a position to capitalize on his birthright and turn it into his professional advantage.

"In a way I sacrificed my anonymity for my father, whereas, he sacrificed me for his fame."

It wasn't long before Jeff caught the attention of Columbia Records A&R executive Steve Berkowitz, who was instantly captivated by his dynamic range as a singer. A courtship ensued and soon Buckley had a cadre of lawyers and advisers grooming the young upstart for what was anticipated as a long and fruitful career ahead. A four-song EP, *Live at Sin-é*, was released in November of 1993 and after spending several months on a solo promotional tour, Buckley put together a band of his own. Bassist Mick Grondahl, drummer Matt Johnson, and guitarist Michael Tighe were recruited and by August of 1994 his first full-length studio album was ready for the world. It was called *Grace*.

Buckley's quartet toured the world for the next year and a half in support of *Grace*, resulting in half a million dollars of debt to show for the effort. At tour's end, drummer Matt Johnson announced his decision to leave the group. A temporary replacement was found in Eric Eidel, before Parker Kindred joined the group full-time. Amid the upheaval, Buckley began work on his second album. It was to be called *My Sweetheart the Drunk*.

At this point Buckley crossed paths with the poetess punk rock icon Patti Smith, who was just emerging after eight years of inactivity, and ended up performing on two tracks from her 1996 LP, *Gone Again*. Also present at those sessions was Tom Verlaine, guitarist and leader of the band, Television. Against the wishes of his record label, who wanted a more commercial presence behind the board, Buckley asked Verlaine to produce his second LP. Sessions in New York and Memphis followed, and after spending $350,000 on the recording no one was happy with the results. Buckley decamped from New York City to Memphis in order to focus on writing more songs. After three months of woodshedding he felt that he was ready to proceed, this time with *Grace* producer Andy Wallace back at the helm, and on the very eve that his band was flying into Memphis from New York City to resume work on *My Sweetheart the Drunk*, Buckley impulsively decided to wade into the Wolf River with all of his clothes on and go for a swim. A steamboat happened by at that exact moment, creating an undercurrent that held him captive beneath the waves and on May 29, 1997, Jeff Buckley drifted off of this mortal coil.

I wanted to be a singer, you know—a chanteuse. – **Jeff Buckley**

Even though he was blessed with the voice of an angel and a rare sensitivity, Buckley could also be prone to vocal histrionics and at times exhibited the petulance of a spoiled child—check out his pile-driving cover of the MC5's "Kick Out the Jams" or the ridiculous over-indulgence of his take on Big Star's "Kangaroo," which repeats the same moronic riff relentlessly for over ten straight minutes.

Stay with me under these waves tonight…
"Nightmares by the Sea" – **Jeff Buckley**

Was Jeff Buckley's death a self-fulfilling prophecy on some level? He certainly appeared to be obsessed with the premature loss of his father and wrestled with those demons throughout the pages of his numerous journals and personal correspondence. Throughout his twenties he fretted that he somehow wouldn't manage to outlive his father's brief 28 years on this planet. Biographer David Browne's *Dream Brother* utilizes the device of alternating chapters between Tim and Jeff's lives to drive home the eerie parallels between the two of them. Perhaps it is only natural that a Scorpio, such as Buckley, would refer time and again to water as a recurring motif; it is his most recurring theme—the ocean, sleeping under a blanket of waves, drowning. Jeff certainly shared Tim's reckless temperament, allegedly going as far as trying heroin on a few occasions ("Mojo Pin") in spite of, or perhaps, because of, the fact that the drug took the life of his father. Some have speculated that Jeff's drowning was a form of suicide, but it would seem to be just one more reckless choice in a life that was strewn with them—death by misadventure. With millions of dollars at stake, and the demands of the world's largest record company bearing down on him, either consciously or unconsciously, Jeff Buckley opted out of the game. And now, with no say in the matter, his catalog continues to grow year after year, as long as there is a profit to be made on the scraps he left behind in his wake.

San Diego Troubadour, September, 2013

TWENTY-FOUR

"May the mother of God
have mercy on you…"
A Conversation with Tony Sheridan

It was the first day of summer on June 22, 1961 when John Lennon, Paul McCartney, George Harrison, and Pete Best found themselves at Fredrich-Ebert-Halle in Harburg, Germany, cutting their very first professional recording. Liverpool's most famous quartet was in the middle of their second (of five) German expeditions, woodshedding six hours a night, eight days a week, at an establishment called the Top Ten club in the Reeperbahn district of Hamburg, infamous for its after-hours offerings of strip clubs, prostitutes, drugs, and organized crime. At a time when the social mores of the era were having the lid blown off conventional attitudes, it was among the denizens of the Reeperbahn that the Beatles truly came of age—due in part to their budding friendship and musical collaboration with fellow Brit Tony Sheridan. Producer Bert Kaempfert heard Sheridan and the Beatles playing their mashed-up version of American rock 'n' roll at the Top Ten club and thought they made a vital sound together, so he assembled a series of recordings, mostly featuring Sheridan's voice and guitar. A 45 rpm single was issued from these sessions on October 23, 1961, coupling an old Scottish folk ballad with a Christian hymn, dressing it up in Levis and black leather jackets: "My Bonnie (Lies

Over the Ocean)" backed with "When the Saints Come Marching In." No one knew it at the time, but it was a record that would change the course of twentieth-century, popular music by inadvertently bringing the Beatles to the attention of NEMS manager Brian Epstein—sparking into action a series of events that led to a worldwide cultural revolution. Sheridan was an essential ingredient in that catalytic flint, causing a musical and cultural explosion.

It's been 50 years since those fabled sessions in Hamburg, and Sheridan is still rocking and rolling in 2012. His life is certainly a compelling saga: from the time of his birth in Norwich, England (May 21, 1940), at the onset of World War II, he was abandoned as an infant and subsequently reunited with his mother years later. Like many of his teenage contemporaries he was deeply affected by the mid-fifties Skiffle craze in Britain. By the age of eighteen, he found himself on the British television program, *Oh Boy!*, playing rock 'n' roll on a weekly basis. In 1967 he was made into an honorary captain of the U.S. Army after touring Vietnam and entertaining the troops. In the 1970s he performed and recorded with Elvis Presley's TCB Band. Moreover, the accumulated wisdom that came from his worldly travels was reflected in his songwriting, particularly on the excellent 2002 compact disc, *Vagabond*. Sheridan eventually settled down near Hamburg in Seestermühe where he continues to enjoy life.

The last time Sheridan was in San Diego I had the chance to sit down and mach schau with him on behalf of my weekly radio program *State Controlled Radio*. His stories had me laughing for hours.

Can you tell me how being from Norwich shaped your world view?

Well, I could talk about that for hours, but being born at the beginning of the Second World War in Britain was not an easy thing. Babies should not be subjected to all that fear and God-knows-what when the bombs are going down. A baby should grow up in a slightly more peaceful atmosphere, one would think…and it was one of the reasons that we later became interested in the infectious essence of rock 'n' roll as we heard it—raw and pure—in 1956.

When we heard that in Britain it changed our lives. There was nothing approaching that before in England and it shook me up. When I was fifteen and sixteen I thought, "Hey! This is the most wonderful thing I've ever heard in my life," and "My God, could I possibly do that myself?" All that went through my mind and very soon I told myself, "Of course you can do that, too. Maybe even better." So a decision came about to do rock 'n' roll very early.

Was Elvis the most important influence for you at that time?

He was the trigger figure. But I came from a classical household where my mother played piano and was a contralto in her spare time, she was also a fervent Christian. I didn't hear anything but classical or sacred music up until my puberty.

Do you have memories from the end of World War II?

The American influence was very strong on us kids, lots of soldiers around in uniforms, but we had seen a couple of films. And the real music came from America. Even Johnny Ray and stuff like that influenced us a great deal. Before rock 'n' roll Johnny Ray was almost a trigger figure but it took an Elvis to do it. The American music that the GIs brought with them, ranging from blues to jazz: Sinatra, Ella Fitzgerald, Billie Holiday. Consciously when you are a kid if you hear that sort of thing, if you hear Glenn Miller, you hear something American. This is so obvious to a kid: that is not British. We associated the music with the better looking uniforms, the nicer badges, their way of walking was somehow a little freer or something, we kids saw that. And we got chewing gum. [laughs]

Speaking of chewing gum, by the time you heard Lonnie Donegan were you familiar with people like Leadbelly and Woody Guthrie?
    Not at that time, because Donegan introduced us more or less to Leadbelly, etc.

What happened when you heard Lonnie Donegan?
    Donegan, who got his name from Lonnie Johnson, played that music very well indeed. Donegan was a bit of a genius. He was that guy who had to happen at that time in order to turn this into something that was important. Looking back it is easy to see the connection between being born and Hitler and the Beatles. Without Hitler there wouldn't have been any Beatles. Simple as that.
    Because if this guy [Hitler] helped cause the Second World War then kids like John Lennon and others wouldn't have been so intimately part of this horrible, loud bombing thing, which just scares the shit out of you at a very early age. Life is just confusion. To grow up with the mentality of deprivation—*I haven't been loved, nobody loves me, I'm a*

horrible guy—that was very prevalent during the war years. Kids were rejected; their mothers had to give them away, put into a child's home. That happened to me. This was the psychological reason for why a lot of things went down later. Like the music. Or your personal relationships with women, they are all intimately connected to your early childhood.

The fact that a few guys came out of the rubble like Lennon and McCartney and a few others, too, the fact that we were given the gift to transform this negativity: war, pain, deprivation…into some kind of musically acceptable energy for the whole world, it was something therapeutic I felt at the time that it came out. Then we were just dealing with our puberty urges and putting most of that energy into the music 'cause the girls weren't really available at that time in history.

How did you get involved with Jack Good and the Oh Boy! *program on ITV?*
Jack Good? You doubtlessly heard about The 2i's Coffee Bar on Old Compton Street [in Soho, famous for many musical discoveries]? That's where we met. One day Jack Good came in and we knew about his show; he had a bit of a reputation of being sort of an *avant-garde* television director/producer who came from Oxford, an intellectual who was deeply and fervently into rock 'n' roll. Jerry Lee, Elvis, Chuck Berry, Fats Domino, Little Richard.

The Everly Brothers?
And then you have the others [laughs]. Eddie Cochran, Gene Vincent. I knew those guys very well.

So well that Sheridan ended up performing on a package tour with both Cochran and Vincent in the spring of 1960 and narrowly missed being in the automobile accident on April 17, 1960, which left Cochran dead and Vincent badly maimed for the remainder of his life. In 2010 Sheridan told RTÈ (Irish Radio):

And then I heard they'd had this accident and that Eddie had been killed. The next day it really hit me; I could've been in that car.

After Cochran and Vincent's car crash Sheridan's next move was to go to Hamburg, Germany.

The subject came up of going over to the red light district and playing every night in a club—not just half an hour or an hour or something, but all night. And that sounded so attractive: "What! Playing all night! Wonderful." Like 'till two in the morning or more. Because previously the longest gig I'd ever had I think was 45 minutes. I was playing with my group, I was on TV. The idea of playing all night to a young audience and being able to play anything I wanted, as loud and as vulgar as I wanted, just to let it all out. That was not allowed in Britain, there was nowhere you could do that. So, something inside of me went "click" and this was the right thing to do and you're now going over to the "enemy." Of course, you're getting back at your mother this way too, for the pain she caused you as a little child. You're getting right back at a few other relatives as well who don't want to see you going over to Germany to play.

I wasn't part of the Beatles by any means, I was just sort of the "house singer" if you like, I was a guy they were looking up to, all of them at the time. And I was asked, "Tony, would you mind playing with this group who would love to back you for the next three or four months? Can you imagine playing with this group and making a go of it?" And I was like, "Yeah! I think so." And the fact that nobody recorded a single evening, that's such a shame when I think about it. In those days it just sort of went past. Everything we did was NOW. It was just a practicing ground, there was nowhere in the world where you could practice [in public] that long and intensively every night. You could play wrong chords [at the expense of the public], sing too loud, sing the wrong melody, forget the words, whatever—it didn't matter. There was nowhere else in the world where you could do that and get away with it. And then, at the other end, you either come out being good—really good—or you realize you haven't got what it takes.

But the thing in Hamburg is that many singers and musicians gave up, more or less, because they felt like they couldn't come up to a certain quality. They weren't having any fun anymore either. When you discover that you're shit I don't think that's very good for the ego. But it certainly saved us from a lot of bad records!

Being a musician has always been a help I've found when getting along with people. You know I went to Vietnam so I did that to myself for another reason...it was a deal.

Part of your karma?
Um, if you want to call it karma, I don't particularly adhere to that word. The thing about karma is you don't need

a word for it. It's a natural balancing out situation. As long as things are fairly well-balanced then everything's all right.

And when they're not, the universe has a way of making sure they go back into balance.
Absolutely. For individuals, groups, nations, and the world itself.

A postscript: Tony Sheridan passed away on February 16, 2013 in Hamburg, Germany at the age of 72. He is survived by several children, including his son, rockabilly singer Tony Sheridan, Jr.

San Diego Troubadour, October, 2012

TWENTY-FIVE

Holding on to Yesterday:
Thinking About Elton John

Rob: top five musical crimes perpetrated by Stevie Wonder in the '80s and '90s—go! Sub-question: is it, in fact, unfair to criticize a formerly great artist for his later-day sins? Is it better to burn out than to **fade away?** – Jack Black (1969-) **as Barry in the film adaptation of Nick Hornby's** *High Fidelity* **(2000)**

On May 17, 1975, *Captain Fantastic and the Brown Dirt Cowboy* by Elton John became the first title in the history of *Billboard's* Top 200 album chart to debut at the number one position the week it was released. That might not be remarkable in the current cultural climate, but it's something that neither the Beatles, nor Elvis Presley achieved at the height of their respective popularities. It also stands to note that for a brief window of time between 1973 and 1976: Elton John hijacked the cultural consciousness of the entire western world. His name, likeness, and music were absolutely unavoidable within mainstream culture, and you either embraced the ubiquitous commercial hype that characterized his entire trip, or you desperately wished for him to disappear as quickly as possible—there wasn't much middle ground. As an eleven-year-old pop freak, with my discriminating wisdom in its earliest developmental stages, I have no problem admitting that in 1975, I unequivocally adored Elton John and his music. I bought the entire package: hook, line, and Stinker. But I figured, like all adolescent crushes, that my appreciation for him was something that would eventually dissipate over time. *Or would it?*

Blessed with a sublime gift for melody, and possessing few peers among his or any other generation, that introverted geek of a compositional genius eventually emerged from his shell, and mutated into one of the most exciting performers of our time. As an entertainer with a flair for the outrageous, and a stylistic proclivity towards being "flash," by 1972 he was dubbed the "Liberace of rock," due to his arch playfulness; he is, without a doubt, as queenly as any "bi-sexual" male within the annals of rock 'n' roll. As the 1997 documentary *Tantrums and Tiaras* amply demonstrates, Elton Hercules John is a diva through and through, with a complex or three firmly intact after all these years.

What makes so much of that candy floss bearable to me is this lone fact: when the man is on his game, his music is as deep and infectious as pop music gets. Elton John has that uncanny ability to reach in there and pluck your heart strings just so, while simultaneously getting everyone in the room to join in on one of those bona fide, block-buster, earworm ditties of melodic perfection. *"One more time now..."* He's better at it than Paul McCartney. That tour bus sequence employing "Tiny Dancer" in the climax of *Almost Famous* says it all: everyone loves to sing along with Elton John. Young Reginald's time spent as a teenager providing a good old knees-up at the local pubs in Stepney and Pinner obviously paid off. In spades, you might say.

It is remarkable, in retrospect, how much *Captain Fantastic and the Brown Dirt Cowboy* defines for me that hysterical, historical, cultural watershed—that exact mid-point in the decade right before punk exploded and its shrapnel went flying everywhere, leaving few survivors in its wake. And yet, everyone I knew who cared a lick about music at the time, possessed a copy of *Captain Fantastic*. It was a matter of cultural allegiance, a true sign of the times, and that rarest of birds: a beautiful work of art that still managed to appeal to a mass audience.

❧

Man on Wire. It is said that what often makes a star most, in the classic Judy Garland sense of the word, is not that certain "something" they possess, but rather that "something" that is missing from their psychological and spiritual makeup. As a performer it's easy to get caught in an unconscious trap, where you need the applause and the approval of the audience to make up for the lack of basic emotional necessities in life (i.e. "Mommy didn't love me, etc."). It's a classic Freudian road show that's been selling out for decades, and Elton John just might fall into that particular type of casting more perfectly than anyone else in the history of show business. If Montgomery Cliff had somehow gotten his shit together, and figured out how **not** to do himself in, he might have survived the way that Elton John has. It might be the reason we still have Elton John here with us. While his "art" may have gone soft over the years, the reason his earliest work burns with such a compelling intensity is that for a while there, he was skirting on the edge of his own psychic ledge, where he might plummet to his death off the high wire at any given moment. That's exciting to watch, and nerve-wracking at the same time, especially if that's **you** up on the wire. In a way, Elton John's output from 1970–76 is very much like walking up on the wire, and eventually you either submit to the void or you choose a less mortal way to gamble with your creativity and sanity. You can only hang out on the trapeze for so long, and then it's time to take stock and figure out how and where you want live. This was apparent by November of 1975, during "Elton John Week" in Los Angeles. After performing for 110,000 fans over two nights at Dodger Stadium, and receiving his own star on Hollywood Boulevard, he attempted suicide at his Bel Air mansion by swallowing 60 Valium and jumping into his swimming pool in front of his mother and grandmother, screaming, "I'm going to die!"

"It was stress," he would later admit. "I'd been working non-stop for five years. But it was typical me. There was no way I was going to kill myself doing that. And, of course, my grandmother came out with the perfect line: 'I suppose we've all got to go home now.'"

❧

Captain Fantastic and the Brown Dirt Cowboy was the second LP I bought with my own pocket money, earned from my after-school paper route. As a budding devotee of the mindless trash filtering through the Top 40 airwaves, I mostly bought 45s up to that point, as those were the songs I was familiar with, and singles were far more affordable than LPs. In 1974, there was a big difference between 69 cents and four dollars. You could buy six singles for the cost of a single LP, and you knew you were getting six songs that you liked. But the payoff for taking a risk on a LP ran much deeper. LPs were more likely to be "art," rather than strictly commerce. As much as I loved extinguishing my quarters on pinball, candy bars, *CREEM* magazine, and Slurpees at the 7-Eleven, I garnered even more of a rush by picking up 45s from the Drug Fair across the intersection on Columbia Pike. But as I shifted my allegiance to the more adult, album-oriented sounds of underground rock radio, I found myself shelling out nearly ten dollars for the purchase of my first LP in 1974, *The Beatles 1967–70* double-gatefold "blue" compilation of their later-day hits, and forever after, I was hooked on the long-playing format. I still love 45s to this day, but when *Captain Fantastic* came out, it was an LP I just *had* to own, and it remains one of my favorite albums ever recorded.

How many records do you have in your **your** collection that you have heard literally hundreds of times and can still say that you're not tired of? A record where you still derive immense joy from the experience of dropping the needle and letting it play through both sides until it reaches the run-out groove on side two?

I wonder if it isn't stagnation of a sort, i.e. arrested development, or merely an exercise in nostalgia. There's nothing like the sensation of watching your childhood innocence recede into the distance. I sometimes wonder if that's the rub for me when I listen to much of Elton John's back catalog, but particularly *Captain Fantastic and the Brown Dirt Cowboy*. To listen to the climax of side one (as I am doing right at this very moment) and all six minutes and 45 seconds of "Someone Saved My Life Tonight"—it's unexplainable: it still sounds magical to me (and how the hell did a nearly seven-minute song make it to #4 on the pop charts?). The ten songs that comprise *Captain Fantastic and the Brown Dirt Cowboy* take me on a singular journey: comforting, stimulating, and soothing in a manner that's incomparable. If I could explain it, I would. But its charms largely remain a mystery to me.

☯

Captain Fantastic and the Brown Dirt Cowboy is an autobiographical song-cycle, a concept album about the humble origins of Elton John's and Bernie Taupin's musical partnership that began in the summer of 1967, when Liberty Records placed an ad in the *New Musical Express*, soliciting "talent." Nothing came of their association with Liberty, except for the label bringing them together. Throughout 1968 and '69, the two budding tunesmiths were staff composers at Dick James Music, unsuccessfully writing songs for other artists, until it was decided by Dick James that the best way to sell their songs was to have Elton sing them himself.

It had already been three years since June of 1965, when Reginald Kenneth Dwight stepped into a professional recording studio for the very first time, with his group Bluesology, to record one of his original compositions, "Come Back Baby." When Bluesology called it quits in 1967, he appropriated the names of fellow band-mates Elton Dean and Long John Baldry, and Elton John was invented. This is the period of time represented by the narrative on *Captain Fantastic*.

There isn't a single misstep in the execution of the writing, performances, or production on *Captain Fantastic*. The packaging is over-the-top value for money, with two booklets and a poster within its gatefold sleeve: the cover art by Alan Aldridge is the absolute height of the form. It's a supremely majestic piece of work, and as good as pop/rock gets in the 1970s.

In a 2006 interview with Cameron Crowe, Elton John said, "I've always thought that *Captain Fantastic* was probably my finest album because it wasn't commercial in any way. We did have songs such as 'Someone Saved My Life Tonight,' which is one of the best songs that Bernie and I have ever written together, but whether a song like that could be a single these days, since it's [more than] six minutes long, is questionable. *Captain Fantastic* was written from start to finish in running order, as a kind of story about coming to terms with failure—or trying desperately not to be one. We lived that story."

Elton's producer Gus Dudgeon remarked to Elizabeth Rosenthal that he thought that the musicians on *Captain Fantastic* were the best Elton had ever played with, lauding their vocal work, and soundly praised Elton and Bernie's songwriting. "There's not one song on it that's less than incredible," said Dudgeon.

To me it's easily the crowning achievement of Elton John's illustrious career. This record is a powerful and ironic summary, serving as **the** demarcation point where the Elton John phenomenon crested—never to reach those dizzying heights again. And just because nothing lasts forever, that high water mark is beyond reproach. It's comparable to having your favorite team win the championship. No matter what happens next year, no one can take away the fact that, for that one season, your team was the best in the world at what they do. In 1975, Elton John had a championship season. He was undefeated and everything he touched turned to gold and/or multi-platinum. Inevitably, however, after a few too many victory parties, the trophy yielded to other contenders, because even the greatest of champions can't expect to hold the title forever.

❀

In August of 1980, Elton John appeared on Tom Snyder's *Tomorrow* program and Snyder asked him who his earliest musical influences were. Elton's camp reply was: "Kay Starr and Jim Nabors." After the laughter died down, he explained that "when I was a lad, there was a woman named Winifred Atwell, a Jamacan lady who played the piano. She was very fat and she used to play two pianos. She used to play honky-tonk on one and then she would go to her other piano and play very classical things. She was the first person I saw, and I loved her. She was honestly my biggest influence to get me to play the piano. After that, it was Jerry Lee Lewis, Little Richard, Fats Domino. Little Richard was really influencial because I'm a vamper. Not a vampire, a vamper. Jerry Lee Lewis is technically the best rock 'n' roll piano player, because he goes all over the keys, and hits the right notes every time. But Little Richard used to stand up and go: 'bang, bang, bang, bang, bang!' And that's exactly what I do.

"A lot of what happened to me is being at the right place at the right time. Persistence. Waiting. And just sheer fortune. I never wanted to be a singer. After I left my old band [Bluesology], I was just an organ player. I just wanted to write music. And then I got pressured into recording my own songs, forming a band, going out on the road to promote them, pressured into coming to America the first time, which is where it all happened. So a lot of it is accident."

❦

Observing artists at the height of their powers is tricky business, because it's all too easy to drop into the habit of expecting them to always be that innovatively ground-breaking, and when they don't fulfill those expectations, it can be extremely disappointing. That's how it goes with expectations, so it's best not to have any, if you can possibly avoid it.

*His fate lay in a wastepaper basket...*While not all popular music is trash, certainly not all trash is popular. But as the most adaptable magpie to ever come down the musical pike, Elton John has the amazing ability to shift with every fad in the popular music firmament as it emerges. No matter what stylistic shifts occur, EJ has managed to remain contemporary by virtue of his production choices and how he presents himself to the public. His skills at mimicry worked particularly to his advantage circa '69–'70, when Elton John was still a studio musician for hire, willing, and able, to do accurate (and anonymous) re-recordings of the pop hits of the day simply to make pocket money, and hone his vocal chops. The proof is in the excellent time capsule compilation *Reg Dwight's Piano Goes Pop*, a collection of tracks recorded for the budget-minded Music for Pleasure label in London, where EJ covers the likes of "Signed, Sealed, Delivered–I'm Yours,"

"My Baby Loves Lovin'," and "United We Stand" (to name but a few of the titles). I particularly love hearing the lyrics to "Young, Gifted, and Black" coming out of 'ole Reggie from Pinner. It's a riot, and again, he's an amazing mimic.

Elton John is one of pop music's ultimate fans, and it shows in his complete assimilation and mastery of adopting any form and melding it into his own work when it suits him. I find this trait to be marvelous during the period where he is emulating Leon Russell, Van Morrison, and the Band, as the stylistic models for *Tumbleweed Connection* and *Madman Across the Water*. The Americana affectations and rustic results are fabulous—or are at least in alignment with the type of free-spirited music I enjoy. And if he's going to copy anybody, those are certainly righteous masters to sit at the feet of. I mean they did write a song called "Levon" (as in Helm) for goodness sake.

This stylistic adaptability was true throughout the entire period of 1970–76, where Elton John moved as comfortably through the singer/songwriter territory of James Taylor/ Carole King, as he did into the glam rock world of T. Rex and David Bowie, sexual androgyny, white soul, funk, R&B, and disco. You name it, and he could adopt a pastiche of that style. He is an adaptive master of them all. Just listen to the range of songs on *Goodbye Yellow Brick Road* alone; it's incredible. And this is true all the way to *Blue Moves*, the last album he made before taking a hiatus from his band, Bernie Taupin's lyrics, and his original producer Gus Dudgeon. *Blue Moves* is the end of an era and a signifier that a new period was beginning. There were no new records from Elton John in 1977, save for the *Greatest Hits Volume II* collection of singles, and he went so far as to announce his "retirement" from the stage at Wembley Arena that November.

Well, that obviously didn't stick because the very next year he was out on tour as "A Single Man," reinventing himself as a solo pianist. The concert film, *To Russia... With Elton*, documents his historic visit to Moscow, as EJ was one of the first western entertainers to perform in the former Soviet Union.

❦

So, Elton John got fed up with the machinations around him, and decided to chuck everything that had been successful up to that point: that's when he started producing himself (with his longtime sound engineer Clive Franks) and his records subsequently became stiff as a board—with very little feel, and NO swing whatsoever. At that precise moment (circa '78), recording technology shifted into the era of automation and drum machines, and the entire vibe of popular music, and subsequently the music of Elton John, changed. Radically. And NOT for the better I might add. In fact, it got worse as the '80s wore on and the machines took completely over, with way too many sounds being triggered by a Fairlight synthesizer, or the gruesome textures of a Yamaha DX-7 keyboard. I think of it as a slight-of-hand, click-track trick, where the shift from analog to digital technology took much of the human element out of making records, resulting in the majority of recordings from this period, up through the present day, sounding stiff, robotic, and devoid of spirit.

But even when Elton brought his producer and his old band back together in 1983, and started writing exclusively with Bernie Taupin again, it was too late. The rot had already set in, and the thing that set Elton apart: his ability to be such a brilliant mimic and adapter to the changing fashions, turned out to be a creative albatross disguised as a lemming. Contemporary pop in the '80s morphed into something so synthetic that you wouldn't dare wish to spend any time with it. Do you want to put on "Sacrifice," "Who Wears These Shoes?" or "Nikita" and see how they stand up to "Love Lies Bleeding" or "Amoreena" in a taste test? I thought not, but those are my sensibilities. It may be that I'm just too old school. I need music to feel expansive, inspirational—of the spirit. And by the 1980s, too much of it felt like its spirit was being strangled in a technological straightjacket, without the ability to breathe or make an unquantified move.

After ten years of making records that sounded sonically stale (1978–88), the next thing to go was the bold, stylistic inventiveness of the composer. By the time Elton John was contracted to churn out soundtracks for the Disney Corporation, he had settled into a comfortable type of formulaic stagnation. If "Circle of Life" needed to be written, it certainly didn't need to be re-written many times over. The paydays must be rewarding, but absolutely nothing of this period inspires me as a listener. But what should I expect from the guy after four decades of being a hit machine? We all fall in love sometimes and everybody gets soft in the middle, eventually. You can't stay 26 forever and keep on cranking out "Bennie and the Jets." Unless you've got a million dollar piano, of course, and there's a gig to do in Vegas.

☯

I can't help but marvel at all those early LPs I missed out on the first time around, and had to go back and discover retroactively: *Elton John* (04.10.70), *Tumbleweed Connection* (10.30.70), *11.17.70* (04.71), *Friends* (04.71), and *Madman Across the Water* (11.05.71). Did you happen to notice that release schedule? He put out five LPs in a nineteen-month period. That's insane.

I sometimes wonder if the guy peaked creatively in 1971 after the rush of wind that brought along *Tumbleweed Connection*, the *Friends* soundtrack, and *Madman Across the Water*. It is another demarcation point of sorts. Elton John had formed a funky little combo for live performances with Dee Murray on bass and Nigel Olsson on drums. That was a fantastic contrast to the heavily orchestrated arrangements of Paul Buckmaster on Elton's studio recordings. With the songs stripped down and funkier in concert, it revealed these tunes to be what they are at their foundation—exquisite, with gorgeous melodies that have a way of weaving Taupin's oblique verse into a sound that fit quite perfectly on the radio, circa '70, '71, and '72. The gospel block chords, his unique way of voicing the harmony—it's beautiful to say the least. And speaking of Taupin, can anyone please explain to me what the hell "Take Me to the Pilot" is all about anyway? How about "Burn Down the Mission?" Does Taupin even know what he's going on about in these lyrics?

There is a soundboard recording of this trio's performance from Tokyo in October of '71 that is so exciting that it ought to be a part of Elton's official catalog. It is **that** good, and it demonstrates what an expressive singer he is, and has been from the get-go. I **love** the timbre of his voice before his lost the higher register of his range. You know, like that part were he sings "the blues-ooze-ooze" on the chorus of "Goodbye Yellow Brick Road?" Nobody sings like that, including the modern-day Elton John.

After 1971, the Elton John machine shifted to a much higher level of worldwide popularity with the addition of guitarist Davey Johnstone, for the album *Honky Château—* his first LP to reach number one on the charts.

Elton John had three number one LPs in 1975 alone, sustaining a seven-album streak where he reached the top of the charts: *Honky Château* (05.19.72), *Don't Shoot Me, I'm Only the Piano Player* (01.26.73), *Goodbye Yellow Brick Road* (10.05.73), *Caribou* (06.28.74), *Greatest Hits* (11.08.74), *Captain Fantastic and the Brown Dirt Cowboy* (05.19.75), and *Rock of the Westies* (10.04.75).

At this point in his career, Elton John was responsible for three percent of the world's total record sales. In addition to achieving seven number one albums in a row, 1975 saw no less than three Elton John singles reach the number one spot on the *Billboard* Hot 100: "Lucy in the Sky with Diamonds" (#1 for two weeks in January '75), "Philadelphia Freedom" (#1 for two weeks in April '75), and "Island Girl" (#1 for three weeks in November '75). The aforementioned "Someone Saved My Life Tonight" reached #4 in August. His incomparable popularity led him to be one of the first white performers to be invited on Don Cornelius' *Soul Train*. He also helped Rocket Records label mate Neil Sedaka achieve a number one single with "Bad Blood" in October '75, and "Pinball Wizard," from Ken Russell's *Tommy*, was a massive turntable hit, even though it was not released as a single. With three number one LPs, and three number one singles, where else was there to go but down?

The commercial descent began when the live LP *Here and There* (04.30.76), peaked at #4. After *Blue Moves* (10.22.76) stalled at #3, and *Greatest Hits Volume II* (09.13.77) creaked to #21, the writing was on the wall. Oversaturation and the times they were a-changing. 1978's *A Single Man* peaked at #15, and 1979's tardy misstep into disco, *Victim of Love*, peaked at #35. The exceptionally spotty LPs, *21 at 33* (#13 in '80), and *The Fox* (#21 in '81), demonstrated a sensibility that wasn't quite in step with the charts, and that continued on 1982's *Jump Up!* (#17). Elton may have continued to have chart hits with some of his singles in the early '80s, but all of those recordings lacked the verve of the original Gus Dudgeon years.

Such is the age of analog. Listen to the records that were produced by Mr. Dudgeon in the '70s. They breathe. Everything was so fresh then, and the productions really do swing. "Have Mercy on the Criminal," check out the propulsion on that track. Gus Dudgeon transformed his work, as did the orchestral arrangements of Paul Buckmaster. The vocal blend of Davey Johnstone, Dee Murray, and Nigel Olsson had a special chemistry. The sound they attain for the backing vocals on "Candle in the Wind" alone is beyond spectacular. They couldn't be substituted and expected to attain the same results. Art and alchemy don't work that way, unfortunately.

There is a *definite* sea change when Elton John fired Dee Murray and Nigel Olsson, in exchange for the expanded lineup of *Rock of the Westies* and *Blue Moves*. There was another shift even more drastic, when he dropped his entire band, announced his retirement, fired his producer, stopped working with his long-time collaborator, and self-produced the first single of his career with the highly ironic "Ego," which stalled in the charts in the spring of '78 at #34 in the U.S. and Britain.

After a season or two at the top, it was time to begin the descent. *Rock of the Westies*, and the highly underrated *Blue Moves*, captured an interesting cross-section of Elton's past eight years. Something old, something new, something borrowed, and the lyrics were definitely blue, with Bernie Taupin working through the downer process of divorcing his wife Maxine and having that personal turmoil reflected in the subject matter of the lyrics. That must have had some commercial ramifications. Oh, and then there was the not-so-small matter of announcing, in the pages of the October 7, 1976 issue of *Rolling Stone,* that he was "bi-sexual." At the time, that was an incredibly bold thing to do, and I completely applaud his candor. It's hard to say how much that statement affected his popularity, but a pop music career can't sustain itself with very many records like "Sorry Seems to Be the Hardest Word." It's a buzzkill, no matter how beautiful the melody and the track are. We came here to party, and you're over there weeping in the corner? It's time to change the channel.

☯

One of the beautiful aspects of hearing Elton John in the context of Top 40 radio, in those early years of the '70s, was hearing "Rocket Man" and "Saturday Night's Alright for Fighting" alongside all the other pop confections of the day. The disposability of pop is something that both Elton and Bernie remarked about with Paul Gambacini in a 1973 interview for *Rolling Stone:*

Bernie Taupin: "Well, as you've said before, a lot of times it's good to write disposable songs anyway. You can write one or two 'classics,' that will last and be covered again in a few years' time, but I think a majority of good pop songs nowadays are disposable. They're songs for the time they're in the charts, and three months later, they're just completely forgotten and nobody bothers with them again. I think that's healthy in a way. You should always have fresh material coming along."

Elton John: "With all due respect to Carole King, *Tapestry* was a great album, but the other two albums after that sounded like they were recorded at the same sessions, but that *Tapestry* was the first ten tracks done and the next 20 were done when everyone was getting increasingly more tired. She should worry, though, having written some of the world's great songs, but I couldn't work with that same line-up on every album."

In an amazing act of projection, that is exactly how I have come to feel about the last three decades of Elton John's musical output. I would love to say that his work on *The Lion King*, *Aida*, *Songs from the West Coast*, or *The Union* are just as vital and inspiring as *Goodbye Yellow Brick Road*, or even *Rock of the Westies*. But I'd be lying to you.

And yet, there is all of that amazing output between 1965 and 1976. It's really one of the greatest bodies of work around from the last 50 years. However, out of those 50 years, 40 of them are not very worthy of attention, and I wish that weren't the case. I feel sullied and disloyal by even suggesting it. I guess it's really a matter of how disposable you want your pop music to be. Sometimes you get lucky and make art at the same time you're just trying to accommodate market conditions. But how much can you really relate to "singing the blues" when your records have sold over 300 million copies? The real message of records like *Too Low for Zero* and *Breaking Hearts* is that you truly cannot go home again. And sometimes, for a kid like me that found so much joy on the playgrounds of past triumphs, it's hard to acknowledge—that championship season, in all of its glory, belongs strictly to the past.

The track "Idol," buried at the end of side four on *Blue Moves*, is the most self-effacing projection of what I feel is exactly what happened to Elton John's own career as an artist. It's an uncanny cabaret/lounge-lizard interpretation of a washed-up has-been, and it's exactly what's about to happen to him as an artist, circa '78. *And I have to say I like the way his music sounded before.* That pretty much sums it up. Cue the credits. Being post-modern was never more ironic, unless you want to follow up a self-parody with a theme for a TV show that doesn't exist. After that, in the era of discotheques, there's nothing left to do but boogie until they announce last call and kick us out of the joint. And closing time is coming soon. Real soon.

> *Oh, he was a light star tripping on a high wire*
> *Bulldog stubborn, born uneven,*
> *a classless creature, a man for all seasons.*
> *'Cos the fifties shifted out of gear,*
> *he was an Idol then, now he's an Idol here*
> *But his face has changed, he's not the same no more*
> *And I have to say I liked the way his music sounded before.*

www.jonkanis.com, July 18, 2014

TWENTY-SIX

Fruits from the Garden of Eden:
Come and Get It
The Best of Apple Records

We want to set up a system whereby people who just want to make a film about anything don't have to go on their knees in somebody's office. Probably yours.
— John Lennon (New York, New York, May 14, 1968)

Its been 43 years since the Beatles announced the formation of their own record label, and in all that time, with a few exceptions, most of the artists who recorded for Apple Records have not been heard from since. That is a real shame for anyone who is deeply interested in late '60s/early '70s pop music, because Apple was a delicious folly that created more than a few master strokes during the glory years of 1968 and 1972. It's a unique window of time where naïve, idealistic, utopian values were at the fore, with a community of like-minded freaks attempting to set up a new kind of artistic collective. Depending upon who is telling the story (such as in *Apple to the Core: The Unmaking of the Beatles* by Robert D. Schonfeld and Peter McCabe), Apple was fraught with organizational anarchy from day one until Allen Klein infamously stepped in to square accounts, and by doing so drove an irreparable wedge between the four principals. Part vanity project, part unintentional welfare line, the freak flag of free enterprise was certainly flying high when all four Beatles chose to thrust themselves into the roles of impresario, sideman, producer, and A&R (artists and repertoire).

Peter Asher (from *Strange Fruit: The Story of Apple Records*): "I think the only plan for Apple was for it to be good music, and ideally, music that wasn't getting an opportunity to be heard in other places. Paul asked me to be part of Apple Records pretty early on. First, he asked if I would produce records for Apple, because that's what I was doing at the time, as a newly anointed record producer and ex-artist. And then he later asked me if I would be head of A&R for the label. And I think the reason that it ended up with such a broad-based and eclectic collection of artists was because they came in from all different sources. There was Paul McCartney saying to sign up Mary Hopkin; Ringo talking about John Tavener; John talking about his stuff with Yoko and other projects that he had; George bringing in Indian music, and Jackie Lomax, and Doris Troy. It really was a case of them having this extraordinary power and influence, and using it pretty wisely. [People were] listening to the Modern Jazz Quartet or Indian music, who wouldn't have otherwise, and I think that's a good thing."

Between 1968 and 1973, Apple Records issued approximately 50 different singles by artists other than the Beatles, and for the generally curious and uninitiated, there is a highly entertaining sampler on offer. *Come and Get It* borrows its title from the Paul McCartney song that he gave to label mates, the Iveys, shortly before changing their name to Badfinger—easily the most successful artist on Apple's roster outside of the Fab Four. *Come and Get It* offers up a number of rarities that I had only heard about through the Beatles grapevine, including Brute Force's "King of Fuh," Ronnie Spector's "Try Some, Buy Some" and "Ain't That Cute" by Doris Troy. A smattering of these tracks are really just teasers for the full-length offerings on hand by Billy Preston, James Taylor, Mary Hopkin, the aforementioned Badfinger, and George Harrison protégé Jackie Lomax (check out his overlooked classic *Is This What You Want?*). Lomax's "Sour Milk Sea" is one of the great Beatle outtakes—a Harrison composition and production that features McCartney on bass, Ringo Starr on drums, and Eric Clapton on lead guitar. It would have sounded fabulous on *The Beatles*, making a far better representation of Harrison's compositional gifts then say, "Piggies."

The mastering and packaging are great, with Top 20 hits rubbing shoulders with novelty curios, political protests, and Hindu chants—an eclectic romp before the dream was officially declared "over."

Larry Kane Interview, New York, New York (May 13, 1968)

John, what is Apple?
John Lennon: It's a company we're setting up which involves records, films, electronics—which make records and films work...and what's it called [to McCartney] manufacturing?
Paul McCartney: Yeah, it's just a few things.

Are you the directors of this?
McCartney: Yeah. But all the profits won't go into our pockets. They will go to help people, but not like a charity.
Lennon: If anyone wants to make a film, and they go to a company, and they get shown into the waste paper bin,

and nothing ever happens! And they go round and make an underground one, and it goes round and round underground and a lot of people never see it. So, if they come to us: *they won't stand a chance*. But we hope to make a thing that's free, that people can just come, and do, and record, and not have to ask "Can we have another microphone?" in the studio because we haven't had a hit yet?

Are the days of the Beatles on stage over?
Lennon: Well, they've been over for the last two years because we've been on land. But, you never know, do you?

Did you enjoy the trip over to India?
McCartney: Yes.
Lennon: The journey was terrible. But the trip was all right.

There was a report that you didn't like it or you didn't have the patience and decided to go home.
Lennon: We were there four months, or George and I were. We lost 13 pounds and we looked a day older.

Do you think this man [Maharishi Mahesh Yogi] is on the level?
Lennon: I don't know what level he's on, but we had a nice holiday in India, and rested to play businessman.

What do you see in the years ahead?
McCartney: An endlessly expanding vista.
Lennon: Apple. We'll try and set it up, and see where it goes. Like a top: we'll set it going, and hope for the best.

Ugly Things, #31, Spring/Summer, 2011

TWENTY-SEVEN

Ken Sharp with Stanley and Simmons
NOTHIN' TO LOSE
The Making of KISS 1972–1975

Has there ever been a more absurd notion in the pantheon of rock 'n' roll than the fire-breathing, blood-squirting quartet of grease-painted mutants that call themselves KISS? While there has always been flamboyance, spectacle, costumes, cosmetics, volume, pyrotechnics, and other forms of lowest-common-denominator elements within the sphere of entertainment, no one has ever alchemized those ingredients in their conceptual crockpot quite as uniquely as KISS.

With the studied nuance of a sideshow carnival barker, *Nothin' to Lose* finds writer Ken Sharp authoritatively trawling through the embryonic days of the KISS phenomenon with a no-stone-unturned "oral history" of what went down in the nether regions of rock, four decades ago. Aided and abetted by founding members Paul Stanley and Gene Simmons (along with the recollections of 200-plus innocent bystanders, including co-founders Peter Criss and Ace Frehley), *Nothin' to Lose* offers precious little in terms of objective analysis—instead opting for a self-aggrandizing, first-person narrative approach that stays true to the Simmons/Stanley model of cocky self-assurance. Of course, this being KISS, they occasionally obliterate that boundary into full-blown obnoxiousness: that perspective depends upon your level of affection for the band and/or a tolerance for ego-driven, male bravado. When Simmons states in an early television interview (on the *Mike Douglas Show*) that he is "evil incarnate," you recognize a comic book boast when you hear one, with his prodigious tongue firmly in cheek. And yet, the guy is reptilian enough to make such a proclamation believable. That much said, *Nothin' to Lose* is a well-organized page-turner, driving home the mythology of a cross-dressing, glam-rock band from New York City who were so dedicated to making it into the upper echelons of rock 'n' roll that they literally did whatever it took to succeed.

Nothin' to Lose demonstrates quite clearly that without the faith and the financial backing of Neil Bogart's Casablanca Records, KISS would most likely have never found their audience. Bogart was a world-class gambler and promotions man, who made a fortune with Buddah Records, selling bubblegum acts to AM radio. Bogart was relentless in his faith, sinking half a million dollars into KISS before ever seeing a return on his investment. Also key to the equation were their co-managers Joyce Biawitz (who would go on to marry Bogart) and Bill Aucoin, a gay television director whose discreet sexual proclivities stood in extreme contrast to his hedonistic, womanizing charges.

Casual readers might find aspects of *Nothin' to Lose* a tad tedious, as it more than successfully conveys what a slog it is for most bands to break into the mainstream. In fact, two and a half years of relentless touring did not result in much business for KISS's first three studio LPs (*KISS*, *Hotter Than Hell*, and *Dressed to Kill*), and their entire career was on the line with the radical decision to take a band with no hits and create a double, live album of previously uncommercial songs. The watershed moment came in the winter of '75 with *Alive!*, a sonic souvenir of KISS in concert, that took them to the next plateau, featuring their Top 20, career-defining hit single "Rock and Roll All Nite."

Excess, duress and conquest: it's all here and while the music of KISS may be anthemic fun, and mega-stupid, *Nothin' to Lose* is an enjoyable romp through a bygone freak show and about as substantive as a swirl of cotton candy. You might feel sick once they pull up stakes, but it certainly was thrilling while the circus was in town.

Ugly Things, #36, Fall/Winter, 2013

TWENTY-EIGHT
Rush *Time Machine* Tour
Irvine Meadows Amphitheatre, Irvine, CA
August 13, 2010

If you were a white suburban American male, it was a simple rite of passage. On your first day of high school, they gave you your math book, your chemistry book, your gym locker combination, and the newest Rush album. All of these things were required to navigate the journey to manhood. That's why, like rings on a tree trunk, you can always tell how old someone is by what their favorite Rush album is, give or take a year. If the album you got with your gym locker combination didn't take, chances are you were converted when you fell in with certain upperclassmen, who would be highly schooled in not only telling you why an older album was better, but possibly how to play some of those spidery riffs.

    – Ward Whipple, from his blog *Everybody's Dummy*

Growing up in the '70s was a peculiar time to be white, male, teenage, and American. Richard Linklater's *Dazed and Confused* did a pretty great job of approximating the era. If you lived in the suburbs of America you took your cultural cues from the radio, and/or whatever your peers were listening to, which more than likely was also the radio. Before MTV or the Internet, how did you find out about new music? The radio. Or magazines. Or, more importantly:

word-of-mouth. If you happened to have older siblings or friends, they might be able to clue you in to what was hip, fashionable, and socially acceptable. Depending upon the crowd you ran with, you might be familiar with all the LPs by Led Zeppelin or Aerosmith or Kiss. Or maybe you ran with a crowd that thought Kool & the Gang and Stevie Wonder was da shit. I loved all of those artists. But to be a progressive rock geek? Before 1980, few of my peers at school were listening to Rush. When I first heard Rush's breakout LP *2112* in 1976, I figured it was just too heavy musically, and lyrically over most people's heads. In retrospect, it's all just a bit too obtuse for me. Is it possible to be profound without being the slightest bit pretentious? Sure. But more than half of the fun of listening to Rush is attempting to sort out exactly what they are going on about in those futuristic conceits, and Neil Peart's "dainty prose."

Ward Whipple: "Like most stereotypes, it's not an exact science. Plenty of American males, white or otherwise, hate Rush, will tell you why, and refuse any counter-claim. Geddy Lee has an annoying, shrill voice: to today's ears he sounds uncannily like Gwen Stefani. Neil Peart is an overrated drummer—if he's so good, he wouldn't need such a huge kit. Alex Lifeson is a pedestrian guitarist: nothing he's done is particularly innovative. Their songs suck, and they have no talent—that's the weakest argument right there, as quality is a matter of opinion, and there is no questioning their technical abilities."

There may not be any "whiter" place in the world than Canada, and when it comes to musical soulfulness, you'd be hard pressed to list more than two or three artists from Canada who remotely possess that African-American dynamic, exemplified by Otis Redding, James Brown, Sly Stone, etc. etc. And yet, Canada produced Neil Young and Joni Mitchell, and that fact alone is incredibly deep. Randy Bachman's pretty soulful too, now that I think about it. But when you come in contact with rawk groups like April Wine and Triumph, or singers such as Anne Murray or Bryan Adams or Celine Dion, the mind boggles at discovering anyone on the planet who can sing or play with a more "vanilla" (i.e. bland) approach to music. Well, Kenny G. comes to mind as well, but that's probably because he's right on the Canadian border, being from Seattle, Washington and all.

But I digress. There was a time in the middle 1970s, when a number of bands deemed "progressive" continued to expand their parameters WAY past that of the three-minute 45 rpm single, using the expanded canvas of the 33 1/3 rpm long-playing album as a means to express ideas that no longer fit snuggly within the confines of Top 40 radio. The Album Oriented Rock station offered something different, more expansive—at least for a while until that format became an anachronism as well, and morphed into the nostalgic hell hole that we now know as Classic Rock Radio.

For some reason the music of Canadian hard-rock trio Rush seems to have a rather polarizing effect on most listeners, who usually fall into the "hate it" or "love it" camp, as exemplified by Mr. Whipple's observations above.

When I was sixteen, I LOVED Rush, and was thrilled beyond belief that I was able to see them in 1980 on their *Permanent Waves* tour, and again in '82 for *Signals*. Those were grand musical experiences, with the type of presentation (and excess) you're not likely to ever see again. In 1978, you could hear a song like "Cygnus X-1 Book I and II" that lasted 29 minutes, containing seven different musical movements. That sort of thing is fairly passé for a sports arena concert circa 2014 (thank you *This Is Spinal Tap*). But it was cool as hell thirty years ago.

☯

However, to see RUSH in 2010? It was completely unthinkable that I would have any desire to see these guys again in this lifetime. There are a number of reasons, but it's mostly because I grew out of my adolescent passion, and just stopped paying attention by 1983.

But my interest in this ultimate of power trios was reignited when I chanced upon a 2009 *Rolling Stone* article relating the tragedies of 1997 that befell drummer and lyricist Neil Peart when his teenage daughter was killed in a car accident—to be followed six months later by his wife of twenty years dying of cancer. At that point, Rush essentially disbanded and Peart dealt with his emotional devastation by embarking upon a solo 50,000 mile trek on his BMW motorcycle. He eventually integrated and processed those tragedies.

Much of this is recounted in the excellent 2010 feature length Rush documentary *Beyond the Lighted Stage*, which will stand as a revelation for anyone who thinks they know what Rush is about. I particularly recommend this film to their detractors, because I understand all too well how easy it is, from a very superficial level of awareness, to write these guys off as a bunch of pretentious pricks. And even though I had long admired Rush's music, I had no idea they had such a tremendous, self-deprecating sense of humor until seeing this film. Catching up with the band in concert this summer also served to fill in some of those gaps in my perception.

A lot has changed in the world of rock 'n' roll since I first witnessed this band, and graduated from high school as part of the class of '82. When I moved from Northern Virginia to San Diego, California, I made some drastic changes to my listening habits, where many of the bands I dug as a teenager in high school were no longer fascinating. Unfortunately, Rush fell into this category. Sure, I still enjoyed their earlier albums, all the way back to their self-titled debut in 1974. But as they mutated their sound into a more keyboard-oriented approach in the era of MTV, mullets, and shoulder pads, they basically lost me after a series of albums (1984's *Grace Under Pressure,* 1985's *Power Windows,* and 1987's *Hold Your Fire*) that were deeply at odds with my developing interest in music from the 1940s, '50s, and '60s. It seemed that as they moved forward in time, I moved backward, and as a consequence, I lost track of them for a couple of decades. A similar thing happened recently with several of my closest friends from high school, getting back in touch after 25 years. Sometimes it's fun to get caught up with people from your past. And so it is with Rush.

I guess much of the impetus for going to see Rush once again came from my seventeen-year-old daughter, Emily, a budding musician in her own right. As she herself is about to enter her senior year of high school, she is exactly the same age I was when I was a fervent Rush fan. There is, in fact, a color photo in my 1981 high school annual where I'm proudly wearing my *Permanent Waves* tour shirt.

After Emily's mother bequeathed her a vinyl copy of *Moving Pictures*, Emily fell in love with it, and when I found out that Rush was performing their 1981 masterpiece in its entirety on this 2010 *Time Machine* Tour, it seemed as though the time was ripe to check them out once again. Part of me had always wished I'd seen them on the *Moving Pictures* tour and now, 30 years later with this *Time Machine* concept, I was finally getting the opportunity. Perhaps time isn't linear after all?

Neil Peart stated in the *Time Machine* program notes that he was inspired by the recent tours of Steely Dan and Todd Rundgren, where they played classic LPs from their back catalog in sequence, and in their entirety (that would be: *The Royal Scam, Aja, Gaucho*, and *A Wizard, a True Star* respectively). He suggested to his Rush band mates that they go out and perform the entire *Moving Pictures* album, noting that this would be a first, as the band had never played the ten-minute long "The Camera Eye" live before. As an audience member who was there "back in the day," I must confess that seeing them now was better than it was in the 1980s, even as I viewed them from the very outer reaches of the lawn section at Irvine Meadows. The technology for presenting this type of amplified, multi-media experience is so MUCH better than it was thirty years ago, and quite simply all three members of Rush (bassist/keyboardist/vocalist, Geddy Lee, and guitarist, Alex Lifeson, included) are even more accomplished at their respective instruments than ever before. As I commented to my daughter after the show, "Geddy Lee is the worst musician of the group and he is absolutely amazing."

And clearly it is Geddy Lee who is the driving force behind the visuals of the band, as Rush created three unique short films (each about five-to-six minutes long) that were played at the beginning of the concert, at the top of the interval, and at the conclusion, after the band had left the stage. These short films set up the evening's construct of the *Time Machine* and created a fresh context for presenting their music in two thousand and ten. With no new album to promote, the band decided to feature the most successful album of their career, but in addition to performing *Moving Pictures,* they also provided a wide swath of songs from every corner of their 36-year journey, without feeling the need to focus on their most popular songs, or sell a new record. They did have a pair of excellent new songs ("Caravan" and "BU2B") that they performed from a work in progress entitled *Clockwork Angels*, and I thought that the new material sounded as good as anything else they performed during the entire evening. (The set list for this performance can be found in the **Appendix** on page 476.)

I have to say I'm sorry for letting Rush slip out of my sight for such a long time, and it's great to have them back on my radar. I look forward to their next long player, and will have to be in attendance when they go out on the road to promote *Clockwork Angels*. Most likely with my daughter in tow.

www.jonkanis.com, August 14, 2010

TWENTY-NINE

Roger Waters *The Wall* Live
Honda Center, Anaheim, California
December 14, 2010

On November 30, 1979, Pink Floyd released their eleventh studio album titled *The Wall*. To date, it has sold in excess of 23 million units worldwide.

Formed in London during 1965, primarily as a vehicle for the stream-of-consciousness perfection of singer/songwriter/guitarist Syd Barrett, the Pink Floyd also included bassist Roger Waters, keyboardist Richard Wright, and drummer Nick Mason. After Barrett left the quartet in 1968, guitarist/vocalist David Gilmour stepped in and the group swung a hard left turn into a zone of self-indulgence (i.e. over-extended space jammage) with twelve, fifteen and twenty-minute rambles typifying the era of 1969–71. Never commercial in the Top 40 sense of the word, the quartet soldiered on to become one of the leading lights in the British progressive rock movement of the 1970s. They maintained just enough box office appeal to retain record company support: being allowed to mature at their own pace as composers, managing the gradual ascent into master status through a series of recording projects and world tours. It was a long-term investment that is largely unheard of in today's music industry. This organic germination period allowed for the development of several masterpieces including the undeniably perfect *Dark Side of the Moon* in 1973, followed in 1975 by the arguably more accomplished *Wish You Were Here.*

When *The Wall* came out I was a sophomore in high school living in the suburbs of Northern Virginia, contemplating another harsh winter in a brutally bland landscape—which in hindsight is probably why I deeply related to the pessimistic musings of the Floyd so well. I had been listening to *Animals* (on vinyl, eight-track, and cassette) since it was released at the beginning of 1977 (it's still my all-time favorite Floyd LP) and after two-and-a-half years of playing catch-up with the afore-mentioned *Dark Side of the Moon* and *Wish You Were Here*, I was impatiently primed for some fresh Floyd. Based on the sales figures, I clearly wasn't alone in the anticipation.

In those grand old days before the Internet, exchanging grass roots information was *way* more of a challenge than it is today. It did, however, allow for many places to retain their provincial charm. Circa '79, my grapevine regarding rock 'n' roll came primarily through the twin pipelines of FM radio (thank you DC 101, WAVA-FM and WHFS-FM) and the monthly issues of *CREEM* and *Circus* magazine that I purchased religiously at my local Drug Fair or 7-Eleven. I also hung out incessantly at every single record store I had any sort of access to, including, but not limited to, Penguin Feather, the Rainbow Tree, Waxie Maxie's, and Giant Music.

The first day of December began a month-long vacation from the academic responsibilities of my year-round school calendar, and the very next day it snowed several inches— the *exact* week *The Wall* hit the stores. But I was determined. Resolute. Having no transport of my own, it appeared that my only recourse was to walk several miles through the snow, with every penny I possessed, and make my way to the Waxie Maxie's record store in Woodbridge. I had waited 30 interminable months for this record and I wasn't about to let a little snow, or the possibility of frostbite, get in my way. Incredibly, I had no way of knowing then (when I finally made it back across the tundra with my treasure in tow), that 30 years on—millions of fans, including myself, would still be listening to this masterpiece of a recording.

I spent the entire month of December, every single day, soaking up all four sides of this double LP opus in sequence, repeatedly trying in vain to wrap my head around the information contained in the grooves and drizzled on the sleeves of the cover art. I peeled off the clear plastic "PINK FLOYD THE WALL" sticker from the outer shrink-wrapping and applied it directly to the front cover, in order to retain the effect of graffiti after opening the package—I wanted the writing to stay on *The Wall*. I listened and I stared at it. I contemplated it. It stared back. And no matter how much time I spent with it that winter, the piece remained an enigma. At least until I heard Roger Waters explain much of the back story on Jim Ladd's syndicated *Innerview* radio program later in the season.

It wasn't long before I spied in one of my periodicals that Pink Floyd would be touring *The Wall* in North America in February of 1980. The only snag was that they would be performing exclusively in New York and Los Angeles. New York! How the hell was I going to get to Nassau, New York, from Northern Virginia? My parents would never have allowed such a thing, and I found myself scheming about how I could hitchhike, or grab a train, or *somehow* get myself up to the Nassau Coliseum. I was obsessed with seeing this performance, and yet I knew in my heart it was completely beyond my means to travel across four states to make an 800-mile roundtrip by myself at age fifteen. And then there was the not-so-small matter of getting a ticket to the show. It was a big enough challenge at home to gain permission to see rock 'n' roll concerts 36 miles away at the Capital Centre in Landover, Maryland—there was NO way I was going to see Pink Floyd in New York.

But hey, I'm not complaining, because over the decades I have been blessed beyond measure to witness thousands of historic performances. And yet, there are always those few exceptions that somehow managed to "get away."

Well, three decades on, in what was the 52nd and last U.S. performance of Roger Waters' current world tour, I managed to see a live performance of *The Wall*! It wasn't Pink Floyd, and it wasn't 1980, but we actually live in a time where the technology has *finally* caught up to the vision and imagination of Mr. Waters, and I have to say that it was, without a doubt, an absolutely mind-blowing experience.

The Wall may very well be the ultimate contemporary artistic expression of anti-war protest. When Waters first conceived of the piece, it started out as a metaphorical continuation of the themes and the personal demons that had plagued his psyche for as long as he had been in the public eye. Water's father, Eric, was a soldier in the British Army who died in combat in Anzio, Italy, in January of 1944. Waters was four months old when he lost his dad, and the anguish and loss that he experienced from never knowing him has been expressed time and again throughout his work. It is that rage and sense of loss that is central to the story of *The Wall*. Ostensibly inspired by the schizo-phrenic deterioration of founding member Syd Barrett, as well as by a general disgust of the more "boorish" members of Pink Floyd's audience, Waters imagined putting a physical wall between himself and the audience—creating a performance art piece that isn't so much a rock 'n' roll concept record as much as it is a meditation on the state of the human condition. A burned-out, beyond-jaded rock star allows his sanity to slip after shutting himself off from anything beautiful in the world. The indignities mount brick-by-brick into a rationale of self-preservation and delusion. The protagonist Pink suffers the fate of a suffocating mother (due, in part, to the absentee father) and is berated and brainwashed into subservience by a totalitarian school system. Oppressed and betrayed by an uncaring wife (somehow mirroring the mother figure), Pink reacts to each of these wounds by cutting himself off from the world at large, and retreating to an inner sanctum of self-protection. At this point, mental collapse is inevitable. Breakthrough or breakdown appear to be Pink's only options.

FEAR BUILDS WALLS

Just as Roger Waters and his Pink Floyd band mates were creating *The Wall*, the group itself was imploding. Keyboardist Richard Wright was ousted and reduced to the status of a paid sideman, as Waters honed his neurotic, control freak nature to the point of tyranny. Ultimately, *The Wall's* commercial success confirmed what Waters already suspected—as the primary architect of *The Wall*, and all the lyrical content on *Dark Side of the Moon*, *Wish You Were Here*, and *Animals*, he felt that he had artistically outgrown Pink Floyd and that it was time to retire the moniker and move on. After one last fractious LP, 1983's *The Final Cut* (which is really sides five and six of *The Wall*), Waters announced that he was leaving the group, believing that with his departure, Pink Floyd would roll over and succumb to a passively honorable death. "Not so" said guitarist David Gilmour and drummer Nick Mason, who eventually re-united with Rick Wright and decided to continue on as "Pink Floyd" without him—an act that Waters considered no less than high treason. Through legal channels, Waters attempted to stop the trio from using the lucrative brand name—but failed.

Waters and Gilmour are the perfect complementary archetypes to one another, with Waters the anal-lytical Virgo of precision and vision (Mr. Left Brain), and Gilmour the deeply intuitive, emotional, psychic Pisces (Mr. Right Brain). Throughout the remainder of the '80s and '90s, the two of them took pot shots at one another in the press as Waters commenced his solo career and "Pink Floyd" continued on without him. Waters would later comment that for Pink Floyd to write, record and tour without him was akin to the Beatles going into a recording studio without John Lennon and still calling themselves the Beatles. As Waters told Sylvie Simmons in her excellent piece for *Mojo* ("Troubles Behind *The Wall*, December 1999), "I didn't decide that the band would have to die. I expressed my view that that would have been the best thing. I would be distressed if Paul McCartney and Ringo Starr made records and went on the road calling themselves the Beatles. If John Lennon's not in it, it's sacrilegious. I don't want to put words into Dave's mouth, but from what I've read, I have a suspicion his view would be that a lot of people would hold the view that it wasn't OK to go on calling the band Pink Floyd when Syd ceased to function. The body of work that the four of us produced together post-Syd has some of that connection to the same things that the Beatles' work has a connection to, and that, for me, makes Pink Floyd important. And to continue with Gilmour and Mason, getting in a whole bunch of other people to write the material, seems to me an insult to the work that came before. And that's why I wanted the name to retire." Two more "Pink Floyd" studio albums followed (1987's *A Momentary Lapse of Reason* and 1994's *The Division Bell*), with Waters pronouncing them a "fair forgery." It became an artistic stalemate where the fans were the real losers in this battle of egos.

So then, imagine everyone's surprise after decades of bickering, that these same four gentlemen would get up on stage together and perform in London's Hyde Park, at the Live 8 concert on July 2, 2005. A truce had been reached to support a worthy cause, but everyone involved went to great lengths to assure that this was strictly a one-time only situation. "Great to see you again, now bugger off." Sadly, that fate was guaranteed when Rick Wright passed away on September 15, 2008.

However, a different sort of miracle occurred on July 10, 2010 in London, when Gilmour asked Waters to perform with him for a charity event supporting the Hoping Foundation (Hope and Optimism for Palestinians in the Next Generation). Not only did Gilmour ask Waters to perform a couple of Pink Floyd songs, he also wanted to do a version of the old Teddy Bears chestnut "To Know Him Is to Love Him." You've got to be kidding? These two warriors, who had been at each other's throats for years, are going to bury the hatchet and make light of all their collective history by singing "To Know Him Is to Love Him?" How ridiculously *wonderful* is that? When Waters initially begged off from singing the number, Gilmour responded by saying that if Waters sang with him at the Hoping benefit, he would come and perform "Comfortably Numb" with him at one of his shows on his *Wall* World Tour. It was an offer that even Waters couldn't refuse, and the existing video is a delight to watch.

Which brings us full circle to the fact that never in my wildest dreams did I fantasize I would get to see *The Wall* performed live in this or any other lifetime. Based on all the current evidence, this 2010 version of *The Wall* is even better than the original. The state-of-the-art technology of digital sound reproduction, lighting, and visual projection has finally caught up to Waters' vision of the piece. The props, the staging, the unique spectacle of having a brick wall engulf the stage over the course of 90 minutes is without parallel in the history of rock 'n' roll. And after 30 years of maturation and working through his issues of loss, abandonment, and anger at the powers that be for the senseless wars they continue to create, *The Wall* has become less a personal expression of agony and more a universal contemplation of the boat that the entire human race is rocking in together. The visual ideas contained within this new presentation of *The Wall* run deeper still as it rams home the insane misery that the acts of war cause to every sentient member of our planet, not to mention the damage it causes our ever-loving Mother Earth. In the final tally, it demands that we change our collective course of action and be willing to drop our walls of protection, so that we might become vulnerable enough to learn the art of love and open up respectful communication with all beings.

When I was fifteen, I totally related to the message of alienation and loss that is central to *The Wall*. But as we have all matured over the past three decades, so has the message that Roger Waters brings to his revamped and revitalized masterpiece. "New and improved" doesn't begin to do the work justice. Again, no one in the history of rock 'n' roll has ever staged a touring production as impressive in its scope as this version of *The Wall*—and I seriously doubt that anyone ever will.

Hats off and much appreciation to Roger, Dave, Rick, Nick, co-producers Bob Ezrin and James Gutherie, conductor Michael Kamen, and all who were involved in creating this work for the ages.

☯

Every gun that is made, every warship launched, every rocket fired, signifies in the final sense A THEFT from those who hunger and are not fed—those who are cold and are not clothed.
— **Dwight D. Eisenhower (1890–1969)**

☯

P.S. These are the songs that played over the PA immediately preceding the performance—no doubt hand-picked by Waters himself: "Mother," *John Lennon*; "Masters of War," *Bob Dylan*; "A Change Is Gonna Come," *Sam Cooke*; "Imagine," *John Lennon*; "Strange Fruit," *Billie Holiday*; "People Get Ready," *the Impressions*.

www.jonkanis.com, December 15, 2010

1) Outside the Wall
2) In the Flesh?
3) The Thin Ice
4) Another Brick In the Wall–Part 1
5) The Happiest Days of Our Lives
6) Another Brick In the Wall–Part 2
7) Mother
8) Goodbye Blue Sky
9) Empty Spaces
10) What Shall We Do Now?
11) Young Lust
12) One Of My Turns
13) Don't Leave Me Now
14) Another Brick In The Wall–Part 3
15) The Last Few Bricks
16) Goodbye Cruel World
Intermission
17) Hey You
18) Is There Anybody Out There?
19) Nobody Home
20) Vera
21) Bring the Boys Back Home
22) Comfortably Numb
23) The Show Must Go On
24) In the Flesh
25) Run Like Hell
26) Waiting for the Worms
27) Stop
28) The Trial
29) Outside the Wall

THIRTY
Mystery, Murder, Mayhem, and Magic
Ecstatic and Overstimulated
at SXSW 2014

Austin, Texas—South by Southwest (SXSW). The world's largest music industry conference celebrated its 28th year of existence this March, and like any ambitious young person seeking to make their way into the wider world, it is clearly experiencing a number of growing pains. Astrologically you could call it the Saturn Return of SXSW. And in that precise sense you could also say that it's time for a huge wake-up call within the industry to reevaluate the role that music plays in the world of art, commercialism, information, and entertainment.

What started out in 1987 as a quaint, regional forum, unspoiled by the trick-turning of commerce, has exploded into a colossal consumer circus, with multi-national corporations co-opting the essence of the event and turning it into a marketing opportunity to expand their demographics, regardless of whether those companies have anything to do with music or the entertainment industry. The original idea behind SXSW was to provide a platform for relatively obscure and unsigned bands to expand their audience and potentially grab that elusive brass ring, the recording contract—a goal that was at one time considered synonymous with "making it" as a musician. And while that romantic notion still exists for some, at the heart of the conference there is a prestige aspect by appearing at SXSW—as this is definitely **the** place to be seen within the music business. However, with the glut of musical acts these days, what kind of absurd fantasy must you entertain to believe that out of 15,000 artists simultaneously on display, somehow **your** band is going to stand out among the field? Ostensibly a **music** conference, SXSW went through a radical reinvention when it added the emerging technological elements of film, media and interactive—where the brightest minds of the Internet network with scores of entrepreneurs and end users in the virtual world of websites and video gaming. SXSW is clearly not just about the music any longer.

As a personification of just how much the values within the music industry have changed since the inception of SXSW, the most popular attraction on day one of the music panels (Tuesday, March 11) was the perpetually inventive Neil Young, making a pitch for his latest business enterprise: the Pono digital music player and online store (Pono is a Hawaiian word meaning "righteous, the One"). His endearing presentation was in tandem with a Kickstarter campaign that had a goal of raising $800,000; in less than a week, the campaign had already raised over four million dollars (and by April 15, 2014 had climbed to six million).

Young's proposal was compelling—similar, I imagine, to when he reinvented Lionel, LLC, the model train company in which he has a twenty percent stake. "Thank you for being here today and for supporting this idea, because rescuing an art form is not something that is really of a high consideration to many of the people in the investment community."

Ever the master storyteller, Young spent the better part of an hour describing his personal journey through the recording technology that took us from analog tape machines of the 1950s and '60s, into the digital realm of the '80s, up through the present day. Young's main emphasis was on how MP3 compression technology approximates a mere five percent of the data that is contained on the master reel of most analog (and many digital) recordings.

"I thought CDs were a little rocky when they first came along," said Young, "because I couldn't hear the echo like I could on the old records and analog tapes. As a musician, I thought I'd just put more echo on [laughter]. *That* was some kind of indicator and we knew *something* was funky."

He continues: "We put out a lot of records during that time and in the studio I noticed that the big new digital machines recorded everything at 16 bit/44.1 kHz. It was a good machine, and I had two of them, so I had a total of 48 tracks. We locked them together and had a lot of control over the sound and we could do a lot of things that we could never do with analog. It was pretty impressive how we could fix all our mistakes—this was in the early '80s.

"I am a fan of listening loud—I love to listen loud. That's what it's really all about for me. I love pure rock 'n' roll really loud. I love to even hear acoustic music really loud. I like to take whatever it is to the limit and then listen to it right there. And when I started doing that with these machines it started to hurt and I couldn't do it for very long so part of the record-making experience that I used to enjoy became painful. And that was a sign to me that something was wrong.

"Then time went by and I got some better machines, but they weren't really that much better to improve it. But

I noticed when I listened to CDs in my car the same thing happened—it hurt my ears a little bit. And then the MP3 came along and that's when the recording industry really went into duress."

By reminiscing about the bygone days of analog recording, Young touched upon what had really changed during the 1990s—the actual music being made because of the shift in recording technology.

"All of the people who work behind the scenes to make records—great producers and arrangers like Jack Nitzsche and Phil Spector—people that used these huge orchestras and played live with twelve tambourines, two pianos, multiple instruments—they were making these great records in the '60s and in the late '50s. Those people were in the studios in Los Angeles playing and they were having the great experience doing that. But all of the musicians and all of those services that used to support the musicians and all of those recording studios started to die—it was the most amazing thing. This vibrant, creative, old culture started to go away and it was because of the MP3 and the cheapening of the quality to a point where [the music] was practically unrecognizable. And the price also went down and then the record company's control of what they could do with the records went away. They could no longer decide how to market the records because they made some stupid deals. They made some very dumb deals with some very smart people. And then, as a result of those deals they were convinced that they could only sell individual tracks [because it was perceived that] the album had no value. Only the individual tracks had value. So, the reason behind the LP going away was the idea 'well, it's all just filler.' Filler—the artist is really just ripping you off. The record company is just really putting one or two good tracks on and the rest of it is just crap. So you don't have to buy this. If you buy an MP3 all you have to do is buy your favorite song and you don't have to get the rest.

"So, as a guy who has been making records for many years already at that point I was pissed off about that because I love making records. That's what I do. I love every song on the record. I love every note on every song on every record [applause]. They meant something to me. They're a family of songs that were telling a story of how I was feeling. And they weren't just filler. I'm not the only one who feels this way. Now, maybe there were some people who did do what they were accused of doing there, but I had never met those people who said 'well, we're going to do eight pieces of crap and two great records.' [laughter] I mean, if they *were* doing it, they weren't loud about it.

"So then the guys at Goldstar Studio, where Jack Nitzsche used to write those great charts and Phil Spector—for whatever good or bad has happened to him for what he has done in the world—was a genius and he was making unbelievable records. **Sometimes art is on a different plane from everything else.** So, here's a genius guy making great records: they're all based on echo. The Goldstar echo chamber was a meat locker and nobody could figure out why it was so magical and why, when you turned it on, your records were so great. I went in there with Buffalo Springfield in 1966 and we made our first record and we had producers who didn't know what they were doing—they were making their first record too—so it was kind of a disaster. But I do remember hearing the echo going 'my God, it's magic.' It really is, you just put your voice in there and suddenly it's like heaven in there. So when echo went away, that wasn't just 'oh, echo's gone.' *That* was a world-class disaster. It was huge for people who cared about sound. And then, because all of that happened, Goldstar closed its doors and sold the meat locker. They sold everything. And that was the end of an era. And then all of the producers and musicians and arrangers and answering services and delivery services for the instruments who used to move around town in their little vans going from one studio to another delivering the musician's instruments to different sessions they all started to go away. They all started to die.

"Now, music is not real estate. It doesn't go up and down that way, so there was really something wrong. And what it was is we were selling shit. People were still buying it because they like music. But they were buying wallpaper. They were buying background sounds. They were buying Xeroxes of the Mona Lisa. They were buying a musical history that's supposed to be preserved for everybody to hear, now preserved as a tiny little piece of crap with less than five percent of the data of the highest resolution in digital that can be recorded today, which I like to use.

"So, five percent is the standard of the world. And motion pictures went into the digital age—those art forms, they went up. A lot of things happened that got better. Cameras got easier to use. Everything went up and music went down. Music went to the bottom. Everyone lost their jobs, that's the true disaster of this. All of these friends that I had and all of these people that I had never met who I loved anyway because they were engineers and producers, all of those people who supported our industry, they all lost their jobs. It's not a bad thing that people make records at home, that's cool. But there is another way to make records, so that went away. That was the collateral damage of the MP3.

"Now I started thinking about that after ten more years of doing this. I've been able to listen to my records and put them out. And I went 'Well, *I* heard it.' It's too bad nobody else will get to hear it unless I put out some vinyl and then they can hear it. And we made vinyl and vinyl became popular and became a little niche. 'Wow, vinyl's popular'—it's starting to get popular, and then in desperation record companies starting making vinyl based on digital files, putting CD masters on vinyl because they thought vinyl was a collectable. They weren't putting it out because of the sound, they were putting it out because it sold. And vinyl was kind of a sham: you were buying a collectable fashion statement.

"So, that's just a little background from my life and where I'm coming from. To think about all those people who don't have jobs and all that music that's out there that was created during that time that is now circulated at five percent of what it's capable of being circulated at. And young people growing up today whose bodies are wide awake, they're sensitive and they can hear. They get something that lets them recognize it. They can identify the name of the song and learn the melody from listening to this. But inside their soul they're just not getting what we got 'cause there's just nothing there for them. The human body is so sensitive—it's a beautiful thing. Whatever you believe about where things come from, the human body is unbelievable. It's so sensitive and when you give it something, it loves it. You give it good food, it grows—it's nourished. And when you give it good input it loves it. When it sees great art it feels good, and we all are like that. So, with our music, we were deprived, getting a miniscule 1/20th of what we were capable of getting what we used to listen to. After one or two listens you got it, you heard it, your body was not getting anything new after that, you've already figured it out: 'that's it, okay I recognize it.' Music even changed a little bit and 'got cool.' Instead of being soulful, which it still is—I love a lot of artists today, I'm not putting them down—I'm just saying that music adapted. It became beat heavy and it became ripe for what the media was selling. It became smart, clever. *Tricky.*

"So, here we are. I started thinking it might be a good idea to try and do something about it. I'd heard all the formats: CDs, MP3s, vinyl, cassettes, eight-tracks, DVD-Audio. And you're probably listening to a lot of MP3s and they're very convenient. And what we've decided to do is to come out with a new system that was not a format, had no rules. Respected the art.

"Respected what the artist was trying to do. Did everything that it could to give you what the artist gave, so that you get the feel. Not just what the artist intended you to feel, but actually what the artist did. And that is what Pono is. Pono plays back whatever the artist decided to do, or the artist's producer decided to do. All of the formats: 44.1 kHz, 48 kHz, 88.2 kHz, 96 kHz, 176.4 kHz, 192 kHz—all of them are all played back on Pono, just like the artist made them. The artist makes the decision. Before the artist makes the decision to put something on a certain resolution level, and then to put something on a CD it has to get 'dummied down' to the resolution of a CD. That's what happened no matter what the artist did. So artists started going 'why the hell should I do that when it's going to go down anyway?' But still some artists continue to record at the higher resolutions thinking that maybe someday, someone would have a chance to hear them.

"And so we started doing that. I moved up to 192 kHz. I've heard about 384 kHz, although I've never heard it. Some scientists say 192 kHz is ridiculous, you can't hear it, it has too much information, it's going too fast, people can't hear it and some producers say that if you can't hear it, it's a waste of time, so we record at 96 kHz. And a lot of records are made at 96 kHz—those are considered high resolution, and they are high resolution. But there is a higher resolution and you can hear the difference. That's what I feel when I listen to it. My body is getting washed, I'm getting hit with something great, I'm not getting a bunch of ice cubes thrown at me, it's water. It's a cool mist. Every part of my body is getting hit with this thing. My soul is feeling it—I'm doing what I used to do. I'm listening, I'm feeling, I'm experiencing—I'm living the music. So that's why I record at 192 kHz. And that's why I transferred everything I did in analog to 192 kHz, so I could have 192 and bring it to you eventually."

Young concludes his pitch with these thoughts: "When a kid hears a song for the first time, you gotta remember: these are young people—they're fresh, they're peaking, all of their senses are there, their vision is great, their hearing is amazing, their physical abilities are at their peak. Everything is tuned in just like nature meant it to be. There's been very little damage. Just so I can sleep at night I want to bring back real music."

By the looks of his Kickstarter campaign Neil Young has clearly gained the confidence of the greatest venture capitalists possible: other fellow music lovers. *That* is capitalistic democracy in action.

❦

After spending a week in Austin I am left wondering: is there any such thing as a "pure" artist any longer? In centuries past artists were subsidized by patrons in order to survive. But in order to eat and pay the rent these days, there seems to be a form of artistic prostitution going on within the music industry, and it's alarming by how accepted that dynamic has become. *Los Angeles Times* pop music critic Randall Roberts writes "Gag me with a Samsung" (one of the major sponsors at SXSW) when quoting keynote speaker Lady Gaga, who is attempting to perpetuate the delusion that "without sponsorships, without these companies [like Doritos] coming together to 'help us,' we won't have any more artists in Austin. We won't have any more festivals, because record labels don't have any money."

That rationalization of corporate whoredom is the reason why many people might be staying away from SXSW next year and long into the foreseeable future. Greg Dohler, drummer with the Baltimore, Maryland post-punk/noise pop band, Small Apartments, has been coming to the event for the past five years with his wife, Cindy France, and they both said they would definitely be taking next year off. "Everything that we love about the festival is just being taken over by all the corporate stuff and it's just gotten too big," says Dohler.

"It reached a tipping point for us this year in terms of the crowds and the marketing presence, so we're not planning to return. It makes me sad because at its best, SXSW is an incredible celebration of our musical heritage, as well as emerging artists. This year I was blown away by a young British band called the Wytches, but I was just as thrilled during a panel to watch James Williamson of the Stooges demonstrate how he wrote 'Search and Destroy.' There is a magical connecting of the musical dots across generations that I have always appreciated at the festival, but this year there were just too many obstacles to enjoying the music."

When SXSW first started, Austin, Texas, was a relatively obscure college town, the state's capitol that plays host to the University of Texas. With a fluctuating population of close to a million inhabitants, Austin has, over the past 25 years, easily become the musical mecca of the United States, with hundreds of local musicians performing every night of the week in countless bars, cafés, restaurants, clubs, theaters, and block parties. The competition is fierce and rising to the top of this particular scene requires not just plenty of talent, but also lots of street hussle, and the ability to network and become well connected in a community where nearly everybody is hip, handsome, stylized and bona fide.

If you're looking for a quiet little place to settle down, Austin isn't it. And if you're seeking a moment of peace and quiet then be sure to steer clear of the greater downtown Austin area during SXSW, because you've never seen more drunken debauchery in your life. San Diego's defunct Street Scene festival at its most raucous, couldn't have held a candle to SXSW. As a matter of fact, add New Orleans' Mardi Gras to your most frantic Street Scene memory, and **maybe** you will have an approximation of what SXSW has grown into.

ꙮ

So, what **was** I doing in attendance at SXSW 2014? It all began innocently enough when Raul Sandelin, director of *A Box Full of Rocks: the El Cajon Years of Lester Bangs* asked me if I wanted to go to SXSW to film and conduct interviews for his follow-up documentary, *The Rock Bards*. Instead of focusing on a singular figure, this film will feature a diverse canon of rock journalists who were active during that classic heyday of gonzo-esque journalism, circa 1966 to 1981—a period beginning with rock's first intelligent publication, *Crawdaddy!*, book-ended by the advent of MTV. I committed to the assignment but didn't quite realize what I had signed on for, and when I checked out the official SXSW website, I found myself both excited and somewhat trepidatious. But I worked through my anxiety and decided to embrace the adventure that lay ahead.

I had grown completely oblivious to the evolving character of SXSW, and didn't realize how much it had changed since I was last in attendance (March of 1992), when SXSW was only six years old. At that time I arrived in Austin on the Greyhound with only an acoustic guitar and a backpack, promoting my first EP, *Walk Without Me*. I was touring the United States and Europe as a gigging musician for the first time, seeking fortune, fame, and experiential wisdom—and boy, was it truly humbling to discover what it takes to make it as a professional musician. Thanks to the mentorship of songwriter and musician Peter Case (whom I joined on a 45-city tour later that year, as road manager and opening act), I gained even more insight. I also spent an evening with the late, great folk musician Bill Morrissey when he played at Marcia Ball's establishment, La Zona Rosa. Bill ended up borrowing my guitar to perform his set when the club did not have one, per his contract rider. I still feel the resonance of his superb mojo every time I play.

Typifying the frenetic pace of SXSW, Bill had his five-piece band waiting for him at a gig in Dallas. He popped down with his girlfriend on a commercial flight to Austin, and zoomed over in a limo specfically to play a quick acoustic set. Then it was back to the airport so he can fly north to Dallas and be reunited with his band, playing his gig there an hour later. That is the speed that things happen at SXSW. After Bill's set, I trucked over to the Terrace and witnessed an amazing gig with John Trudell/AKA Graffiti Man, Michele Shocked, and the magnificent Timbuk3 at the height of their power as a quartet. The guys in AKA Graffiti Man befriended me and gave me a ride in their van back to my lodgings afterwards. The type of camaraderie that exists among Austin musicians was something I had rarely experienced, and I would find out over the next two plus decades that such a night is emblematic of the Austin music community. And hallelujah for that.

☯

SXSW turned out to be a whirlwind of a time with plenty of highlights and by the end of the week my feet were absolutely killing me from all the walking and standing. But, as it's been said before: rock 'n' roll is not a spectator sport—you've got to participate.

My first priority was to capture material for the documentary, and to that end I shot some great footage, starting off with a panel led by San Diego musician Cindy Lee Berryhill honoring the legacy of her late husband, Paul Williams, and *Crawdaddy!* magazine, featuring music journalists Ed Ward, David Fricke, Ann Powers, and Paula Mejia. The camera also captured wonderful interviews with former *CREEM* editors Billy Altman and John Morthland; rock journalist for the *Austin Chronicle* Tim Stegall; *Lincoln Journal Star* arts and entertainment writer Kent Wolgamott; and Lester Bangs biographer (*Let It Blurt*) Jim DeRogatis. Intelligent, insightful and humorous conversations were also captured with Ward and Mejia.

There was a fun panel titled *It's Only Rock & Roll: Fifty Years of the Rolling Stones*, that featured John Doe (of X), Ian McLagan (Small Faces, the Faces, the Rolling Stones), and the MC5's Wayne Kramer. Their stories were highly entertaining.

I met dozens of compelling personalities along the way and heard some truly amazing music throughout the week. Musician Jim Basnight (who is producing a Sonny Boy Williamson documentary) was a joy to hang out with as well as Mark Bjerke, a promoter for the *We Fest* country and western festival that happens every August out of Detroit Lakes, Minnesota. Plenty of people were at SXSW promoting their latest projects: I ran into photographer Bob Gruen, who was signing copies of his *Rock Seen* book, and I spoke at length with the legendary Robert Gordon who was on hand to promote his latest tome *Respect Yourself: Stax Records and the Soul Explosion*. He generously inscribed my copy with: "For Jon—Great films in the Stax Museum!" referring to the five shorts on permanent display that I co-directed in 2004 with David Peck.

There was an opportunity to reunite with many of my fellow musicians and songwriters from the Sturgeon Bay, Wisconsin, Steel Bridge Songfest community who were performing at SXSW this year: pat mAcdonald and melaniejane from Purgatory Hill; Liv Mueller (who just relocated to Austin from Milwaukee); Ruby James, Stephen Cooper, Vee Sonnets, Gregory Roteik, and Zach Vogel of WIFEE and the Huzzband; Dan-O Stoffels, Ellie Maybe and Geri Micheva of the Geri X band; Brett Newski, Walter Salas-Humara, and Alex Mitchard were also on hand playing music and supporting their friends.

Every day and evening had something truly special going on: Tuesday night it was seeing San Diego's Octagrape at the Lit Lounge Upstairs. Bassist Otis Barthoulameu, aka "O" of fluf fame, sat next to me on the flight out to Austin, regaling me with one hilarious road story after another. Right before Octagrape was a rocking trio from San Antonio, Texas, called the Rich Hands. Between bands I dashed across Sixth Street to the venue Friends for their *Sounds from Chile* showcase and caught the amazing Nano Stern, a folk singer from Santiago who completely captivated the room. I then drove south on Congress Avenue across the Colorado River to catch the Steel Bridge reunion at the Swollen Circus show at the Continental Club.

Wednesday night Cindy Lee Berryhill's five-piece Garage Orchestra performed a tight set of great new songs at Esther's Follies. Thursday night Louise Goffin was at the Paramount Theater (with bassist Tom Freund and percussionist Elsa Chahin) performing a fabulous eight-song set of material from her yet-to-be released album *Songs from the Mine*. Friday it was back to the Paramount to see a truly once-in-a-lifetime experience: the official SXSW tribute to the recently departed Lou Reed, who passed away on October 27, 2013. The house band for the night included guitarist Lenny Kaye and bassist

Tony Shanahan from the Patti Smith Group, guitarist Ivan Julian from the Voidoids, and Blondie/Plimsouls drummer Clem Burke. This three-hour-plus performance deserves a glowing review all on its own, but I will say that there were many amazing moments, including an positively EPIC fifteen-minute version of "Sister Ray" by the Baseball Project. Surprise guest Sean Lennon did an unrehearsed version of the Velvet Underground's "What Goes On" that was scorching. Alejandro Escovedo did an awesome job on the eight-minute "Street Hassle" (with a cameo by Louise Goffin), and the entire affair ended with everyone coming onstage for an energetic run through of "Rock and Roll." It was magical and mystical, with a lot of love in the room for Mister Reed—a night to remember for sure. (The set list for this performance can be found in the **Appendix** on page 475.)

☯

On Saturday I spent much of my time south of the river, catching the Geri X band at Aussies Bar and Grill before going to the Whip In to see Louise Goffin with Tom Freund, meeting the delightful Jenni Fender, the marvelous Patrice Pike, and hanging out with the lunatic genius that I've known for 25 years, Mr. Steve Poltz. Everyone was dynamic, energetic, and spot on with their performances. I left with a huge smile on my face before navigating the labyrinth of partitioned one-way streets and endless traffic. Just after losing the light during my interview with Kent Wolgamott at the Convention Center, I went over to the club Parish on Sixth Street to catch Sean Lennon and Charlotte Kemp Muhl's quintet, the Ghost of a Saber Tooth Tiger. They performed a *tremendous* eight-song set, concluding with an intensely rearranged version of the Syd Barrett classic "Long Gone." Their new album, *Midnight Sun,* is well worth checking out. (The set list for this performance can be found in the **Appendix** on page 474.)

By the time GOASTT had finished playing I was pretty much toast but I still headed over to the Star Bar where Geri X and Brett Newski were playing. After helping them load up their van I grabbed a plate of Blue Ribbon Barbeque and walked the twenty blocks back to my car. By this time the downtown Saturday night vibe was positively roaring with revelers and I was **done** with that energy and feeling absolutely fried. However, that didn't stop me from driving south of the river once again to the Continental Club to see local heroes Jon Dee Graham and the Fighting Cocks (his final song "Do Not Forget!" is pure rock 'n' roll street poetry). It was then over to the Saxon Pub on Lamar Blvd. to catch J.D. Wilkes and the Dirt Daubers (from Paducah, Kentucky), before seeing former Dead Boy Cheetah Chrome at 1:00 AM to close out the night and the SXSW festival with a loud and rocking set with his super fine quartet. I cut out after saying my goodbyes to several new friends and managed to squeeze in one last round of drinks back at the Aussie with my soul brother, Dan-O, where we closed the bar, and then it was back to the hotel to collapse and prepare for the two interviews that I had scheduled for the following day.

Of course, it wasn't all fun and games at this year's SXSW and that was reflected in the 7:00 AM Thursday morning phone call from *The Rock Bards'* producer Ed Turner to find out if "I was all right." I had planned on seeing X at the Mohawk the night before and I have Billy Altman to thank for not being in attendance, as I wanted to be well-rested for our interview at 10:30 AM the next morning. I went to bed oblivious to the fact that half past midnight, 21-year-old Rashad Owens had crashed the barricades at Fourth Street and Red River, fatally mowing down two people on a moped and a bicycle, and injuring 21 other pedestrians on the sidewalk. A week later a third fatality was added to the list. Owens is charged with capital murder and aggravated assault: when the aspiring rapper panicked and drove the wrong way down a one-way street after being stopped by Austin police for not having his headlights on. His blood alcohol content was registered at 0.114. The incident cast a pall over SXSW for the remainder of the week.

Austin Chronicle rock journalist Tim Stegall: "I was covering X last night at the Mohawk and standing up in the balcony and I saw the hit and run thing happen on one side of me and X was on the other. And my mind might be playing tricks on me but I swear X was playing "Johnny Hit and Run Paulene" as the car went crashing through the barrier."

Running down our Q&A for *The Rock Bards* film, despite the distress caused by the events of the previous night, Stegall was able to offer up some sage perspective on the role of the critic in society: "You're throwing yourself into the culture, grabbing everything you can and reporting back fearlessly and honestly. And that means that not only should you be praising something if it's worthy of being praised, you should also not be afraid to tell somebody 'sorry your new record fucking sucks. Sell the guitar and amp, go back to working at Walmart.' You should not be afraid to say 'No,

I'm sorry, Taylor Swift is not as good as Joni Mitchell.' Just because this person writes songs does not mean that they're good, and you are being sold a bill of goods. I'll be damned if Lester Bangs would have ever picked up a press release and basically re-wrote it for his review. And he is my benchmark of what a rock critic is supposed to be. There were others who came close to that standard as well: Nick Toches, Nick Kent with the *NME* [*New Musical Express*]. Also, Claude Bessy, who went by the name Kickboy Face, who wrote for *Slash* magazine, which was the original, premier punk rock fanzine back in the late '70s. And you want to talk about a fearless writer? Man, that guy let it all hang out.

"These are people that I revered when I was growing up. But it is primarily Lester Bangs. I had these odd impulses because I'm also a musician as well, playing in a punk rock band called the Hormones. But at the same time I was buying Sex Pistols records and New York Dolls records and whatever else was exciting me at the time. X, for sure. I read the *Rolling Stone Illustrated History of Rock Music* and Lester Bangs had a really interesting article in there about the history of the British Invasion and one phrase in particular caught my eye and it became my motto. Lester wrote right in the middle: 'rock 'n' roll at its core is a bunch of raving shit.' And I fell over laughing and thought 'this guy is speaking my language, man.' Lester was a spontaneous beat poet when he wrote about this stuff. And the language that he used was beautiful. And you felt that when you were reading him—there was something boiling inside him that needed to come out. And that was a joyful thing to read. I felt like pogoing to Lester."

As for how music journalism changed in the post-MTV world, Stegall says "I didn't start seeing a change in rock criticism really, until probably about the mid-'90s. Around that time you started seeing copy space restricted in magazines and we started being told 'Yeah, try to sum up this band in 700 words.' 'What?! How can you tell a story in 700 words?' Jeez, I'm just getting warmed up here. It got to where the layouts of the magazine would be more about having a really nice, big, pretty picture and just a little bit of text there, almost like if you had a caption for the photo. Also the advertising would take up a lot more space. So, that upset me. Nowadays it's almost like being a mechanic—I know I've got 250 words, I'll punch these in here. You end up having to be as succinct as possible. You find yourself cutting out almost every single adjective, every single qualifying word in there. It might be arguable that it makes a better writer out of you. It certainly makes a more concise writer out of you, but I kind of miss the days when I could just go off and tell a story."

By the end of my stay in Austin I came away with an extremely updated perspective—not only on the music industry but on the festival as well. As for how SXSW has changed over the years, journalist John Morthland offers this perspective: "I came here in 1985. SXSW has always grown. Film came along a few years later and interactive right after that so now there's this nine-day run. Interactive is bigger than music now in terms of number of registrants. The original South by Southwest was just music but it also took place during spring break because that's when all the students were out of town so it kept the clubs busy. But as the conference has grown there's been more and more of these day parties and a few years ago it started getting really big. That's when you started getting your Fader Ford and the Rachael Ray Picnic. And what's happened now is people come here for spring break, which is completely the opposite of the way things started. What you have now is all these additional events during the day and at night in clubs that are not SXSW events and all of these are private concerns. You saw Doritos this year—some of the very biggest events are these corporate events that have nothing to do with music but they come because this is where everyone is. And so, as a result, it just keeps attracting more and more people and then more and more non-SXSW events start taking place and it's been snowballing that way for quite a while. You notice a real difference in these last three or four years. It's been very tense and it's hard to have much fun, truthfully. There's just always this sense that something's going to happen. And, of course, this year something really bad did happen.

"So all these extraneous events—that's not South by Southwest. To hold those events, corporations have to go to the city of Austin to get permits and the city is going to have to start looking at its own role in all of this. Whenever something happens most people don't make that distinction. The city is going to have to look into its own heart, it's going to have to cop to its role in this kind of chaos and make the same kind of compromises and accommodations that it expects South by Southwest to make. [Because] it's grown too much for that to be workable any more."

San Diego Troubadour, April, 2014

THIRTY-ONE

Robert Gordon
Respect Yourself
Stax Records and the Soul Explosion

The Satellite record shop on McLemore Avenue in Memphis, Tennessee was an unlikely locale to spark a worldwide musical revolution, but that's exactly what Estelle Axton and her brother Jim Stewart created in 1959 after they recorded and released their first single "Fool in Love" by the Veltones. Two releases later they had a number five R&B smash with Carla Thomas' "Gee Whiz (Look at His Eyes)," and for the next two and half decades, their empire at Stax Records was responsible for some of the greatest sounds committed to magnetic tape anywhere.

When the siblings took over the neighboring Capitol Theatre cinema and turned it into a recording studio, they unwittingly advanced race relations in their fair city by hiring an interracial house band called Booker T. and the MGs. It wasn't long before the Memphis Group was backing a roster of clients that included the likes of Rufus Thomas, Otis Redding, Sam and Dave, Eddie Floyd, Johnnie Taylor, Albert King, William Bell, and Isaac Hayes. If you don't already own the three *Complete Stax/Volt Singles* box sets, you owe it to yourself to pick 'em up and devour them. Pronto.

And if you're the slightest bit curious about how the entire phenomenon came together (and you ought to be), pick up a copy of Robert Gordon's latest tome. *Respect Yourself* is an unrivaled homage to the music and culture of Gordon's hometown, and his lyrical prose beautifully relates how Memphis became the unquestionable birthplace of soul music in America. Gordon's fascinating narrative also makes clear how the music scene of Memphis in the '60s and '70s was a perfect microcosm of the entire country, reflecting the struggle of race relations between blacks and whites into a localized triumph of cooperation and assimilation—with great art resulting from this musical melting pot.

Of course, it wasn't all fun and games at Stax, or across America for that matter. 1968 brought the tragic deaths of Otis Redding, the Bar-Kays, and Dr. Martin Luther King, Jr. Before the season was over, Stax lost the rights to its entire catalog over a legal technicality, when Ahmet Ertegun and Jerry Wexler sold Atlantic Records to Warner Bros. Stewart and Axton managed to bounce back for a second act in the '70s (thanks largely to the mega success of the *Shaft* soundtrack), but nothing was the same after the majority of their catalog was lost. The company eventually filed for bankruptcy in 1975 and the original studio where all of those classic records were made, was demolished in 1989.

But the city of Memphis restored that loss in 2003 when it opened the Stax Museum of American Soul Music, recreating the building where all of that magic originally went down. *Respect Yourself* is much more than a trip down memory lane; it's a fabulous reminder of how beautiful we are as a people when we're able to sit together at the table of brotherhood. And groove with one another.

Ugly Things, #37, Spring/Summer, 2014

THIRTY-TWO
Down on Mudcrutch Farm:
Notes from a Tom Petty Fan

All right, it is Monday morning, May 5th (Cinco de Mayo) and my thoughts go spiraling backward to the fact that I had the supreme pleasure and privilege of witnessing two performances by the band MUDCRUTCH this past Thursday and Friday evenings (May 1st and 2nd) at the Troubadour in West Hollywood, California. In 2008, at this historical juncture in the annals of pop culture (generally), and rock 'n' roll (specifically), there isn't much in the way of NEW MUSIC that comes down the pike and gets this 43-year-old kid very excited. I've wondered, at times, if I've seen and heard too many sounds over the years. How do you stay fresh and excited about a musical genre that may have played itself out years ago? I REMAIN, however, a music fanatic (no two ways about it) and in spite of how weird the music business gets, it is still possible to be surprised and to have my faith in rock 'n' roll re-kindled—because that is exactly what happened for me this weekend at the Troubadour.

Now the name Mudcrutch may hardly be a household word, but Tom Petty certainly is. Both with and without his group, the Heartbreakers, Petty has earned the stature as one of rock 'n' roll's most beloved, successful, and critically recognized songwriters and performers. If there is anything to dislike about the guy, it is the fact that his music is so ubiquitous on classic rock radio that it is easy to dismiss him, due to over-familiarity with his greatest hits. It's not Petty's fault that commercial radio programming is so goddamn static.

Until very recently, Mudcrutch has been nothing more than a footnote in Petty's assent to global stardom, since disbanding nearly forty years ago. With a passionate, regional fan base in their native Gainesville, Florida, the original Mudcrutch commanded audiences of up to 1,000 people, but during their five-year existence, there is scant musical evidence of what they sounded like. A couple of demo tapes and two 45s released in 1971 and 1975 respectively, did little to bolster their commercial status, and the band broke up after Petty was offered a solo deal through Leon Russell and Denny Cordell's Shelter Records. After Mudcrutch keyboardist Benmont Tench put together a quartet for his own recording project, including Mudcrutch guitarist Mike Campbell, bassist Ron Blair, and drummer Stan Lynch: Petty usurped the quartet for his own solo debut and viola!—the Heartbreakers were born (out of three/fifths of the original Mudcrutch).

So now, thirty-two years later, after re-counting the entire Mudcrutch saga for Peter Bogdanovich's excellent, four-hour documentary, *Running Down a Dream*, it appears all that reminiscing inspired Petty to contact Mudcrutch guitarist Tom Leadon and drummer Randall Marsh, asking if they'd be interested in a reunion. Petty told Warren Zanes that "I felt like we had left some music back there, and I wanted to go back and get it."

My initial hope regarding Mudcrutch's reunion was that the band would go back and revisit some of their earlier compositions. But that didn't happen, and in retrospect, I'm glad that they chose to harvest a new crop of material instead: modeled upon the musical heroes who inspired them to play in the first place. In addition to performing thirteen of the fourteen songs on the newly-released (April 29) *MUDCRUTCH* LP, only "Oh Maria" did not get aired. The quintet also celebrated their roots by covering tunes from their original repertoire, when they were the house band at Dub's Diner in Gainesville, playing songs by the Rolling Stones, Little Richard, Bill Monroe, Eddie Cochran, Bob Dylan, the Byrds, and Jerry Lee Lewis. The mixture of rock 'n' roll, bluegrass, rockabilly, and folk is an intoxicating concoction, and totally in keeping with why Bob Dylan once described Petty as "gutbucket." This is American rock 'n' roll at its absolute best. As Petty said from the stage on Thursday night, "This is probably the finest bar band you're gonna hear in West Hollywood tonight." The way they sound on fire tonight, Mudcrutch may be the finest bar band you're ever going to hear. Period.

❧

Now I have to ask: why hasn't Benmont Tench ever sung a lead vocal before this LP? His composition, "This Is a Good Street," is one of the coolest songs I've heard in a long time, and sequenced back-to-back with the instant Petty classic, "The Wrong Thing to Do," it provides more than ample evidence of why this album is worth your attention. Ditto for the album's centerpiece "Crystal River," and a casual re-write of Hank Williams' "Lost Highway" for the album's closer, "House of Stone," which brings the whole thing back from whence it sprang: the hand-carved cradle of down-home, American-roots music.

The band just finished playing thirteen shows, with six sold-out performances at the 500-capacity Troubadour. I hope that after Petty and the Heartbreakers are done playing their greatest hits package out there in the sheds of the world, he somehow manages to make his way back to the bar. Oh, I forgot to mention that in Mudcrutch, Petty plays a Hofner bass, and together with Randall Marsh, they make a wonderfully-understated rhythm section. They certainly make the music swing.

MUDCRUTCH manages to be a tour-de-force record by a brand new band that took thirty-eight years to finally record their debut LP. I will never forget the expression of joy on Tom Leadon's face both nights. Smiling ear-to-ear: a dream was clearly coming true, and it was beyond wonderful to witness. What an amazing experience. Thank you gentlemen for a great pair of shows, and for helping to restore my faith in rock 'n' roll as a positive force in the world.

☯

A personal chronology of Tom Petty and the Heartbreakers:

April 20, 1978: is the first time I spy any footage of TP, in the fairly dismal film *FM*. "Breakdown" is on the original motion picture soundtrack. I win tickets off the radio (DC 101) and catch it at Springfield Mall with my buddy Joe Martin.

April 23, 1983: catch Tom Petty and the Heartbreakers for the first of fourteen times as they headline the "X-Fest" at Jack Murphy Stadium in San Diego, California, hosted by local radio station 91X. Also on the bill are the Stray Cats, the Ramones, Bow Wow Wow, Modern English, and the Flirts. I remember being extremely disappointed at the time that original bassist Ron Blair is no longer with the Heartbreakers, replaced by the otherwise remarkable Howie Epstein.

July 26, 1985: Tom Petty and the Heartbreakers perform at the Greek Theatre in Berkeley, California, in support of their current LP *Southern Accents*. Lone Justice opens the show.

June 9, 1986: Tom Petty and the Heartbreakers with Bob Dylan at the San Diego Sports Arena, San Diego, California. The acoustics at the Sports Arena are legendary for their "muddiness," but that can't cloud the fact that I'm seeing Bob Dylan for the first time with one of my very favorite bands backing him up. It is a perfect musical pairing. After touring New Zealand, Australia, and Japan, tonight is the first date of their North American *True Confessions* tour. It's the only show in which they perform their collaboration, "Got My Mind Made Up." Of personal significance on this day: I meet writer Paul Williams (of *Crawdaddy!* fame) for the first time and we trade Dylan tickets. I gave him a ticket for this show in exchange for…

June 14, 1986: Tom Petty and the Heartbreakers with Bob Dylan at the Greek Theatre, Berkeley, California. I managed to somehow tape-record this show from the third row with

Jerry Weddle's rig, and it felt like Dylan was looking at me the entire time. Taping is too nerve-wracking, dealing with threat of being hassled by security, to enjoy a moment like this. But the show *is* great and the tapes *are* an awesome way to re-live some of your fondest memories.

June 16, 1986: Tom Petty and the Heartbreakers with Bob Dylan at the Pacific Amplitheatre, Costa Mesa, California. The first of two nights in Costa Mesa and I'm beginning to love the album that is being played before every show on this tour: *AKA Graffiti Man* by John Trudell and Jesse Ed Davis. During a rendition of "I've Forgotten More than You'll Ever Know," I lean over to my friend, Steve Kobashigawa and say, "Don't Petty and Dylan sound great singing together?" He replies, "Of course, they do. Petty's been doing Dylan his entire career."

June 17, 1986: Tom Petty and the Heartbreakers with Bob Dylan at the Pacific Amplitheatre, Costa Mesa, California. The second of two nights in Costa Mesa, and the last time I would see Dylan backed up by TP and the Heartbreakers. I absolutely loved these shows and I think this is the finest group of musicians that has ever suppoted Dylan. *So long, good luck, and goodbye.*

October 16, 1992: Columbia Records Celebrates the Music of Bob Dylan, Madison Square Garden, New York, New York. One of the most hyped events in the history of Dylan's career, the array of talent on stage is staggering. George Harrison is the high point of the evening for me, singing "If Not for You" and "Absolutely Sweet Marie."

But Tom Petty and the Heartbreakers do great versions of "License to Kill," "Rainy Day Women #12 & 35," and "Mr. Tambourine Man," with Roger McGuinn on twelve-string. It's too bad about Sinead O'Connor.

March 18, 2002: the 17th Annual Rock and Roll Hall of Fame Induction Ceremony, Waldorf-Astoria Ballroom, New York, New York. For five years (2000–2004) during my time with Reelin' in the Years Productions, I had the pleasure of researching and procuring archival musical footage for the RARHOF, and one of the perks of that gig was attending the ceremony each year. Well, not only attending the ceremony, but also getting to sit in on the rehearsals in the afternoon, and occasionally meeting the inductees—very intimate. The ceremony includes a performance by the original Heartbreakers doing "American Girl," with Ron Blair re-instated in the bass chair, and one last public performance with bassist Howie Epstein on "Mary Jane's Last Dance," before his untimely passing in 2003. Significantly, I get to meet Mike Campbell on this day.

August 25, 2002: Tom Petty and the Heartbreakers at the Coors Amphitheatre, Chula Vista, California. This is part of a small round of shows before kicking off *The Last DJ* tour in the fall. Jackson Browne opens the show.

October 29, 2002: Tom Petty and the Heartbreakers at the Open Air Theatre, San Diego, California. *The Last DJ* tour is in full swing with Jackson Browne again opening the show. I can't report on Jackson's opening set because my RITY associates and I were backstage watching music performance footage from the '50s and '60s with Petty, Campbell, Tench, Blair, Scott Thurston, and a few friends. If I didn't have a picture documenting the moment, I wouldn't believe that I was actually there. It's great to know that people in Tom Petty and Mike Campbell's position remain passionate music fans themselves, and are down-to-Earth enough to hang out with "regular folk." Shocked and stunned.

November 29, 2002: *Concert for George*, Royal Albert Hall, London, England. Thanks to the generosity of several people, but primarily of Mike Campbell, who pulled a few strings on my behalf, I was able to witness what might be the coolest concert ever staged. That is highly subjective, of course, but I doubt that I will personally see a more magnificent or emotional performance than the *Concert for George*. Eric Clapton, Jeff Lynne, Paul McCartney, Ringo Starr, Monty Python's Flying Circus, Ravi and Anoushka Shankar, Michael Kamen, and fellow Traveling Wilbury, Tom Petty—all in attendance to celebrate the music and spirit of George Harrison. The Heartbreakers sound great on "Taxman," "I Need You," and "Handle with Care." You can actually see me in the film being seated during Ravi Shanker's introduction—as I take off my beret and look around, I shake my head and wondered: *what did I do to deserve being in that spot at that moment?* I cried through much of the show and found the entire experience breath-taking. It was truly magical.

March 14, 2004: Rehearsals for the 19th Annual Rock and Roll Hall of Fame Induction Ceremony, Waldorf-Astoria Ballroom, New York, New York.

March 15, 2004: the 19th Annual Rock and Roll Hall of Fame Induction Ceremony, Waldorf-Astoria Ballroom, New York, New York. Tonight George Harrison is inducted into the RARHOF for the second time—the first time was as a Beatle, now he is going in as a solo artist—and Tom Petty is on hand with Jeff Lynne to induct Mr. Harrison. There is a great performance of "Handle with Care," and the jam at the end of the evening on "While My Guitar Gently Weeps," with Prince on lead guitar, is mind-bogglingly great. Check out the video on YouTube.

May 1, 2008: Mudcrutch at the Troubadour, West Hollywood, California. A nineteen-song set performed by the best bar band in the world. I can't believe they did the Stones' "Off the Hook."

May 2, 2008: Mudcrutch at the Troubadour, West Hollywood, California. Another nineteen-song set, this time with Little Richard's "Rip It Up" replacing "Off the Hook." This could be the last time I see Tom Petty, Mike Campbell, Benmont Tench, Tom Leadon, and Randall Marsh together on stage. What a fantastic experience and a great memory! (The set list for both performances can be found in the **Appendix** on page 475.)

Long live rock 'n' roll. Endless gratitude to Mike Campbell, Tom Petty, the Heartbreakers, and Mudcrutch. Gentlemen, you are the absolute best!

www.jonkanis.com, May 5, 2008

THIRTY-THREE
Mike Keneally
Wing Beat Fantastic and
You Must Be This Tall

With the weather turning weird and the weird turning pro, I am happy to inform you of an alternative to soaring in a hot air balloon this Indian Summer: it's called *Wing Beat Fantastic*, the seventeenth solo album by San Diego wunderkind Mike Keneally.

Or perhaps the sensation is more like Charlie Bucket riding in that great glass elevator over the rooftops of London? In lieu of the perfect metaphor, *Wing Beat Fantastic* is an old-school, 40-minute sonic splash into that subterranean lake on the edge of town, right before dusk, known in cinema parlance as "the magic hour." Each time I hit the play button and dive back into its splendor I find this record's charms to be nearly mystical. *Wing Beat Fantastic* establishes a tone and sustains it with all the child-like wonder and masterful flair that has inspired me to declare repeatedly that Mike Keneally is a musical genius. His instinctive grasp of what makes a song work, along with a Herculean ability to play a score of instruments, make comparisons to Stevie Wonder or (especially) Todd Rundgren extremely apt when discussing Keneally's all-around gifts as a musician. The dude really can play anything, but, he's an astute enough producer to draft in collaborators when their tonal color or style better serves the needs of a particular song—most notably percussionist Marco Minnemann. In a back catalog shimmering with rough diamonds and difficult-to-digest-jewels, *Wing Beat Fantastic* is a masterpiece. I find myself wondering if Keneally would have ever made such an accessible musical statement were it not for the obvious, but unlikely, collaboration that resulted out of his long-time association with Andy Partridge, the primary steward of Britain's woefully underappreciated XTC.

Two writing sessions at Partridge's home studio yielded eight collaborations, covering quite the emotional range of material with melodies that are positively sublime, particularly on "Inglow" and "It's Raining Here, Inside." "You Kill Me" is filled with wry observations and the album's title track makes me feel like I'm whirling through space without a tether, such is its propulsion and sense of proportion. I'm also struck by the album's plaintive tone, exemplified by "That's Why I Have No Name" and the emotional narrator in the poignantly desperate "Your House." "Miracle Woman and Man" goes a long way to restoring the balance and the trip reaches a joyous climax in the album's penultimate track "Bobeau," featuring a superb guitar solo from Keneally, and the awesome trombone textures of April West, before the balloon drifts back to terra firma on "Land." Call it oceanic circulation or climate change, *Wing Beat Fantastic* is an invitation to fly, regardless of the weather, and should you not be afraid of heights I will see you in the clouds. Time to hit play again.

San Diego Troubadour, November, 2012

Forget everything about what you think rock 'n' roll, jazz, symphonic orchestral scores, or perhaps even what the *avant-garde* are all about. As the title of Mike Keneally's latest assemblage *You Must Be This Tall* suggests, this is not a work for the immature, insecure, feeble-minded, or under-developed. It might also require the patience of a wise, educated soul or an open-minded Zen neophyte (or perhaps a combination of the two) to appreciate the heady brew that spews forth from the fount of San Diego's most consistently brilliant, musical maverick.

There has always been a part of Keneally's compositional makeup that rips pages wholesale from the textbook of his mentor and bandleader Frank Zappa (i.e., the orchestral splendor of Zappa's *Läther*, *The Grand Wazoo*, and *Uncle Meat* crossed with the improvisatory guitar explosions of the *Shut Up 'n Play Your Guitar* series), spliced together with a deconstructionist bent that can't help but express its composer's deep and abiding love for the Beatlesque pop of XTC. Combine all that (and much more) with a truly magical X factor and you have the mark of a true original.

You Must Be This Tall is largely an *Odds and Sods*-type compendium of songs that couldn't (or wouldn't) find a home among the various projects for which they were originally conceived. But destitute orphans these tracks are not. The introductory title song sounds very much like the overture that it is, having been commissioned for the Netherland's Metropole Orchestra. It is majestically glorious, which is true of most of this album.

A few of the tracks ("Cavanaugh," "Kidzapunk," "Pitch Pipe," and the utterly epic, "The Rider") were conceived while Keneally was out on tour with Dethklok and Joe

Satriani. "Indicator" is an outtake from the sessions with Andy Partridge that produced last year's staggeringly beautiful *Wing Beat Fantastic*. The ultimate track on the album, "Glop," sounds exactly like THAT: a sonic dog pile that shreds and snarls and melodically challenges you at every twist and turn (or eight bars). It's either confounding and/or exhilarating.

Sure, there are bursts of super nova conventional rock music for 24 bars before being swept into a serpentine deconstruction of time shifting, four bars of 9/8, four bars of 4/4, into two measures of atonal scales that slide back into the "rock" section once again. You better have a flexible pelvis if you intend on dancing to this stuff.

You Must Be This Tall is a dense and mystifying piece of work whose dividends may not be immediately accessible. It could take ten spins (or more) before any of these sounds start to make sense. I'd file it under Uneasy Listening. But I'd also add that it's well worth the effort. Meet this album half way and you'll be grinning like a savant in no time. Kudos to Mister Keneally. What will he come up with next?

San Diego Troubadour, December, 2013

THIRTY-FOUR

Angelically High and Lonesome: Remembering Phil Everly
January 19, 1939–January 3, 2014

On January 3, 2014, Phil Everly, of the legendary Everly Brothers, passed away in Burbank, California from complications due to a lifetime of cigarette smoking that resulted in chronic obstructive pulmonary disease. He was two weeks shy of 75.

Along with his older sibling Don, the Everly Brothers significantly changed the course of popular music during six short years at the top of the charts with their unique blend of country, western, rockabilly, and the blues—essentially personifying, as much as anyone, what many people have called "rock 'n' roll music" for over five decades. Their influence is incalculable and it would be impossible to imagine the second half of the twentieth century without their close knit, celestial harmonies. Much like the Wilson brothers (and many others), there's no mistaking the effects that sharing the same DNA has upon harmony singing. Although they're two full years apart in age, sonically they might as well be perfectly matched twins with Don typically taking the bottom register lead vocal and Phil soaring in perfect parallel formation above him. In a word, what they sound like is exquisite timelessness, laced with the sensation of time standing still.

Phil and Don are the sons of Ike and Margaret Everly. Don was born (February 1, 1937) in the now defunct hamlet of Brownie, Tennessee, and Phil (January 19, 1939) in Chicago, Illinois. They spent their childhoods growing up in Shenandoah, Iowa and Knoxville, Tennessee, before attending Indiana State University. Ike was a superb guitarist in his own right (as well as a contemporary of Merle Travis) and taught his sons how to play the guitar and sing before either of them had reached the age of ten. During their time in Iowa, Ike hosted his own radio program and the quartet often performed as the Everly Family. But no matter where their travels took them, all roads eventually led back to the Appalachian hills of Muhlenberg County, Kentucky (the world's largest producer of coal, where the majority of the Everlys live), which also serves as ground zero for the unique musical hybrid that the brothers brought to the world.

In the 1984 BBC documentary *Songs of Innocence and Experience*, the Everlys shared what it was like to come of age in that place and time. Phil: "It was the best of times to sit on the porch and swing up at our Aunt Myrtle's and Uncle Roland's, Nadine's and GW's. We would be playing at night and when we got a little older we started singing a little louder because sometimes that music would attract some of the young girls [laughs] and you had a chance to meet somebody that way."

That "high and lonesome sound" of the Kentucky mountain range is legendary in its sense of conveying a particular flavor of emotion—what some might refer to as being melancholy, although Phil didn't see it that way. "I don't really call it melancholy," he said. "I think it's just a basic truth that life is full of both happy and sad events—you

336

know, love and death, losing and winning, and in this area and this music, people are very honest about it. When you're happy, you sing a happy song and when you're sad, you sing a sad song and you allow yourself to feel."

During their time in Knoxville the Everly Brothers came to the attention of family friend Chet Atkins. Intially a quartet with parents Ike and Margaret, they had transitioned into a self-contained duo by the time Atkins introduced them to publisher Wesley Rose. Rose was not only impressed by their crisp harmonies but also with their original songs, and in 1957 he arranged for a publishing contract with Acuff-Rose, in addition to a recording contract with Cadence Records. Shortly thereafter they relocated to Nashville.

Phil: "Nashville was pretty much the mecca of country music—of course, we were doing a strange brand of country [mixed with] some of the other things that we had been listening to."

Don: "Phil and I wanted to get on records—any way that we could do it was what we wanted to do. We liked all kinds of music at that point. We were trying to make it in the field and appearing at the Grand Ole Opry was considered 'stardom.' Hank Williams, to me, was the first real rock 'n' roll star. To me, he wasn't a real, pure, down-home country musician. He was out there. I think it was a combination of that and black R&B that made rock 'n' roll. And there was something so glamorous about that cowboy suit with the white piping, and the Cadillac, the music, and the whole thing."

Songwriter Boudleaux Bryant: "Chet Atkins had told me that he knew two great singers, a couple of brothers that were a great duet and that if he found the right material he might record them. But that's a pretty hazy thing to try and go into full production with as far as writing goes [laughs].

"But when I first heard them I thought they were wonderful. They had a different quality. There had been many duets before but they had that little extra something and when the two voices came together there was an abstract third 'something' happening that made them just a little touch above most anybody I'd ever heard."

As songwriters, Felice and Boudleaux Bryant supplied Phil and Don with their breakout hit "Bye Bye Love" in March of 1957, where it reached #2 on the pop charts. For the next three years the two couples were an unstoppable team, racking up classic after classic with the following singles; "Brand New Heartache" (1957), "Devoted to You" (#10 in 1958), "Problems" (#2 in 1958), "Poor Jenny" (#22 in 1959), "Take a Message to Mary" (#16 in 1959), "Sleepless Nights," "So How Come (No One Loves Me)," "Love Hurts" (all three from 1960), in addition to a trio of #1 smashes with "Wake Up, Little Susie" (1957), "All I Have to Do Is Dream" (1958), and "Bird Dog" (1958).

Don: "As soon as we could afford it we went and had suits made in New York. We quit dressing in what they call the '50s style now because everybody was wearing it. Your father was wearing it, first of all [laughs]. The last thing you wanted to look like is your father. We went strictly Ivy League: three buttons, button-down collars where everything had a buckle in the back, including your shoes. [laughs]

"Yeah, the whole clothes thing and then the haircuts. I'll tell you, the hassle over haircuts was just immense. The first time we walked through the streets of Hong Kong in the early '60s, before the Beatles, you'd stop traffic. Literally stop traffic. People would stop. And stare."

Phil: "I believe Elvis Presley is still a kind of king. If he hadn't kicked down all the doors none of us could have gotten through."

Don: "Music was going through a real major change then. The era of orchestras was ending. Records were beginning to rock 'n' roll and you either hated it or loved it.

"And we called it rock 'n' roll because of Alan Freed, he named it rock 'n' roll and those were the records that we listened to. I called Little Richard rock 'n' roll. But I also called what Buddy Holly was doing rock 'n' roll.

"At the end of the '50s, it was pretty tumultuous being on the road. The big package tours that we would get on—you would have fifteen to twenty acts and you were playing to 100,000 people a night in these big coliseums, doing three songs, with pandemonium—no one could hear a thing; everybody's screaming and yelling from the time it started 'till the time it ended."

Even though Phil says that performing on a package tour with the likes of Eddie Cochran and Buddy Holly was like "being in a college fraternity," it wasn't all fun and games, especially when it came down to the business side of music.

Don: "It was Us against Them, always. Very few of those rock 'n' rollers from our life ever wound up with any control over anything they did. It wound up that a publishing company had control over what was being released and we disagreed with that entirely. If your publishing company controls your releases they're going to want their songs to be released. So, it all came down to artistic freedom. We had to have it and we got it. But, in the process, all of the people that we were dealing with had to go by the wayside in order for us to pursue it. Because rock 'n' roll wasn't going to stand in that one spot. And let's face it, it didn't."

After a three-year stint with Cadence, the Everlys signed a lucrative contract with Warner Bros. Records in 1960. For another three years the hits just kept on coming. Their first single for their new label "Cathy's Clown" (written by Don and Phil) sold eight million copies, becoming the duo's biggest-selling record.

Other successful singles followed; "So Sad (to Watch Good Love Go Bad)" (#7 in 1960, written by Don), "When Will I Be Loved" (#8 in 1960, written by Phil), "Walk Right Back" (#7 in 1961), "Crying in the Rain" (#6 in 1962, written by Howie Greenfield and Carole King), and "That's Old Fashioned (That's the Way Love Should Be)" (#9 in 1962 and their last Top 10 hit).

In addition to parting ways with Cadence and their publishers at Acuff-Rose, the Everlys career hit a bit of a speed bump for six months when they enlisted into the United States Marine Corps Reserves in November of 1961, rather than be called up into the Army for two years of active service.

Phil: "I had thought this through and the marines sounded like death to me and Don said to me, 'Yeah, but you know they got those shiny helmets.' [laughs] I never saw a shiny helmet. But one thing led to another and we wound up there."

Don: "It was great training. It was something that I think, all in all, helped us in that period of time when life could have been a lot more difficult."

If the Everlys began the '60s commercially with a bang, they would soon find themselves considered passé, due in part to the new wave of troubadours led by Bob Dylan and the incoming British Invasion. The irony was galling— it was as if Phil and Don had hosted the greatest shindig imaginable for six years and after getting the rock 'n' roll party energized they were told to leave their cooler full of cokes on the back porch and take a hike.

Don: "We turned around twice and all of a sudden you had to be English. It was 'in' to be English, especially with the Beatles, and then the Rolling Stones. A lot of good came out of it, but it dominated the airwaves for quite a period. Everybody was saying, 'Geez, the Beatles sound an awful lot like you,' and I said, 'Yeah, well what can I do about that?'

"The other side of the music business is you became very 'square' if you didn't get stoned and you didn't have the really long hair and you didn't have that element about your 'mystique.' I was listening to the music and to me it wasn't revolutionary, it was just louder and had more tracks.

"They didn't know what to think of us at all. I mean, even if we didn't wear tuxedos they didn't know what to think of us. They knew that we were from the '50s, and that was not the '60s, you know? It was that attitude and our songs didn't have any double meanings so we had a hard row to hoe within that era: we also worked Las Vegas and that was really bad. Music quit being something that you could earn an honest living by; it had to be a 'social movement.'"

Phil: "I always felt that the '60s were phony. Through that psychedelic period you still have to get records played and when everybody has an attitude, like they're going for that sort of 'political reform.' I think that the '60s was a very bad period for music."

Even though the Everlys continued to record well into the 1980s, the hits had pretty much dried up in the United States after 1964. In the classic tradition of living a country western/rock 'n' roll lifestyle, both brothers went through a period of drug abuse and became addicted to methamphetamine. They pursued various projects both solo and together in the early '70s, eventually drafting together a touring band led by an unknown pianist and composer named Warren Zevon. Guitarist Waddy Wachtel would join the group shortly thereafter.

Warren Zevon: "The Everly Brothers were looking for a piano player and when I met Phil he said that I could audition for them. Don and Phil were both at the audition and I played 'Hasten Down the Wind.' Phil said, 'Can you play like Floyd Cramer?' I said, 'You bet I can.' Without asking me to play another note, they hired me."

Zevon and Wachtel enjoyed three years on the road with the Everlys, but by 1973 the brothers decided that they needed a rest from the grind as well as each other. What happened next is one of rock's most infamous incidents (as recounted in Zevon's biography *I'll Sleep When I'm Dead*).

Crystal Zevon: "Don and Phil were breaking up, but they had contracted to play a three-night gig at Knott's Berry Farm. Warren wanted me to be there for the Everly Brothers' last performance."

"It was July 14, 1973. We arrived and Don was drinking heavily. I'd seen Don perform with the flu and a temperature of 103 degrees. I'd never heard him hit a sour note or be anything short of professional in front of an audience.

But, this night, he walked onstage dead drunk. He was stumbling and off key and I remember Phil trying to restart songs several times. It was embarrassing.

"The fourth or fifth song they did was "Wake Up, Little Susie," and Don was forgetting people's names and insulting the audience and Phil. Finally, Phil stormed offstage. He smashed his Gibson guitar and said, 'I quit.' It was stunning."

Even though it took a decade, when the duo later reunited in 1983 and performed a triumphant comeback show at London's Royal Albert Hall, the brothers had learned to put things into perspective. Phil: "Don and I had toured for almost sixteen years straight and we'd been working for years and years before that, so we'd done a lot."

Don: "We were working seven, eight, nine months a year—and if you do that for a period of twenty years you've got a big chunk of your life spent traveling, being a duet in the music business. Especially when you do it like Phil and I do—with close harmonies, nose-to-nose. That puts a lot of strain on the relationship.

Phil: "The real pressure for us was the business—we had much more to worry about than some sort of sibling rivalry continuing past adolescence all the way into adulthood. That's a simplistic kind of viewpoint of what led to the ultimate end of the Everly Brothers, but it's untrue.

"You can sing the blues at twenty and be blue. You can be sad at twenty. And when you sing the blues at 40 you've got 40 years of blues and 40 years of sad and it's sadder, but then at 60 it will be some other way. The family made music, dad made music, and he taught us the craft, and actually, I probably believe that it's a family business or otherwise I wouldn't have taught my sons and passed that on. I would like to see my grandchildren learn to play just because it's what my dad taught me.

"His guitar got him out of the coal mines of Kentucky and the guitar he gave us got us all the way to London and the guitar that I've given my son I think is doing very well for him with the girls. So, if he can do the same for his son I think it's a grand kind of thing. But we were, basically, carrying on what the family did.

"I approach my life in this way: yesterday is yesterday and if you take all of your past mistakes and drag them into your present, you're only going to confuse your present. Tomorrow is more important than your yesterday."

Don Everly said he didn't expect to see the day his brother would pass.

"I loved my brother very much," the 76-year-old wrote. "I always thought I'd be the one to go first. The world might be mourning an Everly Brother, but I'm mourning my brother Phil Everly. My wife Adela and I are touched by all the tributes we're seeing for Phil and we thank you for allowing us to grieve in private at this incredibly difficult time."

Phil Everly is survived not only by his brother Don, but also his wife Patti and his two sons, Jason and Chris, both singers and songwriters.

San Diego Troubadour, February, 2014

THIRTY-FIVE

Yoko Ono/Plastic Ono Band
Fox Theatre, Oakland, California
February 23, 2010

Yes, I'm a witch…

Yoko Ono and the Plastic Ono Band, live in 2010: what a concept. Last week on February 18, Yoko Ono celebrated her 77th birthday. And on September 21, 2009, she released a brand new album entitled *Between My Head and the Sky* —it's absolutely fabulous—quite likely the best album of her recording career. Ono has always been unconventional, controversial, and forward-thinking. It's the highest form of irony that her lifelong stance at promoting world peace should be considered so radical a position (and greeted at times with so much hostility) in our contemporary culture. But that's a reflection on the values of society at large.

A week ago Tuesday, on February 16, 2010, Ono performed at the Brooklyn Academy of Music (BAM) with a reconstituted Plastic Ono Band, led by her son Sean Lennon. Also in attendance were Eric Clapton, Klaus Voormann, and Jim Keltner, who turned up to celebrate and perform in the spirit of the original POB circa 1969–70. All accounts of the show appear to be enthusiastically positive, with Ono herself writing two days later on her **Imagine Peace** website:

BAM! Suddenly, the audience started to sing Happy Birthday to me right in the middle of the sing-along GIVE PEACE A CHANCE! That was such a nice surprise. I was so unprepared for it, I don't even remember if I thanked the audience or not. Did I? There was so much love circulating; it didn't seem necessary to say anything…we were family.

The curtain went down after GIVE PEACE A CHANCE. Sean and I looked at each other. Sean's eyes were twinkling. "You were great," said Sean. "So were you." It was a grand moment. We knew we had been witnesses to something that was bigger than both of us.

The day did not start very well. I kept looking up at the sky, wondering when it would stop snowing. I love snow. But I was also concerned if any cars could go near the theatre if it kept snowing. If it was around the corner from my apartment like the Beacon Theatre…but the show was at BAM. Brooklyn!

Weeks before the show, I [imagined that I] was going to give the performance of my life at BAM. Was I crazy?! Actually, I wasn't. The show went over so well, it surpassed our wildest expectations.

Thank you for adding your magic to it. We are a lucky mother-and-son.

A week after the BAM performance, Ono and her band (sans the guest stars) traveled 3,000 miles west to perform at the 2010 Noisepop Festival in the newly renovated Fox Theatre in downtown Oakland, California. The Fox has been closed for forty years and it just reopened a year ago. The building is stunning to behold: a 1930s art deco theatre that has much in common with the Golden State Theatre in Monterey—two fine examples of period architecture.

The performance at the Fox began at 8 PM sharp with the San Francisco noise-pop band, Deerhoof, performing a 45-minute set. They are a talented, super-tight quartet, and they certainly are prolific—out in the lobby they have more than ten CDs available.

Sometimes I am happy and sometimes not. I am, after all, a human being, you know. You get your wisdom working by having different emotions. – **Yoko Ono**

During the interval between acts, a large screen descended as a backdrop for the stage, and instead of the customary rock music blaring out from the PA during the set change, the sound of birds came fluttering out of the speakers, soon to be joined by a looping animated image of Yoko Ono sustaining a perpetual stream/scream of birds coming out of her open mouth. The absence of loud music on the changeover contributed to a vibe *extremely* different from your typical rock 'n' roll concert, making it feel much more like an art piece/happening, which of course it was. Would you expect anything less from Yoko Ono?

After a 30-minute break, the theatre darkened and a fourteen-minute film began, with the audience regaled by highlights from Ono's illustrious life and career. Beginning with home movies of her as a child in pre-World War II Japan, the montage included: clips from various conceptual art performances, samplings of her films from the 1960s, various events from her life with husband and co-creator John Lennon, and examples of the many peace and art projects that she has embarked upon since Lennon's death in 1980. The film was beautifully edited and a fantastic introduction to the evening's performance.

Ono emerged to a standing ovation at 9:35 PM and approached the microphone to sing a lovely, *a cappella* version of her song "It Happened"—originally released as the B-side to her February 1981 single, "Walking on Thin Ice." The audience was wildly enthusiastic and then her band joined her onstage, led by Sean Lennon on electric guitar, to launch into the opening number from her new album, "Waiting for the D Train." It appears that rock 'n' roll and technology have finally caught up with Ono's singularly unique form of vocalizing—because, in 2010, she sounds more contemporary and compelling than ever. If her age has presented any challenges for her, it certainly didn't show in her voice. She sounded truly majestic, alternating between wordless emoting and clear diction, with her singing crisp, tuneful, and melodic. I think the majority of people have misconceptions about Yoko Ono's music and they should check out her new LP—it would be a startling revelation for a lot of people.

☯

Controversy is part of the nature of art and creativity. I just believe in going forward. – **Yoko Ono**

It's obvious that not everyone in the world finds Yoko Ono's pioneering art to be his or her particular cup of tea. With that idea in mind, I refer listeners to Lester Bangs' excellent review of her first *Plastic Ono Band* LP from the March 4, 1971 edition of *Rolling Stone* magazine. If context is indeed crucial to understanding our subjective points of view, then appreciating an *avant-garde* artist might just ask that much more of the listener than the underdeveloped pop music sensibilities of an adolescent.

Bangs: "Anyone performing *avant-garde* music is laying themselves open to a certain amount of hostility and derision at the outset. And if that person also happens to be Yoko Ono, who has not only displayed a gift for hyping herself with cloying "happenings," but also led poor John astray and been credited by more than one insider with "breaking up the Beatles," why, the barbs and jeers can only be expected to increase proportionately. Not only do most people have no taste for the kind of far-out warbling Yoko specializes in; they probably wouldn't give her the time of day if she looked like Paula Prentiss and sang like Aretha.

"On the other hand, not much of her recorded product inspires any sympathy. What it mostly inspires is irritation, even in hardened fans of free music and electronic noise. *Two Virgins, Life with the Lions*, and the distinctly uncatchy "Peace" jingles on the *Wedding Album* were the ego-trips of two rich waifs adrift in the musical revolutions of the Sixties. Dilettante garbage, simply.

"It wasn't until the long freak-out on the back of the *Live Peace in Toronto 1969* LP that Yoko began to show some signs that she was learning to control and direct her vocal spasms, and John finally evidenced a nascent understanding of the Velvet Underground-type feedback discipline that would best underscore her histrionics. That record began to be listenable, even exciting, and the version of "Don't Worry Kyoko" on the back of the "Cold Turkey" single was even better. Now Yoko finally has an album all her own out, and it bodes well for future experiments by the Murk Twins along these lines.

"For one thing, Yoko has excellent backup this time: one track features an Ornette Coleman quartet, and the rest find John, Ringo and bassist Klaus Voormann working out accompaniments that are by turns as frenzied as Yoko herself and quite restrained. It always sounds thought-out, carefully arranged, appropriate: and with Yoko's music, that's saying something.

"This one will grow on you. They haven't ironed out all the awkwardness yet, but this is the first J&Y album that doesn't insult the intelligence—in fact, in its dark, confounding way, it's nearly as beautiful as John's album. Give it a try, and at least a handful of listenings before your verdict. There's something happening here."

Sound as medium has an incredible elasticity. So, of course, it is tempting for artists of other fields to try something with sounds. Why not? We are living in the age when there is no limit in gathering all forms of art and music to mix it together if you so desire.

— **Yoko Ono**

After the relentless workout on "Waiting for the D Train," Sean switched over to bass for the funky title track "BETWEEN MY HEAD AND THE SKY." Afterward, he mostly stuck to electric guitar for the rest of the evening. Next came a ripping version of "Rising," followed by a bouncy "Walking on Thin Ice." Then the band left the stage, and as Lennon picked up an acoustic guitar, he introduced his friend Harper Simon (the son of Paul Simon) to join him on second acoustic as they accompanied Ono on her song, "Will I." It was a lovely downturn in energy and a mellow interlude during an otherwise intense evening.

But it wasn't mellow for long, as the band came roaring back to pump up the energy for the wordless "Moving

Mountains," seguing straight into "CALLING," another highlight from the new album. Lennon sang the repeated line of "The Sun Is Down!" for the duration of the next number, as Yoko stretched out on the floor, stage right, doing yoga postures. I must say that at 77, she's incredibly limber.

Art is like breathing for me. If I don't do it, I start to choke.

– Yoko Ono

Next came one of the highlights of the evening as Lennon introduced the song, "Death of Samantha," by saying "we did this song last week with Eric Clapton, and this is one of my favorites of your's, mom; it's from *Approximately Infinite Universe*, isn't it?" After the song was over, which featured a fantastically fluid and dynamic solo from Lennon on electric guitar, he said "I learned how to play that by watching Eric last time. But I gotta say that it's more fun just playing with all my friends tonight. It's not so nerve-wracking."

Yoko introduced the next song "Mind Train" by saying that when they originally recorded it for the *Fly* LP, it was twelve minutes long. Tonight's version would not be so long, which prompted Sean to pipe in with "Hey, this is San Francisco [sic], the place known for long jams. We might do a twenty-minute version." They instead kept it to about five minutes and it was very cool. After "Mind Train," the band once again left the stage and Lennon announced that he and his mom were going to perform a duet together. He went over to the baby grand piano and played beautifully, as Ono sang the meditative "Higa Noburu"—a wonderful way to end the set.

Remember, each one of us has the power to change the world. Just start thinking peace, and the message will spread quicker than you think. – **Yoko Ono**

After many minutes of applause, the band came back to provide a live soundtrack to Ono's film *FLY*. Then, Deerhoof joined the Plastic Ono Band for a spirited rendition of "Don't Worry, Kyoko (Mummy's Only Looking for Her Hand in the Snow)," before leaving to another standing ovation and coming back for the all-inclusive sing-along of "Give Peace a Chance." After you've got everyone joining in for five minutes on THAT particular number, you can't possibly follow it—and it was the perfect way to end the show. (The set list is in the **Appendix** on page 475.)

Adding to the art-happening ambience of the night, there was a small pen light that said *ONOCHORD OAKLAND y.o. 2010,* sitting on the arm of each person's chair. At the end of the concert, Ms. Ono took a flashlight and shined it at the audience in three sequences: flash, flash-flash, flash-flash-flash, to represent I-LOVE-YOU. Everyone was invited to flash their light back at the stage and at each other. What more could you wish to project, and have others project onto you?

The show was fantastic, historical, and extremely significant personally—well worth driving 1,000 miles for the experience.

A dream you dream alone is only a dream.
A dream you dream together is reality. – **Yoko Ono**

www.jonkanis.com, February 25, 2010

THIRTY-SIX

Robyn Hitchcock with Joe Boyd
Largo, Los Angeles, California
September 23, 2010

Last evening I witnessed a unique event in Los Angeles where one of my favorite musician/songwriters, Robyn Hitchcock, provided the musical accompaniment for a reading by Joe Boyd. Mr. Boyd was reciting excerpts from his 2006 memoir titled *White Bicycles*, sharing stories from his long and distinguished career as a manager, record producer, and film executive.

The presentation began with both gentlemen coming out and Hitchcock stating that "Joe is Dr. Frankenstein, and I am his monster." He explained further that he had stopped listening to music after he turned thirteen—with the exception of the new groups and songwriters that Joe Boyd had a hand in producing. And with that as a means of introduction to an evening dubbed *Chinese White Bicycles*, Mr. Hitchcock launched into "My White Bicycle," the 1967 song by British psychedelic group, Tomorrow. By the song's conclusion, the mood and tone for the evening were properly established, and Mr. Boyd commenced to reminisce.

As the night progressed the audience was treated to one anecdote after another, learning how Boyd put on shows at London's legendary UFO club, back in 1966 and '67 (the launch pad for the original Pink Floyd with Syd Barrett), and how he fell in love with the Birmingham group, the

Jon Kanis

Move, a quintet that Boyd was so entralled with that he tried to convince his boss at Elektra Records, owner Jac Holzman, to sign them to his label. Alas, this was not to be, and as the story wound down, Hitchcock again approached the microphone for a fantastic rendition of the classic 1967 Move single "I Can Hear the Grass Grow."

And that's how it went throughout the next two hours as Boyd and Hitchcock traded licks. Boyd would relate an incident from his life and Hitchcock would respond with a song by that artist. And what a life Boyd has enjoyed thus far: a trip to Scotland that led to meeting and managing the Incredible String Band; stage managing the 1965 Newport Jazz and Folk Festival, site of the infamous controversy where Bob Dylan "turned electric" before a sea of folk purists; managing and producing classic LPs by both Fairport Convention and Nick Drake; assembling the 1973 documentary for Warner Brothers *A Film About Jimi Hendrix*, and finally, concluding with his program notes, a eulogy basically, for the London-based tribute concert on May 10, 2007, for the recently departed Syd Barrett.

All in all, a great night of intimate stories and music—*White Bicycles* is an excellent memoir by someone who was at the heart of swinging London during the mid-late '60s. Bravo.

Set List: "My White Bicycle" *Tomorrow* / "I Can Hear the Grass Grow" *the Move* / "Chinese White" *Incredible String Band* / "It Takes a Lot to Laugh, It Takes a Train to Cry" *Bob Dylan* / "Reynardine" *Fairport Convention* / "River Man" *Nick Drake* / "The Wind Cries Mary" *Jimi Hendrix Experience* / "Bike" *Pink Floyd*.

www.jonkanis.com, September 24, 2010

354

THIRTY-SEVEN

TNP at the Echoplex
Los Angeles, California
November 2, 2010

Well, well, well—it's always a potent experience to cross paths with an old crush, and in this particular case it had been six swift years since last bearing witness to a live performance by the cultural phenom known as **Stew**. Gallons of ink have been spilled in tribute to the conquering, misfit, hero: the guy who managed to create a musical version of his fictionalized life story and sell it to Broadway. The end result, *Passing Strange,* delighted some, but failed to put enough patrons in the seats, even after winning a 2008 Tony award for best Book for a Musical. Nevertheless, when the production of *Passing Strange* ended, Broadway's latest darling was relieved to get back to what he loves doing the most: touring and spontaneously performing with a rock 'n' roll band, without the mandatory commission of churning out the same performance night after night.

"Theater is a tour where you stay in one place," writes Stew in the program notes from his performance at the Getty Museum last Saturday evening. "But it's far more grueling than rock 'cause you're doing the same thing every night— theater is the missionary position of live entertainment. It's nice, but what about a whip on occasion? On a rock tour you can decide one night to do all slow versions if you feel like it, or do covers. Or play way-too-long guitar solos, you can change it up. That way it takes longer for you to go crazy. But it's hard to do that in theater—and believe me we went as far as we could go [during *Passing Strange*] to create the rock 'n' roll vibe—given the restrictions. But at the end of the day you can't stop a Broadway show in the middle to go into a cover of 'Cat Scratch Fever.' Well, you could. But the producers and union would freak."

On Tuesday night at the Echoplex, it was more than apparent that Stew was relishing the lack of constraints that being on the road was affording him with his newly re-constituted Negro Problem.

To start at the beginning…'twas back in 1994 that native Angelino Mark Stewart began the performance art project of TNP with Charles Pagano, Jill Meschke, and Gwynne Kahn, releasing several singles of idiosyncratic pop perfection before that original lineup imploded due to a confluence of conflicting agendas. The first TNP LP, *Post Minstrel Syndrome*, documents the conclusion of the original quartet, effectively marking the exit of Kahn and Meschke and the entrance of Ms. Heidi Rodewald. A second TNP LP was released in 1999, *Joys and Concerns*, and during the course of the following year drummer and singer Charles Pagano also left the fold. For those of you taking notes, an era had clearly ended.

And that became obvious in 2000, when instead of another Negro Problem LP, Stew's next project, *Guest Host*, was released under the moniker of STEW. I'm not sure what the difference is between the material recorded as "The Negro Problem" and the musical entity "Stew." You'd have to ask Stew, 'cuz to me they sound fairly inter-changeable. "Stew" seems to be a bit more stripped down, a sort of TNP unplugged, and *Guest Host* afforded the opportunity for Stew and Rodewald to tour as a duo, a format that they would return to time and again. A prolonged stint at L.A.'s Knitting Factory in June of 2001 provided the basic tracks for the next Stew LP, *The Naked Dutch Painter...and Other Songs*, and quickly on it's heels came another Negro Problem LP, *Welcome Black*. Somewhere during this period, two authorized "bootlegs" of demos and rejected tracks emerged at the merchandise table at gigs: *Sweetboot,* and *Muddy Sweetboot.* I find many of these performances to be some of the most satisfying things that Stew has ever put down in a studio. The spontaneity of recording demos clearly suits Mr. Stewart.

2003 saw the release of another Stew LP, *Something Deeper Than These Changes,* containing the brilliant "Kingdom of Drink." Over the next couple of years Stew and Heidi's paths converged with the folks at the Sundance Institute Theatre Program in Utah, producing the first version of what would become the musical, *Passing Strange,* at the Berkeley Repertory Theatre in 2006. A Public Theater version in New York City emerged in 2007, and by 2008 a production was launched at the Belasco Theatre. In theatre circles, Stew was being celebrated as the latest toast of the town—and had seemingly arrived. But winning a Tony award was not enough of an enticement for audiences to put down their hard-earned cash for a ticket, and the show closed after 165 performances on July 20, 2008. Fortunately, Spike Lee captured the production for posterity before the cast and crew dispersed with the wind.

And good-god-almighty, that is already two years ago. In the duration, Stew and Rodewald redefined their personal perimeters after spending over a decade together as a couple. And they're finding out once again, what it's like to be in a touring band, while keeping their musical collaboration firmly intact.

This latest version of TNP, currently crisscrossing the U.S., features keyboardist Joe McGinty, woodwind player Michael McGinnis, and drummer Greg Joseph. There is also a fantastic trumpet player, a percussionist, and two background vocalists (whose names I didn't catch), that added a fresh dynamic to the proceedings.

Tuesday's program began with McGinty and McGinnis performing a short, understated set, before Lisa Jenio's quartet, Candypants, offered up some levity with a lovely batch of stripped-down material. Then, TNP came out, taking over the entire length of the stage, with Stew resplendent in a black kilt, black shirt, and a necktie of red polka-dotted hearts. You certainly can't accuse the guy of lacking style.

The two-and-a-half hour show began with "Bleed," a sublime, melodic motif that features as the emotional lynch-pin in *Passing Strange*. "Bleed" shares the same music but a different melody and lyric as "Come Down Now," and the two songs serve as twin narratives to a connected story, doubling its resonance.

After "Bleed," the crowd sang along to a radically re-arranged version of "The Re-Hab Song," sounding much like "When the Music's Over" by the Doors. The brand new "Curse" is impressive, before lurching into "Gary Come Home," a song Stew composed for the best friend of *Spongebob Squarepants* (Gary happens to be a snail, should you not catch cartoons on the Nickelodeon channel). "This is a song about Tom Cruise" is how "Ken" is introduced. Plunging into the aforementioned "Kingdom of Drink," this is the first of two emotional high points during the evening's set. The band's ability to be sensitive and support Stew's protagonist gives the performance a dynamic momentum—perfect for swigging and swinging in a metaphorical barroom, where alcohol is both country and king. Stew's forever-morphing, dramatic persona is both menacing and poignant, particularly in the next song, "Speed." It's a continuation of Stew's first-person narrative ability to singularly describe the attraction, and fatal follies, of why some folks indulge in chemical stimulation. In his introduction, Stew said that he couldn't perform the song earlier in Davis, California, where there was a "phalanx of old ladies in the front row. I can't fuck up old ladies." After performing for the patrons at the Getty Museum on Saturday night, he said he felt like "a moving Rothko," imagining those in attendance thinking: "he's compelling, a compelling Negro."

"If you really want to change, you need to be a revolutionary. Americans are too undisciplined to be fascists. Fascism will never happen in America" is how he introduced "Bong Song," with a dedication to Panorama City. By this point, the band sounded like *Da Capo*-era Love with flute and Latin percussion. I found the music not quite as lyrical as Love, but the counterpoints were raggedly exquisite. And I suppose that is a quality that has always been a part of TNP.

There is a sparkling new Negro Problem CD in a black cardboard sleeve to be found at the merch table, and the first mention of its existence comes before the song "Black Men Ski." The LP doesn't appear to have an official title, but Stew referred to it as *Work in Progress*. Next came a pair of duets with one of the background singers on the "Sexy Brooklyn Mami" and "Omnibus." Both songs feature in the new musical, *Brooklyn Omnibus*. "Does anybody know what a bodega is?" asks Stew before going into "Can I Get You

Love?," the second emotional high point of the evening, due to the conversation between the song's two protagonists.

That seems to conclude all the material that was pre-rehearsed. We are now in the realm where "anything goes." Stew refers to the thick, three-ring binder on his music stand for the lyrics to "Comikbuchland," with only Rodewald to accompany his guitar and voice. It is obvious here, and in many other parts of the show, that Stew is damn lucky to have Heidi as his collaborator, because she is frequently the glue that holds this musical enterprise together. "In New York they call this process," says Mr. Glib-Spontaneity before launching into the obscure "Smudges," a song written in the aftermath of the January 1994 Northridge earthquake. "It's funny, most of these songs were written two miles from here. Peter Case called me with a proposal to write two songs for a show at the Getty Museum [in 2003]. The commission was like two months rent in Silver Lake, so I took it." So much for the true-life motivation for "Statue Song."

The standard set closer "Witch" has the entire band back in toto with Stew's guitar strap disconnecting from its body. In response to the cacophony of requests being shouted by the audience, the band slides into a reggae version of TNP's first single "Birdcage," before concluding the night's festivities with "the Tea Party version" of "Mahnsanto." (The set list for this performance can be found in the **Appendix** on page 475.) The band left the stage shortly before midnight and everyone appeared to have had a great time. *Welcome Black*, indeed, TNP. Don't be such a stranger in the future.

www.jonkanis.com, November 3, 2010

THIRTY-EIGHT

Gerry Goffin:
Beyond the Brill Building

It's been said before in these pages, but like a great refrain, it needs to be sung **once more**, with a feeling: *music is a form of prayer.* It's not a toy. It's a talisman not to be trifled with, deserving of your utmost respect. It's magical and mystical—a mysterious temple, capable of giving form to your dreams, and the means for your aspirations to soar. When a really substantive piece of music reaches in and touches your heart, and provides you with whatever it is you need at that moment: solace, understanding, validation, wisdom, forgiveness, celebration (whatever was evoked by the intentions of the composer), then it allows us to revel in the affirmation that we are alive in the here and now. It's alchemy, pure and simple.

When a composition speaks to you and articulates something deep within, it becomes a part of your psyche, often to the point where you might even believe that you yourself wrote it—it conveys your depth of feeling to such a degree. That is what master tunesmiths do: they access that realm of universal feelings, and express them for everyone to share.

If anyone in the course of twentieth century popular music has been able to tap into and express that yearning for love and acceptance; of having the blues because you made a misstep; of feeling desire and being desirable; or wishing for an escape out of the boredom of circumstance, and finding a safe haven in the arms of unconditional love—that person is Gerry Goffin. As the husband and songwriting partner of Carole King, Goffin is responsible for co-writing some of the most beloved songs of the last 50 years. He is a textbook example of taking your dreams to heart, and sharing them with the world—as well as find out that you aren't the only one who needs to be loved, or yearns to live in a world free of fear, bigotry, and hatred. It sounds like a fantasy of what heaven on Earth might look like, and Goffin expressed it time and again, frequently in less than three minutes and thirty-three seconds.

Gerald Goffin was born February 11, 1939, in Brooklyn, New York, and grew up in the borough of Queens. He graduated from Brooklyn Technical High School, enlisted in the Marine Corps Reserve, and spent a year at the U.S. Naval Academy, before resigning from the Navy to study chemistry at Queens College.

It was at Queens in 1958 that Goffin met, and fairly quickly married fellow student Carole King (she had already changed her name professionally from Carol Kline). They immediately started writing songs together, as Goffin told *Vanity Fair* in 2001: "She was interested in writing rock 'n' roll, and I was interested in writing a Broadway play. So we had an agreement where she would write the music to the play, if I would write lyrics to some of her rock 'n' roll melodies. And eventually it came to be a boy-and-girl relationship where I began to lose heart in my play, and we stuck to writing rock 'n' roll."

By 1960 they were staff composers for impresario Don Kirshner's Aldon Publishing at 1619 Broadway, otherwise known as the Brill Building: the most prestigious address in the world if you're a professional songwriter. At Aldon they shared an office with another husband-and-wife, songwriting team: Barry Mann and Cynthia Weil. The competition was fierce to produce a hit song for the recording artists of the day. At the urging of Kirshner, who was pushing for a "follow up" song for the Shirelles, after having a hit with "Tonight's The Night," Goffin and King unwittingly wrote a classic that defines the beginning of the 1960s: "Will You Love Me Tomorrow."

As King wrote in her memoir, *A Natural Woman*, "my grandmother couldn't understand how anyone could earn a living writing songs that appealed to teenagers, but that's exactly what Gerry and I were doing. Though now in his twenties, Gerry hadn't forgotten which three-letter word was foremost in the mind of every teen. It was s-e-x that kids thought about when they listened to lyrics about hearts full of love, hearts breaking, lovers longing, youth yearning, cars, stars, the moon, the sun, and that most innocent of all physical pastimes: dancing. We wouldn't write a song about dancing until the following year, but sex was definitely the implied third character in our first big hit."

When Goffin and King were inducted into the Rock and Roll Hall of Fame in 1990, writer Jon Landau summarized their significance: "As songwriters, Gerry and Carole stand as a great bridge between the Brill Building styles of the late

'50s and early '60s, and the modern rock era. They started looking forward with their first hit [when] they wrote a 'little' song called 'Will You Love Me Tomorrow.' It was the first great '60s record to be written from a women's point of view, and it was the first great ballad directed to a new generation that would soon be labeled 'baby boomers.'

"In 1962, the Drifters recorded their sublime, 'Up On the Roof,' a song that expressed the sensibility that a few years later would be called 'sixties idealism.' And in 1963, Gerry and Carole extended that idealism with the romantically eloquent 'One Fine Day' [by the Chiffons]. By the time they wrote 'Don't Bring Me Down' for the Animals, and 'Goin' Back' for the Byrds, they helped to start an approach that would affect every singer/songwriter to come after them. And in a nice epiphany, in 1967 they closed the cycle they began with 'Will You Love Me Tomorrow' when they wrote '(You Make Me Feel Like) A Natural Woman' for Aretha Franklin."

The significance of Goffin and King's music could not be more lovingly and succinctly put. These are the same sentiments this author heard from the podium in March of 2004, witnessing Goffin and King receive the Grammy Trustees Award from the Recording Academy for their "significant contributions to the field of music." It's nearly as great an honor as John Lennon saying, in 1963, that he wanted Paul McCartney and himself to become "the Goffin and King of England."

❧

Over the span of several years, Goffin and King racked up one classic after another, including four number one hits: "Will You Love Me Tomorrow," by the Shirelles; "Go Away Little Girl," by Steve Lawrence; "Take Good Care of My Baby," by Bobby Vee; and "The Loco-Motion," by Little Eva.

If you listen closely to the lyrics that Goffin was coming up with to match King's "rock 'n' roll melodies," it is easy to hear the yearnings of someone who may have had it made on the material plane, but spiritually was yearning for something else.

"We should have been deliriously happy, and indeed, I was happy," writes King. "In my bubble of contentment, I thought my husband was happy, too. But Gerry was beginning to feel the winds of the societal storm brewing on both coasts. That storm would become a tempest with enough momentum to polarize families across America and around the world."

As King further shares in her autobiography, drugs unwittingly caused the partnership and marriage to unravel: "I don't believe Gerry knew he was dropping acid the first time he ingested it. I believe someone who thought he was doing him a favor slipped it into his coffee. It wasn't a favor. After that, Gerry took LSD many more times on his own. He lost touch with reality at first, for days, then for weeks at a time for many years afterward, with intermittent periods of lucidity, creativity, and wisdom. The appeal for Gerry and others who sought to 'expand' their minds was the notion that lysergic acid diethylamide would make them more creative and metaphysically aware. But people on acid found it difficult to communicate and function in a world dominated by people not on acid."

Doctors diagnosed the 26-year-old Goffin as schizo-phrenic, then manic, treating him with massive amounts of Thorazine, and eventually recommending shock therapy as a solution to his increasingly erratic temperament.

"When Gerry's behavior started to become more irrational, I was afraid he'd do something he'd regret later. I didn't know whether to laugh or cry when he climbed up on a ladder and painted "Love Your Brother" on the side of our house. However, when he attempted (and thankfully failed) to seriously hurt himself, I knew it was time to call for help.

"Shock therapy helped Gerry for a while in 1965, but the circumstances that led to his ingestion of LSD in the first place had not gone away."

By 1967, Goffin was going through some serious changes. Tiring of the plasticity of life in the suburbs, he crafted a beautiful retort to the values of upward mobility in the Monkees #4 smash hit, "Pleasant Valley Sunday": *Creature comfort goals they only numb my soul and make it hard for me to see / My thoughts all seem to stray, to places far away / I need a change of scenery.*

In *Vanity Fair*, Goffin later said that he "wanted to be a hippie—I grew my hair long, and Carole did it modestly. And then I started taking LSD and mescaline. And Carole and I began to grow apart because she felt that she had to say things herself. She had to be her own lyricist."

The disconnect between the two writers is evident in some of the last songs they collaborated on, significantly, three of the tracks on the phenomenal 1969 LP by Dusty Springfield, *Dusty in Memphis*. "No Easy Way Down," "Don't Forget About Me," and "I Can't Make It Alone," speak directly to their circumstances, and choosing to go their separate ways. And although the lyrics are credited to Toni Stern, Carole King's 1971 smash "It's Too Late," appears to be addressing the dissolution of their partnership as well: *It used to be so easy living here with you, but we just can't stay together don't you feel it too, still I'm glad for what we had, and how I once loved you.*

They divorced in 1968. Both went on to continued success as individuals with King having a successful run of hits during the '70s, including the definitive singer/ songwriter LP of the era, *Tapestry*. Goffin released a solo album of his own in 1973, *It Ain't Exactly Entertainment*, and continued to write lyrics into the '90s, enjoying two number one songs with composer Michael Masser: the Oscar-nominated, "Theme from *Mahoghany* (Do You Know Where You're Going To)," by Diana Ross, and "Saving All My Loving for You," by Whitney Houston. Another of his great songs from the 1970s, written with Barry Goldberg, is "I've Got to Use My Imagination," a Top 10 hit by Gladys Knight and the Pips. This song also addresses the pain of a breakup: *I've really got to use my imagination to think of good reasons to keep on, keepin' on / Got to make the best of a bad situation, ever since that day, I woke up and found that you were gone.*

☯

Goffin passed away on June 19, 2014, in Los Angeles, California, at the age of 75. *The Guardian* referred to him as "the poet laureate of teenage pop."

In 1975, Goffin told writer Bruce Pollock: "I can't write under deadlines anymore, but I respect people who can.

Right now I'm just writing what I feel like writing and I keep changing. If I want to write something commercial I don't see anything wrong with it. If I want to write a song that I feel personally, I don't see anything wrong with that either.

"I've written a couple of thousand songs. I write a lot more songs that people don't use—about fifty-to-one. Last year I wrote forty songs in forty days.

"There's also another thing. There's a certain magic that some records have and that some records don't have and that's not a quality you can capture unless everything is going right. There are so many personalities involved, so many variables. Sometimes you can write a mediocre song and it becomes a big hit—it's really hard to talk about.

"I'm not going to say whether my songs were good or bad. If people like them, that's fine, and I'm happy. You've got to realize, when I started writing songs there's been several revolutions that have taken place in pop music, and I think they were all improvements. I've always thought, any way you looked at it, the changes have been for the better."

In a statement, Carole King said: "Gerry Goffin was my first love. He had a profound impact on my life and the rest of the world. Gerry was a good man and a dynamic force, whose words and creative influence will resonate for generations to come. His legacy to me is our two daughters, four grandchildren, and our songs that have touched millions and millions of people, as well as a lifelong friendship. He will be missed by his wonderful wife Michele, his devoted manager, Christine Russell, his five children, and six grandchildren."

San Diego Troubadour, August, 2014

THIRTY-NINE

The Long Goodbye and the Inevitable Winter That's Blowing *Inside Llewyn Davis*

Oh, February! (aka the "death season"), that profound reminder (à la "Turn! Turn! Turn!"), where cyclical regeneration comes stealing like a thief in the night. And rightly so—it's how nature balances its books every year. However, should you find yourself responding to the season with emotional angst, you can always calm that savage beast of a weary psyche with the soothing sound of music. Particularly those organic emanations referred to as "folk music"—that communal repository of ancient yore, dressed up in the finery of ballads, jigs, reels, and dirges, forever championing the grim realities of starvation and deprivation, combined with tales of violent skirmishes that climax in fatalistic dishonor. Ah yes, sharing folk songs together—it's the perfect way to celebrate winter.

And as much as the above paragraph might be an apt metaphorical reference point for their 1996 film, *Fargo*, the long, cruel winter of discontent continues in the wonderfully wily world of sibling auteurs Joel and Ethan Coen— that dynamic duo whose singular style continues to spiral them ever upwards into the highest echelons of cinema with their latest offering: *Inside Llewyn Davis*. Painting a world in sensibilities that are barely recognizable by contemporary standards, they have crafted a love letter to a bygone era that stands in stark contrast to now. And what the hell, it's only been a half-century of turning the calendar page for goodness sake. But consider the profound technological changes that 50 years have wrought regarding the way music is perceived and experienced in our culture. It's a heavy period of transition that we currently find ourselves in the midst of.

The onscreen chyron hips us to the fact that it's 1961 at the Gaslight Café in the Greenwich Village neighborhood of New York City. To be even more precise it is the evening of February 17 and performing onstage is folksinger Llewyn Davis. He is finger-picking his way through the folk standard "Hang Me, Oh Hang Me"—sung from the perspective of a man whose luck is about to run out at the end of a rope. The singer is good and his self-assurance with a murder ballad goes a long way toward purposefully establishing tone, because, as should be clear by now, there are no careless gestures or symbolic frivolity when it comes to the carefully plotted universe of the Coens. More to the point, there is a deliberate, epic fatalism scattered like so many leaves throughout the film's emotional terrain, with our hero perpetually mired in an existential vacuum. And it's no surprise either, as he futilely hacks away at a folk-singing career of diminishing returns—spending his days and nights conjuring an archaic world through song, and strumming endless variations on the themes of murder, loss, and emotional degradation. He's stranded on the edge of a breakthrough, unable to make the leap at becoming self-aware, and fated to repeat this cycle until he figures out how to change it up.

Fare thee well, my honey, fare thee well...

The star of *Inside Llewyn Davis* is, of course, MUSIC—that magical construct of organized sounds and silences, of notes and words that summon untold mysteries. Central to the enigmatic mystery that's *Inside Llewyn Davis* is Davis himself, portrayed brilliantly by the charismatic Oscar Isaac, an unconventionally handsome actor of subtle gifts who also happens to be a sublimely effective musician. Isaac's Davis is woefully self-obsessed and his inability to connect with a wider audience as a folk singer is mirrored (and exacerbated) by the series of mishaps that unfold throughout his days—days so indistinguishable as to mirror weatherman Phil Connors in the movie, *Groundhog Day*.

Inside Llewyn Davis affords you the opportunity to walk a mile in the shoes of another man, only in this case it is six consecutive days and nights with Davis, shuttling up and down Manhattan and embarking on a fruitless journey to Chicago, with nothing to show for the effort but rejection and the impulse to give up on his musical dreams and return to the life of a merchant marine. But life is being so uncooperative at the moment that Davis can't even score a gig as a seaman and he's stuck being a folk singer by default.

Central to the plot's development, of course, are the songs performed throughout, with the libretto serving to emphasize much of the action. Much like Robert Altman's *Nashville*, the Coens had the actors arrange and perform their own material live for the film. Music is an important element in every Coen brothers film (thank you, Carter Burwell), but it is particularly crucial to *Inside Llewyn Davis*. After such a deft series of collaborations on the *The*

Big Lebowski (1998), *O Brother, Where Art Thou?* (2000), and *The Ladykillers* (2004), it made perfectly logical sense to once again enlist musician and producer T Bone Burnett to supervise the performances.

"The conversation expands in really interesting ways once we get T Bone involved," says Joel Coen. "He gets into the story, or the script, and takes it places musically that we wouldn't have thought of, and opens up all these interesting things."

On the film's official website, Burnett shares some of his perspective: "The movie starts out with 'Hang Me,' a song about getting hung. And then it goes into 'If I Had Wings,' and then you come into Llewyn's world and you find out that the guy he performed 'If I Had Wings' with, jumped off a bridge. And then every song is either about death, abortion, or murder. It's separation.

"This sounds like something a press agent would say, but I want to say this very soberly. I cannot think of a precedent in the history of civilization for this performance Oscar Isaac gives in this film. I don't think any actor has ever learned to play and sing a repertoire this thoroughly and compellingly, and be able to film it all live without a click track, without the aid of tuning, without the aid of technology—just a complete analog performance of this character whose music Oscar had never heard a year before he did the film. Unbelievable. Oscar absorbed the guitar playing of Dave Van Ronk and the era—a technique known as Travis Picking—as if he was born to it. He learned all the songs, and he learned to sing 'em so naturally.

"The thing is when we were on the set...in the movie you always have some kind of thumb track or click track or something that sets the tempo so you can cut between takes. But in this case, you know, the Coens decided early on that they just wanted to shoot and record the music live. No playback."

In addition to Isaac's superlative performances throughout the film and on the soundtrack, there are also impressive moments by the Down Hill Strugglers, Stark Sands, Carey Mulligan, and Justin Timberlake, who really shines in his one big scene of the hysterical novelty pastiche "Please Mr. Kennedy," as recorded by the "The John Glenn Singers."

In spite of the legalistic conceit at the end of the film's credits, claiming that there are "no similarities to persons living or dead," nothing could be more patently absurd. The fact remains that Davis is a fictional amalgamation, like most of the characters in *Inside Llewyn Davis*, and you can spend a hefty portion of the film's 105-minute running time playing "spot the doppelgänger," that literary concept where a paranormal double of a living person exists somewhere in the world. *Inside Llewyn Davis* is littered with composite characters very much based upon real events and people, with the obvious nod being Davis himself, whose situations are very much drawn from the late, great Dave Van Ronk as he relates in his superb autobiography, *The Mayor of MacDougal Street*. The Coens pay further homage to Van Ronk by having his version of "Green, Green Rocky Road" play over the film's final crawl. Van Ronk's true-to-life adventures of being a merchant marine and schlepping off to Chicago in the dead of winter, in a failed bid to audition for powerhouse manager Albert Grossman, is recounted in a sequence where Davis carpools to Chicago with a couple of disenfranchised hipsters, which include Roland Turner, a verbose junkie portrayed by the consistently superb John Goodman, and Garret Hedlund, who plays Turner's sulking "valet," Johnny Five. Upon arriving at the legendary Gate of Horn venue, Davis auditions for club manager Bud Grossman (F. Murray Abraham, in a wonderfully callous performance), who tells Davis matter-of-factly after he performs a passionate dirge about a queen who dies during childbirth: "I don't see a lot of money here."

There actually was a folk-singing husband and wife duo in the '60s named Jim and Jean, who recorded for Verve Folkways (Timberlake and Mulligan's characters respectively). Llewyn's miserly record label president, Mel Novikoff (Jerry Grayson), IS Folkways Records' president Moe Asch. Columbia records producer, Mr. Cromartie (Ian Jarvis), IS John Hammond Sr. And, of course, in the penultimate scene of the film, we have Bob Dylan performing "Farewell," in yet another echo within this epic tone poem of death and re-birth. The Coens are clearly giving us a poke in the ribs by taking a folk music purist like Davis (à la Van Ronk) and insinuating it is the night that Robert Shelton of the *New York Times* would show up to write a rave review about the young upstart from Hibbing, Minnesota (the review ran on September 29, 1961). That historical inevitability led to Dylan being signed to a recording contract by Hammond, setting the stage for Dylan's worldwide, one-man revolution, allowing him to escape the comparatively low-rent ghetto of Folkways, Elektra, and other independents—for his ultimate ascent into the big time.

In his memoir *Chronicles Volume One*, Dylan acknowledges the influence and the debt he owes to Van Ronk:

"I'd heard Van Ronk back in the Midwest on records and thought he was pretty great, copied some of his recordings phrase for phrase. He was passionate and stinging, sang like a solider of fortune and sounded like he paid the price. Van Ronk could howl and whisper, turn blues into ballads and ballads into blues. I loved his style. He was what the city was all about. In Greenwich Village, Van Ronk was king of the street, he reigned supreme." Dylan's debt ran even deeper after he lifted wholesale Van Ronk's arrangement of the traditional "House of the Rising Sun" and put it on his own self-titled debut. Van Ronk was miffed but gracious about it and somehow learned to take the matter in stride. It's a lesson in class that Llewyn Davis would do well to take to heart.

"What are you doing?"

The Coens are the Doublemint Twins of cinema and in addition to the above mentioned doppelgängers, there is a "doubling" that runs throughout the film; Timkin and Davis, Jim and Jean, two different tabbies, two sets of dinner guests at Davis' friends, the Gorfeins, Jean's two *other* lovers besides her singing partner Jim Berkey, a pair of women (Jean and his sister Joy) incessantly harping on Llewyn, Jean and Roland independently suggesting that Llewyn is living an excremental existence—the symbolic twinning goes on and on. There is even a callback to their previous film *O Brother, Where Art Thou?* by naming the Gorfein's cat Ulysses, a reference to Homer's *Odyssey* that both films share. And then there's the film's ultimate doubling down by repeating the first scene as the last, suggesting in its oblique way that the first verse had come back around as a refrain, which also serves as a final exclamation point to this cinematic Gordian knot. And most assuredly something in the world of *Llewyn Davis* is coming to pass because each and every breath of this film is spent singing variations on sweet adieu, fare thee well, and goodbye to what has been. Hell, even the last two words of the film are Llewyn saying "au revoir" to the guy from the Ozarks (representing the old guard) who kicks the living daylights out of him for heckling his wife the night before.

Oh, and for all you train spotters out there: as Llewyn nears the end of his cinematic journey he comes across a movie theatre with a one-sheet poster advertising the Walt Disney film *The Incredible Journey*. Although the novel by Shelia Burnford was published in 1961, it was not made into a film until November of 1963. The adventure of three pets (a Labrador, a Bull Terrier, and a Siamese cat) who travel 250 miles through the Canadian wilderness to return to their home, was no doubt part of the inspiration to include a cat named Ulysses as a central plot device as well.

You probably heard that one before, because it was never new and it never gets old and it's a folk song. – Llewyn Davis

The "Neo-Ethnics" vs. the "Pop Folkies"

Historically, much about the Greenwich Village folk scene hinged on the perception of how "authentic" performers appeared to be—the way they sounded, the way they dressed and how affected was their approach to the material. The type of performers featured on ABC-TV's short-lived program *Hootenanny* (1963–64) emphasized the "pop folk" approach, and while that show managed to bring traditional folk songs to a much broader audience, its clean-cut, candyass take on folk music rankled the sensibilities of the "neo-ethnics" like Ramblin' Jack Elliot, Van Ronk, and others.

Van Ronk: "We knew about the Kingston Trio and Harry Belafonte and their hordes of squeaky-clean imitators, but we felt like that was a different world that had nothing to do with us. Most of those people couldn't play worth a damn and were indifferent singers, and as far as material was concerned they were scraping the top of the barrel, singing songs that we had all learned and dropped already. It was *Sing Along with Mitch* and the *Fireside Book of Folk Songs*, performed by sophomores in paisley shirts, and it was a one hundred percent rip-off. They were ripping off the material, they were ripping off the authors, composers, collectors, and sources, and they were ripping off the public."

"When you read about the scene you see this mania for authenticity," says Joel Coen, emphasizing a type of moral stance that many within the folk community felt was imperative. When Bob Dylan stopped writing topical songs adaptable to the civil rights movement (i.e. "Blowin' in the Wind" or "The Times They Are a-Changin'"), many within the traditional folk community felt a sense of betrayal. That feeling was emblematic of how so many people's identities were wrapped up in the political correctness of the scene and that folk musicians must retain their social "integrity." Many of the "neo-ethnic" folkies believed that this ancient language, passed from person to person throughout the ages, held a secret, transformative power and it was not to be trifled with or maligned. Within these circles the politics and the music walked hand in hand. Whether you were fighting for socialism, communism, or civil rights, folk songs became anthems that served as a focal point in the quest for social transformation. But that also begged the question: who are the arbiters of such aesthetics and how does one go about becoming an "authentic" folk singer? For Van Ronk, the answer lay in the record collection of artist and archivist Harry Smith.

Van Ronk: "We were severely limited, because much as we might consider ourselves devotees of the true, pure folk styles, there was very little of that music available. Then a marvelous thing happened. Around 1953, Folkways Records put out a six-LP set called the *Anthology of American Folk Music*, culled from commercial recordings of traditional rural musicians that had been made in the South during the 1920s and '30s. The *Anthology* was created by a man named Harry Smith, who was a beatnik eccentric artist and an experimental filmmaker. Harry had a fantastic collection of 78s and his idea was to provide an overview of the range of styles being played in rural America at the dawn of recording. That set became our bible.

"It was an incredible compendium of American traditional music, all performed in the traditional styles. That was very important for my generation, especially those of us I consider 'neo-ethnics,' because we were trying not only to sing traditional songs but also to assimilate the styles of the rural players. Without the Harry Smith *Anthology* we could not have existed, because there was no other way for us to get hold of that material."

Moving Ahead by Looking Back

There are some who have suggested, or perhaps it's merely wishful thinking, that *Inside Llewyn Davis* will spark a brand new folk boom among the current generation of music fans. Regardless, for T Bone Burnett, this is what lies at the heart of the film: "I don't want to give a lot away but the film is about a time when there's a new moment happening. The old has died, and the new thing hasn't quite been born. We've been in an interregnum now for the past ten years, really, where the old has been dying but is not dead, and the new is being born but it's not yet alive.

"We've been in this brackish water where it's not one thing or another. The old structure that we lived in for my whole lifetime has been dismantled for the most part. But the new structure hasn't taken place. This is an incredibly long conversation that has to do with everything that's going on in the Internet and in music. But at any rate, I feel we're at a time now when the value of music has been brought into question. And this movie speaks very eloquently, I think, about the value of music, and about the value of art throughout culture. We've been in a period of time for the last twenty years really, during which there's been an assault on the arts by the technology community. The technology community has devalued the art, especially music, and has taken over the role of the artist in the society. We're being told now that artists are to crowd-source their work; that artists are to follow the crowd rather than lead the crowd. Well, there's no artist worth his salt that will follow the crowd.

"I'm not interested in any artist who will follow the crowd. Jules Verne put a man on the moon a hundred years before a rocket scientist did. Einstein said that Picasso preceded him by twenty years. The arts have always led the sciences, and they should, too, because the arts are involved with the whole of humanity, the whole of the creation, not just specific parts of it. We can't let the engineers be in control of our society because one thing will happen. We will turn into *The Matrix*. So that's why this film is important to me because it talks about this in a very eloquent way. It's a much more profound way to talk about where we are."

Touché T Bone and, once again, hats off to the Coens, who have crafted the ultimate ode of surrender. And may we all learn to gracefully say "adios" to the traditions of the past that no longer serve our evolutionary ascent.

San Diego Troubadour, February, 2014

FORTY

Epiphanies to Slay the Dragon:
Coming of Age in the Spirit of '76
—A Mashup Mosaic—

THE BIG PICTURE – I
Setting Intentions

What came first, the music or the misery? People worry about kids playing with guns, or watching violent videos—that some sort of culture of violence will take them over. Nobody worries about kids listening to thousands, literally thousands of songs about heartbreak, rejection, pain, misery, and loss. Did I listen to pop music because I was miserable? Or was I miserable because I listened to pop music? – **John Cusack (1966–) as DJ Rob Gordon, in Nick Hornby's** *High Fidelity* **(2000)**

Is this the real life? Is this just fantasy?
Caught in a landslide, no escape from reality.
Open your eyes, look up to the skies and see...

Q: If not Now—when?

As above, so below. I have always been a stickler for determining exactly what "**the truth**" of any situation is. Not that I've always been able to recognize it, or possessed the integrity to act upon it, but as I continue to evolve, my perception of truth morphs over time. My intention is to always be in alignment with my intuitive awareness—what some refer to as the seat of the Soul—and to remain steadfast in having the courage to act upon that truth. And, most importantly, to always perform "right action," by not lying, stealing, or acting in a harmful manner toward others or myself—living in accordance with what I believe to be sound moral principals with a minimal amount of dogma.

Imagine all the people living life in peace. Imagine if each of us were taught how to live by the principals of right action, from the time we were able to speak and reason. To be taught, and know within our hearts, that each and every life form is Divine, and that all beings are sacred. **Paramahansa Yogananda** (1893–1952) writes in his *Autobiography of a Yogi* about establishing a school for young boys in India and teaching them how to meditate by the time they reach the age of five. If the science of yoga and meditation were taught to all children throughout the world, just imagine the sort of culture we would have. It may not be "perfect," but it would certainly be a much more peaceful, conscious, and aware civilization, with respect and love for all beings, as well as the planet.

☯

Q: Is love all you need?
A: I would say awareness is all you need. And that love stems from awareness. – **Allen Ginsberg (1926–1997)**

THE BIG PICTURE – II
Accentuating the Positive, Acknowledging the Negative

Labor to keep alive in your breast, that little spark of celestial fire called conscience. For myself, one of the lessons in truth-seeking began during my time at Peyton Randolph Elementary School in Arlington, Virginia, where my fellow classmates and I were taught about how **George Washington** (1732–1799) could never tell a lie. Our teacher, Mrs. Bryant, told us that when the first U.S. president was a young boy, he chopped down his father's prized cherry tree. And even though he was likely to be punished, he still had the strength of character to admit to the deed: "I cannot tell a lie, Pa." His honesty was rewarded with admiration from his father for telling the truth. It's a strong myth regarding personal character, not to mention ironic, as I would later find out that the cherry tree story is an unsubstantiated myth, or a lie.

To Serve Man. What is the purpose of using revisionist history as propaganda and why do we tell that story, and so many other fabrications, to impressionable children and pawn it off as historical fact? The long answer to that question can be found in **Howard Zinn**'s (1922–2010) excellent book, *A People's History of the United States.* Slavery has existed in many forms throughout the world, and the short answer seems to be that certain segments of society make up for their spiritual deficiencies by controlling and manipulating others. It is (in part) how external power is derived—by holding dominion over peoples, continents, and planetary resources. It also allows for a certain class of people to benefit from the labor and ignorance of others. For want of a better term, I refer to these people as "the ruling class." Others have labeled them "the one percent," "the military-industrial complex of war profiteers," or "the Illuminati." However **you** choose to define these movers and shakers/policy makers, it is in every person's best interest to become informed: to learn the ways of the wider world—or suffer the fate of remaining ignorant, like lambs led to slaughter by an unfeeling group of sociopaths that sometimes double in our society as "politicians."

The United States was founded by the brightest people in the country—and we haven't seen them since.

– **Gore Vidal** (1925–2012)

Knowledge is power. Before reaching the age of twelve, I was taught in public school about the Declaration of Independence, the articles of the Constitution of the United States, and its Preamble. Understanding the ideas contained within these pioneering documents, and the concept of *habeas corpus*, is **crucial** if we are to live in a free and open society—free, that is, from arbitrary state action. A democracy is a form of government in which all eligible citizens participate equally, even when the definition of what constitutes a democracy varies from culture to culture.

Question authority. In addition to the institutionalized mythology of our Founding Fathers, I learned about truth, lies, and ambiguity through my own upbringing. Central to my experience is the fact that I did not meet my biological father until I was 26 years of age—primarily due to the consciousness of the adults involved: my mother, my stepfather Arthur (who raised me from the age of six months onward), and my biological father, Michael. My circumstances while coming of age were veiled in vague half-truths and omissions—an exercise in manipulation until I was old enough to start formulating bolder questions and develop the inner fortitude to seek out those answers for myself.

Question everything. One of the byproducts of my upbringing was to become obsessed with determining what "**truth**" is. While I believe that the truth will set you free from a maze of illusions, those same truths are capable of filling you with a profound sadness and a sense of righteous indignation about what is really going on in the world. I don't particularly care much for dogma. Like nostalgia, dogma equals death of the spirit in the eternal Now—that energetic principle of Life that is ever-changing—and dogma keeps you from stepping into your authentic Self, your true power. But in order to own and be in your authority, it is necessary to **slay the psychological dragon** within your psyche (symbolized by breaking free of your dependence upon parental figures, which includes the government)—and that metamorphosis requires a spiritual transformation to occur.

You cannot define yourself in reference to other external coordinates; you must define yourself internally through your relationship with a higher entity. Think of yourself as a manifestation of some higher thing, some higher frequency. [makes waves with his hands] *This* is the visible realization. And you know that because you can't see atoms can you? And you certainly can't see the forces that hold atoms together. There, in the micro quantum world, lie the answers to everything. We can't understand it with biological rational minds, but when you feel it intuitively, and get yourself in alignment with that stuff, you'll beam like the Sun.* – **Comedian/Actor Russell Brand (1975–)**

THE BIG PICTURE – III
What Are the Possibilities?

Ooh, my soul. Perhaps I've been unwittingly hoodwinked or hypnotized by some nefarious means, but I have always been entranced by the sound of music. As a child, I found it mystifying how waves of sound from the radio or a record player produced such a state of transcendent bliss, filling me with the impulse to dance, sing, and shout to the heavens! In my paradigm, sound vibrations literally create and change the universe—that which I perceive to be consciousness itself. With intense, mindful, thought streams of energy, I intuit that ANYTHING IS POSSIBLE, which is precisely why I feel that musicians and artists of all disciplines must act as *conscious* conduits if they are to affect vibrational change in a deliberate, intentional, and positive manner. Or, in a dense and negative manner—the choice is always yours—so endeavor to choose wisely.

It's all up to what you value, down to where you are. It all swings on the pain you've gone through, getting where you are.
— **George Harrison (1943–2001)**

Music is a moral law. It gives soul to the universe, wings to the mind, flight to the imagination and charm and gaiety to life.
— **Plato (427–347 BC)**

Music in the soul can be heard by the universe.
— **Lao Tzu (6th century BC)**

Music is a higher revelation than all wisdom and philosophy.
– **Ludwig van Beethoven** (1770–1827)

Don't bore us, get to the chorus. – **Steven Tyler** (1948–)

By the time I was ten, whenever I had the opportunity, I would stay in my room on Sunday afternoons and listen to all three hours of *American Top 40*, the syndicated radio program hosted by **Casey Kasem** (1932–2014), occasionally taking notes on what was in the charts that week. As kitschy as much of it is, pop music in the '70s was wonderfully diverse. In any given hour on the Top 40, you could hear country/western, R&B, singer/songwriters, soul, disco, arena rock, middle-of-the-road ballads, and novelty songs. It was certainly NOT the ghetto of segregation that radio devolved into by the early 1980s, where the primary concern for programmers was segmenting the audience for greater ease in targeting their advertising demographics.

Watching television is like taking black spray paint to your third eye. – **Bill Hicks** (1961–1994)

However, it wasn't JUST music I was hypnotized by. There was also the compulsive junk-food junkiedom of the "idiot box" (i.e. television) as well. Like millions of contemporaries, my psyche, personal habits, and thought patterns were in large measure a by-product of a media-drenched culture. There's no denying or negating that fact—it simply is— with the jury still out on how that impacts society-at-large. I suspect that it would have been of great personal benefit while coming of age to have a mentor on hand with the cognition of a **Marshall McLuhan** (1911–1980), a **Paddy Chayefsky** (1923–1981), or a **Joseph Campbell** (1904–1987); a noble steward who is capable of staving off your naiveté and explaining just how much sway the media holds in molding and shaping the collective consciousness of the human race—not to mention being able to explain exactly what "the medium is the message" signifies. How much the media affects your consciousness depends largely on **you**, but it took me the greater part of 30 unconscious years before I began to figure that out for myself, and stopped swallowing information from the Box wholesale, undigested—mindlessly repeating with parrot-like precision such queries as "How do **you** spell relief?" and knowing, unequivocally, that the answer is "R-O-L-A-I-D-S."

I love to accentuate the positive whenever possible. Seriously, it's all I wish to do in this lifetime. But I find that rather hard to accomplish with the TV blathering on in the background. To me, TV is a magnet for banality and negativity. The vibrational frequency of television commands your awareness and holds it hostage at a very base level.

In 1976, **Tom Snyder** (1936–2007) interviewed Marshall McLuhan and asked him "what would happen if you shut off television for 30 days in the entire United States of America?" McLuhan: "There would be a kind of hangover effect, because it's a very addictive medium. You take it away and people develop all of the symptoms of a hangover—it's very uncomfortable. It was tried two or three years ago in Germany and in Great Britain, they actually paid people to not watch TV for a couple of months. And they discovered that they had all the withdrawal symptoms of drug addicts. TV is a very, very involving medium and it is a form of 'inner trip.' And so, people do miss it." Snyder: "The thought just occurred to me that if you turned off television there would be a lot of people who would say, at the end of the 30-day period, we will not permit you to turn it back on. Do you think that could happen?" McLuhan: "A great many of the teenagers have stopped watching television—they're saturated—saturation is a possibility. As for the possibility of reneging on any future TV, I doubt it. Except through saturation. But TV is so demanding, and therefore so soporific that it requires an enormous amount of energy to participate in. You don't have that freedom of detachment. One of the effects of television is removing people's private identity. They become corporate peer group people just by watching it. They lose interest in being private individuals. This is one of the hidden and perhaps most insidious aspects of television."

Here's a query: How might events from the past be healed, in order to move forward from the psychic shackles that linger in the unconscious shadows?

Terence McKenna (1946–2000): "What civilization is, is six billion people trying to make themselves happy by standing on each other's shoulders and kicking each other's teeth in—it's not a pleasant situation. And yet, you can stand back and look at this planet and see that we have the money, the power, the medical understanding, the scientific know-how, the love, and the community to produce a kind of human paradise. But we are lead by the least among us, the least intelligent, the least noble, the least visionary. And we do not fight back against the dehumanizing values that are handed down as control icons. Culture is not your friend.

"Culture is for other people's convenience and the convenience of various institutions: churches, companies, tax collection schemes, what have you—it is not your friend. It insults you, it disempowers you, it uses and abuses you. None of us are well-treated by culture. And yet we glorify the creative potential of the individual, the rights of the individual. We understand the felt presence of experience as what is most important. But the culture is a perversion. It fetishizes objects, creates consumer mania, it preaches endless forms of false happiness, endless forms of false understanding in the form of squirrelly religions and silly cults. It invites people to diminish themselves and dehumanize themselves by behaving like machines. Meme processors of memes passed down from Madison Avenue and Hollywood.

"And I think that the way we counteract all of that is by creating art. Man was not put on this planet to toil in the mud. Or, the god who put us on this planet to toil in the mud is no god I want to have any part of: it's some sort of Gnostic demon. It's some kind of cannibalistic demiurge that should be thoroughly renounced and rejected. By putting the art 'pedal to the metal' we maximize our humanness and become much more necessary and incomprehensible to the machine."

☯

We'd all love to see the plan. – **John Lennon (1940–1980)**

On November 27, 1976, Paddy Chayefsky's *Network* premieres: "And here's that mad prophet of the airwaves, **Howard Beale!**"

"Edward George Ruddy died today. Edward George Ruddy was the chairman of the board of the Union

Broadcasting System and he died at eleven o'clock this morning of a heart condition and woe is us—we're in a lot of trouble. So, a rich, little man with white hair died. What has that got to do with the price of rice, right? And why is that woe to us? Because you people and 62 million other Americans are listening to me right now; because less than three percent of you people read books; because less than fifteen percent of you read newspapers. Because the only truth you know is what you get over this tube.

"Right now there is an entire generation that never knew anything that didn't come out of this tube. This tube is the gospel, the ultimate revelation. This tube can make or break presidents, popes, prime ministers—this tube is the most awesome goddamn force in the whole godless world and **woe is us if it ever falls into the hands of the wrong people** and that's why woe is us that Edward George Ruddy died.

"Because this company is now in the hands of CCA—the Communication Corporation of America. There's a new chairman of the board, a man called Frank Hackett, sitting in his office on the twentieth floor. And when the twelfth largest company in the world controls the most awesome goddamn propaganda force in the whole godless world, who knows what shit will be peddled for truth on this network. So, you listen to me: television is not the truth. Television is a goddamn amusement park. Television is a circus, a carnival, a traveling troupe of acrobats, storytellers, dancers, singers, jugglers, sideshow freaks, lion tamers, and football players. We're in the boredom-killing business. So, if you want the truth, go to God. Go to your gurus. **Go to yourselves**, 'cause that's the only place you're ever going to find any real truth. Man, you're never going to get any truth from us. We'll tell you anything you want to hear, we lie like hell, we'll tell you that Kojak always gets the killer, and nobody ever gets cancer in Archie Bunker's house, and no matter how much trouble the hero is in, don't worry, by the end of the hour he is going to win—**we'll tell you any shit you want to hear.**

"We deal in illusions man, none of it is true. But you people sit there day after day, night after night, all ages, colors, creeds—we're all you know. You're beginning to believe the illusions we're spinning here, you're beginning to think that the tube is reality and that your own lives are unreal. You do whatever the tube tells you. You dress like the tube, you eat like a tube, you raise your children like a tube, you even think like a tube. This is mass madness, you maniacs. In God's name, you people are the real thing—we are the illusion. So, turn off your television sets, turn them off now, turn them off right now, turn them off and leave them off, turn them off right in the middle of the sentence I am speaking. Turn them off!"

☯

Snapshot #1 – Saturday, January 3, 1976

The conceits are unbelievable. The yuletide log had sung its song, with its dying embers dancing in anticipation of a glorious New Year ahead. Glorious because 1976 was destined to be a year of significant change. The air was crackling, and there was no escape from the public relations blitzkrieg surrounding the United States of America's 200th trip around the Sun.

In **Frank Zappa's** (1940–1993) song, "Poofter's Froth Wyoming Plans Ahead," (from the exceptional *Bongo Fury* LP), he warns that the advertising campaign for America's bicentennial has been in the planning stages for years—selling patriotism in every imaginable form, with the balloon and bunting brigade in full-swing and doing its absolute damndest to persuade the nation to feel good about itself. Particularly after the recent one-two debacles of the Nixon administration's Watergate scandal, preceding a clear and utter failure at being able to spin anything positive out of the "conflict" in Southeast Asia—other than being able to announce the withdrawal of U.S. military personnel. With inflation, unemployment, gas shortages, and political unrest in an election year, there was a perpetual need for a fresh beginning in America: to regain a sense of domestic optimism for the future. To that end, incumbent president **Gerald Ford** (1913–2006) even ran an ad during his election campaign on the "Peace" platform. It was such a lovely fantasy for the unelected commander-in-chief to foist upon his constituents.

Thunderbolt and lightning, very, very frightening me! It was the first Saturday of the year, and I was enjoying a solitary afternoon in my room, preparing to complete my stint at elementary school and finish off the sixth grade. But something occurred that day that changed me forever. The radio was tuned to WPGC, the local Top 40 station, and with zero fanfare I experienced "Bohemian Rhapsody" for the first time. It was the lead single by the British quartet Queen, from their fourth long-playing album, *A Night at the Opera*, and the track had just been released as a 45 rpm disc that week. At the time, listening to *A Night at the Opera* seemed an adolescent rite of passage, and in

1976 it sounded unbelievably surreal, an experience rife with immense ramifications. Having your mind blown by "Bohemian Rhapsody" was akin to the delayed gratification of smoking marijuana for the first time—you don't really feel its effects. But when I heard it again the following hour (it was already in heavy rotation), I sat stunned by the radio after all five minutes and 55 seconds of the track played out ("any way the wind blows…"). Strike the gong and the spell was broken, my disbelief shattered, destroyed by a manic station ID and a frantic flurry of advertisements. I clicked off the pablum and instinctively *knew* what my next course of action had to be: I HAD to track down a copy of that record. It was a mandatory matter of acquisition and it needed to happen right this minute. Ah, compulsive obsessions—where *do* they come from?

With no time to ponder such things, I grabbed a dollar from my dresser, put on my coat and asked/told my mom that I needed to go to Drug Fair and I would be back in fifteen minutes. Even though the temperature outside was 46 degrees under grayish skies (the reason I was indoors listening to the radio in the first place), I was oblivious to the chill in the air as I ran as fast as possible for the mile it took me to reach my destination. I bounded through the glass doors and veered toward the right, where cameras, watches, and other cheap electronic devices shared floor space with several rows of LPs, and a vertical wire rack displaying the latest singles. I quickly ran my eyes down the length of the perch and there it was, toward the bottom, sporting an Elektra Records paper sleeve (with its distinctive lime green butterfly on the label)—the object of my quest. I grabbed a copy of the record, on sale for sixty-nine cents, walked over to the cash register, and slid my dollar to the man behind the counter. I jittered nervously in place as he handed me my change, and picking up the 45 between my thumb and forefinger, I ran all the way home. Flying up the stairs to my bedroom, I tore off my coat and put the record on the platter, giving the A-side several listens before flipping it over out of curiosity and checking out what was on the B-side: drummer **Roger Taylor**'s (1949–) "I'm in Love with My Car." I couldn't wrap my head around the sentiment *at all* and took it to be some kind of three-minute joke.

Still, it rocked like nobody's business, and it had those trademark, larger-than-life, Queen vocal harmonies. Satirical or not, however, it wasn't going to hold a candle to what was on the A-side. But then again, what can? **Freddie Mercury** (1946–1991), the fabulously gay and grandiose lead singer and pianist of Queen, had composed an absolute masterpiece of angst, frustration and existential liberation— the ultimate adrenalized release from a self-imposed rock 'n' roll prison. Bassist **John Deacon**'s (1951–) understated support suits the song perfectly, and guitarist **Brian May**'s (1947–) electrifying signature solo is as exquisite a musical expression as there has ever been. The performance is as triumphant as it is ruminating and melancholy, and **Roy Thomas Baker**'s (1946–) production is magnificence personified. Even though my eleven-year-old psyche couldn't completely come to grips with the obscure storyline or the consequences of what it meant to kill a man, I certainly could identify with the errant longing expressed in the lyric "I sometimes wish I'd never been born at all…" How universally human is that? Then there is that operatic middle section before a climax without parallel—and pray

tell: how horrendous (or egotistical) did your actions have
to be for Beelzebub to set aside a special devil just for *you*?
THAT had to be a joke, right? In a year of celebrations,
disappointments, discoveries, and transitions, crossing the
borderline of childhood into the Dark Wood realm of adult
concerns, it was the perfect introductory soundtrack to
inaugurate the fireworks of 1976.

Snapshot #2 – Friday, April 16, 1976

It was the most surreal experience. I was sitting in front of
the television on the afternoon of Good Friday, watching
the local ABC affiliate channel seven, because they were
showing Richard Lester's classic 1964 film, *A Hard Day's
Night*, starring the Beatles. Even though I barely remembered the Beatles before they officially broke up in 1970 (to
pursue individual projects), I was already a freak about their
music, and was following all four solo careers as much as the
radio, and my budget, would allow.

Every afternoon, Monday through Friday, from three to
five PM (right before the local news), channel seven would
program old movies, and as a gimmick to entice viewers, they
called their segment *Money Movie Seven*. The host, Johnny
Batchelder, sat in a director's chair on a cheap set, randomly
picking names out of the local phone book and calling them
live on air. If the caller could correctly guess the amount of
money in the jackpot, they would win that amount. Each
time a caller made an incorrect guess, the jackpot grew by
another $10. Before the last commercial break, someone won
$237. According to the rules, the prize amount went back to
the starting point of $77—double sevens for channel seven.

Mr. Batchelder held the *White Pages* on his lap and addressed the camera to say it was time to pick another caller and give them a chance to win the jackpot. At that exact moment he started dialing the phone, my father walked through the front door from work. Amazingly, as I sat watching the television screen, the phone started ringing in the kitchen. I ran over to the phone excitedly, not believing the synchronicity, and lifted it off the cradle: "Hello, Jackson residence." I continued watching the TV in the living room as Johnny spoke to the camera and to me in my earpiece simultaneously: "Hello, I am calling from *Money Movie Seven*. Is Mister Arthur Jackson at home?"

My father hadn't even taken his coat off yet as I handed him the phone while jumping up and down saying "77 dollars! 77 dollars! 77 dollars!" He gave me a "hush" gesture as he lifted the phone to his ear. I darted my eyes between my father and the television, and watched as the exchange took place. My father finally responded with the answer that I had been feeding him for over 45 seconds and Mr. Batchelder said "Congratulations! You are the winner here on *Money Movie Seven*! Please stay on the line so that we can get all your personal details." And with those words the climax of *A Hard Day's Night* came on the screen, with the Beatles in a TV studio performing "I Should Have Known Better." It was an unusually exciting way to end the film and my dad was $77 richer, thanks to my Beatles obsession.

You got to have a Jones for this, a Jones for that—but this running with the Jones, boy just ain't where it's at. Later that weekend I discovered a copy of Boz Scaggs' *Silk Degrees* in my Easter basket, in addition to a bunch of chocolate to get all wired up on. Thanks, ma.

THE BIG PICTURE – IV
An All-American Mongrel Boy

Snapshot #3 – Sunday, July 4, 1976

1976 was the Chinese year of the Dragon—a year I spent pedaling my bike and teeter-tottering on the chasm between eleven and twelve, when I learned about the eternal song and dance of responsibility, and its subsequent reward of remuneration, by delivering copies of the *Washington Star* and folding pizza boxes after school at **The Broiler** on Columbia Pike in Arlington, Virginia. My best friend and partner-in-crime at school, Jimmy Burke, had connected me with both gigs, and I leaped at the opportunity to make some dough of my own. My intuition and desire to be an independent person of means must have been working overtime, no doubt influenced by the fact that my family's infrastructure was on the brink of collapse.

My mother and stepfather had initiated divorce proceedings in the spring of '76 and their official announcement to my two younger brothers and myself just happened to neatly coincide with the outbreak of my adolescence: that social-sexual-intellectual playground of awakening where we begin to consciously wonder about the world we inhabit, attempting to understand how the whole kit-and-caboodle came into being in the first place. You know, that Divine Comedy of human interaction that we collectively refer to as civilization or society.

Being born in the District of Columbia, I was acutely aware, early in life, how our collective institutions (i.e. family, schools, churches, government, banks, corporations, mass-media, etc.) shape our culture and reflect the consciousness of its citizens. These institutions impact every person's existence, and I am *particularly* aware of how the privileges I possess as a "free white male" influence my experience. I am not among the majority in gender nor ethnicity, but somehow, the Anglo-Saxon cultural values of a predominately white patriarchy have presided over this continent, and much of the globe, for well over five centuries.

Conventionally considered a "Caucasian," I am actually of "mixed" race due to a confluence of genetic influences: Cherokee, Dutch, French, Irish, Welsh, English, German, and 50 percent Slovakian. By nationality, I am considered an "American," although I tend to think of myself as a citizen of the world or, better yet, a child of the universe. My social and spiritual obligations and responsibilities are to the planet and the whole of humanity—rather than attached to a special interest group that champions jingoism, which in my mind has become synonymous with nationalism. Preserving and promoting the cultural values of a nation is one thing; imposing those values onto another culture is imperialism under the guise of globalization. Imperfect as it may be to possess aversions of any sort, if there's one thing I can't stand it is flag-waving. A flag is many things but it is primarily a symbol—and symbols are extremely potent objects in this world, particularly when you project an ideology upon them and manage to coerce others, through either propaganda or intimidation, into your fundamentalist viewpoint.

☯

Bill Hicks asks a reasonable question: *What business is it of yours what I do, read, buy, see, say, think, who I fuck or what I take into my body—as long as I do not harm another human being on this planet?*

They say that patriotism is the last refuge to which a scoundrel clings. Steal a little and they throw you in jail, steal a lot and they make you king. – **Bob Dylan (1941–), paraphrasing Samuel Johnson (1709–1784) and Eugene O'Neill (1888–1953)**

I was but nineteen-years-old when my dear old dad (technically my stepfather) shuffled off this mortal coil at the tender age of 55. But while he was here he repeatedly emphasized two things: 1) obtain a quality education, and 2) you can achieve **anything** in this life once you put your mind to the task. Those are two rock solid pieces of advice that I live out every day.

It was a *profound* experience to come of age during the season of America's bicentennial. But as we propel ourselves forty years past that historical landmark I am still left wondering: how did we arrive at this particular place in time, and what does the future hold based on the sum of knowledge that we possess as a race? What is **truth?** What is an illusion? Why are we taught the pledge of allegiance as children? What constitutes a democracy? What do the words "life, liberty and the pursuit of happiness" truly mean? Is it possible to nail down such an ephemeral construct as "freedom?" Do we really possess such a thing as free will, and if so, is it possible to have that quality of consciousness usurped by conditioning and enculturalization? And in the final analysis, does Love really conquer All?

We recently concluded one epoch in human history, as recorded by the Mayan calendar, and the world obviously did not come to an end on the Winter Solstice of 2012. Rather, we began a new cycle. But can any of us declare with certainty where our exact locale is as we continue to explore the physical and psychic frontier between the known and the unknown universe? Is there really such a thing as a true North Star to fix our gaze upon, and guide us on this journey? I am a firm believer in the notion that in order to know where you are going, you have to know where you have been. To arrive at any potent conclusions it is necessary to apply some critical thinking skills to your perceptual awareness. By definition, critical thinking would involve observation, interpretation, analysis, inference, evaluation, explanation and metacognition. These are not skills that were reinforced or encouraged during my years of study in public education. Moreover, they became by-products of a personal crusade dedicated to the vigilant principle of defining for myself what reality and truth are. If it is true that the personal can be political, I also contend that the personal can be the universal, as the tools of science, reason, and intuition, demonstrate how the macro contains the micro, and vice versa.

We are all influenced by what we are exposed to, right? It is called enculturalization: proximity to information, exposure to ideas, what kind, how much, and how that information is applied.

I also feel that music education is of supreme importance. Learning to be an active participant, expressing yourself through sound, and truly learning how to LISTEN. I am grateful to have grown up in an era where music was neither competition (ala *American Idol*), nor used as a passive, wallpaper fashion accessory.

Music is a sanctuary and church pew. I started listening to rock 'n' roll and pop music as an alternative to the rather dry hymnals of the United Methodist church that I was baptized in. By the age of twelve I felt that some of these congregations needed better songs to sing. However, if there is anything I am proud of and relate to as being from "America," it is the traditional music that is indigenous to this continent.

Baby Boom Go Boom. I was born in the last year of the post-World War II baby boom (1946–1964), and I maintain the point of view that anyone who was twelve-to-sixteen during 1965, '66, or '67 was pretty frickin' fortunate if you look at the pop charts of those years compared with the pop charts of, say, '88, '99, or 2014. Not to say that there isn't anything enjoyable on Top 40 radio today—because there is, but you just can't match the quality of the output from 1966 to '76, '86, '96, or 2006. You're pretty much comparing apples—and onions.

I have long enjoyed the idea that where you are at the age of twelve really defines so much of your cultural aesthetics and preferences. I found it easy in 1985 to go back and appreciate the music of 1955 or 1945, but remaining open to new music coming out in '95, or 2005, or 2014? It's not as easy a task. For a kid coming of age in 1985, or 1995, or 2005, you can always go backward and discover how great *Rubber Soul* is, even though you might have been raised on Eminem, LMFAO, Usher, or Justin Bieber. All pop music is marketed for a demographic between the ages of eight-to-sixteen, emotionally and mentally. For this reason, most young adults lose interest in pop music by the time they turn twenty, because they are no longer being spoken to with the conditioned response of pop music, i.e. its social engineering. By the time you're twenty, it's time to start putting away such childish things.

Or is it? What if your most passionate obsession in life is music itself? Something that feeds the soul, emotions, and intellect, in ways that no other form succeeds at? "Music is the greatest form of communication we have," says **Sir Elton John** (1947–) and I believe that **Reginald** doth speak the truth. So where do you go with all of that passion when you are no longer spoken to by Contemporary Hits Radio?

For me, I was eighteen when I moved from the east coast to the left coast, and by going 3,000 miles westward, I dropped a slew of listening habits and formed a multitude of new ones. A big part of turning eighteen was the adventure of exploring the rich history of recorded sound that goes back to the turn of the century. I started devouring any and all books, records, magazines, films, and videos I could find that connected me to the rich legacy of documentation that exists for twentieth century culture—and I hope that passionate level of curiosity never ends.

When all was said and done that spring, my parents went through five different divorce decrees, before concluding that what was best for all parties was for my two brothers and myself to stay together under the guardianship of my step-father, and that we would spend time on the weekends and holidays with our mother. Just like **Van Morrison** (1945–) sang at the time, 1976 was turning out to be a heavy period of transition for us all.

THE BIG PICTURE – V
Revisiting the Meaning of Patriotism in a Free World

Dangerous consequences will follow when politicians and rulers forget moral principles. Whether we believe in God or karma, ethics is the foundation of every religion.
— His Holiness the XIV Dalai Lama (1935-)

While some people think that dissent is unpatriotic, I would argue that dissent is the highest form of patriotism. In fact, if patriotism means being true to the principles for which your country is supposed to stand, then certainly the right to dissent is one of those principles. And if we're exercising that right to dissent, it's a patriotic act. — Howard Zinn

An Overview to the Politics of Dancing. Here are the rules that the State has devised for the general population, as filtered through the sensibilities of **Robert Shea** (1933–1994) and **Robert Anton Wilson** (1932–2007) in *The Illuminatus Trilogy* (1975):

DEFINITIONS and DISTINCTIONS

Free Market: That condition of society in which all economic transactions result from voluntary choice without coercion.

The State: That institution which interferes with the Free Market through the direct exercise of coercion or the granting of privileges (backed by coercion).

Tax: That form of coercion or interference with the Free Market in which the State collects tribute (the tax), allowing it to hire armed forces to practice coercion in defense of privilege, and also to engage in such wars, adventures, experiments, "reforms," etc., as it pleases, not at its own cost, but at the cost of "its" subjects.

Privilege: From the Latin *privi*, private and *lege*, law. An advantage granted by the State and protected by its powers of coercion. A law for private benefit.

Usury: That form of Privilege or interference with the Free Market in which a State-supported group monopolizes the coinage and thereby takes tribute (interest), direct or indirect, on all or most economic transactions.

Landlordism: That form of Privilege or interference with the Free Market in which one State-supported group "owns" the land and thereby takes tribute (rent) from those who live, work, or produce on the land.

Tariff: That form of Privilege or interference with the Free Market in which commodities produced outside the State are not allowed to compete equally with those produced inside the State.

Capitalism: That organization of society, incorporating elements of tax, usury, landlordism, and tariff, which thus denies the Free Market while pretending to exemplify it.

Conservatism: That school of capitalist philosophy, which claims allegiance to the Free Market while actually supporting usury, landlordism, tariff, and sometimes taxation.

Liberalism: That school of capitalist philosophy, which attempts to correct the injustices of capitalism by adding new laws to the existing laws. Each time conservatives pass a law creating Privilege, liberals pass another law modifying Privilege, leading conservatives to pass a more subtle law recreating Privilege, etc., until "everything not forbidden is compulsory" and "everything not compulsory is forbidden."

Socialism: The attempted abolition of all Privilege by restoring power to the coercive agent behind Privilege, the State, thereby converting capitalist oligarchy into Statist monopoly. Whitewashing a wall by painting it black.

Anarchism: That organization of society in which the Free Market operates freely, without taxes, usury, landlordism, tariffs, or other forms of coercion or Privilege. Right Anarchists predict that in the Free Market people would voluntarily choose to compete more often than to cooperate. Left Anarchists predict that in the Free Market people would voluntarily choose to cooperate more often than to compete.

☯

It's about whose side the government is going to be on. Is it going to be on the side of the largest financial institutions and the largest banks on Wall Street, the ones that can hire a lot of lobbyists and lawyers, or is it going to be on the side of real people? We can't have capitalism if there aren't rules. Nobody should be able to steal your purse on Main Street, or steal your pension on Wall Street. – **Senator Elizabeth Warren, Democrat, Massachusetts, speaking with Stephen Colbert (May 21, 2014)**

Have you ever read the Orwellian double-speak of the *Patriot Act*? It essentially codifies, by "legal means," the ability to reenact **Franz Kafka's** (1883–1924), *The Trial*, on American soil. Combined with the National Defense Authorization Act (NDAA), we have lurched another step closer to overt totalitarianism—and both documents are a vile desecration of every ideal that America is supposed to stand for, according to the Founding Fathers, and the United States Constitution. **George Bush, Jr.** (1946–) signed off on the *Patriot Act* behind closed doors in the dead of night on October 26, 2001. **Mr. Barack Obama** (1961–) has extended and co-signed the travesty annually since taking office in 2009.

Or, to frame the POV another way, here's **Emmett Grogan** (1942–1978) in his classic 1972 bio/novel *Ringolevio—A Life Played for Keeps*: "Kenny didn't like those people, especially the ones with two last names, whose people had come over on the Mayflower or something and whose English Protestant ethnic and ancestral background gave them inherited money and a patronizing attitude toward people like him. They got a real good education where they learned how to steal legitimately from everybody, more and better than any of the great, hard-earning crooks in the country, who at least worked for a living and simply accepted the possibility of punishment as a hazard of their occupation. The highfaluters robbed people blind and never got caught because they and their kind made the rules—and if you make the rules you don't have to break any, you just change them when they interfere with your larceny."

Absolute power corrupts absolutely. Most people prefer not to make waves, but by the very definition of the word "democracy," everyone has to be involved. Otherwise, you have the power of the state controlling/dominating the people, instead of **We the People** controlling the state's power. Because there are NO secrets in a free, open, and democratic society, in order to have a "democracy," you must have full disclosure from your governmental representatives.

On April 27, 1961, **John Fitzgerald Kennedy** (1917–1963) made an address titled "The President and the Press," to the American Newspaper Publishers Association. This is what he had to say about censorship and a free press: "The very word 'secrecy' is repugnant in a free and open society; and we are as a people inherently and historically opposed to secret societies, to secret oaths, and secret proceedings.

"We decided long ago that the dangers of excessive and unwarranted concealment of pertinent facts, far outweighed the dangers which are cited to justify it. Even today, there is little value in opposing the threat of a closed society by imitating its arbitrary restrictions.

"Even today, there is little value in insuring the survival of our nation if our traditions do not survive with it. And there is very grave danger that an announced need for increased security will be seized upon by those anxious to expand its meaning to the very limits of official censorship and concealment. That, I do not intend to permit to the extent that it is in my control.

"And no official of my Administration, whether his rank is high or low, civilian or military, should interpret my words here tonight as an excuse to censor the news, to stifle dissent, to cover up our mistakes or to withhold from the press and the public the facts they deserve to know.

"For we are opposed around the world by a monolithic and ruthless conspiracy that relies on covert means for expanding its sphere of influence—on infiltration instead of invasion. On subversion, instead of elections. On intimidation, instead of free choice. On guerrillas by night, instead of armies by day.

"It is a system, which has conscripted vast human and material resources into the building of a tightly knit, highly efficient machine that combines military, diplomatic, intelligence, economic, scientific and political operations.

"Its preparations are concealed, not published. Its mistakes are buried, not headlined. Its dissenters are silenced, not praised. No expenditure is questioned, no rumor is printed, no secret is revealed.

"No president should fear public scrutiny of his program. For from that scrutiny comes understanding; and from that understanding comes support or opposition. And both are necessary.

"I am not asking your newspapers to support the administration, but I am asking your help in the tremendous task of informing and alerting the American people. For I have complete confidence in the response and dedication of our citizens whenever they are fully informed. Not only could I not stifle controversy among your readers—I welcome it.

"This administration intends to be candid about its errors. For as a wise man once said: 'An error does not become a mistake until you refuse to correct it.' We intend to accept full responsibility for our errors; and we expect you to point them out when we miss them. Without debate, without criticism, no administration, and no country, can succeed—and no republic can survive.

"That is why the Athenian lawmaker Solon decreed it a crime for any citizen to shrink from controversy. **And that is why our press is protected by the First Amendment**— the only business in America specifically protected by the

Constitution. Not primarily to amuse and entertain, not to emphasize the trivial and sentimental, not to simply 'give the public what it wants'—but to inform, to arouse, to reflect, to state our dangers and our opportunities, to indicate our crises and our choices, to lead, mold, educate, and sometimes even anger public opinion.

"This means greater coverage and analysis of international news—for it is no longer far away and foreign, but close at hand, and local. It means greater attention to improved understanding of the news, as well as improved transmission. And it means, finally, that government at all levels, must meet its obligation to provide you with the fullest possible information outside the narrowest limits of national security.

"And so it is to the printing press—to the recorder of man's deeds, the keeper of his conscience, the courier of his news—that we look for strength and assistance, confident that with your help, man will be what he was born to be: free and independent."

☯

Why does the U.S. federal government possess so many secrets? **In a true democracy there are no secrets,** but it should be obvious by now that we do not live in a democracy. In a democracy you have a fully informed populace that is participatory in all areas of civic life. The idea of jeopardizing "national security" is a smoke-screen ruse to protect the government's black ops programs. Generally speaking, most people in this country do not understand or participate in civics. Most people do not want their bubbles of illusion burst, because as we know, the "**truth**" is hard to swallow. In today's world of media saturation and disinformation, the "truth" is also nearly impossible to discern. The 1997 film *Wag the Dog* demonstrated beyond a doubt that in today's world of technology, ANYTHING can be fabricated by digital/CGI means, and made to look as "real" as the most hi-tech special effects in a big budget Hollywood film. The events of 9/11 were orchestrated in such a manner. Anyone sophisticated enough to understand what *Wag the Dog* demonstrated (in terms of creating false flag events to precipitate an act of war against another nation) is capable of understanding how those who control the media are able to manipulate the consciousness of the masses through those very same means. These false flag events keep people preoccupied from the real issues of domestic control and domination, because they're in fear for their own lives. Ordinary civilians, who ought to be up in arms and demonstrating against the fact that their domestic resources are being usurped, and the lives of innocents are being destroyed by policy-making politicians, who stand to make a buck from the bloodshed of others. These war-profiteers consider any amount of "collateral damage" acceptable on the chess board of war—especially if they are not personally at risk or vulnerable. There are many excellent summations of how the powers that be operate these maneuvers with cold-blooded efficiency, and I recommend reading **William Cooper**'s (1943–2001) *Behold a Pale Horse*, and **John Coleman**'s (1935–) *The Committee of 300: The Conspirator's Hierarchy*. If you believe in vetting information when authors make outrageous claims and accusations, these books have footnotes galore, verifying their sources.

☯

The Telegraph ran a piece in April 2014, reporting that a "major study finds the U.S. is an oligarchy," meaning a "group of a few rule or command the many." That's hardly a newsworthy item unless your head is completely buried in the sand. That is what the Occupy Wall Street movement was all about, bringing awareness to the masses regarding how the majority of the planet is controlled by an elite ruling class. This isn't a matter of "theory." It's fairly obvious that we currently exist within a culture where the power to control the resources of the planet effectively rests with a very small number of special interest groups and elites. Royalty, wealth, family ties, and corporate or military control distinguish these people. **Aristotle** (384–322 BC) pioneered a term to be used as a synonym for rule by the rich—**plutocracy.**

Snapshot #4 – Monday, May 31, 1976

This Ain't the Summer of Love. One of the side effects to my parents' splintering marriage was being left to fend for myself and do whatever I wanted to much of the time. The freedom was exhilarating, but the downside was a sense of abandonment, and that's where music (and the media) became a type of surrogate guardian. The tube and the radio seemed to be in collusion with one another, with several TV themes becoming Top 10 hits that season: *S.W.A.T.*, *Happy Days*, *Laverne & Shirley*, *Baretta*, and *Welcome Back, Kotter*. Strangely, all those programs were on ABC-TV.

Much more significantly, it was in May of '76 that I discovered *CREEM* magazine ("America's Only Rock 'n'

Roll Magazine") and read my first issue from cover to cover. Robert Plant and Jimmy Page from Led Zeppelin were on the cover in a classic shot by photographer Neil Zlozower. You could pick *CREEM* up at the 7-Eleven for a buck, and I became addicted to the irreverent, aggressive, testosterone-influenced reportage exemplified by the magazine's editor at the time: Lester Bangs. *CREEM* magazine destroyed whatever was left of my innocence. I was an intellectual sponge and grateful to meet my latest mentors. From this point forward, rock 'n' roll would take center stage in my consciousness. It wasn't long before girls and marijuana would soon join that holy triumvirate.

But first I need to finish the sixth grade, with two major events happening before summer vacation. My music teacher, Carleen Hardesty, asked me if I would represent our school in the Arlington All-County Chorus. There were ten of us, and I was the only boy. Even though it was frightening to be on stage (particularly with all those girls), I was inspired by my teacher's confidence in me. That experience changed my life, and for that I'm forever grateful to Ms. Hardesty.

☯

At the same time my homeroom teacher, Mr. Smith, asked a girl from our class and me to represent our school by spending one full day on a plantation. The object was to educate us through simulating the experience of what it was like to live 200 years ago in Virginia before electricity, running water, indoor/outdoor plumbing, washing machines, canned food, refrigeration, TV, radio, etc. After spending a day in scratchy woolen clothes that smelled like they had never been washed, I performed a score of chores like picking vegetables, milking a cow, and eating a gruel of unseasoned beans as our daily meal—I couldn't wait to get back to the twentieth century. Whatever the challenges of the modern-day world, I was impatient to use a proper toilet, wash with soap and hot water, eat a cheeseburger and French fries, and listen to Aerosmith again.

On the morning of Memorial Day, my Cub Scout troop met at the Tomb of the Unknown Solider. We were all dressed up in our uniforms to watch the changing of the guards, and out of the blue, there was the president, **Gerald Ford** walking among us, flanked by Secret Service men, saying good morning and shaking our hands. I got to meet the only president in the history of our country not elected into office. That's, of course, if you don't include **George W. Bush** in 2001.

Snapshot #5 – Wednesday, June 30, 1976

School's Out for Summer! And the next adventure would be an extended stay in Michigan to visit my mom's side of the family where my eldest cousin Kathy was graduating from Muskegon Senior High School. As the familial weirdness continued, I spent a couple of weeks with my Aunt Nancy, who exposed me to Bruce Springsteen's *Born To Run* and Bob Seger's *Live Bullet,* in a car ride across the state back to Detroit. I also spent an inordinate amount of time listening to *Frampton Comes Alive!*, along with several Richard Pryor, George Carlin, and Cheech & Chong records.

Significantly, I witnessed my first two concerts this month: **Harry Chapin** (1942–1981) at the Pine Knob Theatre in Flint, Michigan, and **Elton John** (1947–) at the Capital Centre in Landover, Maryland. I also saw **Neil Diamond** (1941–) in August at the Capital Centre, and by the end of the summer, I was completely addicted to attending rock 'n' roll shows and conspired to be in attendance at as many as I could from that point forward. (Set lists for these peformances can be found in the **Appendix** on pages 473-474.)

Snapshot #6 – Sunday, July 4, 1976

The fourth of July—what a time! The hype was incredible. EVERYTHING was red, white, and blew.

Despite the imperfections, I am grateful I live in a culture that purports to allow free speech. I was exceptionally lucky to take innumerable field trips and grow up with the Smithsonian, the Air and Space Museum, planetariums, art galleries, national monuments, colonial architecture, and Robert E. Lee's plantation literally in my back yard.

We played with fireworks in our side yard and as dusk approached we all climbed into the car and watched the bicentennial celebration from the rooftop of a local hospital my Uncle Bill had access to. Despite the family traumas, it was an exciting time to be alive.

I would hear ELO's "Strange Magic" and it seemed to capture the vibe of the era beautifully, with a lyric mourning the loss of a dream. Our utopian fantasy of changing the world didn't quite work out the way we had hoped. So, now what do we do?

Right after the fourth of July, the radio started playing "Magic Man" by a group from Seattle called Heart. I loved the texture of their guitars and they sounded heavier than anything else on the Top 40 at the time. I went over to Jimmy Burke's one afternoon. He handed me a copy of *Dreamboat Annie* and said, "my sister bought this last night. Do you think she got ripped off?" After listening to side one and gazing at the glamour shots of the Wilson sisters for fifteen minutes, I distinctly decided that she did not get ripped off, and I couldn't wait until I possessed a copy of my own. Another record we listened to was the latest from Kiss called *Destroyer*. Jimmy thought they had "sold out" because they recorded a soppy ballad called "Beth," but it turned out to be their highest charting single, and expanded their audience by millions. In retrospect, I find it amazing that we (a couple of eleven-year-olds) were contemplating the idea of integrity in art, by wondering if our musical heroes had somehow sold out their work (and their fans) by making commercial concessions. If Jimmy and I were anything, we were precocious. Thank you mass media.

THE BIG PICTURE – VI
The Founding Fathers and The Fool on the Hill

History is a nightmare from which I am trying to awake.
      – **James Joyce (1882–1941), from** *Ulysses* **(1922)**

Captain America to Billy the Kid in *Easy Rider*: "We blew it."

Ideal: existing as an archetypal idea of, or relating to, philosophical idealism. **Utopian:** proposing or advocating impractically ideal social and political schemes. **Crackpot:** a person who is crazy or very strange, one given to eccentric or lunatic notions. **Visionary:** having or showing clear ideas about what should happen or be done in the future. (All definitions according to the conventions of *Webster's* dictionary.)

If *anything* in life can be considered "true," then certainly the maxim of "context is crucial" must rank among the top tier of truisms. And while guidebooks and maps are all well and good for traversing the known landscape, how do you navigate your way along a path that has yet to be forged? Perhaps an even more pertinent question might be: how does creative innovation manifest itself, and what does it mean to be in touch with your own genius? We humans are peculiar social animals, with some mighty bizarre beliefs and rituals. Surely we require a specific context to our current Earthly circumstances if we are to consider the "radical" notion (and the action required) of how to improve our collective lot in life, making the world a better place to flourish. I feel there's a lot of work to be done to correct the imbalances and the perverse value system maintained by the current power-elite. The social paradigms we are enmeshed within seem way more oppressive than permissive. That said, I am reminded of another maxim: *Be the change you wish to see*—because you always have to start with yourself before you can effect any positive change in the broader world that we share.

The bells are ringing. It may be considered passé (or worse) to espouse the act of projecting peace and love upon all of your fellow human beings. However, embodying the values of a peace-loving-bohemian-hippie-freak of nature need not be locked into any specific epoch. The outmoded evolutionary theory, "survival of the fittest," is nothing more than a nasty rationalization of why certain segments of our civilization insist on repeating the same violently regressive behavior, simply because it is what they have been taught— handed down as "tradition." Ignorance is not bliss, ladies and gents—it is fatal, and what sort of future awaits the people of planet Earth if we continue to carry forth the myopic neuroses of war, racism, greed and blind aggression? Is there a glimmer of a chance that the smartest monkey from the concrete jungle can somehow transcend the mire of conditioned response, and make the evolutionary leap to a higher rung of awareness? I put in a communiqué to **Dr. Ivan Pavlov** (1849–1936) on that particular subject and I'm still awaiting his response…

For anyone who has studied the patriarch's official version of what gets passed off as world his-story for the past 2,000-plus years, it would appear we've been in a continuous series of bloody conflicts. And after spending a lifetime or three in the library, processing all of that information, it becomes a mental high-wire act to retain your sanity in the face of all the evidence. It also requires a busload of faith and hope that somehow the hundredth monkey theory will apply to the human race, and we will inevitably achieve a critical mass, transmuting into a race of compassionate, loving super-beings—as Divine and creative as anyone has ever been. That might come off as some kind of delusional, new-age fantasy, but I say, dream big with your eyes open or remain asleep. The brutal alternatives of avarice without compassion hold no sway with my head, heart, or soul.

If being "realistic" means accepting barbarism as a way of life, I prefer the point of view that planet Earth was never intended to be a way station for brute savages, regardless of how much money or technology they possess.

You're watching the What to Think *network...*

Meanwhile, the entertainment propaganda that passes for "news and information," within the media sewage system, continues to inform our lives to such a degree that most of us scarcely know what to think about our world. If you are looking for a spot-on metaphor for the technological chains of our contemporary existence, you need not look any further than the brilliantly executed *The Matrix* (1999), by the Wachowski Brothers. As for further repercussions of what potential futures await, check out the films *Masked and Anonymous* (2003) or *Children of Men* (2006). Works such as these, as well as the classic novels of **George Orwell** (1903–1950), *1984* and *Animal Farm* in particular, are meant to be cautionary tales, not self-fulfilling prophecies—which is what they are in a state of becoming if apathy and ignorance continue unabated among the general population.

Others say don't hate nothing at all except hatred. – **Bob Dylan**

So, what are **you** going to choose for your motivating principles as you move throughout this small slice of infinity? This post-modern society of ours is screaming for a series of vitalizing transmutations to occur.

The bottom line is: you are what you think you are, and you are more than what you think you are. If you can get the world at large to concur with who your sense of Self is and create a consensus reality together at the same time, that's a bonus. And not only that, you get what you deserve. The cosmic law of karma, or "what goes around, comes around" is exemplified in the quotation: "Whatsoever a man soweth, that shall he also reap" (Galatians 6:7). Certain scenarios might require lifetimes to settle the score, but I trust that eventually everything will balance out in the end.

I heard it was you talking 'bout a world where all is free, it just couldn't be and only a fool would say that.
— **Walter Becker (1950–) and Donald Fagen (1948–)**

And now a word about the Founding Fathers. I love the crazy, patch-work quilt of ethnicity that makes up the whole of America, and Washington, D.C. seemed like a microcosm of the world. There was a Saturday morning cartoon segment on ABC-TV in the early '70s called *Schoolhouse Rock* that was a wonderful primer employing the mnemonics of song to learn aspects of grammar, math, science, and history. One of my favorite songs from the series, "Melting Pot," was about the origins of America and its cultural diversity, exploring the notion of Ellis Island and the Statue of Liberty, helping out the poor huddled masses, yearning to be free. It's a hell of a story.

But talk about the power of myth. It is amazing to think of the stories that get handed down as gospel regarding the

Founding Fathers: **George Washington, Thomas Jefferson** (1743–1826), **Benjamin Franklin** (1706–1790), and the rest of the rich, white, slave-owning, plantation owners who also served as the statesmen/architects for this country.

However, what doesn't get taught in our public schools at all is the role the occult played in the establishment of the United States of America. British author and scholar David Ovason has written a superb book titled *The Secret Architecture of Our Nation's Capital* that spells out quite clearly how most of the important leaders of the United States were Freemasons, and how the District of Columbia's most significant buildings have their origins in specific rites and rituals, all centering around astrology and intentional magic—rituals that Calvinists and Protestants back in the day would most assuredly have referred to as "witchcraft."

On page 68 of Ovason's book there is an illustration of a Masonic apron that was a gift from the French general Lafayette to George Washington, displaying many Masonic symbols of the occult, including a pentangle, the Moon, the Sun, and other arcane objects. Much like Paris, France, Washington, D.C. is considered a "Virgo" city by virtue of the fact that many of the groundbreaking ceremonies and architectural monuments were initiated when either the Sun, or the Moon, or other important planetary bodies were in the heavenly sign of Virgo. Also, there are over twenty important public buildings, including the Library of Congress, that contain hidden cosmological symbolism. *The Secret Architecture of Our Nation's Capital* is a dry, yet fascinating exploration of Freemasonry rituals that provides excellent references, verifying how our Founding Fathers consistently and intentionally employed foreknowledge of astrological cycles to manifest a very specific type of republic—one that benefits the aristocracy, or "ruling class."

THE BIG PICTURE – VII
Epiphanies are a Swing Set for Your Mind

Epiphany—*noun*, a sudden, intuitive perception of, or insight into, the reality or essential meaning of something, which is usually initiated by some simple, homely or commonplace occurrence or experience.

All truth passes through three stages. First, it is ridiculed. Second, it is violently opposed. Third, it is accepted as being self-evident. – **Arthur Schopenhauer (1788–1860)**

Some people have a deep, abiding respect for the natural beauty that was once this country. [Trash hurled at the feet of a tearful **Iron Eyes Cody**] *And some people don't. People start pollution. People can stop it. This has been a Public Service Announcement from Keep America Beautiful.*

I don't believe in "my country right or wrong." My country wrong needs my help. – **Peter Tork (1942–)**

Cosmologically speaking. History records innumerable facts and tells us much about who we think we are as a race of beings. However, those subjective narratives of what we tell ourselves about the nature of reality are usually revisionist and oftentimes couched in a hidden agenda, dependent upon who is doing the storytelling. Beyond the obvious physical subsistence needs of air, water, food, and protection from the elements, there are also the social, psychological, emotional, and spiritual aspects to our existence that are easy to speculate about, yet difficult to quantify, measure, and identify. We define who we are to ourselves and to each other by our belief systems and the paradigms that we co-create together. It stands to reason that in order to live a fully conscious existence, we must commit some energy to understanding who, what, and where we believe ourselves to be in the universe.

In the Foreword to **Barbara Hand Clow**'s (1943–) extraordinary book, *The Pleidian Agenda*, gravitational physicist **Brian Swimme, Ph.D** (1950–) writes about the traditional cosmological task of learning how to "enter the universe," and what it means to learn "the ways of the wider world. We've amassed storehouses of information concerning the universe and how it operates, and all of this is to be drawn upon to learn how to act intelligently in the universe."

Modern scientific evidence supports the idea that humanity, in one form or another, has been on this planet for a minimum of 50,000 years (if not significantly longer), and for the majority of that time, to the best of our knowledge, we've relied on artistic, oral traditions to pass on information in the form of stories, poems, songs, and ritualistic dancing. But a cosmological split between the old world and the new occurred in 1543 when Polish astronomer **Nicolaus Copernicus** (1473–1543) decreed that the Sun, and not the Earth, was the center of our universe. Swimme: "We now accept this as true but we need to remember that the entire culture was based on the assumption that Earth was at the center. One result of this transformation was to cast all speculative cosmological works into the trash bin. As a canon of the church, Copernicus refused to publish his findings until he was on his deathbed. And what he feared would happen indeed did take place: the scientific content of his research was accepted and the cosmological orientation of the entire medieval world was slowly but decisively rejected. The modern world, based on a split between science and religion, had its beginning here. Henceforth, religion would be increasingly viewed as a repository of truths concerning the behavior necessary to get to heaven; science, on the other hand, would come to be understood as a method for discovering the truth about the physical universe, a universe no longer considered to be filled with spiritual realities, but composed entirely of crass matter." This idea of science as the ultimate barometer of evaluating and measuring "**truth**" is the lynchpin to understanding our contemporary society.

And now a word about Energy. Energy exists in four basic forms: heat, light, chemical energy, and electrical energy. According to the first law of thermodynamics, energy can be changed from one form to another, but it cannot be created or destroyed. Nothing remains static in the universe. Everything is in a state of flux. Or, the only constant is change. Another aspect regarding energy, according to Newton's Third Law of physics: "for every action, there is an equal and opposite reaction." Are any of these constructs relevant to our ideas regarding karma or reincarnation?

God bless H.G. Wells? Even though I may lack the scientific tools at the moment to prove it, I intuit that outside the realm of the third dimension, all space/time events happen simultaneously—it is our minds and level of awareness (i.e. state of consciousness) that perceive events to be of a sequential nature, with time flowing strictly in one particular direction. For all we know, time may very well be the invention of human thought. I find the notion of time travel fascinating, and love any narrative (such as the Montauk Project or the Philadelphia Experiment) that allows for the idea of time and the seriality of events to be bent forwards, backwards, or sideways. I feel that the majority of human beings (particularly myself) greatly misunderstand the machinations of space and time. And although it may be beyond the current ken of science (or then again, maybe not), I accept the possibility that there may be up to twelve or more different dimensions for human beings to exist within—with some of those realms possibly being astral, ethereal, spiritual, or metaphysical in nature. Until each of us develops the consciousness of an avatar, these ideas remain speculative. I've read some pretty far-out texts, but I propose that if you can think of an idea, then on some level of reality it becomes "true," if only in the consciousness of the perceiver. Without empirical evidence or the rationalist consensus of others, constructs of this sort are often dismissed with words like "delusional," "crazy," or "insane." Ultimately, who among us gets to choose what the last word, or authority, is on any idea? Each individual, that's who. But the trick remains of how to beware (**be aware**) of the cause and effect of ideas, thoughts and the impulses that lead to action.

Thoughts *are* things and when you invest enough energy into a thought construct, it becomes dense enough to formulate itself into a physical manifestation of that thought. That is a major aspect of what we collectively refer to as "reality." There is a social contract, developed over the centuries, that most people adhere to in the name of going with the flow. We call that "law abiding." When our attitudes, beliefs and behavior benignly contradict that social contract, we often refer to those types of people as "eccentric." When the social contract is violated by acts of perceived malice, we refer to those types as "criminals."

How on Earth did we get here and how did it all begin? Where do our notions of who we are as a race come from anyway? With very few exceptions, such as village elders and shamans, most of our collective mythologies involve narratives handed down by either the church and/or the state. With seven billion souls congregating on this rock that orbits a star, there must be at least that many versions of the story—seven billion explanations as to who and what humanity is. Is there such a thing on Gaia as Absolute Truth? In our current third-dimensional realm of dualism, where every perspective is relative to the perceiver, I say only those who can prove omnipotence can have an absolute handle on Anything/Everything. More to the point, you have your version of "reality" and I, of course, have mine—is there truly a place where the twain shall meet? If our perception is to evolve beyond fundamentalist fascism, how do we determine for ourselves what "right action" is? Is tolerance for contradictory viewpoints necessary for harmony and balance to occur in the world? For, as the Bard once wrote: "Nothing is really good or bad in itself—it's all what a person thinks about it." (*Hamlet*, Act 2, Scene 2).

Morals, as well as its kissing cousin, Values, form the basis from which such relative distinctions are made. Anyone who feels that an unexamined life is not worth living would do well to take a look/see within their own heart and decide just what it is that they stand for in the grand tally of existence. Certainly we were all given the choice to create an existence beyond being pawns or benefactors in a Ponzi scheme? At what point in history did it become necessary to draw a line in the sand and choose a side? *Where does the boundary lie, who sets it and why?* Epiphanies can be borne from such ponderings.

Archetypal energy. I am greatly indebted to the pioneering work of professor Joseph Campbell and the ideas that he put forth in his groundbreaking books, particularly *The Hero with a Thousand Faces* and *The Power of Myth*. Campbell, a professor at Sarah Lawrence College, was in turn a scholar of Swiss psychologist **Carl Jung** (1875–1961), who understood all too well about the potency of myth and the use of archetypes in order to define our sense of Self throughout the ages. Jung's work in the development of humanist psychology stressed the vital importance of a completely integrated psyche that embraces and is aware of all aspects of duality. In Jung's mode of thought, a human being's capacity to remain in balance is paramount to one's spiritual, mental, physical and emotional wellbeing. Each person has a light and a shadow side to their psyche that must remain in balance: a Yin to complement the Yang, a feminine aspect in tandem with the masculine, and a conscious awareness that co-exists with the unconscious.

As a protégé and peer of **Sigmund Freud** (1856–1939), the Austrian neurologist who became known as the Founding Father of psychotherapy, Jung developed a deep, intuitive understanding into the human condition by a persistent analysis of how humans think, feel, and behave. Jung was also a practitioner of the occult and employed various divination systems throughout his career to arrive at his profound conclusions regarding the universe. Those systems included the tarot, astrology, and empirical shamanism. The discoveries that Jung made about the psyche and human nature are reflected in the work of many other scholars, notably the observations of philosopher, ethnobotanist, and writer Terence McKenna, one of the twentieth century's boldest provocateurs, due to his paradigm-busting insistence that humankind needs to evolve as quickly as possible in order to avoid the ecological terrors that otherwise await. As I write these words in the spring and summer of 2014, the Pacific Ocean is filling with millions of gallons of radioactive waste due to the core meltdown of the Fukishima nuclear power plant in Tokyo, and it is impossible to ascertain what the full range of implications are. Perhaps we have already unwittingly created our endgame on planet Earth due to arrogant, egocentric, unscientific carelessness.

I am by no means an expert when it comes to quoting chapter and verse from the *Talmud*, *Quran*, *Bhagavad-Gita*, or the *Bible*. But what I do know from a bit of comparative religions study is that every one of these holy texts provides a moral framework for how to live. Each path offers something unique and at the same time, shares universal principals. But one of the aspects that ties all of these religions, in fact all religions together, is that they are all dogmatic in the sense that their spiritual laws, ideals and parables are immutable— they are static and do not allow themselves (or their strict practitioners) to morph with a constantly changing universe. Multiply that aspect with the inability to discern between prose that is taken literally, and poetry that is to be interpreted metaphorically, and you have the denotation disconnect that has caused incalculable wars since the dawn of man. How did homo erectus become such a violent animal in spite of his advanced forebrain, with an ability to reason in ways that no other creature on this Earth can?

If you take the *Bible* literally, according to some interpreters, human beings have been on this planet for a mere 6,000 years. If you accept that idea as being true, then I suspect some further research might be in order. That would appear to be as realistic as literally believing that planet Earth was formed by an omnipotent creator in less than a week.

Seth, The 12th Planet, reading the signs. I've read some pretty far out books over the years that claim to be channeled or dictated by entities that exist in other dimensional realms. Many of these books share the flavor of an extremely well written science fiction novel. Regardless of how much, or how little, scientific evidence is available to corroborate such information, the ideas contained in these works are worth considering, if only for the fact that it opens the conscious mind to broader possibilities. These works create pathways within the imagination that can unleash hidden potential in revolutionary ways. With the introduction of this novelty, new worlds are formed and the shift in our collective paradigm can be as great as the understanding that the world isn't flat at all. In fact, it's a sphere within a complex interacting system that is interdependent with an infinite amount of other energies.

THE BIG PICTURE – VIII
Conspiracy Therapy 101, or Was Jesus Really a Capricorn?

If leaders may lie, then who should tell the truth?
— Desmond Tutu (1931–)

Don't follow leaders, watch the parking meters. "Who governs? Who really rules? To what extent is the broad body of U.S. citizens sovereign, semi-sovereign, or largely powerless? These questions have animated much important work in the study of American politics."

These questions are the opening gambit to the ground-breaking 2014 study entitled *Testing Theories of American Politics: Elites, Interest Groups, and Average Citizens* by Princeton University professor Martin Gilens and Northwestern University professor Benjamin I. Page. This 42-page study provides much empirical evidence within established academic circles, of what has been dismissed repeatedly as "conspiracy theory" by those who do not wish to have their cover blown: i.e. the Power Elite/Ruling Class.

"The central point that emerges from our research is that economic elites and organized groups representing business interests have substantial independent impacts on U.S. government policy, while mass-based interest groups and average citizens have little or no independent influence. Our results provide substantial support for theories of Economic Elite Domination and for theories of Biased Pluralism."

Does the National Security Agency equal the State's attempt at creating another form of totalitarianism?

The actions taken by Mr. Edward Snowden to reveal the lengths that the United States government has taken to spy on foreign nationals and law-abiding citizens of its own country strike me as a stance of desperation that ought to be applauded in the name of full disclosure and true democracy in action. The U.S. government and its representatives believe that every means justifies its end—even if that means suspending the U.S. Constitution! God forbid that Mr. Snowden's actions may have saved us from suffering the totalitarianism of martial law. In the name of freedom and true justice, why should the idea of full disclosure represent such a threat? I interpret Mr. Snowden's actions as a threat to fascism, which our government inches closer to with each passing day. *Thank God and the Founding Fathers for the First Amendment.* Free speech is our saving grace, and creating a respectful dialog with one another is our only chance at rising above the sociopaths in positions of power and the greedy rationalizations that justify any and all crimes against humanity.

Conspiracy Theory—*noun* 1) a theory that explains an event as being the result of a plot by a covert group or organization; a belief that a particular unexplained event was caused by such a group. 2) the idea that many important political events and economic and social trends are the products of secret plots that are largely unknown to the general public. (definition according to *dictionary.com*)

I have this feeling man, 'cause you know just a handful of people actually run everything—that's true, it's provable. I'm not a conspiracy nut. It's provable. A handful—a very small elite run and own these corporations, which include the mainstream media. I have this feeling that whoever is elected president, like Clinton was, no matter what promises you made on the campaign trail—blah, blah, blah—when you win, you go into this smoky room with the twelve industrialist-capitalist-scumfucks who got you in there. You're in this smoky room and this little film screen comes down and a big guy with a cigar goes: "Roll the film." And it's a shot of the Kennedy assassination from an angle that you've never seen before that looks suspiciously

off the grassy knoll. And then the screen goes up and the lights go
up and they go to the new president: "Any questions?" "Uh, just
what my agenda is..." "First, we bomb Baghdad." "You got it."
– **"The Elite" by Bill Hicks (from** *Rant in E Minor*)

Here's a short laundry list of the most popular "conspiracy
theories" around—it could be a hundred times longer: What
are Chemtrails and why are airplanes visibly filling our skies
with toxins? What is the purpose of genetically modified
organisms (GMOs) and what does GMO food do to your
body? Who are those responsible for the events involving
the Pentagon and the Twin Towers on September 11, 2001
(9/11)? Are the conclusions drawn by the U.S. government
regarding 9/11 responsible for an illegal series of wars in the
Middle East and are those policies responsible for the deaths
of hundreds of thousands of innocent people? What are the
black ops programs of the Central Intelligence Agency (CIA)
and the Federal Bureau of Investigation (FBI) all about? Are
there secret mind-control programs, such as MK-ULTRA,
that involve the use of Lysergic acid diethylamide (LSD-25)?
Were the moon landings faked and what are the space
programs of the National Aeronautics and Space Administration (NASA) all about? Why is fluoride added to the
water supplies of various municipalities and what role does
it play in suppressing the pineal gland? What is Manifest
Destiny? Does the royal bloodline of the British aristocracy
descend from reptiles? Who really killed John and Robert
Kennedy? Why was John Lennon assassinated? Are there
pedophiles in the upper echelons of world government? Are
those same government officials involved in Satan worship?
Is the *Protocols of the Learned Elders of Zion* a hoax or a

genuine agenda? What is the purpose of the secret society of the Freemasons? What is the Philadelphia Experiment and the Montauk Project? Is time-travel technology possible? Does that involve life forms that originate from a planet other than Earth (aliens/extraterrestrials)? What is Area 51 and the Roswell, New Mexico incident of 1947 about? What is the controversy regarding the nation state of Israel and its extended conflict with Palestine? What is the Bilderberg Group and the Council on Foreign Relations, and what is their relationship to the Federal Reserve System, the World Bank, the Internal Revenue System, and the suspension of the gold and silver standard into a fiat economy? Did Jesus and Mary Magdelene have a child together? Coke or Pepsi?

How many of the above-mentioned narratives can be vetted and/or disproved? And if they can be proven to be true, then what exactly does it mean if time travel is possible or extraterrestrials exist? Is it important if your governmental representatives are lying to you and that the culpability is enough to destroy individuals, nation states, economies, and quite easily the planet itself?

There is ample "evidence" supporting and debunking each of the above-mentioned constructs. How do you pick and choose what to believe and base your worldview upon? What does your life experience teach you about the nature of truth, how to perceive reality, and the types of action that one must take?

☯

Alvy: *I'm sorry, I can't go through with this. I can't get it off my mind, Alison! It's obsessing me!*

Alison: *I'm getting tired of it, I need your attention.*
Alvy: *But it doesn't make any sense. He drove past the book depository and the police said conclusively that it was an exit wound. So how was it possible for Oswald to have fired from two angles at once? It doesn't make sense! I'll tell you this. He was not marksman enough to hit a moving target at that range. But if there was a second assassin – that's it!*
Alison: *We've been through this.*
Alvy: *They recovered the shells from that rifle.*
Alison: *All right, then what are you saying now? That everybody on the Warren Commission is in on this conspiracy, right?*
Alvy: *Well, why not?*
Alison: *Earl Warren?*
Alvy: *Hey, honey, I don't know Earl Warren.*
Alison: *Lyndon Johnson?*
Alvy: *Lyndon Johnson is a politician! You know the ethics those guys have. It's a notch underneath child molester.*
Alison: *Then everybody's in on the conspiracy. The FBI and the CIA and J. Edgar Hoover, the oil companies and the Pentagon and the men's room attendant at the White House?*
Alvy: *I would leave out the men's room attendant.* – **Woody Allen** and **Carol Kane** in *Annie Hall* (April 20, 1977)

Alvy: *I distinctly heard it. He muttered under his breath, "Jew."*
Rob: *Alvy, You're crazy.*
Alvy: *No, I'm not. We were walking off the tennis court. He was there and me and his wife. And he looked at her, and then they both looked at me and under his breath he said, "Jew."*
Rob: *Alvy, you're a total paranoid.*

Alvy: *How am I a paranoid? I pick up on those kind of things. I was having lunch with some guys from NBC, so I said "Did you eat yet, or what?" And Tom Christie said, "No. Jew?" Not "Did you eat?" But "Jew eat?" You get it?*
Rob: *Max.*
Alvy: *Stop calling me Max.*
Rob: *Why? It's a good name for you. Max, you see conspiracies in everything.*
Alvy: *No, I don't. I was in a record store, listen to this. So I know, there's this tall, blond crew-cutted guy and he's looking at me in a funny way and smiling and he's saying, "Yes, we have a sale this week on Wagner." Wagner, Max. So I know what he's really trying to tell me. Very significantly, Wagner.* - **Woody Allen** and **Tony Roberts** in *Annie Hall* (April 20, 1977)

Getting Hip to the Three Sisters. **George Carlin (1937–2008)**: "I don't really, honestly, deep down believe in political action. I think the system contracts and expands as it wants to. It accommodates these changes. I think the civil rights movement was an accommodation on the part of those who own the country. I think they see where their self-interest lies; they see a certain amount of freedom seems good—an illusion of liberty—give these people a voting day every year so that they will have the illusion of meaningless choice. Meaningless choice—that we go, like slaves, and say 'Oh, I voted.' The limits of debate in this country are established before the debate even begins and everyone else is marginalized and made to seem either to be communist or some sort of disloyal person—a 'kook'—there's a word, and now it's 'conspiracy.' See, they made that something that should not be even entertained for a minute: that powerful people might get together and have a plan! Doesn't happen! You're a 'kook!' You're a 'conspiracy buff!'"

Mr. Carlin continues: "There's a reason education sucks and it's the same reason it will never, ever be fixed. **Because the owners of this country don't want that.** I'm talking about the real owners now—the big, wealthy business interests that control things and make all the important decisions.

"Forget the politicians. They are irrelevant. The politicians are put there to give you the idea that you have freedom of choice. You don't. You have no choice! You have OWNERS! They OWN YOU. They own everything. They own all the important land. They own and control the corporations. They've long since bought and paid for the Senate, the Congress, the state houses, the city halls, they got the judges in their back pockets and they own all the big media companies, so they control just about all of the news and information you get to hear. They've got you by the balls.

"They spend billions of dollars every year lobbying to get what they want. Well, we know what they want. They want more for themselves and less for everybody else, but I'll tell you what they don't want: they don't want a population of citizens capable of critical thinking. They don't want well-informed, well-educated people capable of critical thinking. They're not interested in that. That doesn't help them. That's against their interests.

"They don't want people who are smart enough to sit around the kitchen table and think about how badly they're getting fucked by a system that threw them overboard 30 fucking years ago. They don't want that!

"You know what they do want? They want obedient workers. People who are just smart enough to run the machines and do the paperwork and just dumb enough to passively accept all these increasingly shitty jobs with the lower pay, the longer hours, the reduced benefits, the end of overtime and the vanishing pension that disappears the minute that you go to collect it. And now they're coming for your Social Security money. They want your retirement money. They want it back so they can give it to their criminal friends on Wall Street, and you know something? They'll get it. They'll get it all from you sooner or later because they own this fucking place! **It's a big club, and you ain't in it! You and I are not in the big club.**

"By the way, it's the same big club they use to beat you over the head with all day long when they tell you what to believe. All day long beating you over the head with their media telling you what to believe, what to think, and what to buy. The table is tilted folks, the game is rigged, and nobody seems to notice, nobody seems to care. Good, honest, hard-working people—white collar, blue collar, it doesn't matter what color shirt you have on. These are people of modest means who continue to elect these rich cocksuckers who don't give a fuck about you.

"They don't care about you at all. And nobody seems to notice, nobody seems to care, and that's what the owners count on. The fact that Americans will probably remain willfully ignorant of the big red, white, and blue dick that's being jammed up their assholes everyday, because the owners of this country know the truth: it's called the 'American Dream,' because you have to be asleep to believe it."

THE BIG PICTURE – IX
Hermetically Into the Light

So, as I occasionally ask myself, and others, what's it going to be: hope or despair? Fear? Or love? Giving up and abandoning my ideals and the hope for a better world isn't an option. I believe that we have it within ourselves to put those "better angels of our nature" to the fore, because we are capable of achieving true greatness as a race when we remain focused and aware and cooperative with one another. My feeling about the archetypal nature of human beings is that if we courageously choose strength and kindness towards ourselves, then we will cease to create needless conflicts with others—but in order to do that we have to accept and embrace every aspect of our human nature. Which also requires the courage to face and understand who we are as a collection of molecules, atoms, and belief systems.

Do we have it within ourselves to evolve to the next level of being? To develop the consciousness and value system of an avatar, to the point where we individually and collectively transcend the shackles of tyranny, domination and disregard towards other sentient beings? To question all that we believe and perceive about the nature of what "reality" is, we have to understand and be in touch with our own feelings—which also happens to be the prerequisite of empathizing with other living creatures. How does one evolve from a **Siddhartha** into a **Buddha**? Where does one learn to behave like a **Christ**? How does one learn to utilize Love as the underlying principle of every thought and every deed? Authentic history can be important, because the wise ones throughout the ages assert repeatedly that anything is possible. So dare to dream the impossible dream, for as **Basil King** (1859–1928) once famously stated: "Be bold and mighty forces will come to your aid."

The world is like a ride at an amusement park and when you choose to go on it you think it's real because that's how powerful our minds are. And the ride goes up and down and round and round and it has thrills and chills and is very brightly colored and it's very loud. And it's fun—for a while. Some people have been on the ride for a long time and they begin to question: "Is this real or is this just a ride?" And other people have remembered and they come back to us and they say "Hey, don't worry, don't be afraid, ever. Because this is just a ride." **And we kill those people.** [laughs] *"Shut him up. We have a lot invested in this ride. Shut him up. Look at my furrows of worry. Look at my big bank account. And my family. This has to be real." It's just a ride. But we always kill those good guys who try to tell us that, you ever notice that, and let the demons run amuck. But it doesn't matter because it's just a ride and we can change it any time we want. It's only a choice—no effort, no work, no job, no savings of money—it's a choice right now between fear and love. The eyes of fear want you to put bigger locks on your door and buy guns and close yourself off. The eyes of love instead see all of us as One. Here's what we can do to change the world right now to a better ride: take all that money that we spend on weapons and defense each year and instead spend it feeding and clothing and educating the poor of the world, which it would do many times over, with not one human being excluded, and we can explore space together—both inner and outer—forever, in peace.*
– **Philosopher King/Comedian Bill Hicks (1961–1994)**

Promote tolerance, compassion, kindness, and love. Eradicate all forms of hatred, racism, aggression, and greed. **ALL** life is sacred.

See you down the road my fellow beings. Peace.

www.jonkanis.com, May 30, 2014

APPENDIX

Sessionography
Selected Recordings (1984–2015)

All lyrics and music composed by Jon Kanis unless otherwise indicated.

The Bangles Christmas Tape
"Most Likely You'll Go Your Way (and I'll Go Mine)" (Bob Dylan)
Recorded November 1984 at Cactus Clown Studio, Eagle Rock, California.
Produced, engineered, and mixed by Darian Sahanaja.
Personnel: Jon Kanis (vocals), Steve Kobashigawa (electric bass), Darian Sahanaja
(keyboard, tambourine, vocals), Nick Walusko (guitar).

Demo Session
"Love Minus Zero/No Limit" (Bob Dylan)
Recorded November 1984 at Cactus Clown Studio, Eagle Rock, California.
Produced, engineered, and mixed by Darian Sahanaja.
Personnel: Jon Kanis (acoustic guitar, vocals), Darian Sahanaja (tambourine).

It's Happening!
"That's Not Me" (Brian Wilson, Tony Asher)
Taped December 16, 1985 at Pasadena Community College, Pasadena, California.
Pilot episode written and directed by Domenic Priore. Personnel: Jon Kanis (tambourine),
Darian Sahanaja (organ, vocals), Nick Walusko (electric guitar, lead vocal).

Demo Session
"C'Mon Everybody" (Eddie Cochran, Jerry Capehart) (two takes), "Welcome to the
Working Week" (Elvis Costello), "She's the One"/"The Preacher's Daughter" (Bruce
Springsteen), "I'm In Love With a Girl" (Alex Chilton), "No More to Say" (David
Brauner), "New Amsterdam" (Elvis Costello), "Silence of My Name" (two takes), "I Go
to Pieces" (Del Shannon), "Honey Don't" (Carl Perkins), "Girls Talk" (Elvis Costello)
Recorded May 7, 1987 at Studio Sound 3, San Diego, California.
Produced by Jon Kanis. Engineered by Corey Fayman.
Personnel: Jon Kanis (acoustic guitar, vocals), Jeff Ilses (electric guitar).

Demo Session
"Baby, Let's Play House" (Arthur Gunter), "Sweet, Sweet Dreams,"
"Where I Wish You Were," "Desire," "Arlington"
Recorded June 19, 1987 at Studio Sound 3, San Diego, California.
Produced by Jon Kanis. Engineered by Corey Fayman.
Personnel: Jon Kanis (acoustic guitar, vocals), Corey Fayman (drums).

Demo Session
"It's You My Love," "Walk Without Me," "60 Minutes or More," "Take a Look at Me"
Recorded November 27, 1987 at the Clairemont Mystery House, San Diego,
California. Produced, engineered, and mixed by the Mystery Guy. Personnel:
Jon Kanis (acoustic guitar, vocals), Mystery Guy (electric guitar, electric bass).

Demo Session
"Think It Over," "Waste of Time," "What's It All About?"
Recorded December 4, 1988 at Studio Sound 3, San Diego, California.
Produced by Jon Kanis. Engineered by Corey Fayman.
Personnel: Jon Kanis (acoustic guitar, vocals).

Demo Session
"Hold My Hand" (Neil Innes), "Poem + Untitled Song," "Alba Rhythms," "Why Don't
You Love Me?" (Hank Williams), "Where I Wish You Were," "The Letter" (Wayne
Carson Thompson), "Poem" + "Every Candle Upon My Cake," "Poem," "My Funny
Valentine" (Richard Rodgers, Lorenz Hart), "Arnold Layne" (Syd Barrett)
Recorded February 4, 1990 at Studio Sound 3, San Diego, California. Produced by
Jon Kanis. Engineered by Corey Fayman. Personnel: Jon Kanis (acoustic guitar, vocals).

Demo Session
"Walk Without Me" (two takes), "My Favorite Shirt," "Lay Your Life On the Table,"
"Easy To Remember"
Recorded April 1990 at 1332 Bancroft Street, San Diego, California.
Produced by Jon Kanis. Engineered by Charlie Schorner.
Personnel: Jon Kanis (acoustic guitar, vocals).

KCR 1260 AM • Floral Bouquet
Recorded March 13, 1990 at San Diego State University, San Diego, California.
Hosted by Matt Fidelibus and Mike Moon. Conversation, live and pre-recorded
music with Jon Kanis (acoustic guitar, vocals), Bart Mendoza (acoustic guitar, vocals).

KCR 1260 AM • Floral Bouquet
Recorded April 23, 1990 at San Diego State University, San Diego, California.
Hosted by Matt Fidelibus and Mike Moon. Conversation, live and pre-recorded
music with Jon Kanis (acoustic guitar, vocals), Bart Mendoza (acoustic guitar, vocals).

WFMU 91.1 FM • *The Music Faucet / A Tribute To Bob Dylan*
"Baby Let Me Follow You Down" (traditional), "Love Minus Zero/No Limit"
(Bob Dylan), "I Remember You" (Bob Dylan), "Don't Think Twice, It's Alright"
(Bob Dylan), "I Believe in You" (Bob Dylan), "It Ain't Me Babe" (Bob Dylan),
"Ain't No Man Righteous, No Not One" (Bob Dylan), "The Water Is Wide"
(traditional), "Political World" (Bob Dylan), "Dignity" (Bob Dylan), "Babe You're
Not the One" (Steven Keene), "Steven Keene's Blues" (Steven Keene), "Arlington,"
"I Shall Be Released" (Bob Dylan)
Recorded May 26, 1991 at WFMU Studios, East Orange, New Jersey. Hosted by
Nicholas Hill. Conversation, live and pre-recorded music in honor of Bob Dylan's
50th birthday with Clinton Heylin, Tim Hill (acoustic guitar, vocals), Jon Kanis
(acoustic guitar, vocals), Steven Keene (acoustic guitar, vocals).

Walk Without Me EP (MJK Records 101) • (January 1992)
Side 1: "Walk Without Me," "My Favorite Shirt," "Waste of Time"*
Side A: "Arlington,"* "Where I Wish You Were," "Think It Over"*
Recorded February 1989 [*] and December 1991 at Cactus Clown Studio, Eagle Rock,
California. Produced by Darian Sahanaja and Nick Walusko. Engineered and mixed
by Darian Sahanaja. Personnel: Jon Kanis (vocals), Steve Kobashigawa (electric
bass, harmony vocals), Darian Sahanaja (keyboards, drums, vocals), Nick Walusko
(guitars, drums, vocals).

KSDT 95.7 FM • *Jessica's Tulip Time*
"My Favorite Shirt," "A Day in the Life" (John Lennon, Paul McCartney),
"Waste of Time"
Recorded February 13, 1992 at the University of California San Diego, La Jolla,
California. Hosted by Jessica Ballenger. Conversation, live and pre-recorded music
with Jon Kanis (acoustic guitar, vocals).

Various Artists *Staring at the Sun Volume 2* CD
The Shambles *Reviving Spark* CD (Blindspot Records 0004) • (1993)
"It Is & It Isn't"
Recorded October 26, 1992 at Blitz Studio, San Diego, California. Produced by
Jon Kanis. Engineered by Richard Livoni. Personnel: Bill Calhoun (Vox organ),
Kevin Ring (electric guitars, vocals), Jon Kanis (acoustic guitar, tambourine, vocals),
David Klowden (drums), Bart Mendoza (vocals), Mark Zadarnowski (electric bass).

Various Artists *Staring at the Sun Volume 2* CD (Blindspot Records 0004) • (1993)
"Waste of Time" (same info as *Walk Without Me* EP).

Various Artists *That Sounds Like Fun!* Rock & Roll House Cassette
(Snap!! Tapes Fun 002) • (1993)
"Arlington" (same info as *Walk Without Me* EP).

Jon Kanis

Various Artists *Staring at the Sun Volume 3* **CD (Blindspot Records 003)** • **(1994)**
"L.P. in a Bottle"
Recorded February 6 and 13, 1994 at Box Studio, San Diego, California.
Produced by Jon Kanis and Gar Wood. Engineered and mixed by Gar Wood.
Personnel: John Chilson (drums), Paul Howland (electric bass), Jon Kanis (acoustic guitar, vocals), Ray Martinez (electric guitar), Bart Mendoza (vocals), Gar Wood (guitar solo).

KCR 1260 AM • *Floral Bouquet*
"It Is & It Isn't," "Forget (That I Even Mentioned It),"
"Cynthia Mask" (Robyn Hitchcock), "Tim"
Recorded May 18, 1995 at San Diego State University, San Diego, California.
Hosted by Mike Moon. Conversation, live and pre-recorded music with Jon Kanis (acoustic guitar, vocals).

KCR 1260 AM • *Floral Bouquet*
Recorded September 25, 1995 at San Diego State University, San Diego, California.
Hosted by Mike Moon. Conversation, live and pre-recorded music with Jon Kanis (acoustic guitar, vocals).

Demo Session
"Forget (That I Even Mentioned It)," "The Colorist," "Give," "Tim," "That,"
"Everything Remains," "Secret Society," "Fear"
Recorded July 4,1996 at the Art-Union Building, San Diego, California.
Recorded by Jon Kanis. Personnel: Jon Kanis (acoustic guitar, vocals).

The Shambles *Clouds All Day* **CD (Blindspot Records 10)** • **(1996)**
"Change" (Kevin Ring), "Moments" (Kevin Ring)
Recorded 1996 at Blitz Studio, San Diego, California. Produced by Richard Livoni and the Shambles. Engineered and mixed by Richard Livoni. Personnel: Kevin Ring (electric guitars, vocals), Jon Kanis (vocals), Richard Livoni (electric guitar), Trace Smith (drums), Bart Mendoza (guitar, vocals), Mark Zadarnowski (electric bass).

Various Artists *The Who Tribute Quadrophenia* **CD (Flavor Japan)** • **(1996)**
"Is It in My Head?" (Peter Townshend)
Recorded 1996 at Blitz Studio, San Diego, California. Produced by Richard Livoni and The Shambles. Recorded and Mixed by Richard Livoni. Personnel: Kevin Ring (electric guitars, vocals), Jon Kanis (vocals), Bart Mendoza (guitar, vocals), Gregory Page (vocals), Joel Valder (drums), Mark Zadarnowski (electric bass).

A Pair of Opposites **EP (MJK Records 102)** • **(January 1997)**
"Everything Remains," "Forget (That I Even Mentioned It)," "That," "The Colorist," "Tim," "Give"
Recorded August 1996 at Blitz Studio, San Diego, California. Produced by Jon Kanis. Engineered and mixed by Richard Livoni. Personnel: Mike Draper (electric guitar),

Jon Kanis (acoustic guitar, percussion, vocals), Mike Keneally (electric guitar, electric piano, Hammond B3 organ), Cecilia Kim (cello), John Lang (acoustic bass, electric bass), Bill Ray (drums, percussion), Bob Tedde (vocals).

Various Artists *Staring at the Sun Volume 4 It Came from San Diego* **CD (Blindspot Records 005)** • **(1998)**
"Forget (That I Even Mentioned It)" (same info as *A Pair of Opposites* EP).

Yourself Presents • *Cable Access Television*
"It Is & It Isn't," "Forget (That I Even Mentioned It)," "Everything Remains," "Give"
Recorded November 7, 1998 at Cox Studios, El Cajon, California.
Personnel: Jon Kanis (acoustic guitar, vocals).

KPBS 89.5 FM • *The Lounge*
Recorded June 22, 2001 at San Diego State University, San Diego, California.
Hosted by Dirk Sutro in conversation with Jon Kanis. Topic: Pete Townshend and The Who. Live music with Gary Shuffler and Andrew McKeag.

Demo Session
"Dreamery," "A.C. in Michigan," "Popsong 2002," "Tibeatan Hell-O,"
"Allegro 132" (two mixes), "Swampy Sea," "Piece of Mindish," "Shapes,"
"The Sun #19," "Don't Stand There," "ALVIN!," "Poppins," "CutPaste,"
"Bolan," "New Song 7/3," "Waltzing Matilda" (two mixes), "The Moon #18,"
"Don't Stand There (MJK2 version)," "Jon Is My Buddy," "Friday the 13th,"
"Friday the 13th (MJK2 version)" Recorded 2002–2003 at Studio Los Kanis
B Street Bar and Grille, San Diego, California by Jon Kanis.
Personnel: Jon Kanis (guitar, vocals), Mike Keneally (guitar, vocals).

Demo Session
"Butterfly," "Beer Run" (Todd Snider), "Don't Stand There," "Swampy Sea,"
"Lay Your Life on the Table," "Love" (John Lennon), "Make It" (two takes),
"Real Gone," "The Sun," "With a Girl Like You" (Reg Presley)
Recorded March 21, 2004 at 4860 Art Street, San Diego, California.
Produced by Jon Kanis. Engineered by Andrew Trinkle.
Personnel: Jon Kanis (acoustic guitar, vocals).

Demo Session
"Swampy Sea," "Don't Stand There," "Butterfly," "Love" (John Lennon), "Real Gone"
Recorded May 15 and August 2004; San Diego, California. Produced by Jon Kanis
and Mike Keneally. Engineered by Andrew Trinkle and Mike Keneally. Personnel:
Jon Kanis (acoustic guitar, vocals), Mike Keneally (guitar, keyboards, vocals).

KSDS 88.3 FM • *Every Shade of Blue on Jazz 88*
Recorded August 21, 2004 at San Diego City College, San Diego, California.
Hosted by T. Topic: the *American Folk Blues Festival*. Conversation and
pre-recorded music with Jon Kanis and David Peck.

Jon Kanis

Cabalistic Dispatch double LP (MJK Records 00018-9) • (July 17, 2005)
Side 1: "Invocation" (Jon Kanis, Mike Keneally), "Don't Stand There,"
"Forget (That I Even Mentioned It)," "The Colorist," "Think It Over" Side 2: "Fear,"
"A.C. in Michigan," "The Sun #19," "Everything Remains" Side 3: "Butterfly,"
"Questions for a Swami," "Make It" (Jon Kanis, Mike Keneally), "Real Gone," "Give"
Side 4: "That," "Shine On" (Jon Kanis, Mike Keneally), "Lay Your Life on the Table,"
"The Return of the Edmund Fitzgerald"
Recorded September 1, 2004–April 28, 2005 at Doubletime Studio, El Cajon,
California. Produced by Jon Kanis and Mike Keneally. Engineered by Jeff Forrest and
Richard Livoni. Mixed by Jeff Forrest and Jon Kanis. Personnel: Mike Draper (electric
guitar), Nathan Hubbard (drums, percussion, vibes/marimba), Jon Kanis (acoustic
guitar, electric bass, percussion, vocals), Jesse Keneally (vocals), Mike Keneally (electric
guitars, electric bass, Hammond B3 organ, electric piano, keyboards, drums, vocals),
Cecilia Kim (cello), Steve Kobashigawa (electric bass), John Lang (acoustic bass, electric
bass), Bill Ray (drums, percussion), Layne Sterling (vocals), Bob Tedde (vocals).

Demo Session
"Campfire," "Plane Wreck at Los Gatos (Deportees)" (Woody Guthrie, Martin
Hoffman), "Look Away, Johnny Stash," "All Is Not Lost"
Recorded August 2, 2005 at Doubletime Studio, El Cajon, California. Produced by
Jon Kanis. Engineered by Jeff Forrest. Personnel: Jon Kanis (acoustic guitar, vocals).

What's The Problem? a film about STEW by Jeffrey Winograd
"Give" Recorded August 21, 2005 at Studio Los Kanis B Street Bar and Grille,
and Balboa Park, San Diego, California. Segment directed by Rebecca Rodriguez.
Interview regarding the music and career of Mark Stewart and the Negro Problem.
Personnel: Jon Kanis (acoustic guitar, vocals).

Demo Sessions
"Folsom Prison Blues" (Johnny Cash), "Look Away, Johnny Stash" (two takes),
"Campfire," "Whistle Stop at Sparky's" (2 takes), "She Said She Said" (John Lennon,
Paul McCartney), "Jimmy Burke the Newsboy"
Recorded December 22, 2005 at Doubletime Studio, El Cajon, California. Produced
by Jon Kanis. Engineered by Jeff Forrest. Personnel: Jon Kanis (acoustic guitar, vocals).

"Look Away, Johnny Stash," "Campfire," "Whistle Stop at Sparky's," "Jimmy Burke
the Newsboy," "The Wedding March" "Lester Bangs," "Friday the 13th," "I Believe
in You" (Bob Dylan), "For Emily Anne," "Tangled Up in Blue" (Bob Dylan), "Dark
Horse" (George Harrison), "Pigs on the Wing" (Roger Waters), "Make It"
Recorded December 29, 2005 at 3073 B Street Apt. #7, San Diego, California.
Recorded by Jefferson Jay. Personnel: Jon Kanis (acoustic guitar, vocals).

"Rip It On–Bye!"
Recorded February 11, 2006 at the B Street Vault, San Diego, California. Produced
and engineered by Jon Kanis. Personnel: Jon Kanis (acoustic guitar, vocals).

Steel Bridge Songfest II Sessions
"Destiny's Right Hand" (Jon Kanis, pat mAcdonald),
"Two Six-Packs and a Bottle of Wine" (pat mAcdonald, Eric McFadden)
Recorded June 6, 2006 in Room 124 of the Holiday Motel, Sturgeon Bay,
Wisconsin. Engineered by Steve Hamilton.
Personnel: Jon Kanis (acoustic guitar, vocals).

Various Artists *Songs from the Holiday, Vol. 1* **CD** • (2011)
"Holiday Motel" (Jon Kanis, Allan MacPhee)
Recorded June 7, 2006 in Room 124 of the Holiday Motel, Sturgeon Bay,
Wisconsin. Recorded by Steve Hamilton. Personnel: Chris Aaron (acoustic guitar),
Jon Kanis (acoustic guitar, vocals), Cathy Bratten (harmony vocal), Allan MacPhee
(harmony vocal).

Steel Bridge Songfest II Sessions
"Through These Eyes" (Jon Kanis, Liv Mueller)
Recorded June 8, 2006 in Room 124 of the Holiday Motel, Sturgeon Bay,
Wisconsin. Recorded by Steve Hamilton.
Personnel: Jon Kanis (acoustic guitar, vocals), Liv Mueller (vocals).

"Common Sense" (Chris Aaron, Jon Kanis, Ilan Laks, Anna Saks)
Recorded June 8, 2006 in Room 124 of the Holiday Motel, Sturgeon Bay,
Wisconsin. Recorded by Steve Hamilton. Personnel: Chris Aaron (acoustic
guitar), Jon Kanis (acoustic guitar, vocals), Ilan Laks (acoustic guitar, lead vocal),
Anna Saks (vocals).

BZoO Homegrown Radio • *State Controlled Radio* #28 (08.29.06)
"Los Gringos Stonedo" (Chris Aaron), "Whistle Stop at Sparky's,"
"Jimmy Burke the Newsboy," "Rip It On–Bye!," "Trouble in Mind"
(Richard M. Jones), "Look Away, Johnny Stash," "Campfire,"
"Whistle Stop at Sparky's (Reprise)," "Battle Hymn of the Republic"
(Julia Ward Howe, William Steffe)
Recorded August 23–25, 2006 at Appleton, Wisconsin.
Produced by Chris Aaron and Jon Kanis. Engineered by Chris Aaron.
Personnel: Chris Aaron (acoustic guitar, vocals), Jon Kanis (acoustic guitar, vocals).

The Assumptions Demos
"Better Late than Never," "Cocktail Dancing," "Deep Dish Sonic Sage," "Devil's
Play" (two versions), "George's Tune," "Hail Caesar!," "Into Freedom," "The
Magdalene," "Once in a While," "3," "The Utopian Wedding Song," "Velvet
Warning," "Who's Mentoring the Store, Merlin?," "Why Are You," "Wished"
(all lyrics and music by Layne Sterling)
Recorded January–April, 2007 at the B Street Vault, San Diego, California.
Produced and engineered by Jon Kanis. Personnel: Jon Kanis (guitar, electric bass,
keyboards, drums, vocals), Layne Sterling (guitar, keyboards, vocals).

Demo Session
"Below the Fold," "Jimmy Burke the Newsboy," "Campfire"
Recorded February 23–24, 2007 at the B Street Vault, San Diego, California.
Produced and engineered by Jon Kanis.
Personnel: Jon Kanis (guitar, electric bass, keyboards, drums, vocals).

Everything Is Under Control (theme for State Controlled Radio)
Recorded March 11, 2007 at the B Street Vault, San Diego, California.
Produced and engineered by Jon Kanis.
Personnel: Jon Kanis (electric guitar, electric bass, keyboards, drums).

Demo Session
"Solicitude," "Quick!"
Recorded March 14, 2007 at the B Street Vault, San Diego, California.
Produced and engineered by Jon Kanis.
Personnel: Jon Kanis (guitar, electric bass, keyboards, drums, vocals).

Demo Session
"Where Is Joe Strummer When You Need Him?"
Recorded March 23, 2007 at the B Street Vault, San Diego, California.
Produced and engineered by Jon Kanis.
Personnel: Jon Kanis (acoustic guitar, electric bass, keyboards, drums, vocals).

Various Artists *Steel Bridge Songs: Selections from Steel Bridge Songfest Vol. 1* CD
(SB 2006) • (June 2007)
Produced by pat mAcdonald and Chris Aaron.
Production Assistance by Steve Hamilton and Jon Kanis.

Various Artists *Staring at the Sun Volume 6* CD
(Blindspot Records 109) • (May 2008)
"Make It" (same info as *Cabalistic Dispatch* LP).

The Assumptions LP (LS.d Records 00141) • (July 18, 2008)
"Velvet Warning," "The Magdalene," "Deep Dish Sonic Sage," "3," "Better Late
than Never," "Into Freedom," "Cocktail Dancing," "Hail Caesar!," "Why Are You,"
"Once in a While," "Wished," "Who's Mentoring the Store, Merlin?" (all lyrics and
music by Layne Sterling). Recorded July 16–19, 2007 at Big Fish Studio, Rancho
Santa Fe, California, and December 3–11, 2007 at Signature Sound, San Diego,
California. Produced by Mike Keneally. Engineered by Ben Moore, Mike Harris,
Jon Kanis. Mixed by Mike Harris. Personnel: Brian Cantrell (drums, percussion),
Jon Kanis (electric bass, vocals), Mike Keneally (guitars, keyboards, electric bass,
percussion, vocals, orchestration), Layne Sterling (guitar, vocals), Sara Sterling
(vocals, vocal arrangements).

The Jeremy Band *All Over the World* CD (JAM Records 3714) • (April, 2014)
"Come on Over," "Come Clean," "Home," "Where There's a Will,"
"Chain Reaction" (all lyrics and music by Jeremy Morris)
Recorded July 29, 2009 at Lestats, San Diego, California. Produced by Jeremy
Morris. Personnel: Jeremy Morris (electric guitar, lead vocals), Bart Mendoza
(electric guitar, vocals), Jon Kanis (electric bass), Dave Dietrich (drums, percussion).

Listening to Rocks EP
"Come Correct" (David Rizzuto), "Capitalist Plot" (Roger Morrsion),
"Wail" (Jon Kanis, Roger Morrsion, David Rizzuto, Brad Smith),
"Where Is Joe Strummer When You Need Him?," "Doorbell" (Joe Con),
"2010" (Jon Kanis, Roger Morrsion, David Rizzuto, Brad Smith)
Recorded January 26, 2010 at CHAOS Recorders, Escondido, California.
Produced by Listening to Rocks and Christopher Hoffee.
Engineered and mixed by Christopher Hoffee.
Personnel: Jon Kanis (electric bass, vocals), Roger Morrsion (electric guitars, vocals),
David Rizzuto (electric guitars, vocals), Brad Smith (drums, percussion).

Various Artists Glass Flesh 4: A Tribute to the Music of Robyn Hitchcock CD •
(October 31, 2011)
"Fifty-Two Stations" (Robyn Hitchcock)
Recorded March 1, 2010 at CHAOS Recorders, Escondido, California.
Produced by Jon Kanis and Christopher Hoffee. Engineered and mixed by
Christopher Hoffee. Personnel: Christopher Hoffee (baritone guitar, keyboard,
vibraslap, drums), Jon Kanis (acoustic guitar, electric bass, vocals).

The Assumptions Demos
"Machines & Mystics" (Layne Sterling), "A Song for Gary" (Layne Sterling)
Recorded March 6, 2011 at the C Street Vault, San Diego, California.
Produced and engineered by Jon Kanis.
Personnel: Jon Kanis (electric bass), Layne Sterling (acoustic guitar, vocals).

Demo Sessions
"Going Gaga for the American Dream," "Time to Get It Right,"
"The American Dream Continued"
Recorded March 6, 2011 at the C Street Vault, San Diego, California.
Produced and engineered by Jon Kanis.
Personnel: Jon Kanis (guitar, electric bass, keyboards, drums, vocals).

"[The Human] Race [Is A] Riot"
Recorded May 1, 2011 at the C Street Vault, San Diego, California.
Produced and engineered by Jon Kanis.
Personnel: Jon Kanis (guitar, electric bass, drums, vocals).

Jon Kanis

Demo Sessions
"Cosmic Mirror/Cosmic Mate"
Recorded April 13, 2012 at the Vault on Broadway, San Diego, California.
Produced and engineered by Jon Kanis.
Personnel: Jon Kanis (guitar, electric bass, drums, vocals).

"I Love You More Than Words Could Ever Say"
Recorded February 11, 2013 at the Vault on Broadway, San Diego, California.
Produced and engineered by Jon Kanis.
Personnel: Jon Kanis (guitar, electric bass, drums, vocals).

"Valentine's Day on Planet Xena" (Frankie Frey, Jon Kanis)
Recorded February 13, 2013 at the Vault on Broadway, San Diego, California.
Produced and engineered by Jon Kanis.
Personnel: Jon Kanis (guitar, electric bass, drums, vocals).

"Please"
Recorded February 15, 2013 at the Vault on Broadway, San Diego, California.
Produced and engineered by Jon Kanis.
Personnel: Jon Kanis (electric bass, drums, vocals).

Steel Bridge Songfest 9 Sessions
"Welcome Home" by the Come Ons, written by Stephen Cooper, Jon Kanis, and Jimm McIver in the diner area and room 124 of the Holiday Music Motel, Sturgeon Bay, Wisconsin, on 06.09.13 at 10:35 PM. Engineered and mixed by Steve Hamilton 4:00–5:00 AM and 1:15–1:30 PM on 06.10.13. Personnel: Stephen Cooper (lead vocal), Steve Hamilton (tambourine), Jon Kanis (electric bass, acoustic guitar, lead and harmony vocals, handclaps), Jimm McIver (electric guitar, acoustic guitar, harmony vocals, handclaps), Vee Sonnets (organ), Dan-O Stoffels (drums).

"Transformation Day" by the Dagaz, written by Danielle French, Jon Kanis, and Vee Sonnets on the front lawn and in room 230 of the Holiday Music Motel, Sturgeon Bay, Wisconsin, on 06.10.13 at 6:27 PM. Engineered and mixed by Steve Hamilton noon–1:00 PM on 06.11.13. Personnel: Danielle French (acoustic guitar, lead vocal), Jon Kanis (acoustic guitar, lead vocal), Manny Sanchez (drums), Ronnie Sanchez (electric bass), Vee Sonnets (electric guitar). Vocal choir: Danielle French, Vincent Gates, Shiri Gross, Haydee Irizarry, Jon Kanis, Ellie Maybe.

"Jack & the Fox" by the Drunken Coyotes, written by Mike Bleck, Jon Kanis, Kory Murphy, and Troy Therrien on the front lawn of the Holiday Music Motel, Sturgeon Bay, Wisconsin, on 06.10.13 at 11:00 PM. Engineered and mixed by Steve Hamilton 10:00–11:00 PM on 06.11.13. Personnel: Mike Bleck (vocals), Wally Ingram (drums), Jon Kanis (electric bass, vocals), Kory Murphy (electric guitar, vocals), Troy Therrien (lead guitar, vocals).

"I Won't Leave It Alone" written by Craig Greenberg in room 230 at the Holiday Music Motel, Sturgeon Bay, Wisconsin, on 06.11.13. Engineered and mixed by Dan-O Stoffels from midnight–1:30 AM on 06.12.13. Personnel: Danielle French (glockenspiel, vocals), Craig Greenberg (toy piano, lead vocal), Jon Kanis (electric bass, vocals), Vee Sonnets (electric guitar), Dan-O Stoffels (drums).

"Battle of the Bridges" written by Clayson Benally, Robin Bienemann, Landon Capelle, and Vincent Gates at the Holiday Music Motel, Sturgeon Bay, Wisconsin, on 06.12.13. Engineered and mixed by Dan-O Stoffels from 2:30–5:00 PM on 06.13.13. Personnel: Clayson Benally (drums, vocals), Robin Bienemann (electric guitar, vocals), Landon Capelle (rapping), Vincent Gates (guitar, vocals), Jon Kanis (electric bass).

"Like a Satellite" written by Charles Boheme, Lena MacDonald, Caleb Navarro, and Walter Salas-Humara at the Holiday Music Motel, Sturgeon Bay, Wisconsin, on 06.12.13. Engineered and mixed by Billy Triplett in Room 237 and 238, assisted by Steve Smith from 3:30–5:00 PM on 06.13.13. Personnel: Charles Boheme (acoustic guitar), Jon Kanis (electric bass), Tarl Knight (keyboards, vocals), Lena MacDonald (lead vocal), Caleb Navarro (acoustic guitar), Walter Salas-Humara (drums).

"Under the Bridge" written by Carley Baer, Robin Bienemann, Shiri Gross, and Jon Kanis. Written and recorded in the upstairs hallway of the Holiday Music Motel, Sturgeon Bay, Wisconsin, on 06.13.13 at 4:30 PM. Field recording by Robin Bienemann. Personnel: Carley Baer (vocal), Robin Bienemann (guitar), Stephen Cooper (saxophone).

"The Bridge of Cruelty" by the Banditos, written by John Hvezda, Jon Kanis, and Troy Therrien in the entrance of the Holiday Music Motel, Sturgeon Bay, Wisconsin, on 06.12.13 at 5:03 PM. Engineered and mixed by Steve Hamilton 2:30–4:00 PM on 06.15.13. Personnel: Jeneda Benally (trills), John Hvezda (acoustic guitar, lead vocal), Wally Ingram (percussion), Haydee Irizarry (vocals), Jon Kanis (electric bass, vocals), Manny Sanchez (percussion), Troy Therrien (lead guitar).

"Call Me at 3 AM" by Gi Gi Lee, written by Louise Goffin, Craig Greenberg, Jon Kanis, and Corinne Lee in room 230 at the Holiday Music Motel, Sturgeon Bay, Wisconsin, on 06.13.13 at 2:56 AM. Engineered and mixed by Billy Triplett in Room 237 and 238, assisted by Steve Smith 3:30–5:30 PM on 06.14.13 and 12:30–2:30 PM on 06.15.13. Personnel: Louise Goffin (lead vocal, organ), Craig Greenberg (lead vocal, Wurlitzer), Jon Kanis (electric bass, tambourine), Freddie Lee (electric guitar), Dan-O Stoffels (drums), Clayson Benally (tambourine). Vocal choir and hand claps: Stephen Cooper, Vincent Gates, Statler Gause, Louise Goffin, Craig Greenberg, Shiri Gross, Haydee Irizarry, Jon Kanis, Liv Mueller, Andrea Wittgens.

Dark Songs Songfest 5 Sessions
"In Lieu of Deed" by the Untouchables, written by Charlie Cheney, Jon Kanis, and Rick Wood in room 123 at the Holiday Music Motel, Sturgeon Bay, Wisconsin, on 10.27.13 at 11:30 PM. Engineered and mixed by Dan-O Stoffels in Room 237 (basic tracking) and Room 236 (vocals, keyboard) 3:00–4:30 AM on 10.28.13. Personnel: Charlie Cheney (electric guitar, vocals), Jon Kanis (electric bass, keyboard, vocals), Rick Wood (electric guitar), Jamey Clark (drums).

"Squeal Like a Pig, Die Like a Rat" by Nick and His Goomahs, written by Tomcat Joe, Andrea Wittgens, and Dan Smrz in room 229 at the Holiday Music Motel, Sturgeon Bay, Wisconsin, on 10.27.13. Engineered and mixed by Steve Hamilton in the Morgue noon–3:00 PM on 10.28.13. Personnel: Tomcat Joe (lead vocal, electric guitar, lead guitar), Andrea Wittgens (vocals, organ), Dan Smrz (drums), Stephen Cooper (saxophone), Jon Kanis (electric bass), Carley Baer (vocals).

"Grandma!!" by Hump the Homeless, written by Liv Mueller and Jimm McIver in room 123 at the Holiday Music Motel, Sturgeon Bay, Wisconsin, on 10.28.13. Engineered and mixed by Steve Hamilton in the Morgue 10:00 PM–11:00 PM on 10.28.13. Personnel: Liv Mueller (vocals, electric guitar), Jimm McIver (vocals, electric guitar), Jon Kanis (electric bass), Dan Smrz (drums).

"Let's Go for a Ride" by the Kandy Kanes, written by Stephen Cooper, John Hvezda, and Zach Vogel in room 122 at the Holiday Music Motel, Sturgeon Bay, Wisconsin, on 10.28.13. Engineered and mixed by Steve Hamilton in the Morgue 2:30 AM–6:00 AM on 10.29.13. Personnel: Stephen Cooper (lead vocal), Zach Vogel (lead guitar, tambourine, background vocals, tambourine), Jon Kanis (electric bass, tambourine, background vocals), Jamey Clark (drums).

"Devil Dreams on a Idle Horse" by Hold On, written by James Hall, Holly Olm, and Mike Bleck in the lobby of the Holiday Music Motel, Sturgeon Bay, Wisconsin, on 10.28.13. Engineered and mixed by Dan-O Stoffels in Room 237 (bass and drums) and Room 236 (vocals, acoustic guitar, lap steel) 11:00 PM–midnight on 10.29.13. Personnel: Mike Bleck (lead vocal), Holly Olm (vocals), James Hall (guitar, vocals), Jon Kanis (electric bass), Chris Aaron (lap steel), Jamey Clark (drums).

"Devil in My Head (a trilogy in four parts)" by Kookoo Ka-Ju, written by Jon Kanis, Tomcat Joe, and Dan Smrz in room 123 of the Holiday Music Motel, Sturgeon Bay, Wisconsin, at 1:37 PM on 10.29.13. Engineered and mixed by Dan-O Stoffels in Room 237 (bass, drums, electric guitars) and Room 236 (vocals, acoustic guitar) 2:00 AM–4:00 AM on 10.30.13. Personnel: Jon Kanis (lead vocal, acoustic guitar), Tomcat Joe (electric bass, vocals), Mojo Perry (electric guitars), Dan Smrz (drums).

"Party in the Dark" by peeooseooaplsieato, written by Kim Manning and Vee Sonnets in room 124 of the Holiday Music Motel, Sturgeon Bay, Wisconsin, in the wee hours of 10.30.13. Engineered and mixed by Dan-O Stoffels in Room 237 (bass, drums, keyboard, electric guitar) and Room 236 (vocals) 4:00 AM–5:30 AM on 10.30.13. Personnel: Kim Manning (lead vocal), Vee Sonnets (keyboard), Jon Kanis (electric guitar, vocals), Tony Menzer (electric bass), Zach Vogel (drums). Chorus: Landon Capelle, Stephen Cooper, John Hvezda, Danielle French, Jimm McIver, Jaybo, Tony Menzer, Kory Murphy, Zach Vogel.

"Killer Carnie" by Killer Carnie, written by Jon Kanis, Kory Murphy, and Holly Olm in the lobby of the Holiday Music Motel, Sturgeon Bay, Wisconsin, at 5:00 PM on 10.30.13. Engineered and mixed by Dan-O Stoffels in Room 237 (bass, drums) and Room 236 (vocals, acoustic guitar, keyboard) 11:15 AM–midnight on 10.30.13. Personnel: Holly Olm (lead vocal), Kory Murphy (acoustic guitar), Jon Kanis (electric bass), Zach Vogel (drums).

"O! the Horror" by Ellie Maybe, written by Ellie Maybe at the Holiday Music Motel, Sturgeon Bay, Wisconsin, on 10.30.13. Engineered and mixed by Dan-O Stoffels in Room 236 12:45 AM–2:30 AM on 10.31.13. Personnel: Ellie Maybe (lead vocals, harmony vocals, electric bass), Jon Kanis (harmony vocal).

"Angelyne" by the Mystery Trip, written by Kory Christopher, Jon Kanis, Kim Manning, and Vee Sonnets in room 124 at the Holiday Music Motel, Sturgeon Bay, Wisconsin, at 6:30 PM on 10.31.13. Engineered and mixed by Steve Hamilton in the Morgue 3:30–5:00 AM on 11.01.13. Personnel: Kory Christopher (acoustic guitar), Jon Kanis (harmony vocal, electric bass) Kim Manning (lead vocal), Vee Sonnets (guitar), Zach Vogel (drums), Steve Hamilton (Sandman).

A Box Full of Rocks: the El Cajon Years of Lester Bangs • (December 20, 2013)
Produced, written, and directed by Raul Sandelin. Production Assistant Flavia Lacerda. Cinematography by Tony Butler, A.J. Johnson, Dylan Sandelin, Joe Minnich, Andrew Gil. Editing by Tony Butler, Xavier Green, Matt Ramos. Sound Design by Jack Butler, A.J. Johnson, Michael Smith-Ramos. Featuring: Sydney Brown, Jack Butler, Jim Derogatis, Rob Houghton, Jon Kanis, Steve Kelly, Gary Rachac, Jerry Raney, G. Carrol Rice, Mindy Solis, Mike Stax, Milt Wyatt, Dominic Lerma as "Lester." Excerpts from Lester Bangs' writings read by Jon Kanis.

A Box Full of Rocks: the El Cajon Years of Lester Bangs
Original Motion Picture Soundtrack • (Road Ahead Productions) (February 2014)
"It Is & It Isn't" (same info as *Staring at the Sun 2* CD)
"Let It Blurt" (Lester Bangs, Robert Quine, Jody Harris, David Hofstra)
"A Box Full of Rocks Part 1" (Lester Bangs, Jon Kanis)
"A Box Full of Rocks Part 2" (Lester Bangs, Jon Kanis, Raul Sandelin)

Jon Kanis

Recorded January 13–14, 2014 at CHAOS Recorders, Escondido, California. Produced by Christopher Hoffee and Jon Kanis. Engineered and mixed by Christopher Hoffee. Personnel: Christopher Hoffee (elecric guitar, keyboards, percussion, drums), Jon Kanis (acoustic guitar, electric bass, vocals), Matt Lynott (drums).

Sessions for *Fundamentalism Is the Only Way*
"Fundamental in the Key of 'F,'" "Ready. Fire! Aim…," "I Love You More Than Words Could Ever Say," "Empire," "Devil in My Head" (Jon Kanis, Tomcat Joe, Dan Smrz), "Make a Wish," "Where Is Joe Strummer When You Need Him?," "Follow Up," "Jimmy Burke the Newsboy," "Solicitude," "Lahiri," "Welcome Home" (Stephen Cooper, Jon Kanis, Jimm McIver), "The Twelfth of December" Recorded September 2013–June 2015 at CHAOS Recorders, Escondido, California. Produced by Christopher Hoffee and Jon Kanis. Engineered and mixed by Christopher Hoffee. Personnel: Cerphe Colwell (announcer), Christopher Hoffee (electric guitar, slide guitar, keyboards, organ, ARP Synthesizer, min-Moog, Space Wurlitzer, finger cymbals, maracas, tambourine, cowbell, handclaps, drums, vocals), Jon Kanis (six and twelve-string acoustic guitars, electric bass, mini-Moog, piano, Wurlitzer, Philharmonic, Folktek Omnichord, autoharp, handclaps, vocals), George Korg (drums), Matt Lynott (drums, percussion, marimba), Jamie Shadowlight (violin), Brad Smith (drums, percussion).

The Rock Bards (aka Ticket to Write)
"The Past Is Not Made to Last (Who Loves Ya, Baby?)," "Empire," "Dweller on the Threshold" Recorded May 2, 3, and 8, 2014 at CHAOS Recorders, Escondido, California. Produced by Christopher Hoffee and Jon Kanis. Engineered and mixed by Christopher Hoffee. Personnel: Christopher Hoffee (electric guitar, slide guitar, piano, tambourine, handclaps, drums, backing vocals), Jon Kanis (acoustic guitars, electric guitar, electric bass, handclaps, vocals), Sneaky Pete (pedal steel).

All-American Mongrel Boy (1989–2014) (MJK Records/Road Ahead) • (June 2014)
"Where Is Joe Strummer When You Need Him?," "Welcome Home" (Stephen Cooper, Jon Kanis, Jimm McIver), "Arlington," "Through These Eyes" (Jon Kanis, Liv Mueller), "It Is & It Isn't," "Walk Without Me," "That," "Follow Up," "Dweller on the Threshold," "Holiday Motel" (Jon Kanis, Allan MacPhee), "A.C. in Michigan," "The Sun #19," "The Colorist," "Make It" (Jon Kanis, Mike Keneally), "Real Gone," "Think It Over," "The Past Is Not Made to Last (Who Loves Ya, Baby?)," "The Return of the Edmund Fitzgerald (Albert Hofmann Mix)" Recorded February 1989–May 2014. Compilation produced by Jon Kanis and Christopher Hoffee. Mastering by Christopher Hoffee. Original tracks produced by Christopher Hoffee, Jon Kanis, Mike Keneally, Liv Mueller, Darian Sahanaja, Nick Walusko. Personnel: Chris Aaron (acoustic guitar), Cathy Bratten (vocals), Bill Calhoun (Vox organ), Kevin Donaker-Ring (electric guitars, vocals), Mike Draper (electric guitar), Christopher Hoffee (electric guitar, slide guitar, keyboards, piano, Space Wurlitzer, tambourine, handclaps, drums, vocals), Nathan Hubbard (vibes/marimba, drums, percussion), Jon Kanis (six and twelve-string acoustic guitars, electric

bass, Wurlitzer, Philharmonic, vibraslap, percussion, vocals), Mike Keneally (electric guitars, electric bass, Hammond B3 organ, electric piano, keyboards, Mellotron, backwards electric guitars, drums, vocals), Cecilia Kim (cello), Steve Kobashigawa (electric bass, harmony vocal), David Klowden (drums), George Korg (drums), John Lang (acoustic bass), Allan MacPhee (vocals), Bart Mendoza (vocals), Liv Mueller (vocals), Bill Ray (drums, percussion), Darian Sahanaja (keyboards, drums, vocals), Nick Walusko (guitars, drums, vocals), Mark Zadarnowski (electric bass).

Steel Bridge Songfest 10 Sessions
"Puente de Acero" by Los Enemigos, written by Lumberjack Cash, Jon Kanis, and Walter Salas-Humara in room 126 of the Holiday Music Motel, Sturgeon Bay, Wisconsin, on June 8th, 2014 at 10:00 PM–midnight. Engineered and mixed by Dan-O Stoffels 1:00-3:00 AM on 06.09.14. Personnel: Walter Salas-Humara (drums, lead vocal), Jon Kanis (electric bass, harmony vocal, keyboard), Lumberjack Cash (electric guitar, vocals, and Español rap).

"Automatic" by the Shifters, written by Jon Kanis, Lantz Laswell, and Ronnie Sanchez in room 127 of the Holiday Music Motel, Sturgeon Bay, Wisconsin, on June 9th, 2014 at 10:00 PM–1:30 AM. Engineered and mixed by Steve Smith in the Tambourine Collaboratory 3:00-6:30 AM on 06.10.14. Personnel: Jon Kanis (electric guitar, lead vocal), Lance Laswell (keyboard, lead vocal), Ronnie Sanchez (electric bass, vocals), Vee Sonnets (lead guitar), Manny Sanchez (drums).

"Get on to It" by Shiri and the Get-On-Its, written by Tomcat Joe and Shiri Nicole in room 4 of the Tambourine Collaboratory of the Holiday Music Motel, Sturgeon Bay, Wisconsin, on June 11th, 2014. Engineered and mixed by Steve Hamilton in Sausage Studio from 11:30 PM–1:15 AM on 06.12.14. Personnel: Shiri Nicole (lead vocal), Tomcat Joe (electric guitar, vocals), Jon Kanis (electric bass, backing vocals), Clayson Benally (drums, backing vocals), Vee Sonnets (lead guitar, backing vocals).

"Deep Mirror" by the Lobbyists, written by Jon Kanis, Barrett Tasky, and Victoria Vox in the lobby and room 236 of the Holiday Music Motel, Sturgeon Bay, Wisconsin, on June 11th, 2014 at 11:00 AM–3:00 PM. Engineered and mixed by Dan-O Stoffels and Barrett Tasky 1:00–3:00 PM on 06.12.14. Personnel: Carley Baer (vocals), Jon Kanis (electric bass), Sarven Manguiat (acoustic guitar), Manny Sanchez (drums), Barrett Tasky (electric guitars, keyboard), Victoria Vox (ukulele, vocals).

"Love Come Rescue Me" by Megachurch, written by James Hall, Eric McFadden, Liv Mueller, and Andrea Wittgens in room 230 of the Holiday Music Motel, Sturgeon Bay, Wisconsin, on June 12th, 2014. Engineered and mixed by Steve Hamilton in Sausage Studio from 10:45 AM–1:00 PM on 06.15.14. Personnel: James Hall (vocals, guitar), Eric McFadden (vocals, electric guitar), Liv Mueller (vocals), Andrea Wittgens (vocals), Jon Kanis (electric bass, vocals), Kip Wilde (drums, organ), Delphine de St. Paer (vocals), Tomcat Joe (vocals), Victoria Vox (vocals).

Education>Information>Entertainment>
Five Years of State Controlled Radio:

#001 • 02.14.06	A Valentine Card from CA to VA (3 hrs)	
#002 • 02.21.06	Sophomore (2 hrs)	
#003 • 02.28.06	4321 Fairmont Avenue	
	A Tribute to Megalopolis (2 hrs)	
#004 • 03.07.06	Words and Music by Robyn Hitchcock (3 hrs)	
#005 • 03.14.06	Make Mine a Double (2 hrs)	
#006 • 03.21.06	Picking Posies for a Springtime Rendezvous	
	Words and Music by Jon Auer and Ken Stringfellow (2 hrs)	
#007 • 03.28.06	How Sweet to Be an Idiot	
	Words and Music by Neil Innes (2 hrs)	
#008 • 04.04.06	Words and Music by Peter Case • Part I (2 hrs)	
#009 • 04.11.06	Words and Music by Peter Case • Part II (2 hrs)	
#010 • 04.18.06	Words and Music by Buddy Blue (1957–2006) (2 hrs)	
#011 • 04.25.06	Schizoid (2 hrs)	
#012 • 05.02.06	Words and Music by Scott Miller (2 hrs)	
#013 • 05.16.06	Happy Birthday to the Amazing Three:	
	Steve, Nick, and Darian (2 hrs)	
#014 • 05.23.06	To Austin...and Back (2 hrs)	
#015 • 05.30.06	Words and Music by Gregory Page (2 hrs)	
#016 • 06.06.06	Words and Music by pat mAcdonald • Part I (2 hrs)	
#017 • 06.13.06	Words and Music by pat mAcdonald • Part II (2 hrs)	
#018 • 06.20.06	Greetings from Sturgeon Bay, Wisconsin • Part I (2 hrs)	
#019 • 06.27.06	Greetings from Sturgeon Bay, Wisconsin • Part II (2 hrs)	
#020 • 07.04.06	I Kept a Promise to Myself (2 hrs)	
#021 • 07.11.06	Heart (2 hrs)	
#022 • 07.18.06	Shine on You Crazy Diamond: A Tribute to Syd Barrett (2 hrs)	
#023 • 07.25.06	Illuminati and the Sun (2 hrs)	
#024 • 08.01.06	Lionhearted in the Twilight Zone (2 hrs)	
#025 • 08.08.06	Words and Music by Will Sexton (2 hrs)	
#026 • 08.15.06	Ode to LS.d (layne sterling • dragon) (2 hrs)	
#027 • 08.22.06	It's Johnny's Birthday • Words and Music by Jon Kanis (2 hrs)	
#028 • 08.29.06	A Stop in Appleton (2 hrs)	
#029 • 09.05.06	"Mission Accomplished" (2 hrs)	
#030 • 09.12.06	myspace is your space • part I (2 hrs)	
#031 • 09.19.06	myspace is your space • part II (2 hrs)	
#032 • 09.26.06	Words and Music by Andy Partridge or	
	Colin Moulding • XTC • Part I (2 hrs)	
#033 • 10.03.06	It's Johnny's Birthday • Words and Music by	
	John Lennon (Joko segment #1) (2 hrs)	

#034 • 10.10.06	Words and Music by Andy Partridge or
	Colin Moulding • XTC • Part II (2 hrs)
#035 • 10.31.06	Trick or Treat/Samhaim Samhaim
	no disambiguation on hallow's eve (2 hrs)
#036 • 11.07.06	It's Joni's Birthday • Words and Music by Joni Mitchell (2 hrs)
#037 • 11.14.06	It's Neil's Birthday • Words and Music by Neil Young (2 hrs)
#038 • 11.21.06	Pass the Beats: Giving Thanks for
	The Beat Generation • Part I (2 hrs)
#039 • 11.28.06	Pass the Beats: Giving Thanks for
	The Beat Generation • Part II (2 hrs)
#040 • 12.05.06	Cleansing the Doors of Perception (2 hrs)
#041 • 12.12.06	A Conversation with Neil Innes (2 hrs)
#042 • 12.19.06	The Immense Superiority of Michael Joseph Keneally I (2 hrs)
#043 • 12.26.06	The Immense Superiority of Michael Joseph Keneally II (2 hrs)
#044 • 01.02.07	The Immense Superiority of Michael Joseph Keneally III (2 hrs)
#045 • 01.09.07	A Prayer for the New Year (2 hrs)
#046 • 01.16.07	I Have a Dream (2 hrs)
#047 • 01.23.07	1-2-3-Go! (2 hrs)
#048 • 01.30.07	1972: A Season to Remember (3 hrs)
#049 • 02.06.07	Brothers and Sisters: A Celebration of Being
	Black in the 21st Century • Part I (2 hrs)
#050 • 02.13.07	What's Your Movie? SCR 1 Year On... (2 hrs)
#051 • 02.20.07	Let It Down: A Tribute to George Harrison (3 hrs)
#052 • 02.27.07	Brothers and Sisters: A Celebration of Being
	Black in the 21st Century • Part II (2 hrs)
#053 • 03.06.07	Choose Your Seat: The 36th Anniversary of *Soul to Soul* (2 hrs)
#054 • 03.13.07	The Magic Number Nine (2 hrs)
#055 • 03.20.07	Spring Springs Eternal (2 hrs)
#056 • 03.27.07	From Mr. Frantic Past *Captain Fantastic*:
	A Back Alley Tour of Elton John's Career
	on the Occasion of His 64th Birthday (3 hrs)
#057 • 04.03.07	Passover (2 hrs)
#058 • 04.10.07	The Illegal Revenue Service (2 hrs)
#059 • 04.17.07	Ram on Into the Aries Twilight (2 hrs)
#060 • 04.24.07	April Showers (2 hrs)
#061 • 05.01.07	May Flowers/Beltane (2 hrs)
#062 • 05.08.07	Let George Do It • George Carlin Turns 70 (2 hrs)
#063 • 05.15.07	The *Lifehouse* Method (2 hrs)
#064 • 05.22.07	Words and Music by Bob Dylan (2 hrs)
#065 • 05.29.07	Dream Brother • Words and Music by Jeff Buckley (2 hrs)
#066 • 06.05.07	The Age of Aquarius • Part I (2 hrs)
#067 • 06.12.07	The Age of Aquarius • Part II (2 hrs)
#068 • 06.19.07	Jeff Beck: The World's Greatest Living Guitarist (2 hrs)

#069 • 06.26.07   Lowell George Puts on His Sailin' Shoes (2 hrs)
#070 • 07.03.07   Birth (and Re-Birth) of a Nation (2 hrs)
#071 • 07.10.07   No Fixed Agenda, Take 71 (2 hrs)
#072 • 07.17.07   Speaking Your Mind (2 hrs)
#073 • 07.24.07   Life (2 hrs)
#074 • 07.31.07   ...and Death (2 hrs)
#075 • 08.07.07   A Long Day's Journey Into Joe Jackson (2 hrs)
#040 • 08.11.07   Cleansing the Doors of Perception
   (The premiere of SCR for Hamilton's Tavern
   2nd Saturday celebration = HT2S) (2 hrs)
#076 • 08.14.07   Stew *Is* the Negro Problem (2 hrs)
#077 • 08.21.07   A Toast to All My Family and Friends (2 hrs)
#078 • 08.28.07   A Conversation with Tony Sheridan (2 hrs)
#079 • 09.04.07   Back to School (2 hrs)
#066 • 09.08.07   The Age of Aquarius (HT2S) (2 hrs)
#080 • 09.11.07   Nine-Eleven (2 hrs)
#081 • 09.18.07   A Mystery Date with James Marshall Hendrix
   (1942–1970) Part I (2 hrs)
#082 • 09.25.07   Learning How to *SMiLE* (2 hrs)
#083 • 10.02.07   A Conversation with Bart Mendoza (2 hrs)
#084 • 10.09.07   Dr. John Winston O'Boogie Lennon, I Presume
   (Joko segment #2) (2 hrs)
#085 • 10.13.07   Double Live Gonzo
   1 Year on at Hamilton's Tavern (HT2S) (3 hrs)
#086 • 10.23.07   Julian Cope Is *Head-On* and *Possessed* (2 hrs)
#087 • 10.30.07   Dia de los Muertos (2 hrs)
#088 • 11.06.07   Casting a Vote for the Plimsouls (HT2S) (2 hrs)
#089 • 11.13.07   A Conversation with the Truckee Brothers (2 hrs)
#090 • 11.20.07   A Conversation with Cindy Lee Berryhill (2 hrs)
#091 • 11.27.07   A Mystery Date with James Marshall Hendrix
   (1942–1970) Part II (2 hrs)
#092 • 12.04.07   Memories of El Monte, Phaze I of Frank Zappa's
   Conceptual Continuity (2 hrs)
#001 • 12.08.07   Hamilton's Holiday on Ice (HT2S) (2 hrs)
#093 • 12.11.07   Project/Object, Phaze II of Frank Zappa's
   Conceptual Continuity (2 hrs)
#094 • 12.18.07   Stagecraft, Phaze III of Frank Zappa's
   Conceptual Continuity (2 hrs)
#095 • 12.25.07   The Present-Day Composer Refuses to Die,
   Phaze IV of Frank Zappa's Conceptual Continuity (2 hrs)
#045 • 01.01.08   A Prayer for the New Year (take two) (2 hrs)
#096 • 01.08.08   A Conversation with Jon Auer (2 hrs)
#046 • 01.15.08   I Have a Dream (take two) (HT2S) (2 hrs)

#097 • 01.22.08	A Conversation with Steve Poltz (2 hrs)	
#098 • 01.29.08	Make a Wish (2 hrs)	
#099 • 02.05.08	Fat Tuesday (HT2S) (2 hrs)	
#100 • 02.14.08	A Century of Sound (1908–2007) (Two–Year Anniversary of SCR) (4 hrs)	
#101 • 02.22.08	One Toke Over the Line (2 hrs)	
#102 • 02.29.08	2012: Taking a Leap of Faith (2 hrs)	
#103 • 03.07.08	Happy Birthday Commander Gilmour (2 hrs)	
#104 • 03.14.08	The Luck of the Irish (HT2S) (2 hrs)	
#105 • 03.21.08	Eating Chocolate Cake in a Bag The Ballad of John and Yoko (Joko segment #3) (2 hrs)	
#106 • 03.28.08	Steven Tyler Turns Sixty (3 hrs)	
#107 • 04.04.08	Mystery Dance (2 hrs)	
#108 • 04.11.08	Embrace the Enigma (HT2S) (2 hrs)	
#109 • 04.18.08	Nashville (2 hrs)	
#110 • 04.25.08	A Conversation with Tommy Womack (2 hrs)	
#111 • 05.02.08	A Conversation with Will Kimbrough (2 hrs)	
#112 • 05.09.08	The South Shall Rise Again (HT2S) (2 hrs)	
#113 • 05.16.08	Breaking the Sound Barrier in '66 (Happy Birthday Craig Arthur Jackson) (2 hrs)	
#114 • 05.23.08	Down on Mudcrutch Farm (2 hrs)	
#115 • 06.01.08	Q: Did I Lose You? A: Amnesia? (there's no place like home…) (2 hrs)	
#116 • 06.07.08	What Sort of Symbol *Is* Prince Rogers Nelson? (2 hrs)	
#117 • 06.14.08	Happy Birthday Bun E. Carlos! (HT2S) (2 hrs)	
#118 • 06.21.08	20th Century Man: Words and Music by Raymond Douglas Davies (2 hrs)	
#119 • 06.30.08	I Love You Emily Anne (2 hrs)	
#120 • 07.06.08	Seven–Seven–Seventy (Happy Birthday Scott Andrew Jackson) (2 hrs)	
#121 • 07.12.08	All the World's a Stage starring Bon Scott as King Leer (07.09.46–02.19.80) (HT2S) (2 hrs)	
#122 • 07.20.08	Getting the Led Out from A to Zed • Part I (2 hrs)	
#123 • 07.27.08	Getting the Led Out from A to Zed • Part II (2 hrs)	
#124 • 08.03.08	Getting the Led Out from A to Zed • Part III (2 hrs)	
#125 • 08.09.08	Glam Slam (Glam Rock circa 1970–75) (HT2S) (2 hrs)	
#126 • 08.17.08	Getting the Led Out from A to Zed • Part IV (2 hrs)	
#127 • 08.24.08	The Reconstruction of 4 Out of 5 Doctors • Part I (2 hrs)	
#128 • 08.31.08	The Reconstruction of 4 Out of 5 Doctors • Part II (2 hrs)	
#129 • 09.07.08	Basking in the Moment: The Life and Times of Henry Diltz • Part I (2 hrs)	
#130 • 09.14.08	Basking in the Moment: The Life and Times of Henry Diltz • Part II (2 hrs)	

#131 • 09.13.08	I Shall Be Re-Released	
	(or No One Sings Dylan Like Dylan…) (HT2S) (2 hrs)	
#132 • 09.21.08	Mr. Joe Fuckin' Perry (2 hrs)	
#133 • 10.05.08	Down in the Root Cellar Beyond the Blues • Phase I (2 hrs)	
#134 • 10.12.08	Ladies & Gentlemen: Lenny Bruce! (10.13.25–08.03.66) (2 hrs)	
#135 • 10.19.08	"Freebird!" (HT2S) (2 hrs)	
#136 • 10.26.08	The Art of Diplomacy (2 hrs)	
#137 • 11.02.08	Tipping Point (2 hrs)	
#138 • 11.09.08	Cosmic American Music: The Return of Gram Parsons (2 hrs)	
#139 • 11.16.08	I Often Dream of Robyn Hitchcock (2 hrs)	
#140 • 11.23.08	11.22.63 (2 hrs)	
#141 • 11.30.08	Lighting Up with Cheech y Chong (2 hrs)	
#142 • 12.07.08	The Unfathomable Depths of Dennis Wilson (2 hrs)	
#143 • 12.13.08	Don't Forget the Motor City	
	(aka Motown Dance Party) (HT2S) (2 hrs)	
#144 • 12.21.08	Solstice (2 hrs)	
#145 • 01.04.09	The King of Tupelo (2 hrs)	
#146 • 01.11.09	Go West Young Man and Start Again starring	
	Walter Becker and Donald Fagen • Part I (2 hrs)	
#147 • 01.18.09	Rising to the Occasion (A New Birth of Freedom?) (2 hrs)	
#148 • 01.25.09	Up on the Roof (the 40th Anniversary of	
	The Beatles Rooftop Concert) (2 hrs)	
#149 • 02.02.09	Groundhog Day (2 hrs)	
#150 • 02.08.09	L-O-V-E (Three–Year Anniversary for SCR) (HT2S) (3 hrs)	
#151 • 02.15.09	Go West Young Man and Start Again starring	
	Walter Becker and Donald Fagen • Part II (2 hrs)	
#152 • 02.22.09	Down in the Root Cellar Beyond the Blues • Phase II (2 hrs)	
#153 • 03.01.09	Can Blue Men Sing the Whites? (2 hrs)	
#154 • 03.08.09	Garage Sale (2 hrs)	
#155 • 03.15.09	No Fixed Agenda, Take 2 (Swimming in Pisces) (2 hrs)	
#156 • 03.22.09	Get a Job (2 hrs)	
#157 • 03.29.09	No Fixed Agenda, Take 3 (2 hrs)	
#158 • 04.05.09	Happy Birthday Peter David Case (PC Turns 55) (2 hrs)	
#159 • 04.12.09	926 East McLemore Avenue (aka Soulsville U.S.A.	
	the home of Stax/Volt Records) (HT2S) (2 hrs)	
#160 • 04.19.09	Record Store Day (2 hrs)	
#161 • 04.26.09	Gator by the Bay (2 hrs)	
#162 • 05.09.09	Rogue Dead Guys (HT2S) (2 hrs)	
#163 • 05.17.09	A Conversation with Mike Stax • Part I (2 hrs)	
#164 • 05.24.09	A Conversation with Mike Stax • Part II (2 hrs)	
#165 • 05.31.09	A Conversation with Mike Stax • Part III (2 hrs)	
#166 • 06.07.09	Words and Music by James Paul McCartney • Part I (2 hrs)	
#167 • 06.14.09	Words and Music by James Paul McCartney • Part II (2 hrs)	

#168 • 06.21.09   Have a Drink on Me
(aka *The Days of Wine and Roses*) (HT2S) (2 hrs)
#169 • 06.28.09   A Celebration of Doc Pomus (06.27.25–03.14.91) (2 hrs)
#170 • 07.05.09   Michael Joseph Jackson (08.29.58–06.25.09) (2 hrs)
#171 • 07.11.09   Arrogant Bastards: Rock's Cockiest Front Men
(and Women) (HT2S) (2 hrs)
#172 • 07.19.09   Words and Music by James Paul McCartney • Part III (2 hrs)
#173 • 07.26.09   Letting Yer Freak Flag Fly (2 hrs)
#174 • 08.02.09   A Conversation with Barry and the Remains • Part I (2 hrs)
#175 • 08.09.09   A Conversation with Barry and the Remains • Part II (2 hrs)
#176 • 08.16.09   Getting Back to the Garden: Celebrating the 40th
Anniversary of the Woodstock Music and Art Fair
(Four Days of Peace and Music) (HT2S) (3 hrs)
#177 • 08.23.09   Action Painting at Its Finest • Phase I (2 hrs)
#178 • 08.30.09   Action Painting at Its Finest • Phase II (2 hrs)
#179 • 09.06.09   Words and Music by Roger Waters
(born 09.06.43) (2 hrs)
#180 • 09.13.09   Words and Music by Hank Williams Sr.
(09.17.23–01.01.53) (2 hrs)
#181 • 09.20.09   Words, Music, and Stories by Shel Silverstein (2 hrs)
#182 • 09.27.09   Staying Till the End of the Movie (2 hrs)
#183 • 10.04.09   *Quadrophenia* (2 hrs)
#184 • 10.10.09   Three Is a Magic Number: Celebrating the 3rd Anniversary of
Hamilton's Tavern (HT2S) (3 hrs)
#185 • 10.18.09   Happy Birthday Laura Nyro (10.18.47–04.08.97) (2 hrs)
#186 • 10.25.09   Neil Young Archives #1/Lighting South Towards Buffalo and
Springfield (1963–1968) (2 hrs)
#187 • 11.01.09   Neil Young Archives #2/It's a Solo Trip (1966–1971) (2 hrs)
#188 • 11.08.09   Neil Young Archives #3/Requiem for the Rockets or
Don't Spook the Horse (1963–1971) (2 hrs)
#189 • 11.15.09   Neil Young Archives #4/In the Middle of the Road and
Aiming for the Ditch (1969–1973) (2 hrs)
#190 • 11.22.09   Giving Thanks for Neil Young (HT2S) (3 hrs)
#191 • 11.29.09   Words and Music by Randy Newman (2 hrs)
#192 • 12.06.09   Tom Petty Is Alive and Well • Part I (2 hrs)
#193 • 12.12.09   Tom Petty Is Alive and Well • Part II (HT2S) (3 hrs)
#144 • 12.20.09   Encore presentation of Solstice (revised) (2 hrs)
#045 • 12.27.09   A Prayer for the New Year (take three) (2 hrs)
#194 • 01.03.10   Twenty Ten and Back Again
(Fortune Is the End of the Beginning) (2 hrs)
#195 • 01.09.10   Words and Music by David Bowie (HT2S) (4 hrs)
#196 • 01.17.10   Packed with Nouns:
A Conversation with Charlie Cheney (2 hrs)

#197 • 01.24.10	Beyond Hectoring: the Words and Music of	
	Warren Zevon (01.24.47–09.07.03) (2 hrs)	
#198 • 01.31.10	*Ugly Things* #29 with Mike Stax • One (2 hrs)	
#199 • 02.07.10	*Where the Action Is!* with Mike Stax • Two (2 hrs)	
#200 • 02.14.10	A Valentine from Me to You: Kiss Me You Fool!	
	(Four-Year Anniversary of SCR) (HT2S) (3 hrs)	
#201 • 02.21.10	Yoko Ono and the Plastic Ono Band (2 hrs)	
#202 • 02.28.10	Mission Statement (2 hrs)	
#203 • 03.07.10	Arthur Lee and Love (2 hrs)	
#204 • 03.14.10	Johnny the Fox Meets Thin Lizzy (HT2S) (2 hrs)	
#205 • 03.21.10	Viva la Revolución (2 hrs)	
#206 • 03.28.10	Whatcha See Is Whatcha Get (2 hrs)	
#207 • 04.04.10	*SMiLE* It's Springtime! (2 hrs)	
#208 • 04.10.10	Alex Chilton Is More than a Big Star (HT2S) (3 hrs)	
#209 • 04.18.10	Specs: the Jack Nitzsche CV • Part I (2 hrs)	
#210 • 04.25.10	Specs: the Jack Nitzsche CV • Part II (2 hrs)	
#211 • 05.02.10	Zeitgeist or Gestalt? (2 hrs)]	
#212 • 05.08.10	Stone the Crowes (the Black Crowes) (HT2S) (3 hrs)	
#213 • 05.16.10	The Time Machine (singles from *Billboard's* Hot 100	
	for the week ending 05.15.71) (3 hrs)	
#214 • 05.23.10	The Time Machine (singles from *Billboard's* Hot 100	
	for the week ending 05.17.80) (3 hrs)	
#215 • 05.30.10	Looking Forward, Looking Back (2 hrs)	
#216 • 06.06.10	The Time Machine (singles from *Billboard's* Hot 100	
	for the week ending 06.04.66) (2 hrs)	
#217 • 06.12.10	Let's Have a Party to Cure the Summertime Blues	
	(the last SCR 2nd Saturday at Hamilton's Tavern) (3 hrs)	
#218 • 06.20.10	The Clock Is Ticking (2 hrs)	
#219 • 08.01.10	Fifty-Nine/Pearls Before Swine (2 hrs)	
#220 • 08.08.10	Ode to LS.d (take two) (2 hrs)	
#221 • 08.15.10	Flipping Yer Wig! A Conversation with Peter Case (2 hrs)	
#222 • 12.31.10	Auld Lang Syne (2 hrs)	
#223 • 01.31.11	So Long, Donnie (3 hrs)	
#224 • 02.07.11	Words and Music by Bob Marley	
	(02.06.45–05.11.81) (3 hrs)	
#225 • 02.19.11	High 5ive—a Gathering of the Tribes	
	(Five-Year Anniversary of SCR) (3 hrs)	
#226 • 03.04.11	No Fucking Around: It Came from San Diego • Part I (3 hrs)	
#227 • 03.12.11	No Fucking Around: It Came from San Diego • Part II (3 hrs)	
#228 • 03.19.11	The Time Machine (singles from *Billboard's* Hot 100	
	for the week ending 01.03.76) (3 hrs)	
#229 • 03.27.11	E.C. Was Here, Clapton Is God and	
	Slowhand Turns Another Page (3 hrs)	

#230 • 04.23.11	Mercury Stations Direct (3 hrs)
#231 • 04.29.11	Happy Birthday Sir Duke Ellington
	(04.29.1899–05.24.1974) (3 hrs)
#232 • 05.06.11	Bob Seger: Rock and Roll Never Forgets (3 hrs)
#233 • 05.15.11	A Conversation with Gary Heffern (3 hrs)
#234 • 05.22.11	Seven Decades of Robert Allen Zimmerman or
	I'm Only Bob Dylan When I Have to Be • Part I (3 hrs)
#235 • 05.23.11	Seven Decades of Robert Allen Zimmerman or
	I'm Only Bob Dylan When I Have to Be • Part II (3 hrs)
#236 • 05.24.11	Seven Decades of Robert Allen Zimmerman or
	I'm Only Bob Dylan When I Have to Be • Part III (3 hrs)
#237 • 05.30.11	A Conversation with Jim McInnes (3 hrs)

archival projects> producer/director:

Billy Joel Featurette • Songwriter Hall of Fame, New York, New York
A three-minute film presentation in the Imperial Ballroom of the Sheraton Hotel
to honor Billy Joel with the Johnny Mercer Award on June 14, 2001. Produced
and Directed by David A. Peck for Reelin' in the Years Productions. Production
Assistance: Jon Kanis.

Soulsville U.S.A. / A Journey Through the Soul of America
Five short films on the history of American Rhythm and Blues music on permanent
exhibition (as of November 2002) at the Stax Museum of American Soul Music,
Memphis, Tennessee. Produced and Directed by Jon Kanis and David Peck for
Reelin' in the Years Productions. Graphics and Post-Production by Media 101.
Executive Producer/Legal by Mark R. Crosby on behalf of the Stax Museum of
American Soul Music.

Film #1 • *Do You Love Me? (1955–1963)* • (6:13)
1) Drown in My Own Tears/ *Ray Charles*
2) Lonely Teardrops/ *Jackie Wilson*
3) Do You Love Me?/ *The Contours*
4) Prisoner of Love/ *James Brown & the Famous Flames*

Film #2 • *Land of 1,000 Dances (1964–1966)* • (8:49)
1) Land of 1,000 Dances/ *Wilson Pickett*
2) When a Man Loves a Woman/ *Percy Sledge*
3) Love Attack/ *James Carr*
4) Hold What You've Got/ *Joe Tex*
5) Going to a Go-Go/ *The Miracles*
6) Reach Out (I'll Be There)/ *The Four Tops*
7) Get Ready/ *The Temptations*
8) Papa's Got a Brand New Bag/ *James Brown & the Famous Flames*

Jon Kanis

Film #3 • *Say It Loud! (1967–1969)* • (11:20)
1) Sweet Soul Music/*Arthur Conley*
2) Tell Mama/*Etta James*
3) I Heard It Through the Grapevine/*Marvin Gaye*
4) Since You've Been Gone (Sweet, Sweet Baby)/*Aretha Franklin*
5) Choice of Colors/*The Impressions*
6) Say It Loud! (I'm Black and I'm Proud)/*James Brown*
7) Dance to the Music/*Sly & the Family Stone*
8) Proud Mary/*Ike & Tina Turner*
9) It's Your Thing/*The Isley Brothers*

Film #4 • *What's Going On? (1970–1972)* • (11:06)
1) I Want You Back/*The Jackson 5*
2) Back Stabbers/*The O'Jays*
3) Superstitous/*Stevie Wonder*
4) I'll Be Around/*The Spinners*
5) Ain't No Sunshine/*Bill Withers*
6) What's Going On?/*Marvin Gaye*
7) War/*Edwin Starr*
8) Freddie's Dead/*Curtis Mayfield*
9) Thank You (Falettinme Be Mice Elf Again)/*Sly & the Family Stone*
10) Get Up (I Feel Like Being a) Sex Machine/*James Brown*

Film #5 • *Tear the Roof Off the Sucker (1973–1975)* • (10:49)
1) Lady Marmalade/*Labelle*
2) Never, Never Gonna Give You Up/*Barry White*
3) Once You Get Started/*Rufus featuring Chaka Khan*
4) Midnight Train to Georgia/*Gladys Knight & The Pips*
5) If You Don't Know Me by Now/*Harold Melvin & The Bluenotes*
6) Love to Love You Baby/*Donna Summer*
7) Tear the Roof Off the Sucker/*Parliament-Funkadelic*

The American Folk Blues Festival 1962–1966 • Volume One
Various Artists DVD (Hip-O Records B0000750-09) • (08.26.03)
Produced by Janie Hendrix, Jon Kanis, John McDermott, and David Peck for Reelin'
in the Years Productions in association with Experience Hendrix; distributed by
Universal Music Enterprises. Audio Engineering and Restoration by Eddie Kramer.

1) Call Me When You Need Me/*T-Bone Walker* (1962)
2) Hootin' Blues/*Sonny Terry & Brownie McGhee* (1962)
3) The Blues Is Everywhere/*Memphis Slim* (1962)
4) I Can't Quit You Baby/*Otis Rush* (1966)
5) Another Night to Cry/*Lonnie Johnson* (1963)
6) Women Be Wise/*Sippie Wallace* (1966)
7) Hobo Blues/*John Lee Hooker* (1965)

8) Five Long Years/*Eddie Boyd* (1965)
9) Shakey's Blues/*Walter "Shakey" Horton* (1965)
10) Hoodoo Man Blues/*Junior Wells* (1966)
11) Mean Stepfather/*Big Joe Williams* (1963)
12) Going Down to the River/*Mississippi Fred McDowell* (1965)
13) Weak Brain and Narrow Mind/*Willie Dixon* (1964)
14) Nine Below Zero/*Sonny Boy Williamson* (1963)
15) Spann's Blues/*Otis Spann* (1963)
16) Got My Mojo Working/*Muddy Waters* (1963)
17) Bye Bye Blues-Finale/*Entire Cast* (1963)
18) Walking the Floor Over You-Off the Hook/*Earl Hooker* (1969)

The American Folk Blues Festival 1962–1966 • Volume Two
Various Artists DVD (Hip-O Records B0000751-09) • (08.26.03)
Produced by Janie Hendrix, Jon Kanis, John McDermott, and David Peck for Reelin'
in the Years Productions in association with Experience Hendrix; distributed by
Universal Music Enterprises. Audio Engineering and Restoration by Eddie Kramer.

1) Bye Bye Bird/*Sonny Boy Williamson* (1964)
2) My Younger Days/*Sonny Boy Williamson* (1964)
3) Come on Home Baby/*Sunnyland Slim* (1964)
4) Nervous/*Willie Dixon* (1962)
5) Mojo Hand/*Lightnin' Hopkins* (1964)
6) Black Snake Blues/*Victoria Spivey* (1963)
7) Everyday I Have The Blues/*Memphis Slim* (1963)
8) Don't Throw Your Love on Me So Strong/*T-Bone Walker* (1962)
9) Tall Heavy Mama/*Roosevelt Sykes* (1966)
10) Sittin' And Cryin' the Blues/*Willie Dixon* (1963)
11) Murphy's Boogie/*Matt "Guitar" Murphy* (1963)
12) Stranger Blues/*Sonny Terry & Brownie McGhee* (1962)
13) Shake For Me/*Howlin' Wolf* (1964)
14) I'll Be Back Someday/*Howlin' Wolf* (1964)
15) Love Me Darlin'/*Howlin' Wolf* (1964)
16) Down Home Shakedown/*Big Mama Thornton* (1965)
17) All Your Love/*Magic Sam* (1969)
18) Magic Sam's Boogie/*Magic Sam* (1969)

The American Folk Blues Festival 1962–1966 • Volume One
Various Artists CD (Hip-O Records B0001030-02) • (08.26.03)
Produced by Janie Hendrix, Jon Kanis, John McDermott, and David Peck for Reelin'
in the Years Productions in association with Experience Hendrix; distributed by
Universal Music Enterprises. Audio Engineering and Restoration by Eddie Kramer.

1) Shake For Me/*Howlin' Wolf* (1964)
2) I Can't Quit You Baby/*Otis Rush* (1966)

3) Another Night to Cry/*Lonnie Johnson* (1963)
4) Women Be Wise/*Sippie Wallace* (1966)
5) Everyday I Have the Blues/*Memphis Slim* (1963)
6) Don't Throw Your Love on Me So Strong/*T-Bone Walker* (1962)
7) Hoodoo Man Blues/*Junior Wells* (1966)
8) Black Snake Blues/*Victoria Spivey* (1963)
9) Mojo Hand/*Lightnin' Hopkins* (1964)
10) My Younger Days/*Sonny Boy Williamson* (1964)
11) Five Long Years/*Eddie Boyd* (1965)
12) Going Down to the River/*Mississippi Fred McDowell* (1965)
13) Sittin' and Cryin' the Blues/*Willie Dixon* (1963)
14) Nine Below Zero/*Sonny Boy Williamson* (1964)
15) Love Me Darlin'/*Howlin' Wolf* (1964)
16) Got My Mojo Working/*Muddy Waters* (1963)

Reelin' in the Years Productions Demo Reel • (2003)
A twenty-minute musical journey through the world's largest music footage library, hosted by Steven Van Zant. Produced and Directed by Jon Kanis and David Peck for Reelin' in the Years Productions. Featuring clips from the RITY library of: ABBA, AC/DC, Aerosmith, the Beastie Boys, the Beatles, Chuck Berry, Black Sabbath, James Brown, David Cassidy, John Coltrane, Dave Clark Five, Nat 'King' Cole, Elvis Costello and the Attractions, Cream, Miles Davis, Eagles, Ella Fitzgerald, Foo Fighters, Aretha Franklin, Marvin Gaye, Isaac Hayes, the Jimi Hendrix Experience, Lauryn Hill, John Lee Hooker, Howlin' Wolf, Ice-T, Billy Idol, Janet Jackson, the Jam, KC & the Sunshine Band, the Kinks, Roland Kirk, the Knack, Lenny Kravitz, Cyndi Lauper, Led Zeppelin, John Lennon, Little Steven and the Disciples of Soul, Bob Marley and the Wailers, Paul McCartney and Wings, George Michael, Bette Midler, Thelonious Monk, Keith Moon, Alanis Morissette, Muddy Waters, Harry Nilsson, Nirvana, Outkast, Iggy Pop, Pretty Things, Prince, Public Enemy, Radiohead, the Ramones, Red Hot Chili Peppers, Otis Redding, R.E.M., the Rolling Stones, Linda Ronstadt, Run-D.M.C., Santana, Sex Pistols, Simon and Garfunkel, Britney Spears, the Sugarhill Gang, Them, Big Mama Thornton, the Troggs, Ike and Tina Turner, T-Bone Walker, the Who, Sonny Boy Williamson, Stevie Wonder, Neil Young.

Little Steven: *We are all grateful to David Peck. We all know him as a man of his word. A modest man. A man who will always listen to reason. But he has the coolest footage in the world—that being the case, he must share it. Let others see it. He must let us draw water from the well. Certainly, he can present a bill for such services. After all, we're not communists.*

The American Folk Blues Festival 1962–1969 • *Volume Three*
Various Aritsts DVD (Hip-O Records B0002937-09) • (2004)
Produced by Janie Hendrix, Jon Kanis, John McDermott, and David Peck for Reelin' in the Years Productions in association with Experience Hendrix; distributed by Universal Music Enterprises. Audio Engineering and Restoration by Eddie Kramer.

1) Hound Dog/*Big Mama Thornton* (1965)
2) Gulfport Boogie/*Roosevelt Sykes* (1965)
3) Out of Sight/*Buddy Guy* (1965)
4) Feel So Good/*Dr. Isaiah Ross* (1965)
5) Flip, Flop and Fly/*Big Joe Turner* (1966)
6) All Night Long/*Skip James* (1967)
7) Crow Jane/*Skip James* (1967)
8) Got Sick and Tired/*Bukka White* (1967)
9) Death Letter Blues/*Son House* [1967]
10) Wild About You/*Hound Dog Taylor and Little Walter* (1967)
11) Wang Dang Doodle/*Koko Taylor and Hound Dog Taylor* (1967)
12) Stranger Blues/*Sonny Terry and Brownie McGhee* (1967)
13) Burnt Child (Afraid of Fire)/*Sonny Terry and Brownie McGhee* (1967)
14) Gonna Move Across the River/*Sonny Terry and Brownie McGhee* (1967)
15) The Blues Ain't Nothin' but a Woman/*Helen Humes* (1962)
16) Earl's Boogie/*Earl Hooker* (1964)
17) Long Distantce Call/*Muddy Waters* (1968)
18) Got My Mojo Working/*Muddy Waters* (1968)

The American Folk Blues Festival 1962–1969 • *Volume 2*
Various Artists CD (Hip-O Records B0003224-02) • (2004)
Produced by Janie Hendrix, Jon Kanis, John McDermott, and David Peck for Reelin' in the Years Productions in association with Experience Hendrix; distributed by Universal Music Enterprises. Audio Engineering and Restoration by Eddie Kramer.

1) Hound Dog/*Big Mama Thornton* (1965)
2) Stranger Blues/*Sonny Terry and Brownie McGhee* (1967)
3) All Night Long/*Skip James* (1967)
4) Keep It To Yourself/*Sonny Boy Williamson* (1963)
5) Your Funeral And My Trial/*Sonny Boy Williamson* (1963)
6) Flip, Flop And Fly/*Big Joe Turner* (1966)
7) I'll Be Back Someday/*Howlin' Wolf* (1964)
8) Nervous/*Willie Dixon* (1962)
9) Got Sick And Tired/*Bukka White* (1967)
10) Death Letter Blues/*Son House* (1967)
11) Wild About You/*Hound Dog Taylor and Little Walter* (1967)
12) Wang Dang Doodle/*Koko Taylor and Hound Dog Taylor* (1967)
13) Long Distantce Call/*Muddy Waters* (1968)
14) Walking the Floor Over You-Off the Hook/*Earl Hooker* (1969)
15) All Your Love/*Magic Sam* (1969)
16) Bye Bye Blues-Finale/*Entire Cast* (1963)

Jon Kanis

Soul to Soul • Various Artists
DVD and CD (Rhino Home Video R2 970327) • (05.2004)
Original film produced by Tom Mosk and Richard Bock. Executive Producer:
Edward Mosk. Directed by Denis Sanders. Re-issue produced by Jon Kanis
and David Peck for Reelin' in the Years Productions. A&R for Rhino: Robin
Hurley. DVD Post Production and Sound Restoration: David May and Ted Hall.
Manufactured and marketed by Warner Strategic Group.

1) Introduction with *The Kumasi Drummers*
2) Soul to Soul/*Ike and Tina Turner*
3) Run, Shaker Life/*Voices of East Harlem*
4) *Ishmael Adams and the Damas Choir*
5) Jungle Strut/*Santana*
6) Black Magic Woman/Gypsy Queen/*Santana*
7) Sit Yourself Down, Jolico, No No No/*Voices of East Harlem*
8) The Price You Gotta Pay to Be Free/*Les McCann and Eddie Harris*
9) Hey Jorler/*Les McCann and Eddie Harris with Amoah Azangeo*
10) Freedom Song/*Roberta Flack*
11) Tryin' Times/*Roberta Flack*
12) Soul To Soul /*Voices of East Harlem*
13) When Will We Be Paid?/*The Staple Singers*
14) Are You Sure?/*The Staple Singers*
15) He's Alright/*The Staple Singers*
16) *Kwa Mensah*
17) Ooh Poo Pah Do/*Ike and Tina Turner*
18) I Smell Trouble/*Ike and Tina Turner*
19) I've Been Loving You Too Long/*Ike and Tina Turner*
20) River Deep–Mountain High/*Ike and Tina Turner*
21) In the Midnight Hour/*Wilson Pickett*
22) Funky Broadway/*Wilson Pickett*
23) Land Of 1,000 Dances/*Wilson Pickett*
24) Choose Your Seat and Set Down, Walk All Over God's Heaven/*Voices of East Harlem*
25) Soul to Soul (2004)/*Earl Thomas*

archival projects > consultant/research:

The 15th Annual Rock and Roll Hall of Fame Induction Ceremony,
Waldorf-Astoria Ballroom, New York, New York • (March 6, 2000)
Film research, consulting, and licensing by Jon Kanis and David Peck for Reelin'
in the Years Productions for use in VH-1 telecast and permanent exhibition film
in Cleveland, Ohio. Inductees: Hal Blaine, Eric Clapton, Nat 'King' Cole, King
Curtis, Clive Davis, Earth, Wind & Fire, Billie Holiday, James Jamerson, the Lovin'
Spoonful, the Moonglows, Scotty Moore, Earl Palmer, Bonnie Raitt, James Taylor.

Jimi Hendrix • *Experience* DVD • (2000)
(MCA 440-053-194-9) Produced by Janie Hendrix and John McDermott. Audio
remastering by Eddie Kramer. Film research, consulting, and licensing by Jon Kanis
and David Peck for Reelin' in the Years Productions in association with Experience
Hendrix under exclusive license to MCA Records.

The 16th Annual Rock and Roll Hall of Fame Induction Ceremony,
Waldorf-Astoria Ballroom, New York, New York • (March 19, 2001)
Film research, consulting, and licensing by Jon Kanis and David Peck for Reelin'
in the Years Productions for use in VH-1 telecast and permanent exhibition film in
Cleveland, Ohio. Inductees: Aerosmith, Chris Blackwell, Solomon Burke, James
Burton, the Flamingos, Michael Jackson, Johnnie Johnson, Queen, Paul Simon,
Steely Dan, Ritchie Valens.

The 17th Annual Rock and Roll Hall of Fame Induction Ceremony,
Waldorf-Astoria Ballroom, New York, New York • (March 18, 2002)
Film research, consulting, and licensing by Jon Kanis and David Peck for Reelin'
in the Years Productions for use in VH-1 telecast and permanent exhibition film in
Cleveland, Ohio. Inductees: Chet Atkins, Issac Hayes, Brenda Lee, Tom Petty and
the Heartbreakers, Gene Pitney, the Ramones, Jim Stewart, Talking Heads.

The Doors • *Soundstage Performances* DVD • (2002) • (Eagle Vision 300179)
Produced by Stephanie Bennett. Executive Producer: Danny Sugerman. Consulting
by Jon Kanis and David Peck for Reelin' in the Years Productions in association with
The Doors Music Company.

The 18th Annual Rock and Roll Hall of Fame Induction Ceremony,
Waldorf-Astoria Ballroom, New York, New York • (March 10, 2003)
Film research, consulting, and licensing by Jon Kanis and David Peck for Reelin'
in the Years Productions for use in VH-1 telecast and permanent exhibition film in
Cleveland, Ohio. Inductees: AC/DC, Benny Benjamin, the Clash, Elvis Costello
and the Attractions, Floyd Cramer, Steve Douglas, Mo Ostin, the Police,
the Righteous Brothers.

Led Zeppelin • *DVD* • (May 26, 2003) • (Atlantic R2 970198)
Produced by Jimmy Page and Dick Caruthers. Film research and licensing by Jon
Kanis and David Peck for Reelin' in the Years Productions on behalf of Australian
Broadcasting Corporation and SVT.

Dusty Springfield • *Reflections* DVD • (2003) • (White Star D3098)
Produced by Gregory Hall. Executive Producer: Barbara Hall. Film research,
consulting, and licensing by Jon Kanis and David Peck for Reelin' in the Years
Productions on behalf of TROS, Carlton International, and Tom Jones Enterprises.

The 19th Annual Rock and Roll Hall of Fame Induction Ceremony,
Waldorf-Astoria Ballroom, New York, New York • *(March 15, 2004)*
Film research, consulting, and licensing by Jon Kanis and David Peck for Reelin'
in the Years Productions for use in VH-1 telecast and permanent exhibition film in
Cleveland, Ohio. Inductees: Jackson Browne, the Dells, George Harrison, Prince,
Bob Seger, Traffic, Jann S. Wenner, ZZ Top.

Ike and Tina Turner • *The Legends Live in '71* DVD • (2004) (Eagle Vision 30085-9)
Produced by Phil Galloway and David Peck. Consulting and research by Jon Kanis
for Reelin' in the Years Productions. DVD includes a bonus music video for Ike and
Tina Turner's performance of "Soul to Soul," directed by Jon Kanis and David Peck
(08.12.04).

AC/DC • *Family Jewels* DVD • (March 28, 2005) (Epic E2D 58843)
Produced by John Jackson. Film research and licensing by Phil Galloway, Jon
Kanis, and David Peck for Reelin' in the Years Productions on behalf of Australian
Broadcasting Corporation.

awards:

June 1981 • Most Outstanding Literary Contribution
Gar-Field Senior High School, Woodbridge, Virginia

June 1982 • Most Outstanding Literary Contribution
Gar-Field Senior High School, Woodbridge, Virginia

January 31, 2004 • Keeping the Blues Alive Achievement in Film Award from the
Blues Foundation for *The American Folk Blues Festival 1962–1966 Volumes One &*
Two. Gibson Guitar Lounge, Memphis, Tennessee

February 8, 2004 • The 46th Annual Grammy Awards • nomination from the
Recording Academy (R.I.A.A.) for Best Long Form Music Video for *The American*
Folk Blues Festival 1962–1966 Volume One. Staples Center, Los Angeles, California

2004 • Honorable Mention from *MOJO* Magazine Music Awards for *The American Folk Blues Festival 1962–1966 Volume One*

2005 • Winner of Best Music Anthology DVD Award from *DVD Entertainment Awards* for *The American Folk Blues Festival 1962–1969 Volume Three*

2005 • Winner of Best Compilation/Collection of Clips Award from the *Home Media Retailing* Awards for *The American Folk Blues Festival 1962–1969 Volume Three*

August 26, 2014 • Journalist of the Fucking Year Award from *San Diego Troubadour* magazine

multi-media performance/installation art:

18 Spirits, a Multi-Media Performance Collage by Jon Kanis with Cindy Wieber, Steve Snyder, Marc Intravia, Mark DeCerbo, Larry Grano, and Dean Schanbaum at Sushi Community Space/Reincarnation Building, San Diego, California (08.27.00).

There's No Business Like Show Business by Jon Kanis, as part of the Hovercraft Project, 3643 1/2 Sixth Avenue, San Diego, California (09.19.03–04.30.05).

A Royal Flush by Jon Kanis, a solo art installation at the Ruby Room, 1271 University Avenue, San Diego, California (08.26.11–08.26.13).

Keep Your Eyes on the Pies: a Pop Culture Pizzeria by Jon Kanis, a solo art installation at Sicilian Thing Pizza, 4046 30th Street, San Diego, California (03.07.15–).

set lists:

Peter Case with Los Lobos, First Avenue, Minneapolis, Minnesota (08.12.92): Vanishing Act / Poor Old Tom / Walk in the Woods / This Town's a Riot / Never Coming Home / When You Don't Come / Power, Love and Money / Old Part of Town / A Million Miles Away / My Lonely Sad Eyes / Breakin' the Chain / Dream About You / Put Down the Gun / Hidden Love / I Shook His Hand / Encores (with Los Lobos): Marie, Marie / Come On Up / Dizzy Miss Lizzie

Peter Case with Los Lobos, First Avenue, Minneapolis, Minnesota (08.13.92): Vanishing Act / Poor Old Tom / Walk in the Woods / Lakes of Ponchartrain / Walkin' Bum / Never Coming Home / When You Don't Come / Old Part of Town / A Million Miles Away / Dream About You / Beyond the Blues / Hidden Love / I Shook His Hand / Encores (with Los Lobos): Marie, Marie / Come On Up / Wild Thing

Peter Case with Los Lobos, Shank Hall, Milwaukee, Wisconsin (08.14.92): Vanishing Act / Poor Old Tom / Walk in the Woods / Lakes of Ponchartrain / Walkin' Bum / Never Coming Home / When You Don't Come / Old Part of Town / More Than Curious / A Million Miles Away / Dream About You / Blue Wing / Beyond the Blues / I Shook His Hand

Peter Case with Los Lobos, Majestic Theatre, Detroit, Michigan (08.15.92): Vanishing Act / Put Down the Gun / Walk in the Woods / Walkin' Bum / Never Coming Home / When You Don't Come / A Million Miles Away / Dream About You / Old Part of Town / Poor Old Tom / Travellin' Light / Beyond the Blues / I Shook His Hand

Peter Case, Pal Cezaar, Jon Kanis, Aldo Perez, the Bottom Line, New York, New York (08.19.92): 1st set: Vanishing Act / Dream About You / Walk in the Woods / Lakes of Ponchartrain / Walkin' Bum / Poor Old Tom / Never Coming Home / When You Don't Come / Why? / A Little Wind (Could Blow Me Away) / A Million Miles Away / Beyond the Blues / Hidden Love / Moves Me Deeply / Pedro / I Shook His Hand / Blue Wing / Old Part of Town 2nd set: Charlie James / More Than Curious / Power, Love and Money / Hidden Love / Why? / A Little Wind (Could Blow Me Away) / Blue Wing / Breakin' the Chain / Rovin' Gambler / Moves Me Deeply / Never Coming Home / Put Down the Gun / Think It Over *Jon Kanis* / My Lonely Sad Eyes *Aldo Perez* / Beyond the Blues

Peter Case, Cactus Café, Austin, Texas (09.11.92): 1st set: Blind Luck / Poor Old Tom / Broke Down Engine / Last Time I Looked / It Don't Matter What the People Say / Charlie James / Working for the Enemy-Suitcase / More Than Curious / Why? / A Little Wind (Could Blow Me Away) / Breakin' the Chain / Old Part of Town / Rovin' Gambler 2nd set: Vanishing Act / Dream About You / Old Blue Car / Walk in the Woods / Entella Hotel / Never Going Home / When You Don't Come / Horse and Crow / Ice Water / Steel Strings / A Million Miles Away / Travellin' Light / Walkin' Bum / Beyond the Blues / Hidden Love / Lakes of Ponchartrain / 4th of July/Christmas Rag / I Shook His Hand

Peter Case, Bluebird Cafe, Nashville, Tennessee (09.16.92): Charlie James / Blind Luck / Poor Old Tom / Breakin' the Chain / Walk in the Woods / Never Coming Home / When You Don't Come / Why? / A Little Wind (Could Blow Me Away) / A Million Miles Away / Old Part of Town / Beyond the Blues / Hidden Love / Rovin' Gambler / I Shook His Hand / Horse and Crow / Ice Water

Peter Case, Variety Theatre, Atlanta, Georgia (09.17.92): Blind Luck / Poor Old Tom / Broke Down Engine / Last Time I Looked / It Don't Matter What the People Say / Vanishing Act / Dream About You / A Million Miles Away / A Little Wind (Could Blow Me Away) / It's All Mine / Just Hanging On / Charlie James / Working for the Enemy-Suitcase / More Than Curious / Beyond the Blues / Hidden Love / Moves Me Deeply / I Shook His Hand / Never Coming Home / Horse and Crow

Peter Case, 40 Watt Club, Athens, Georgia (09.19.92): Blink Luck / Poor Old Tom / Walk in the Woods / Never Coming Home / When You Don't Come / Vanishing Act / Dream About You / Echo Wars / A Million Miles Away / Why? / A Little Wind (Could Blow Me Away) / Old Part of Town / Beyond the Blues / Hidden Love / Two Angels / I Shook His Hand / It Don't Matter What the People Say / Horse and Crow / Ice Water

Peter Case, McCabe's Guitar Shop, Santa Monica, California (09.26.92):
8 PM set: Blind Luck / Poor Old Tom / Lakes of Ponchartrain / Walk in the Woods / Charlie James / Working for the Enemy-Suitcase / Breakin' the Chain / Never Coming Home / When You Don't Come / A Little Wind (Could Blow Me Away) / Why? / Vanishing Act / Dream About You / A Million Miles Away / Last Time I Looked / Beyond the Blues / Hidden Love / Moves Me Deeply / It's All Mine / I Shook His Hand / Two Angles / Horse And Crow
10:30 PM set: Roving Gambler / Wonderful 99 / Walk in the Woods / Charlie James / Working for the Enemy-Suitcase / More Than Curious / Why? / A Little Wind (Could Blow Me Away) / Vanishing Act / Dream About You / Broke Down Engine / Last Time I Looked / A Million Miles Away / Beyond the Blues / Never Coming Home / Hidden Love / Moves Me Deeply / Breakin' the Chain / I Shook His Hand / It's All Mine / Blue Wing / Horse and Crow / Ice Water

Peter Case, Canal Street Tavern, Dayton, Ohio (10.10.92)
1st set: Blind Luck / Poor Old Tom / Roving Gambler / Walkin' Bum / Punch and Socko / Walk in the Woods / Entella Hotel / Why? / A Little Wind (Could Blow Me Away) / Vanishing Act / A Million Miles Away / Blue Wing / Travellin' Light

Harry Chapin with Tom Chapin, Pine Knob Theatre, Flint, Michigan (06.17.76): Dreams Go By / W*O*L*D / Could You Put Your Light on, Please / Saturday Morning / Short Stories / On the Road to Kingdom Come / I Wanna Learn a Love Song / Mr. Tanner / Someone Keeps Calling My Name / Better Place to Be / Let Time Go Lightly / Cat's in the Cradle / If My Mary Were Here / Taxi / Circle / Encore: 30,000 Pounds of Bananas

Concert for George, Royal Albert Hall, London, England (11.29.02): Sarveshaam *Ravi Shankar* / Your Eyes *Anoushka Shankar* / The Inner Light *Jeff Lynne* / Arpan *Anoushka Shankar, conductor* // Intermission // Sit on My Face *Monty Python's Flying Circus* / The Lumberjack Song *Monty Python's Flying Circus* / I Want to Tell You *Jeff Lynne* / If I Needed Someone *Eric Clapton* / Old Brown Shoe *Gary Brooker* / Give Me Love (Give Me Peace on Earth) *Jeff Lynne* / Beware of Darkness *Eric Clapton* / Here Comes the Sun *Joe Brown* / That's the Way It Goes *Joe Brown* / Horse to the Water *Sam Brown and Jools Holland* / Taxman *Tom Petty and the Heartbreakers* / I Need You

Tom Petty and the Heartbreakers / Handle with Care *Tom Petty and the Heartbreakers with Jeff Lynne* / Isn't It a Pity *Eric Clapton and Billy Preston* / Photograph *Ringo Starr* / Honey Don't *Ringo Starr* / For You Blue *Paul McCartney* / Something *Paul McCartney and Eric Clapton* / All Things Must Pass *Paul McCartney* / While My Guitar Gently Weeps *Eric Clapton* / My Sweet Lord *Billy Preston* / Wah-Wah *Eric Clapton and Jeff Lynne* / I'll See You in My Dreams *Joe Brown*

Neil Diamond, Capital Centre, Landover, Maryland (08.10.76): Street Life / Beautiful Noise / Stargazer / Surviving the Life / Lady-Oh / If You Know What I Mean / Kentucky Woman / Solitary Man / Cherry, Cherry / Sweet Caroline / The Last Picasso / Longfellow Serenade / Morningside / Play Me / Glory Road / Rosemary's Wine / Song Sung Blue /Cracklin' Rosie / Holly Holy / I Am...I Said / Be / Dear Father / Lonely Looking Sky / Sanctus / Skybird / Be (Reprise) / Encore: Brother Love's Traveling Salvation Show / I've Been This Way Before

The Bob Dylan 30th Anniversary Concert, Madison Square Garden, New York, New York (10.16.92): Gotta Serve Somebody *Booker T. & the MGs* / From a Buick Six *Booker T. & the MGs* / Lay Lady Lay *Booker T. & the MGs* / Boots of Spanish Leather *Carolyn Hester, Nanci Griffiths* / See That My Grave Is Kept Clean *John Hammond* / Like a Rolling Stone *John "Cougar" Mellencamp with Al Kooper* / Leopard-Skin Pillbox-Hat *John "Cougar" Mellencamp* / Blowin' in the Wind *Stevie Wonder* / Wanted Man *George Thorogood* / I Want You *Sophie B. Hawkins* / Foot of Pride *Lou Reed* / War *Sinead O'Connor* / Masters of War *Eddie Vedder, Mike McCready* / The Times They Are A-Changin' *Tracy Chapman* / It Ain't Me, Babe *Johnny Cash, June Carter Cash* / What Was It You Wanted *Willie Nelson* / I'll Be Your Baby Tonight *Willie Nelson, Kris Kristofferson* / Highway 61 Revisited *Johnny Winter* / Seven Days *Ronnie Wood* / Just Like A Woman *Richie Havens* / When My Ship Comes In *The Clancy Brothers, Tommy Makem* / Just Like Tom Thumb's Blues *Neil Young* / All Along the Watchtower *Neil Young* / I Shall Be Released *Chrissie Hynde* / Love Minus Zero/No Limit *Eric Clapton* / Don't Think Twice, It's Alright *Eric Clapton* / Emotionally Yours *The O'Jays* / When I Paint My Masterpiece *The Band* / You Ain't Goin' Nowhere *Shawn Colvin, Mary Chapin Carpenter, Rosanne Cash* / If Not For You *George Harrison* / Absolutely Sweet Marie *George Harrison* / License To Kill *Tom Petty and the Heartbreakers* / Rainy Day Women #12 and #35 *Tom Petty and the Heartbreakers* / Mr. Tambourine Man *Tom Petty and the Heartbreakers, Roger McGuinn* / Song To Woody *Bob Dylan* / It's Alright Ma (I'm Only Bleeding) *Bob Dylan* / My Back Pages *Bob Dylan, Eric Clapton, George Harrison, Roger McGuinn, Neil Young* / Knockin' on Heaven's Door *Everyone* / Girl from the North Country *Bob Dylan*

The Ghost of a Saber Tooth Tiger, Parish, Austin, Texas (03.15.14): Too Deep / Xanadu / Animals / Midnight Sun / Golden Earrings / Johannesburg / The Devil You Know / Long Gone

The Elton John Band Louder Than Concorde But Not Quite As Pretty, Capital Centre, Landover, Maryland (06.30.76): Grow Some Funk of Your Own / Goodbye Yellow Brick Road / Island Girl / Rocket Man / Hercules / Bennie and the Jets / Funeral for a Friend/ Love Lies Bleeding / Love Song / Lucy in the Sky with Diamonds / Don't Let the Sun Go Down on Me / Holiday Inn / Empty Sky / Captain Fantastic and the Brown Dirt Cowboy / Someone Saved My Life Tonight / Philadelphia Freedom / We All Fall in Love Sometimes/ Curtains / Saturday Night's Alright for Fighting / Encore: Your Song / Pinball Wizard

Mudcrutch, the Troubadour, Los Angeles, California (05.01.08): Shady Grove / Orphan from the Storm / Six Days on the Road / Scare Easy / Most Likely You Go Your Way (and I'll Go Mine) / This Is a Good Street / Lover of the Bayou / Queen of the Go-Go Girls / Off the Hook / Summertime Blues / June Apple / House of Stone / Love Please Come Home / Crystal River / Topanga Cowgirl / The Wrong Thing to Do / Bootleg Flyer / Encore: Rainy Day Women #12 & 35 / High School Confidential

Mudcrutch, the Troubadour, Los Angeles, California (05.02.08): Shady Grove / Orphan from the Storm / Six Days on the Road / Scare Easy / Most Likely You Go Your Way (and I'll Go Mine) / This Is a Good Street / Lover of the Bayou / Queen of the Go-Go Girls / Rip It Up / Summertime Blues / June Apple / House of Stone / Love Please Come Home / Crystal River / Topanga Cowgirl / The Wrong Thing to Do / Bootleg Flyer / Encore: Rainy Day Women #12 & 35 / High School Confidential

The Negro Problem with Candypants, the Echoplex, Los Angeles, California (11.02.10): Bleed / The Re-Hab Song / Curse / Gary Come Home / Ken / Kingdom of Drink / Speed / We've Just Had Sex / Bong Song / Black Men Ski / Sexy Brooklyn Mami / Omnibus / Can I Get You Love? / Comikbuchland / Smudges / Statue Song / Witch / Birdcage-Buzzing / Mahnsanto

Yoko Ono/Plastic Ono Band with Deerhoof, Fox Theatre, Oakland, California (02.23.10): It Happened / Waiting for the D Train / BETWEEN MY HEAD AND THE SKY / Rising / Walking on Thin Ice / Will I / Moving Mountains / CALLING / The Sun Is Down! / Death of Samantha / Mind Train / Higa Noburu / Encores: Fly / Don't Worry, Kyoko (Mummy's Only Looking for Her Hand in the Snow) / Give Peace a Chance

Lou Reed SXSW Tribute, Paramount Theatre, Austin, Texas (03.14.14): Sweet Jane *Alejandro Escovedo and Richard Barone* / Cool It Down *The Bizarros* / Romeo Had Juliet *Cheetah Chrome* / Femme Fatale *Cindy Lee Berryhill* / Vicious *BP Fallon with the Strypes* / Oh! Sweet Nuthin' *Bobby Bare Jr.* / I'm Waiting for My Man *Garland Jeffreys* / Perfect Day *Louise Goffin* / I Love You, Suzanne *Rosie Flores* / Waves of Fear *The Fauntleroys* / Coney Island Baby *Steve Wynn and the Miracle 3* / Candy Says

Jon Kanis

Sharon Needles / Smalltown *Joe Dallesandro* / White Light/White Heat *Alejandro Escovedo and Richard Barone* / All Tomorrow's Parties *Richard Barone with Cindy Lee Berryhill* / Rock and Roll Heart *Chuck Prophet* / Sally Can't Dance *Jesse Mallin* / Real Good Time Together *The Fleshtones* / Walk on the Wild Side *Suzanne Vega* / Kill Your Sons *Wayne Kramer* / Pale Blue Eyes *Lucinda Williams* / Run, Run, Run *The Black Lips* / Sister Ray *The Baseball Project* / Satellite of Love *Spandau Ballet* / What Goes On *Sean Lennon* / I'll Be Your Mirror *Richard Barone* / Street Hassle *Alejandro Escovedo with Louise Goffin* / Rock and Roll *Finale with Everyone*

Rush with Saxon at the Capital Centre, Landover, Maryland (09.26.80): 2112 (Overture, The Temples of Syrinx, Presentation, Soliloquy, Grand Finale) / Freewill / By-Tor And The Snow Dog / Xanadu / The Spirit of Radio / Natural Science / A Passage to Bangkok / The Trees / Cygnus X1 Book I: The Voyage / Cygnus X1 Book II: Hemispheres / Closer to the Heart / Beneath, Between and Behind / Jacob's Ladder / Working Man / Finding My Way / Anthem / Bastille Day / In the Mood / Drum Solo / Encore: La Villa Strangiato

Rush with Rory Gallagher at the Capital Centre, Landover, Maryland (11.29.82): The Spirit of Radio / Tom Sawyer / Freewill / Digital Man / Subdivisions / Vital Signs / The Camera Eye (abbreviated version) / Closer to the Heart / Chemistry / The Analog Kid / Broon's Bane / The Trees / Red Barchetta / The Weapon / New World Man / Limelight / Countdown / Encores: 2112 (Overture, The Temples of Syrinx) / Xanadu / La Villa Strangiato / In the Mood / YYZ-Drum Solo

Rush Time Machine **at Irvine Meadows Amphitheater, Irvine, California** (08.13.10): The Spirit of Radio / Time Stand Still / Presto / Stick It Out / Workin' Them Angels / Leave That Thing Alone / Faithless / BU2B / Freewill / Marathon / Subdivisions / Intermission / Tom Sawyer / Red Barchetta / YYZ / Limelight / The Camera Eye / Witch Hunt (Part III of *Fear*) / Vital Signs / Caravan / Drum Solo (10:12 PM to 10:20 PM) / Closer to the Heart / 2112 (Overture, The Temples of Syrinx) / Far Cry / Encores: La Villa Strangiato / Working Man

ACKNOWLEDGEMENTS

It's impossible to thank everyone who helped to turn this project into a reality. But first, and absolutely foremost, I must thank Ms. Frankie Frey. Without her encouragement, support, and talents as an art director, designer, and editor, this book would literally not exist. The same goes for the companion CD to this book *All-American Mongrel Boy (1989–2014)*. I can't thank her enough. So, thank you, thank you, THANK YOU Frankie! I love, love, love you!

Thanks are also due to John Chilson (*Schlock*), Mike Stax (*Ugly Things*), and Liz Abbott & Kent Johnson (*San Diego Troubadour*) for giving my words such righteous and groovy places to hang. Additionally, thanks to Tom Stanton of *East End Lights*, *Subliminal Tattoos,* and the *San Diego Reader*.

Without the early academic encouragement of my teachers Martha Smith, Judy Powers, and Ed Johnson, I would never have continued to pursue the act of writing. One mentor I've never met face-to-face, is author Michael Ventura. I'm enternally grateful for the wisdom that is shared in his marvelous essay *The Talent of the Room*. My thanks go out to songwriter extraordinaire Peter David Case, for passing on Ventura's timeless observations, as well as providing so many valuable life lessons between 1989 to the present.

My deepest appreciation and a perpetual hug go out to pat mAcdonald for all his inspiring words, his friendship, and for demonstrating how to create a community in this crazy world we share. FYI, should you have read all of pat's **Foreword**, my extensive interview with the incomparable mister mAcdonald will appear in volume three of *Encyclopedia Walking*.

A HUGE thanks to Liz Abbott, Dirk Dawson, Risa Goldberg, Jeff Lee, and Ward Whipple for assisting with the final proofing, and to Joan Vokac for her production expertise.

For their friendship and support over the span of years during which these pieces first found publication, my love and gratitude go out to Chris Aaron, Jon Auer, Nancy Avery, Tommy Ballew, Emily Belt, Cindy Lee Berryhill, Joyce & Rich Bont, Robin Brack, Robert Calkin, Brian Claffey, Cerphe Colwell, Tracey Contreras, Bill Costa, Alan & Michele Davison, Dirk Dawson, Harpo & Sue Delguidice, Henry Diltz, Karen Eng, Cal Everett, Joe Ferrelli, Rebecca Fitzpatrick Talley, Susan Fleshman, Louise Goffin, Chuck Good, Katy Hamilton, Christopher Hoffee, the Jackson Family, Melanie Jane, Jefferson Jay, Michael & Jussara Kanis, Bob Kastl, Steven Keene, Mike Keneally, Eugene King, Steve Kobashigawa, Steve Laub, Jeff Lee, Lisa Maxwell Alastanos, Tim McDonnell, Jim McNabb, Ben Moore, Roger & Sara Morrison, Lisa O'Hara, Leanne Pearl, Victor Penalosa, George Pittaway, Dominic Priore, Kevin Ring, Darian Sahanaja, Jeff Severson, Brad Smith, Layne Sterling, Ken Stringfellow, Rebecca Tabatzky, Ed Turner, Nick Walusko, Cindy Wieber, Laura Jane Willcock, and Paul Williams.

Last, but certainly not least, thank **you** for taking the time to explore and share these ideas and stories with me.

CPSIA information can be obtained
at www.ICGtesting.com
Printed in the USA
FSOW04n2212300915
11668FS